Praise for

HOTBED

"In Joanna Scutts's capable hands, the individual lives of the members of the Heterodoxy Club become a prism through which to examine the defining issues of New York City in the early 1900s, from suffrage to workers' rights, from racism to sexism. Incredibly resonant in today's times, and a profound read."

—Fiona Davis, *New York Times*–bestselling author of *The Lions of Fifth Avenue*

"Scutts treats these world-changing feminists and activists as they treated each other: with clarity, candor, and warmth. *Hotbed* is both a formidable work of scholarship and a transporting tour de force of storytelling. The women of the secret club known as Heterodoxy would surely have recruited Scutts as one of their own."

—Janice P. Nimura, author of *The Doctors Blackwell*

"*Hotbed: Bohemian Greenwich Village and the Secret Club that Sparked Modern Feminism* is a spirited, inspiring history of a little-known enclave of feminist movers and shakers in an expertly evoked early twentieth-century Greenwich Village. How I long to visit! But then, reading Scutts's book, I almost feel as if I have. Deeply researched and deftly rendered, *Hotbed* is a must-read for anyone seriously interested in feminism, feminist history, and the power of the city to help women change their lives."

—Lauren Elkin, author of *Flâneuse*

HOTBED

HOTBED

Bohemian Greenwich Village and the Secret Club that Sparked Modern Feminism

JOANNA SCUTTS

SEAL PRESS

NEW YORK

Seal Press
Hachette Book Group
1290 Avenue of the Americas, New York, NY 10104
www.sealpress.com
@sealpress

Printed in the United States of America

First Edition: June 2022

Published by Seal Press, an imprint of Perseus Books, LLC, a subsidiary of Hachette Book Group, Inc. The Seal Press name and logo is a trademark of the Hachette Book Group.

The Hachette Speakers Bureau provides a wide range of authors for speaking events. To find out more, go to www.hachettespeakersbureau.com or call (866) 376-6591.

The publisher is not responsible for websites (or their content) that are not owned by the publisher.

Print book interior design by Trish Wilkinson

Library of Congress Cataloging-in-Publication Data

Names: Scutts, Joanna, author.
Title: Hotbed : bohemian Greenwich Village and the secret club that sparked modern feminism / Joanna Scutts.
Description: First edition. | New York : Seal Press, 2022. | Includes bibliographical references and index.
Identifiers: LCCN 2021050666 | ISBN 9781541647176 (hardcover) | ISBN 9781541647169 (ebook)
Subjects: LCSH: Heterodoxy (Club)—History. | Feminism—New York (State)—New York—History—20th century. | Greenwich Village (New York, N.Y.)—History—20th century.
Classification: LCC HQ1906.N5 S39 2022 | DDC 305.420907471—Cdc23/eng/20211118
LC record available at https://lccn.loc.gov/2021050666

ISBNs: 9781541647176 (hardcover), 9781541647169 (ebook)

LSC-C

Printing 1, 2022

To Ali, Lucy, Grace, Sarah, and Susan,
My own charmed circle,
In love & friendship

CONTENTS

Introduction

A LITTLE WORLD FOR US

ON SATURDAY AFTERNOON, IN A PLACE THAT FEELS, JUST then, like the brightly pulsing center of the universe, a group of women gathers to talk about the world, and their place in it. They haven't come far—physically, at least. Most have walked: from shared apartments, boardinghouses, and cooperative lodgings, or from red-brick mansions and smaller family homes, to a townhouse on MacDougal Street, in the middle of a busy, scruffy block just below Washington Square Park, the heart of the bohemian New York neighborhood they call Greenwich Village.[1] In the basement is a restaurant that everyone knows simply as Polly's, its walls painted with sunny yellow chalk paint and hung with local artists' work, and its wooden tables crammed close together. The whole point is to overhear your neighbors' conversations, lean over, and join in. It's what makes the Village the Village, this contagious buzz, sitting elbow to elbow with artists and radicals and waiting for the chef, an anarchist poet, to bang down your plate of goulash or liver and onions with his signature hiss *"bourgeois pigs."*[2] Short-haired young women in loosely tied, batik-print tunics smoke cigarettes and flirt with long-haired young men in wire-rimmed spectacles, tweed coats, and soft-collared shirts. Upstairs, the Liberal Club bills itself as

"A Social Center for Those Interested in New Ideas," and next door, in the Washington Square Bookshop, browsers hang out for long enough that the owners protest they aren't running a lending library.[3] The Village isn't a tourist attraction, at least not yet—it's a place to live, to be, to *become*. Uptown, there might be more "light and space and air," but downtown "there is another and larger and altogether incalculable element, which we might call sentiment,—atmosphere."[4]

At the head of the table in Polly's, a pretty woman in her early forties with a pile of dark-gold hair raps a gavel on the tabletop and brings the meeting to order. The women around the table describe themselves as "the most unruly and individualistic females you ever fell among," and pride themselves on their voracious interests and varied outlooks.[5] They are "Democrats, Republicans, Prohibitionists, socialists, anarchists, liberals and radicals of all opinions."[6] Sometimes they accuse each other of being "cranks on certain subjects," but no woman obsessed by a single issue lasts long in their proudly eclectic meetings.[7] To give each other space to doubt and to disagree, the women keep no records of their meetings. They give their secret, unruly club a name that celebrates the difference of opinion: *Heterodoxy*.

One thing distinguishes the chatter at this gathering from the usual lunchtime buzz: the voices are exclusively feminine. This doesn't mean it's much quieter than any other afternoon or that there's no argument (or, indeed, flirting). But it does change the atmosphere, just a little. In almost every other club and society and discussion group in the bohemian Village, political or artistic or purely social, men are part of the conversation, and their voices tend to carry. It is hard to talk over them, to interrupt or correct, without being labeled stubborn or strident. Among women, it is easier to be heard. At heart, that is the simple idea that the club's founder, Marie Jenney Howe, uses to gather the prominent women of her acquaintance into yet another club. What it will become—a network of mutual support whose legacy runs long and deep in the lives of its members—she has no idea, on that first Saturday afternoon.

The women around the table belong to many other groups: leagues, associations, societies, and organizations of all stripes crowd their schedules. They are veterans of social reform efforts and tireless in their work for an array of causes. It's how women, denied the vote, get things done. This club is different, however, because it isn't trying to *do* anything or change anything. A unique hybrid of the politically oriented Progressive Era women's clubs and the freewheeling, mixed-sex discussion groups that proliferate in Greenwich Village in the early 1900s, Heterodoxy is "the easiest of clubs . . . no duties or obligations."[8] It offers a place to meet that is free of rules and formality, a place where ideas burst forth from intimacy. It's enough to be, as one member puts it, "women who did things, and did them openly."[9] It's enough simply to show up.

There are twenty-five charter members of Heterodoxy, one of whom is so proud of that distinction that she says she wants it carved on her tombstone.[10] Most of them are public figures, in the way that women in professional fields at the time could often be, purely for doing their jobs. For being, if not the first or the only woman in their profession, then among the first and among the few. The majority are college educated—placing them among a tiny, elite percentage of American women—and several hold even rarer graduate degrees in law, medicine, and the social sciences. There are pairs of sisters and pairs of lovers; women entwined by family and marriage; and those who have studied together, worked together, and marched side by side for the vote. They already know each other by reputation, if not personally— an exposé of the group calls it the "de facto star chamber council of the prominent women of New York."[11] Together, in that room, they represent something new, and they know it.

> As I look round and see your faces—
> The actors, the editors, the businesswomen, the artists—
> The writers, the dramatists, the psychoanalysts, the dancers.
> The doctors, the lawyers, the propogandists [*sic*]
> As I look round and see your faces
> It really seems quite common to do anything!
> Only she who does nothing is unusual.
>   —Paula Jakobi entry, "Heterodoxy to Marie" scrapbook

Forging such exceptional lives, well outside the mainstream of expectations for women of their era, can feel daunting and isolating. It is easier in the company of others.

Yet despite the enormous impact of the club on the lives of its members, and the fame of those members in their day, the most basic facts about Heterodoxy remain elusive. We don't know exactly where and when the club first met, only that it was sometime in 1912, probably in the spring, although some historians date it to the fall.[12] Polly's restaurant at 135 MacDougal Street, and the Liberal Club upstairs, which are usually identified as its first meeting places, did not open until 1913.[13] We know that the women met on Saturday afternoons, every other week, skipping the summer months when members went out of town to mini-Village enclaves in actual villages, including nearby Croton-on-Hudson and Provincetown, Massachusetts. At some point, meetings moved to Tuesday evenings. There were modest dues, a couple of dollars a year plus eighty-five cents for the meal, and the topic for discussion was agreed in advance. The meetings could stretch on for several convivial hours.[14]

Because of the lack of records, we don't know what was discussed at any particular meeting, nor who attended, though we can gather something of the meetings' shape. The aim was not "mere clever conversation" but an organized discussion on a specific subject, from psychology to childbirth techniques, pacifism to anthropology, labor organizing to education reform. Guest speakers, frequently invited, included Margaret Sanger, the poet Amy Lowell, Emma Goldman speaking on "Anarchy," and Edith Ellis, a lesbian writer in an open marriage with the scandalous sexologist Havelock Ellis, speaking on the topic of "Love." Every now and again, the doors would be opened to men for what were jokingly called husbands' evenings. "We thought we covered the whole field," one member recalled, "but really we discussed ourselves."[15]

After the second full year of Heterodoxy's existence, the *New-York Tribune* ran a story that claimed to blow the lid off this secretive club, divulging the names of several prominent members who belonged to the group and guests who had addressed it. The paper appeared impressed, or bewildered, that the club could operate without bylaws or written rules and that its criteria for membership were so vague—it was open to "advanced" women, but that meant pretty much whatever the members wanted it to mean. The only other rule was the limit of forty people per meeting, a practicality to make discussion possible—although the gatherings could still be raucous. According to the *Tribune*, Heterodoxy was by this time meeting at the Greenwich Village Inn, at 79 Washington Place, just off Washington Square—another of "Polly's" restaurants, a bigger space that reflected the growing fame of both the restaurateur, Polly Holladay, and the Village itself as a hotbed of countercultural ideas.

Unlike most clubs and institutions in that rapidly evolving quarter, which ran with enthusiasm for a year or two, Heterodoxy weathered the gentrification of the bohemian Village, the upheaval of World War I, and the tyranny of the first Red Scare, during which several of its members were harassed, surveilled, and arrested. It held together through the passage of the Nine-teenth Amendment, which splintered so many women's rights organizations, and of Prohibition, which drove much of the ar-tistic energy of the Village underground or overseas. It lived on beyond the death of its founder, the onset of the Depression, and the scattering of key members to Paris, New Mexico, Hol-lywood, or simply uptown. After a quarter century, it dimmed its lights only with the advent of another world war.

DRAWING HETERODOXY TOGETHER more strongly than any other idea was *feminism*: a new word in America in the early 1910s, if not exactly a new idea. Newspapers and magazines de-voted extensive space to defining, explaining, and ridiculing the word, adapted from the French *féminisme*, and before long it was part of the common lexicon—a word that, depending on your point of view, spelled doom or liberation. Those opposed to wom-en's rights seized on *feminism* as a catchall term for everything they feared: "non-motherhood, free love, easy divorce, [and] eco-nomic independence for all women."[16] In an era consumed by the debate over women's right to vote, anti-suffragists fulminated that feminism was the secret end goal of the suffragists, and that the vote was a slippery slope straight to the hell of gender equal-ity. "The implication," as one Heterodoxy member put it, was that feminism was "something with dynamite in it."[17]

Its ambassadors were certainly treated as explosive. "Here she comes, running, out of prison and off pedestal, chains off, crown off, halo off, just a live woman," wrote Heterodoxy member Charlotte Perkins Gilman, imagining the feminist as a refugee from the patriarchy and the harbinger of a new dawn.[18] When the silent film star Theda Bara declared to a newspaper, "I have the face of a vampire, but the heart of a feministe [*sic*]," she was engaging in a prescient form of celebrity branding and lending the term a frisson of her own. The imprimatur of the notorious "vamp" made the feminist sexy, mysterious, threatening, and thrilling. Of course she was a sensation.[19]

The women of Heterodoxy played a major part in defining—and embodying—feminism for the American public. Indeed, in some ways, to embody feminism *was* to define it. In the absence of any specific political agenda, feminism was a broad and protean identity that often began as a feeling of kinship with other unorthodox women. Novelist, poet, and screenwriter Alice Duer Miller, a member of the club who published a popular column of comic suffrage verse in the *New-York Tribune* (under the title "Are Women People?"), imagined that kinship literally, as knowledge passed down the female line:

> Mother, what is a Feminist?
> A Feminist, my daughter,
>   Is any woman now who cares
>   To think about her own affairs
> As men don't think she oughter.[20]

To Edna Kenton, another Heterodoxy writer, feminism was a spiritual experience, a journey of the soul, "a great personal, joyous adventure with one's untried self," and promised an exuberant range of benefits for the whole human race. "Feminism Will Give—Men More Fun, Women Greater Scope, Children Better Parents, Life More Charm," her article claimed in its headline.[21] Heterodoxy's founder Marie Jenney Howe understood feminism as the quest to become "not just our little female selves, but our whole, big, human selves."[22] That meant more than "a changed world." It meant "a changed psychology, the creation of a new consciousness in women." In other words, feminism was always both personal and political. "The essence of this new consciousness," she concluded, "is woman's refusal to be specialized to sex."[23]

Most club members shared this optimistic, egalitarian vision of feminism, which emphasized the shared humanity of men and women—but it was not a simple idea, and they discussed and debated what "feminism" meant many times over the years. Others in the club argued that there was something irreducibly different and powerful about femininity (often conflated with the ability to bear children), which ought to be recognized in its own right. However they defined it, through their books, articles, speeches, plays, and activism, Heterodoxy members worked tirelessly to spread feminism beyond their radical quarter. For a while, their nickname as club members—"Heterodite"—was a synonym for "feminist."[24]

It can be difficult, at more than a century's distance, to understand how far outside the mainstream Heterodoxy members dwelt. In their personal and professional lives, as well as their political activism, they formed a tiny and tight-knit minority. At a time when fewer than 2 percent of American women got divorced, fully one-third of the group slipped their marital bonds, and several were in long-term relationships, more or less openly, with other women. Those who loved men dreamed of more equal, friendly, and respectful partnerships to replace the patriarchal structure of dependence; the right to keep their own names; and the freedom to have sex without having children. Heterodites who were mothers, to biological or adopted children, generally had much smaller families than the average and started them later in life. In a culture that saw child-rearing as a job for women only and, ideally, a woman's only job, they struggled to find ways to balance families and careers.

Yet although Heterodoxy's interests, opinions, and activism ranged widely, it remained a club for a certain kind of woman: highly educated, outspokenly feminist, economically independent, with the leisure, desire, and means to pay dues and attend meetings. In New York in the 1910s, such a woman was almost always white, at least middle class, and Protestant. The Heterodites' rebellion against marriage and their embrace of professional careers resonated very differently for less privileged women. For Black women, marriage itself could be a gesture of defiance against a culture that disparaged them as sexually "loose" and their relationships as inherently unstable, while for working-class and immigrant women, toiling in factories was a matter of survival, not a blow for freedom. The club members were aware of these differences in circumstances and outlook and worked to overcome them, but connection was a messy, imperfect business, and blind spots remained.

This is a story about feminism, its insights and its exclusions, in its first American incarnation. It's also a story about how history is written: what matters and what doesn't in the stories we tell; who gets forgotten and why. Heterodoxy members were involved in multiple causes and many were active public figures for decades, publishing memoirs, novels, and reams of journalism, winning Pulitzer Prizes and numerous other accolades. Although several of them have been the subjects of biographies, many of these are out of print and, today, hardly any club members retain the level of fame that makes their names instantly recognizable.[25] This book, therefore, does not single out any women, but combines elements of biography and cultural history in an effort to bring Heterodoxy to life as a vibrant whole.

Given the club's size, its long history, and the many achievements of its members, however, Heterodoxy in its entirety is an unwieldy subject. I have therefore chosen to focus on the first turbulent and transformative decade of the club's existence, from 1912 until the early 1920s, which was also the heyday of this particular incarnation of Greenwich Village as America's countercultural epicenter. This approach highlights the causes that most animated the club in the early years: women's rights, both political and professional; socialism and labor organizing; sexual

Charlotte Perkins Gilman in 1900, shortly after she published *Women and Economics*. (*Credit: Library of Congress*)

autonomy and access to birth control; the anti-lynching crusade and larger efforts toward racial justice; and the avant-garde artistic movements, especially in theater and visual arts, that were intertwined with these social and political battles. Although I include sketches of as many club members as possible, I focus on the women who were particularly influential in Heterodoxy and their wider community in the 1910s. These were the women who shaped America's understanding of feminism, either by examining it as a theory or proclaiming it as an identity.

Of all the public feminists in Heterodoxy, the most famous in her own time was Charlotte Perkins Gilman, who is remembered today mainly for her novella *The Yellow Wallpaper*, published in 1892. A vivid depiction of a woman's mental deterioration under masculine medical oppression, the story was inspired by Charlotte's own experience of crippling postpartum depression. Shortly after it appeared, Charlotte and her husband divorced—a scandalous step made infamous by her refusal to treat it as a tragedy. In order to focus on her writing, Charlotte sent her nine-year-old daughter across the country to California to live with her ex-husband and his new wife (who was her close friend), eliciting a vicious public response. Her feminism focused on women as rational, independent human creatures and rejected the idea that motherhood was any kind of blissful, natural destiny. She repeatedly argued that the isolated domestic realm of the family, so worshipped by the Victorians, was unnatural and inefficient: it made it impossible for women to achieve their potential, and it exposed children to the risks of cruel or neglectful parenting. She advocated instead for communal living and the outsourcing of domestic labor to trained and well-paid professionals. But feminist principles were no guarantee of family harmony: Charlotte's daughter Katharine, who lived into her nineties, remained resentful of her mother's abandonment to the end of her life.[26] To combine fulfillment in their career with happiness at home was a struggle that preoccupied the Heterodites, in which there were often no good choices.

The most visible feminist cause of the day, the vote, was only a small part of the grand social revolution that Charlotte Perkins Gilman advocated. At the turn of the century, her book *Women and Economics* became a bible for progressive young women.[27] The prosaic title concealed a radical vision for overturning the patriarchy, in which the author compared marriage to prostitution and insisted that women's freedom rested on economic independence. By the time Heterodoxy began to meet, Charlotte was an international celebrity. She called herself a woman "at large," a giant in the vanguard of her transformative era. When she gave a "background talk" at Heterodoxy on her childhood and feminist beginnings, the theme was "inherited rebelliousness."[28]

One eager early reader of *Women and Economics* was a twenty-nine-year-old Unitarian minister from Syracuse, New York, named Marie Hoffendahl Jenney. At the turn of the twentieth century, she was living in Des Moines, studying and preaching among a network of forward-thinking women known as the "Iowa Sisterhood," who were fighting for women to have a more visible and influential role in church leadership. Despite their mentorship, the young minister found herself restless and unfulfilled. Her work was often tedious and the local community resistant to female authority. She had pledged loyalty to a supposedly progressive church that, year after year, refused to grant women any real power or leadership. More fundamentally, she was beginning to doubt what Christianity taught about the innate differences between men and women. These differences underpinned the whole structure of Western society at the turn of the century, denying women a voice in public and the power to change their circumstances. To many people, they still seemed as fixed and unchangeable as the tides, even as women made incremental gains, professionally and politically.

But, Marie was beginning to wonder, what if they could be overturned—a revolution, not gradual reform, in the very concept of gender? What if Jesus could be thought about not as a man, exactly, but as an "ethical ideal" who was free from "sex bias"? A figure who embodied both masculine and feminine virtues, self-reliance combined with self-sacrifice? This nonbinary Jesus seemed perfectly suited to the new era of equality that Marie hoped would dawn with the twentieth century. But no doubt church leaders would balk at such a bold re- (or de-)gendering of the Son of God. If she was to think her way out of the polarity of gender toward a vision of universal humanity, she would need a new guide. When she read Charlotte's book, Marie sent the author a heartfelt letter declaring herself not just an admirer but a "disciple." She thanked her for writing *Women and Economics*, but more deeply, for *seeing* her, for giving her a language and a theory with which to comb out her tangled beliefs about women and society. In bold, romantic terms she begged to be recognized in return: "I want you to write me. You will, won't you! Perhaps you are flooded with letters. Never mind. They don't care as I care."[29] Their friendship would continue by letter for a decade before they met in person.

When Heterodoxy first met in 1912, Charlotte Perkins Gilman, at fifty-one, was the club's second most senior member: the actress Mary Shaw, famed for her roles in Henrik Ibsen's plays, was six years older. They set the club's standard for notoriety. "Already the air was being charged for the new day," Heterodite

Marie Jenney Howe, the founder of Heterodoxy, was a Unitarian minister, suffrage activist, and writer. (*Credit: Susan B. Anthony House and Museum*)

Zona Gale wrote of Charlotte. "But her mind was one of the first in America to catch the fire."[30] If Charlotte lit the club's intellectual torch, however, it would be Marie's emotional warmth, her "genius for friendship," and her "great mother-heart" that sustained it. "Here's to Marie," said one member, "who in the midst of this strange universe and this cold city created a little world for us."[31]

Marie moved to New York in 1910 and quickly became an organizer in the suffrage movement. Through her activism, she met many of the women who would become core members of Heterodoxy. Most members of the club were involved in the fight for the vote, seeing it as an essential tool (or a weapon) to advance equality, even if they didn't believe it would be enough by itself to truly liberate women. One of the club's most visible members was the beautiful and quotable Inez Milholland, a lawyer and committed suffragist as well as a newspaper darling, whose early death in 1916 amplified her fame by turning her into a martyr for the movement. Her close friend and fellow lawyer Crystal Eastman came to believe that World War I and the political repression it unleashed in America was an even more urgent cause, which led her to cofound the organization that became the American Civil Liberties Union (ACLU). Grace Nail Johnson, the only Black member of Heterodoxy and the wife of civil rights leader James Weldon Johnson, pushed her peers to foreground race in their understanding of equality, while Elizabeth Gurley Flynn and Rose Pastor Stokes, working-class union activists and ardent socialists, kept class and labor issues front and center.[32]

The majority of Heterodoxy's members were writers, and their collective output of articles, nonfiction books, memoirs, novels, plays, and poetry is enormous. Among the club's many journalists, Rheta Childe Dorr, Bessie Beatty, and Madeleine Doty took daring trips to Europe during World War I and reported from Russia in the throes of revolution, while Mary Heaton Vorse chronicled labor battles back home. Dr. Sara Josephine Baker overhauled New York's public health policies and slashed the city's infant mortality rate, while Mary Ware Dennett, the divorced mother of teenage boys, championed sex education and birth control. The writer Susan Glaspell, along with her friends in Heterodoxy and the wider Village, founded the Provincetown Players theater company and was responsible for much of its best work, exploring daring new ideas about gender and relationships onstage. Elsie Clews Parsons, a feminist anthropologist and ethnographer, wrote widely about the evolving structures of family life under feminism and studied Native American cultures in the American Southwest—an area to which the wealthy, restless Mabel Dodge was also drawn after several years as an arts patron and salon hostess in the heart of the Village. Filling out the membership roster were actresses, anarchists, psychologists, poets, teachers, lawyers, socialites, and socialists—few of whom can be classified with just one label.

Together, the women of Heterodoxy pushed each other toward a new way of living. Everything from the way they dressed to the company they kept and the causes they championed was self-consciously new, and the daily pursuit of the future could be exhausting. They needed each other: as inspiration and support, as friends and lovers and rivals. Elizabeth Gurley Flynn, a leader since her teens in the radical Industrial Workers of the World (IWW) and a believer in class solidarity above all, was at first skeptical of the benefits of a women-only organization. Her membership in Heterodoxy proved to be a transformative experience. "It has been a glimpse of the women of the future, big spirited, intellectually alert, devoid of the old 'femininity' which has been replaced by a wonderful freemasonry of women," she wrote. She referred to the club as "this charmed circle," a group touched by magic.[33]

What remains to be discovered of Heterodoxy in the following pages is how this extraordinarily fertile network of friendship grew far beyond the formal structure of meetings to give shape and meaning to its members' lives. Friendship is an elusive subject for history because we tend to take it for granted, to view it as something organic, unspoken, a connection that doesn't require work or analysis. Its story must be pieced together through the evidence of meetings, shared projects, and long associations; through public tributes or private expressions of affection. Biographers often treat friendship as subordinate to romantic or familial relationships, and less important than the influence of mentors and teachers in shaping a person's life. But our friends have a profound influence on our work and our beliefs, on the way we live every day. For the women in this book, friendship was a bolstering, emboldening force. I invite you to treat the women in this book as they treated one another—not as role models or heroines, statues at whose feet we are supposed to sit, but as friends: flawed, frustrating, and human.[34]

Chapter 1

WAY DOWN SOUTH
IN GREENWICH VILLAGE

HETERODOXY'S FOUNDER MARIE JENNEY HOWE WAS A FEW months shy of her fortieth birthday when she arrived in New York from Cleveland, Ohio, in the fall of 1910. Six years earlier, she had married her longtime admirer, Frederic C. Howe, whom she first met during her time in seminary in his hometown of Meadville, Pennsylvania. He had judged her "too beautiful to be a minister" and could not comprehend her longing for a career; when he proposed, she turned him down, and he later admitted he had wanted his "old-fashioned picture of a wife, rather than an equal partner."[1] But the couple stayed in touch, and following her disillusioned departure from the ministry, some years later, Marie reconsidered. Once they were married, she steadily pushed back against her husband's opposition to the idea of women in public life, increasingly active in the suffrage movement in Ohio and later in New York.

Fred, a well-connected liberal political activist, was a great believer in the democratic potential of the American city, which he called "the hope of the future," where "life is full and eager."[2] After several years working with the influential reformist mayor of Cleveland, however, he tired of acrimonious municipal politics, and the couple decided to move to New York, in part based on Marie's "decided preference" for the city.[3] New York was the country's foremost crucible of urbanist theory. Fred quickly rose to prominence as a writer and reformer, and was eventually appointed Commissioner of Immigration of the Port of New York, the busiest in the world, where he was responsible for processing the thousands of people disembarking daily at Ellis Island in search of a new life in America. Marie took up a role as a suffrage leader for the district covering Greenwich Village. Although she struggled with chronic illness, she was able to combine her experience in the pulpit and her passion for women's rights to become a popular speaker and organizer, and she worked hard to convert her husband and his political allies to the suffrage cause.[4]

Fred and Marie threw themselves into the progressive life of their new city. After a stint in the Chelsea Hotel, the couple moved to an apartment at 31 West Twelfth Street, on the wealthy northern edge of Greenwich Village. There, they welcomed crowds of idealistic guests, including many of the founding members of Heterodoxy. "Brilliant young people, full of vitality, ardent about saving the world," Fred called them.[5] Playing the role of hostess to the downtown radicals offered Marie a way of combining her ministering instincts with her zeal for social change. Meanwhile, Fred became the director of the People's Institute at Cooper Union, on the eastern edge of the Village, a "kind of popular university" that invited progressive speakers, and ran classes and lectures for workers and new immigrants on everything from urban planning to foreign policy to feminism.[6]

When Fred and Marie arrived, the Village was largely an Italian neighborhood, bordered by other ethnic enclaves, some growing and some shrinking. The residents of Little Africa, a lively, raffish nineteenth-century haven for free Black families and interracial households, studded with "black-and-tan" dive bars, were migrating north, to the midtown Tenderloin and to Harlem, which in the 1920s would blossom into a new, distinctly African American bohemia.[7] The Lower East Side, meanwhile, was becoming an increasingly Eastern European and Jewish quarter. Fleeing famine, poverty, and antisemitic violence, hundreds of thousands of refugees, especially from Russia, sought safety and opportunity in the biggest immigrant city in the world, and they brought with them an infectious revolutionary spirit. For reformers and radicals in New York in the early twentieth century, there was nowhere else to be but Greenwich Village. From a slow beginning in the early years of the century to a heyday that coincided with, and that is impossible to untangle from, Heterodoxy's earliest and most vibrant years, the scruffy, dense, and tucked-away neighborhood was home to a remarkable flowering of creative and activist energy.

Writers on the Village are always leading us *down*—down the rabbit hole, into the underworld, where something illicit and exciting is germinating, where life is shabby and crowded and free. Mary Heaton Vorse, a writer and Heterodoxy member who had lived in the area since 1900, begins her warmhearted satirical novel *I've Come to Stay* with an invitation, or a lure: "Down below Washington Arch, at the end of the Avenue, lies Washington Square. . . . It takes only a minute to walk from the north to the south, but whether you pass the hotels—west, or choose the way past the Benedict—east, you have left New York and gone into that mythical spot called Greenwich Village."[8] Edith Unger, a sculptor who ran what she claimed was the first tearoom in the Village, set the tone with the words inscribed—backward, for maximum outsider confusion—over her door: ELOH TIBBAR EHT NWOD. Imitators proliferated at an astonishing rate—the Purple Pup, the Dutch Oven, the Crumperie, the Samovar, Christine's, Grace Godwin's Garret—the vast majority of them run by women. Bobby Edwards, the Village's self-styled troubadour, celebrates the freedoms the area offered women in particular in his poem "Way Down South in Greenwich Village." "'Neath the guise of feminism, / Dodging social ostracism, / They get away with much / In Washington Square."[9]

It is difficult to imagine now, walking the well-heeled district of boutiques waving the deep purple flags of New York University, but the Village, as it was called mainly by its bohemian inhabitants, was once cheap, seedy, and out of the way. No subway line went there until the Seventh Avenue line extension to Christopher Street–Sheridan Square opened in 1917. Greenwich Village's hard-to-access location and quirky geography shaped it as much as the literary and political daydreams of its residents. "Under scientific scrutiny, it is an indefinite area below Fourteenth Street, winding around a variety of irregular streets," explains Mary Heaton Vorse's narrator. "It comprises some studio buildings, a few eating places, a club or two, and that is all one can say of its geographical confines. It is nothing much to look at; yet it has already passed into tradition."[10] Washington Square Park was "bounded on the north by a sparse fringe of fashionables who live in mellow brick houses," the settings for Henry James novels, while to the south and east, immigrants crowded into tenements, and apartment buildings nudged up against stores and small-scale factories. "Satin and motorcars on this side, squalor and push carts on that," as the modernist writer and longtime Village resident Djuna Barnes put it.[11] Yet in the optimistic eyes of the bohemians, there was harmony despite the extremes. "One group of people melts gradually into another group or is superimposed on it until one has that intangible thing called atmosphere—poor abused word."[12]

Several of Heterodoxy's core membership lived on the wealthy northern side of the park: suffragist Inez Milholland with her parents, siblings, and servants at 9 Washington Square North, and on the same block as Marie Jenney Howe, the flamboyant

Mabel Dodge in a magnificent apartment on the corner of Fifth Avenue and Twelfth Street, where she held weekly salons. Rose Pastor Stokes, one of the few members of the club who was both Jewish and from a working-class background, lived with her millionaire husband in a brownstone at 88 Grove Street. One of Heterodoxy's pairs of sisters, née Inez and Daisy Haynes, were both long fixtures in the neighborhood: Daisy ran a shop on Thompson Street (also her married name) selling "quaint and curious things," while Inez moved frequently before settling with her husband, journalist Will Irwin, in a four-story house on West Eleventh Street, which was remodeled by an architect friend to embody the colorful, modern Village style. "We painted the walls, all over the house yellow and the woodwork green," Inez recalled. "We took out the sleazy, rococo gas chandeliers [and] established electric lights."[13] Younger Heterodites, no doubt picking up tips from their friends about availability and sympathetic landlords, moved around the neighborhood with footloose frequency, often staying only a few weeks or months at one address before moving on.

The addresses of Heterodoxy members sometimes overlap: playwright Susan Glaspell and feminist leader Henrietta Rodman lived, at different times, at 42 Bank Street, while journalists Madeleine Doty and Mary Heaton Vorse both belonged to a socialist housing collective at 3 Fifth Avenue that was called (with frank unconcern for future historians) simply "A Club."[14] Madeleine later shared a third-floor walk-up apartment at 12 Charles Street with Crystal Eastman and Ida Rauh—all three were graduates of New York University School of Law (as was suffragist Inez Milholland) and active in a number of progressive and artistic ventures in the Village. Crystal reported to her mother that Madeleine had "frank gray eyes and an open smile and much the same charm as a young boy has. I shall like her, and there won't be any emotional strain either way."[15] But the shared quarters didn't last long before Crystal moved out to live with her beloved and strikingly handsome younger brother, Max, who brought his own brand of emotional strain to her friend group, professing his love for Inez Milholland before marrying Ida Rauh in 1911.

This was the charm of life in the Village for bohemian women: creating their own gatherings, communities, and living arrangements, where—liberated from the parlors and chaperones of their upbringings—they could talk freely about anything, with anyone. In their dining room at 1 Patchin Place, a picturesque tucked-away street opposite the notorious Jefferson Market Courthouse, two Smith graduates—a couple known as "the two Elizabeths"—hosted a gathering every Thursday evening, beginning sometime in late 1910. Lit by candles and fueled by coffee, the after-dinner talks around their dining room table ran deep into the evening, and shared commitments blossomed quickly into intimacy. The group was almost exclusively female and united by "a loosely-held attitude towards women's rights," recalled one of the two men allowed to attend regularly, who added that "conversation was the flickering flame that held the group together." A smaller counterpart to Heterodoxy, and including several members who belonged to both groups, the Patchin group also prided itself on its eclectic range of subjects and its witty repartee: "One could air serious as well as amusing opinions, provided they were treated lightly and deftly."[16]

Not long after becoming a regular at "Patchin," writer and Heterodoxy member Katharine Anthony moved into the communal all-female household. The women had "a joint kitchen and dining room with a real cook and excellent food and think they have solved the problem of life in a big city," one of the "Elizabeths," progressive educator Elisabeth Irwin, jokingly told her college alumnae magazine.[17] In 1915, her partner Elizabeth

Westwood died suddenly, aged just thirty-five, and within a few months, Katharine and Elisabeth had become a couple. They moved several times around the Village before landing at 23 Bank Street, where they would live out their lives together. The path from shared ideals to shared beds was a short one in the Village.

The journalist and poet John Reed—"Jack" to his friends—also romanticized the Village, America's "Quartier Latin," as a place to escape middle-class morality. He would become romantically entangled with more than one Heterodoxy woman, and in 1918, wrote his account of the Russian Revolution, *Ten Days that Shook the World*, while living on Patchin Place. When he first arrived in the Village as a recent Harvard graduate, he found a world gloriously free of social constraint. Despite the dust, smells, cockroaches, inadequate plumbing, and unreliable gas at "Forty-Two Washington Square," he extolled that freedom in verse: "But nobody questions your morals, / And nobody asks for the rent,— / There's no one to pry if we're tight, you and I, / Or demand how our evenings are spent."[18] But the pleasures of the Village—sex, booze, friendship, poetry—were more than simply indulgences. Certainly, the opportunity to sit up late drinking with unchaperoned, unmarried women of one's own class was a new and intoxicating experience, but it wasn't simply hedonism. These pleasures were symbolic of a different set of values, far removed from those that governed most of America, and a new way of living that championed equality, cosmopolitanism, freedom of speech and ideas, secularism, and socialism. The self-proclaimed feminists of the Village, men and women, embraced a new form of fellowship between the sexes that was fairer and freer and more *fun* than the ones they'd grown up with. In the epicenter of American bohemia, they took the feminist theory of women's humanity and equality and attempted to put it into practice.

Patchin Place, one of Greenwich Village's most iconic streets, was home to several Village radicals, including John Reed and the writer Djuna Barnes, and a Heterodoxy-like discussion club at the residence of Elisabeth Irwin. (*Credit: Jessie Tarbox Beals, New-York Historical Society*)

By the time Heterodoxy playwright Susan Glaspell settled in the Village in 1913, the scene, sets, and main characters were established.

> One could turn down Greenwich Avenue to the office of *The Masses*, argue with Max [Eastman], or Floyd [Dell], or Jack Reed; then after an encounter with some fanatic at the Liberal Club, or (better luck) tea with Henrietta Rodman, on to the Working Girls' Home (it's a saloon, not a charitable organization) or if the check had come, to the Brevoort.[19]

Her description, one of innumerable miniature guided tours offered by writers in these years, evokes a world in which social, political, and professional pursuits bled into each other. The "Working Girls' Home" was the joking nickname that Mary Heaton Vorse bestowed on the rough-and-tumble O'Connor's Saloon, on a corner of Christopher Street, where you could get hard-boiled eggs with your beer, and where John Masefield, "perhaps England's greatest living poet," had tended bar.[20] The Brevoort Bar was a swankier affair, in the basement of an imposing black-brick hotel dating to 1835, which loomed on the corner of Fifth Avenue and Eighth Street (or, as the stationery styled it, "[Le] Coin de la 5me Avenue et de la 8me Rue"). Continuing the Left Bank Paris pastiche, the staff wore chic striped waistcoats and the bar was well stocked with absinthe.[21] Ambrose, the poseur hero of Mary Heaton Vorse's Village novel, is a regular: "Like all its patrons he grumbled at it, called it monotonous, crowded, smoky, full of slummers; threatened to find another hangout, and never, when he could afford it, went anywhere else."[22]

Among the neighborhood's numerous temples of talk, the most important to its social life and its later mythology was the Liberal Club. In the middle of the row of buildings on

MacDougal Street that housed a shifting array of spaces for eating, drinking, performing, and gathering, the club was a vital social center for the Village as a whole. Its two adjoining parlors had a stripped-down elegance, with high ceilings, big windows, fireplaces, bare wood floors, an old piano, and wooden furniture painted, in the established bohemian style, in bright, clashing shades of orange and yellow. On the walls were political cartoons and paintings by American artists—Charles Demuth, Marsden Hartley, Art Young—who were not yet famous, whose colorful, off-kilter works were inspired both by the Cubists in Paris and by the gritty vistas of urban and industrial US cities.[23] A far cry from an older kind of political club like the staid Gramercy Park organization from which it had broken away, the downtown Liberal Club was "possessed of quite the best dancing floor one might desire."[24] It boasted its own drama troupe and threw fundraising costume balls in nearby Webster Hall that were known as "Pagan Routs."[25] The idea of a political club that was also a dance hall and an avant-garde theater would have seemed odd anywhere in New York in 1903. In 1913, in the Village, it felt inevitable.

Numerous Heterodoxy women were members of the Liberal Club and involved in its organization, but none was more influential than Henrietta Rodman, a high school English teacher and outspoken feminist who is often credited with spearheading the club's move from Gramercy Park to Greenwich Village, and thus with launching the neighborhood as a byword for cultural rebellion. The writer Floyd Dell, who arrived in New York in 1913 and quickly established himself at the heart of the Village's literary culture, created a memorable picture of Henrietta in his memoir, as "a Candide in petticoat and sandals"—that is, an optimistic dreamer who had "an extraordinary gift for stirring things up."[26] Certainly Henrietta cut a distinctive figure in her turban, loose gown, and flat lace-up boots: the picture of a feminist bohemian who cared nothing for corseted convention. But as an educator and organizer, her activism and her politics were more purposeful than this description suggests.

The idea that women's power lies in "stirring things up," of being the catalyst for change, but not carrying it through themselves, was one that feminists frequently encountered. In seeking reasons for the Liberal Club's defection to the Village, scandal-hungry newspapers seized on Henrietta's secret marriage to Herman de Fremery, who worked at the American Museum of Natural History. The *New York Times* suggested that the pair were living in a ménage à trois with Herman's common-law wife, and that Henrietta was also involved, in unspecified ways, in another divorce in the club's ranks. Invoking the buzzword "free love" (gasp!), the paper insinuated that it was sexual immorality that enticed the liberals downtown. The story was quickly enshrined in myth, despite the paper's quick retraction ("De Fremery Marriage: The Times Finds Published Details Are Erroneous."); Henrietta's secrecy was in fact due to the Board of Education's ban on married teachers, which she would soon devote her energies to overturning.[27] Other causes cited for the exodus of ultra-liberals to MacDougal Street include the blackballing of the anarchist Emma Goldman and the refusal to admit W. E. B. Du Bois as a member. The new Liberal Club did include in its membership rolls Heterodoxy's Stella Ballantine, who was Emma Goldman's niece and loyal supporter, but not Du Bois or any other Black people.[28]

Like many cultural shifts in the history of New York, the Liberal Club's move really began as a story about real estate. The younger, more radical wing of the club wanted to create an open, relaxed social center, which was impossible to do in a private apartment in a wealthy uptown residential neighborhood. According to the new club's secretary, a breakaway group began looking for "a house in some picturesque quarter" near Washington Square; among them was the "jaunty and hirsute" Ernest

Holcombe, who was married to Grace Potter, a Heterodoxy member who would become one of America's first psychoanalysts. Before long, Polly Holladay, "a robust young woman with prominent eyes and chin" and "a frequenter of rebel balls," approached the group to propose joining forces—her eponymous restaurant in the basement, the club upstairs. Once they'd found the house on MacDougal Street, "a hardwood parquet floor for dancing was put down, and a player-piano was bought on the installment plan." By the end of 1913, Polly's restaurant and the club were well established, with Heterodoxy members comprising around two-thirds of the female membership.[29] Henrietta Rodman served on the club's scrupulously co-ed executive board.[30]

The more scandalous myth of the Liberal Club stuck because it conformed to a story the Village loved to tell, in which members of the upstart new generation overthrew an older, more entrenched and conservative one. And although the details here were inaccurate, they betrayed a larger truth about how the city was changing, with cracks opening all over: between stuffy midtown and anything-goes downtown, between the nineteenth century and the twentieth, between reformers and revolutionaries. The liberal center was under assault from the energized Left, whose knack for pageantry, stunts, and celebrity made up for a lack of money and traditional authority.

The Liberal Club's in-house theater was a self-consciously modern and proudly amateur undertaking. The performances were primarily "satirical little comedies making fun of ourselves," like Floyd Dell's *St. George in Greenwich Village*, which Henrietta Rodman asked him to write for the club's opening in November 1913.[31] The play took aim at several of the neighborhood's favorite topics of discussion and belief, including Montessori education, anarchism, futurism, and suffrage. The play was mounted without a stage, curtain, or any lights, and the cast—which included Heterodoxy actress Helen Westley, a "femme fatale" with "coal-black hair and black, slinky dresses"—invented their own words when they forgot the script.[32] Familiarity with the local scene made improvisation easier, and the jokes were readily at hand. Their self-conscious laughter was a way for the bohemian Villagers to reaffirm the in-joke identity of the neighborhood. "It was only in the privacy of our Liberal Club little theatre, amongst ourselves, that I made fun of the suffrage movement," Floyd Dell noted. "I would not have thought of doing so in *Vanity Fair*."[33] The question was whether that spirit could spread beyond the borders of Washington Square.

The gatherings at the Liberal Club have, like Heterodoxy meetings, vanished into myth, but in the pages of *The Masses* magazine, a vibrant record survives of the Village's political and artistic preoccupations during the 1910s. Founded in 1911 as a rather earnest socialist weekly, *The Masses* passed after a year or so into the hands of Max Eastman, thanks to his sister Crystal's energetic promotion of his talents. In September 1912, Max, then a lecturer at Columbia University, was informed that he'd been "elected" editor of the magazine—"No pay."[34] He proved to be a talented leader, adept at staying ahead of the conversation and—no less important—delegating work to eager associates, who included both Jack Reed and Floyd Dell. From its headquarters at 91 Greenwich Avenue, the monthly magazine was distributed across the country as an organ of avant-garde ideas. *The Masses* advanced feminist theories, supported suffrage and the labor movement, and published stinging satirical cartoons, poetry, and political commentary on every subject that preoccupied the leftists, progressives, and radicals of the day.

The Masses owed a great deal to the labor and vision of Heterodoxy women, who were editors and frequent contributors. Inez Haynes Gillmore (later Irwin), a well-known and popular short story writer, was recruited early on as fiction editor by Piet Vlag, the socialist writer (a different one) who started the magazine.

"I had almost as much qualification for such a position as for work on the atomic bomb," she claimed—and at first recoiled from the responsibility of taking a red pen to an author's work, knowing only too well how much it could hurt. Before long, however, she began to relish her power, cutting and rewriting "as though I had been born in an editorial chair."[35] Inez brought in her friend Mary Heaton Vorse as a fellow editor, and manuscript review sessions happened collectively, often at Mary's house. In "a cozy room, soft, yellow light, lots of tobacco smoke," writers read their work aloud to the assembled audience of contributors and editors. It was no place for a sensitive ego. "The poor author would feel more and more like a worm," Mary recalled. "You could see him looking wildly around to see if there was a swift exit." This "dismemberment," usually by the artists—who were always locked in rivalry and jockeying for page space with the writers—was often brutal but potentially exhilarating. "There was no greater reward than having them stop their groans and catcalls and give close attention, then laughter if the piece was funny, finally applause."[36] It almost made up for the lack of pay.

Along with Mary and Inez, Heterodoxy members Elsie Clews Parsons, Helen Hull, Alice Duer Miller, Mabel Dodge, and Margaret Widdemer wrote for the magazine, and one-off pieces also came in from labor activists Rose Pastor Stokes and Elizabeth Gurley Flynn, and from Susan Glaspell, who went on to write a play, *The People*, set in "the office of a publication which is radical and poor," with a woman writer as a central character.[37] Heterodoxy contributions reflected the eclecticism that characterized both the magazine and the club: sentimental fiction, daringly intimate poetry, reportage, opinion pieces, satire, and personal essays. Other women whose contributions were vital but unsung included Dolly Sloan, the indefatigable office manager, a tiny, fierce, working-class woman whose husband, John, was one of the magazine's leading artists. Dolly made sure the bills were paid on time and kept the operation afloat, always insisting she was the only practical one among the staff.

Ironically for a socialist magazine, *The Masses* was heavily dependent on the support of wealthy backers, among them Alva Belmont, the fabulously wealthy dowager who was a major supporter of suffrage efforts in New York and had taken Max Eastman's ex-girlfriend Inez Milholland under her wing. When Max and Inez bumped into each other in the lobby of the Hotel Manhattan shortly after he became editor of *The Masses*, he confessed that the magazine he'd been invited to run was in danger of running into the ground. Inez invited him to dinner at Mrs. Belmont's mansion, promising that the heiress would open her purse for the cause. "She doesn't know anything about socialism," she told him. "Just tell her it's a fight and she'll like it." After the meal, whether she was charmed or convinced, or both, by the ardent young socialists, Alva agreed to give *The Masses* two thousand dollars—about four times a good annual salary at the time. Inez's new boyfriend, after what we can only assume was an uncomfortable pause, offered a thousand dollars of his own to the magazine.[38]

In its manifesto, *The Masses* set itself "against rigidity and dogma wherever it is found," which translated into a determined openness to different points of view as long as they were, in some way, radical and new. And stating its side in one of the era's most relentless ideological battles, it declared itself "A Revolutionary and Not a Reform Magazine." Mary Heaton Vorse neatly summed up the overlap of political and creative causes in both the Village and the pages of *The Masses*: "Everybody a Liberal, if not a Radical—and all for Labor and the Arts."[39] That combination was important. It was an axiom of Village life that new ideas about politics and society were inseparable from innovations in painting, theater, dance, literature, and sculpture. There was no contradiction between marching for the vote one day, treading the creaky boards at a little theater the next, and disappearing into an art studio on the third. Max Eastman's wife Ida Rauh, for example, who graduated from law school but never practiced, was at once a prominent labor activist, talented sculptor, birth control advocate, suffragist, and an actress and director with the Provincetown Players.

Ida also came from a wealthy family in Manhattan and did not need to support herself. But whether or not they had to earn a living, Heterodoxy women saw their creative and political work as the source of their identity, and their bond. On the shared ground of economic independence, an actress and a child psychologist, a textile artist, a labor organizer, and a satirical poet could meet and make friends. Being "women who did things—and did them openly," drew the club members tightly together and helped fuel their involvement in other causes.

For women artists who needed to make a living, commercial disciplines like cartooning, illustration, photography, and interior design were more welcoming than the arena designated as "fine" art. Women thronged the ranks of the "decorative" or "applied" arts—everything from basket weaving to interior design, bookbinding to stage and set decoration, jewelry to textiles to ceramics. For artistic Heterodites, the sacrifice of prestige was counterbalanced by economic independence, the value on which their feminism hinged.

Within Heterodoxy, in addition to Daisy Haynes Thompson, with her eponymous curiosity shop, and the political cartoonist Lou Rogers, there was Ami Mali Hicks, a textile artist and one of the most established of the female artisans and shopkeepers in the Village. Ami created decorative rugs, scarves, tunics, and wall hangings in botanical prints in her studio at 158 West Eleventh Street. Around 1917, the Village photographer Jessie Tarbox Beals created a portrait of Ami and her artwork for one of her postcards promoting picturesque Village life. The artist, tall and in her midforties, with her hair loosely braided around her head, rather awkwardly shows off a tufted rug to the camera. She is wearing a quintessential Village outfit: a square-necked flowing tunic in a paisley fabric, embroidered at the collar, hem, and cuffs, and belted over a long skirt and narrow, lace-up boots—clearly, no corset is constraining her breath. A rack behind her displays similar tunics on hangers, and a rattan chair and wooden table are draped and piled with scarves and more rugs. Over her shoulder hangs a display of batik wall hangings. Batik, the technique of applying wax to fabric to create a pattern before dyeing it, had recently come into vogue, and Ami joked about the way that a method so fundamental to her art was suddenly treated as a rare talent. "I am always being asked in prayerful accents, 'Oh, do you do batik?' And I always want to answer, 'My dear, do pianists play sonatas?'"[40]

But Ami, too, was a political activist, a committed suffragist, and a seeker of alternative ways of living and thriving under

Ami Mali Hicks in her studio, photographed by Jessie Tarbox Beals. (*Credit: New-York Historical Society*)

capitalism. There was, for her, no disjunction between art and politics. It was in her studio in 1910 that she and six other friends founded Free Acres, an unincorporated community in New Jersey where inhabitants could own property but not land, which was collectively held. The community was a small but enduring experiment in putting into practice the theories of Henry George, the progressive economist who argued for a single tax on land values as a way to fight inequality and allow all Americans, not just property-owners, to benefit from large-scale improvement projects like the railways. His theories attracted a cultlike following in the wildly unequal Gilded Age, especially among workers and socialists, and he had a particularly enthusiastic following in Heterodoxy—in which both his daughter, Anna George de Mille, and granddaughter, the dancer and Broadway choreographer Agnes de Mille, were members.

Inez Irwin remembered the short Greenwich Village heyday, between roughly 1912 and the end of World War I, as "full of hope and freedom" and the most exciting time of her life. "Great movements were starting everywhere," she wrote. "Everyone was fighting for something. Everyone was sure of victory. I used to say that a speaker with a megaphone could go to the intersection of Forty-Second Street [and] Broadway . . . and announce, 'I am here to gather recruits for a movement to free . . .' and before he could state the object of his crusade, he would be in the center of a milling crowd of volunteers."[41] In these and other memories of the Village, it is the energy of the time and place that lingers, more than the substance of the fight. It's understandable that long after those dreamed-of revolutions had flared and failed, and youthful zeal had faded, the survivors would cast the Village as a locus of passion rather than concrete action. Of course, there were dilettantes and hangers-on, there for the much-derided "atmosphere," especially once the neighborhood was more accessible and more hospitable to tourists. But it is worth remembering that in the year of Heterodoxy's founding, the Socialist candidate for president garnered nearly one million votes, and left-wing radicals had good reason to believe that their movement was ascendant. Ida Rauh bet a friend in 1912 that within ten years the United States would be a socialist republic.[42] Radicals truly believed that the balance of power was on the verge of a profound shift. Although their political fights would range widely, it was the woman's vote—thanks to the leadership of Marie Jenney Howe—that was for many of them the obvious place to start.

Chapter 2

THE TYPE HAS CHANGED

A FEW DAYS BEFORE THE PRESIDENTIAL ELECTION OF 1908, the businessmen of New York City staged a vast, seven-hour parade in support of the soon-to-be-victorious Republican candidate William Howard Taft. On a bright, blustery Halloween morning, more than sixty thousand men representing forty-three professions—from Wall Street bankers and brokers strewing ticker tape to milliners sporting different styles of hat—marched uptown from the financial district. Thousands more supporters lined the streets, huddled against the wind, waving flags. When the parade reached Fifth Avenue, it was suddenly enlivened by a new sound. From a window above the street, a group of women waved flags and hollered, "Votes for women!" through a megaphone.

According to a reporter, a "simply stunning" Vassar senior leaned out of the window and launched into a speech on suffrage, which halted the masculine march in its tracks. The men took one look at her "and stopped to listen, as any sane man would." Alarmingly, a group of marchers broke free of the parade and ran into the building and up the stairs to find the women, but this interruption didn't faze "the young orator," who kept talking for twenty minutes. Then she thanked her audience and added politely, "May I ask you kindly to clear the room?"[1] It appears they left without a fuss.

The parade heckler was twenty-two-year-old Inez Milholland, whose beauty and charisma soon made her a star of the suffrage movement. She was a quintessential New Woman—the fun-loving and free-spirited figure who was ubiquitous in the media; rather like "millennial" a century later, it was a label that marked both a generation and an attitude.[2] By the time she joined Heterodoxy, four years after making a splash at the Taft parade, Inez had become the embodiment of the modern, fashionable suffragist. A cartoon by Boardman Robinson, a radical artist for *The Masses* and other newspapers whose wife, Sally, was also a Heterodoxy member, illustrates the transformation.

THE TYPE HAS CHANGED.

Village radical artist Boardman Robinson illustrated the evolution of the women's rights activist in this newspaper cartoon. (*Credit:* New-York Tribune, *February 24, 1911*)

Called "The Type Has Changed," it shows a flat-footed frump, mannish, bespectacled, and dour, next to a fashionable young woman displaying graceful curves, high heels, low neckline, and a rampantly feathered hat. Both women wear a suffrage ribbon pinned to their chests, but on the older "type" it hangs limp, while on the younger it flutters amid the folds of her scarf like a fashion accessory. There is a gap between them like a cold shoulder: an inch or two on the page, but miles in real-life outlook and status.

Since the deaths of Elizabeth Cady Stanton and Susan B. Anthony in the first decade of the twentieth century, the American suffrage movement had struggled to move forward. The leaders of the dominant group, the National American Woman Suffrage Association (NAWSA), emphasized respectability and women's moral superiority, which made the movement palatable to thousands more supporters. But concrete political progress had stalled. By the end of 1910, only five western states—Wyoming, Colorado, Utah, Idaho, and Washington—had granted women the vote. The issue had been put in front of male voters in a referendum no less than fifty-five times, and only twice had the women prevailed.[3]

The fight for the vote was still being led by members of the generation that had attended or been inspired by the landmark meeting at Seneca Falls in 1848, widely credited with launching the women's rights movement. They favored tactics that were stuck in the previous century: endless petitions, endless meetings, endless speeches on the same points, for the same faithful listeners. Meanwhile, the world had moved on. New technology made it possible to share information much faster, over much bigger distances, than ever before, and photography, now much easier to reproduce, became more common in daily life. With the surge of visual imagery, glamour and celebrity began to infuse the culture, and a younger generation of activists realized that in the new century, the messenger was going to matter as much as the message.

Heterodoxy's other Inez, the writer Inez Haynes Irwin, was thirteen years older than Milholland. She remembered from her college years how viciously the old "type" of suffragist was lampooned for daring to talk while men didn't want to listen. "In the comic weeklies, Priscilla Jawbones, a tall, thin female of great strength and appalling ugliness, was the figure at which all these jokes were hurled," she recalled, adding that "the woman-believer in the movement was a cartoon figure until the last decade of the fight."[4] Ironically, Inez Milholland also resembled a cartoon figure, but not a comic one: she looked to a besotted news media like a real-life Gibson Girl, the ubiquitous fantasy figure sketched by Charles Dana Gibson, with her lithe body and piled crown of hair.

Inez's beauty was a boon to the modern suffrage movement as editors scrambled to put her face on the cover of their pictorial sections and held her up as a fashion icon. When she landed back in New York in September 1910 after a summer in Europe, where she had joined the suffrage fight in London, a *New York Times* reporter was there to greet her and described her up-to-the-minute ensemble. "Miss Milholland scampered down the gangway from the great liner, in a tailored suit, hobble skirt, trimmed with silk. She had on a Turkish turban, with a long Oriental veil, which was tossed carelessly about her neck." Reporters soon realized she could also be relied on for a juicy quote. "It might be considered good politics," Inez suggested to one, if the leaders of the movement "put their most attractive members forward when seeking to influence legislators."[5] In the ensuing months, she would lead parades dressed as Joan of Arc, and her combination of socialite glamour and socialist convictions made her a household name.

Inez had grown up in an environment that combined wealth and progressive zeal. She was the eldest of three children of John Milholland, a mercurial social reformer who made a fortune with an invention that cut through the clog of urban life: a pneumatic tube network under the streets that could zap messages in metal tubes across the city at breathtaking speed. He launched the system in New York by sending a family Bible (wrapped in an American flag) from midtown down to Bowling Green in forty seconds, a journey that took a bicycle messenger nearly twenty minutes. Pneumatic tubes were soon transmitting five million letters a day in New York, operating like the email of their day, making John Milholland a Progressive Era tech baron.[6] He expanded to cities across the United States and Europe, launching new systems with publicity stunts like hurtling puppies, kittens, and bowls of goldfish safely through the tubes.

When Inez turned thirteen, in the summer of 1899, John moved his family to London. The Milholland mansion was easy stone-hurling distance from Kensington Palace, and Inez became an eager recruit of the British suffragettes, whose tactics blended window smashing provocation with public pageantry. It was an intoxicating combination. When she returned to the United States to enroll at Vassar College, her English accent and cosmopolitan flair made Inez irresistible to her sheltered classmates—and to the American press, which assumed, or hoped, that she was more radical than she actually was. When one newspaper reported that she'd been jailed for her activism, her mother, Jean, wrote in to correct the record: Inez had not broken the law, and she was a born and bred New Yorker. "If she be a Suffragette at all, she is very much an American one."[7]

But even as a law-abiding American "suffragette," Inez knew how to make trouble. Vassar was an elite, conservative college, led by a president, James Monroe Taylor, who fiercely opposed woman suffrage and banned all activism for the vote on campus, insisting that it was his college's job to educate women, not to reform society. He had reckoned without "the idol of the whole undergraduate body," who made it perfectly clear that he could not have one without the other.[8]

On a sunny June afternoon at the end of her junior year, Inez led dozens of students and visiting alumnae off campus to the nearest place they could hold a suffrage meeting—a nearby cemetery. There, in a symbolically charged venue conspicuously close to the college, she gathered her fellow students "to listen to impassioned outpourings about the wrongs of their sex while seated on cherub-carved tombstones."[9] The students laid out a picnic and strung a yellow banner between the gravestones that read COME, LET US REASON TOGETHER, a verse from Isaiah that suffragists adopted as a plea for mutual respect.

The guest of honor was Harriot Stanton Blatch, a Vassar alumna thirty years Inez Milholland's senior who was back on campus to give a speech at her alumnae luncheon. As Elizabeth Cady Stanton's daughter, Harriot had grown up in the American women's rights movement. As an undergraduate, she had chafed at Vassar's refusal of politics, calling it "an institution composed entirely of a disfranchised class," which nevertheless refused to take "any interest whatsoever in its own political freedom."[10] She married an English socialist and spent twenty years in England, where she developed an inclusive and class-conscious view of suffrage; although she was a fierce guardian of her mother's legacy, she disagreed with the elder Stanton's desire to restrict voting to educated, literate women. On her return to America in 1902, Harriot brought a new vision of the movement with her: inclusive, confrontational, and media savvy. Inez's graveyard rally heartened her with its unprecedented show of defiance. She was joined there by two core members of her new organization, the Equality League of Self-Supporting Women (soon renamed the Women's Political Union): the labor leader Rose Schneiderman and bona fide feminist icon Charlotte Perkins Gilman.

The year Inez graduated, President Taylor gave a speech praising Vassar's conservatism, noting waspishly that the college "does not love notoriety for the undergraduate, and declares it to be unhealthful, intellectually and socially."[11] But in opposing suffrage, Vassar's president was swimming against a steadily strengthening tide. By the time a newspaper called Inez Milholland "one of the most fascinatingly persistent young radicals who ever mounted a suffragette banner on a mortar-board," that combination of accoutrements was more common than ever before.[12] Women's colleges were vital in fostering the relationships that spurred graduates to undertake activist careers, and campus connections became nodes in larger webs of feminist friendship. Within Heterodoxy, the majority of members, especially the younger generation, had forged friendships on the campuses of colleges like Vassar, Radcliffe, Smith, Barnard, and Bryn Mawr and were connected through close-knit alumnae and sorority networks.

But women's colleges were exclusive and elite spaces—many banned Black and Jewish students from attending—and resistant to political change. When Inez Haynes Irwin and a friend founded the College Equal Suffrage League at Radcliffe in 1900, she faced an uphill task getting undergraduates involved. According to Dr. Sara Josephine Baker, one of the league's earliest members who would go on to join Heterodoxy, "When asked to become a member, the average college woman acted as if you had suggested she play Lady Godiva at a stag-picnic."[13] Raised in a wealthy family in upstate New York, "Dr. Jo," as she was known, originally intended to go to Vassar as her mother had. The deaths of her father and brother while she was in her teens, however, meant she needed to earn money, and economic pressure was part of what led her to the Women's Medical College at the New York Infirmary, founded by the pioneering sisters Elizabeth and Emily Blackwell (the other part, she admitted, was "her native stubbornness," which made her want to study medicine "at all costs and in spite of everyone").[14] In 1911, another soon-to-be Heterodite, the journalist Mabel Potter Daggett, described sitting with a "woman physician"—quite likely Dr. Jo—at a Kappa Kappa Gamma sorority gathering. Having "withdrawn with our tea cups to the sofa," the friends observed with dismay the students' lack of interest in winning the vote. "You are a suffragist and I am a suffragist," Mabel quotes her doctor friend as saying, "but there is only one other woman here whose name is written in the cause."[15]

At the time, only 5 percent of the roughly forty thousand women enrolled in US colleges were members of the Equal Suffrage League. Mabel, writing in her sorority magazine, nonetheless insisted that "a college woman who is not a suffragist to-day is in a most anomalous position," and advanced the argument that the suffrage was not only a right of citizenship but a vital tool to achieve reforms like child labor legislation. But the suffragists recruitment methods were not always so high-minded. In 1909, Crystal Eastman coerced her handsome brother into taking a leading role in the new Men's League for Woman Suffrage. Max was dispatched to tour women's colleges and was credited with inspiring a rash of new on-campus suffrage clubs.[16] "It was never a question of making people believe in the benefits of women's freedom," he explained in *The Masses*. "It was a question of making them *like the idea*."[17]

In 1909, having squeezed everything she could from Vassar, the "orator, suffragette, lawyer in embryo" Inez Milholland was ready to make her mark on a larger canvas.[18] A week after graduation, she sailed to London and threw herself once again into the increasingly visible and uncompromising suffrage battle there. On her return to America, she was in the papers every few weeks, usually identified as a "Suffragette" or a Vassar grad, but soon simply as herself, no explanation needed. In October, her petition to study law at Harvard was denied by its trustees, even though the faculty and the college president were on her side. The anti-suffrage *New York Times* gave "Miss Milholland" space to mock the forces marshaled against her—in particular, the trustee who admitted he was against women's rights because he was suspicious of all progress, including railways and telephones. Two days later, the paper printed an even longer article about Inez's battle with Harvard, recapping her Vassar career and the already notorious graveyard rally. Laying out her plans to go to NYU if Harvard wouldn't budge, Inez explained that she wanted to study law first and foremost to help the suffrage cause and then because "I want to be self-supporting." She added, "I don't have to, of course, but for my own self-respect I feel I must be."[19] The yoking of self-support with self-respect was a privileged position, but it was deeply felt by a generation of women who, like Inez, absorbed their feminism from Charlotte Perkins Gilman and who were searching for an arena beyond marriage in which to make their lives matter.

There can be few more glaring illustrations of the disparity between men's and women's public roles in this era than the first suffrage parade, organized in the same year that sixty thousand men filled the streets for Taft. Just twenty-three women, most of them socialists, dared to assemble under hand-embroidered banners to illustrate "the entire femininity of the movement," and thus presumably lessen the shock of their presence. As they marched, they chanted a rhyming slogan that soon appeared on banners and postcards, framing the vote as a right wrongfully denied to people who were otherwise full participants in society: "For the long work day / For the taxes we pay / For the laws we obey / We want something to say."[20] Nevertheless, they were swiftly moved on by the police. Women's public speaking was still so repellent to the leaders of the mainstream American suffrage movement that they refused to endorse or participate in outdoor rallies and meetings, tactics popular with the British suffragettes that had yet to find traction with American activists. The fierceness with which the old-fashioned American leaders denounced the very idea of public protest shows how important decorous, ladylike behavior had been to the movement—and how vital, to an insurgent new generation, its overthrow now became.

The next year, a few hundred women turned out to march. Dr. Jo Baker was among them, and she compared her excitement and apprehension to "early Christian martyrs lining up for the grand march into the Colosseum." There was no telling how the watching crowds might react to "a group of women making a public show of themselves." At first, it seemed as though her worst fears of public ridicule were justified. When the "fifty courageous men" marching with the parade stepped into line, "we all heard a roar of laughter go up and pursue them like a vanishing wave." But as it turned out, it wasn't the parade itself that the crowd found funny, but the fact that one of the male supporters had accidentally snatched up the wrong sign and was striding along under a banner demanding MEN CAN VOTE—WHY CAN'T WE?[21]

In a remarkably short space of time, however, mass parades became a keystone of suffrage activism, much of it led by Harriot Stanton Blatch and her Women's Political Union—a name that deliberately echoed the headline-grabbing British organization, the Women's Social and Political Union. Suffragists adopted sunshine yellow, eye-catching and optimistic, to symbolize the movement, and the 1910 parade in New York included a convoy of one hundred cars draped in yellow banners and flowers. Participants sold lemonade and sandwiches wrapped in yellow paper.[22] The press eagerly covered the parades but also published worried editorials warning women against too much exertion and excitement. In 1910, the participants were said to be "resolute, but a good deal scared." The following year, the numbers and confidence of participants had risen, though they

were contested: the organizers claimed five thousand marchers; the *New York Times*, just three thousand. Nevertheless, they
acknowledged it as "the biggest thing in the way of a procession which the woman suffragists have ever had in the United
States."[23] There were floats and marching bands, followed by
women arrayed by their professional affiliations: milliners and
dressmakers, workers and farmers, physicians and lawyers. Leading
the actors was Heterodoxy's Fola La Follette, one of Marie Jenney
Howe's closest friends and the daughter of the famous progressive Wisconsin senator Robert La Follette, while Ami Mali Hicks
marched under the banner of women artists. Dr. Jo Baker recalled
"we college women . . . did our parading as a solid phalanx of academic caps and gowns."[24] Harriot Stanton Blatch, arrayed in her
pink and gray Vassar master's degree robes, instructed the women,
"March with head erect. Eyes to the front. Remember, you march
for the mightiest reform the world has ever seen."[25]

By 1912, parade participation had ballooned to ten thousand.
Participants were urged to wear white dresses and straw hats,
which were sold in advance to raise money and create a uniform
effect.[26] That same year, hundreds took part in an after-dark
march, in further defiance of social norms for women's behavior
in public. Captured on camera by Village photographer Jessie
Tarbox Beals, the marchers wore yellow hats and carried specially
designed battery-powered lights resembling Chinese lanterns.
From floats, "beauteous maidens" threw the crowd candies, each
wrapped up in a suffrage verse.[27] These parades, more than any
other activity, cemented the new image of the movement and its
ambassadors. Bold and fun-loving, but essentially law-abiding,
they were reformers, not revolutionaries.

Although they mostly trained their cameras on the affluent
white organizers and society women at the front of the march,
newspapers also recorded the presence of other groups, including Jewish and Italian factory workers, in the suffrage parades.

Inez Milholland, on horseback, led the 1913 suffrage parade in Washington, DC, which was attacked by an angry mob. (*Credit: Library of Congress*)

Mabel Ping-Hua Lee, a young woman from Chinatown, was profiled in one newspaper as an active participant, even though, as a second-generation Chinese immigrant, she was doubly barred from the vote.[28] One of the reports on the 1911 event noted that "there were several negro women in the parade." These women did not, however, enjoy the dignity of being named or photographed.[29] In the next year's much larger march, a disruptive mob singled out Black participants and "mistreated a Negro girl until the division marshal beat them off with a flagpole." The police, according to the suffragists' own indignant reports, did nothing to intervene.[30] White suffragists rarely acknowledged that the risks of marching, or speaking out in public, were very different for a working-class African American woman than they were for an Inez Milholland, and that the police could be just as much of a threat as a mob. They sidelined or excluded Black women, who nonetheless continued to participate in parades, in

New York and in other cities, and fought to be treated fairly and recognized for their contributions.[31]

Even white leaders sympathetic to racial justice failed to understand how the fight for the vote intersected with other issues of injustice. In an early issue of *The Crisis*, the magazine of the National Association for the Advancement of Colored People (NAACP), Inez Milholland's mother wrote a column presenting suffrage as a white women's cause that African Americans would do well to join. Arguing that the vote was "certainly the most vital, as well as the most important, of interests of the New Woman Movement," she chided Black women for not doing more to advance the cause instead of confining their efforts "within their own circle and among their own race." Urging them to "come forward and help share with their white sisters their responsibilities, and seek to obtain for both recognition as citizens possessed of political rights," she offered no promise that those white sisters might, in turn, help to recognize Black civil rights. Although Mrs. Milholland did suggest that an added benefit of women's suffrage would be to help "[secure] to the Negro of the South the political freedom to which he is justly entitled," it was left unspecified how this would happen.[32] W. E. B. Du Bois frequently gave space in *The Crisis* to the suffrage cause, devoting an entire issue to it in 1912 and again in 1915, when the issue featured a Votes for Women Symposium and a cover depicting Abraham Lincoln looking over Sojourner Truth's shoulder. But he also pushed the movement on its exclusions and compromises. When the organizers of the mass suffrage march in Washington, DC, planned to segregate Black activists at the back of the parade, the magazine initiated a letter-writing campaign in protest. According to *The Crisis*, "telegrams and protests poured in," so the policy was changed to allow the women to march instead with their state or professional delegations.[33]

As the marches grew in scope and attendance, activists whole-heartedly embraced spectacle, and the suffrage movement gained new energy and traction. "It was extremely alive, original, fertile in tactics and strategy," recalled Inez Irwin.[34] In New York, so-called sandwichettes strode the city wearing sandwich boards with suffrage slogans; others set up makeshift podiums on street corners in busy business districts. "You drove out in a wagon or car, pulled up at the curb on Columbus Circle or Union Square, and stood up and harangued anybody you could get to listen to you," recalled Dr. Jo Baker. "Orating" in the financial district, to an audience of male Wall Streeters on their lunch break, meant facing a crowd of hecklers, whose arguments were as absurd as they were loud. "To listen to them you would have thought every woman in the country who ever stepped out the door of her house was wantonly neglecting three pairs of ailing twins," the doctor sighed.[35] Elsewhere, women scattered leaflets from the cockpits of biplanes and wore gowns in suffrage yellow to fund-raising balls. They took automobile tours around parts of the country where the technology was still a novelty and organized stunts like cross-country hikes, performances, parties, and pag-eants involving hundreds of people. The events were designed to be seen, photographed, and discussed even more widely in the media—to go viral, 1910s-style.

Onstage and in film, too, a new vision of suffrage activism combined style and conviction, humor and rage. As the coun-try's theatrical heart and a hub of the fledgling movie industry, New York was the epicenter of that strategy, and several super-stars of the early 1900s stage—Ethel Barrymore, Maxine Elliott, and the vaudeville queen Lillian Russell—all turned out for the suffrage cause. A number of well-known actresses lent glamour to Heterodoxy meetings, chief among them the stage veteran Mary Shaw, billed as "America's leading emotional actress," who could draw audiences and attention purely on the strength of her name. Several times she reprised the title role, which was written for her, in (no relation) George Bernard Shaw's scandalous prostitution drama *Mrs. Warren's Profession*, and she was known for her roles in Henrik Ibsen's plays, which revolutionized the way women's lives could be portrayed onstage.[36] Several younger Heterodite performers were active in the suffrage cause, particularly Fola La Follette, Ida Rauh, and Beatrice Forbes-Robertson Hale, who had been an actress and suffragette in London before moving to New York. The club's other actress members included Margaret Wycherly, Eleanor Lawson, Helen Westley, Vida Sutton, and Virginia Kline, who acted in Ibsen plays with Mary Shaw and told the suffrage magazine the *Woman Voter* that "I believe in suffrage for women because I believe in progress for man!"[37] And though she was not a professional actress, Inez Milholland appeared in several pageants, tableaux, and films in support of the cause.

After Harriot Stanton Blatch joked to an audience of suffragists that they should "form a stock company and go from place to place playing propaganda plays to convert all the world to suffrage" (and in the process "make fortunes"), Marie Jenney Howe did exactly that.[38] In early March 1912, just as Heterodoxy was beginning, she assembled the country's first dedicated, volunteer suffrage theater company, though she credited the idea to Beatrice Forbes-Robertson Hale, who had belonged to a similar acting club in London. The 25th District Players' first season of one-act plays featured the work of Mary Shaw, Ida Rauh, and Marie herself, while Fola La Follette and Vida Sutton were among the actresses. Marie's position as leader of the 25th District of the Woman Suffrage Party of New York nominally allied her with the mainstream organization, NAWSA, but her district, encompassing the Village, was known as the most radical in the city and nicknamed the "Fighting 25th." Marie's innovative tactics were designed to attract attention and funds to the cause, and drew on the theatrical talents and milieu of Heterodoxy and the Village.

Suffrage infiltrated the theater in the 1910s through the substance of the performance as well as in the convictions of performers. Skits and satires were enormously popular, taking up anti-suffrage arguments and shredding them with a merciless smile. A one-act comedy by the prominent British suffragette Cicely Hamilton, *How the Vote Was Won*, was typical of the tongue-in-cheek genre. The play dramatized a familiar anti-suffrage argument—that women didn't need the vote because men supported them—by imagining the reaction of one man when all his previously self-supporting female relatives start turning up in his living room demanding that he provide for them. Not surprisingly, he rushes to Parliament to demand votes for women, where he's joined by all the other men in the city, who are facing similar demands. Fola La Follette had been making a name for herself with readings of the play since 1910.

Fola's husband, the playwright George Middleton, dedicated his one-act suffrage farce, *Back of the Ballot*, to "my friends the Antis," and summed up the approach of the suffrage satirists: "When argument fails, try laughter." Mary Shaw likewise believed that satire was a powerfully effective dramatic and political tool, doing more good than "much lauded plays that run the tear ducts dry"—despite the fact that such plays had made her career. Her suffrage satire *The Parrot Cage*, first performed at the Berkeley Theatre in January 1913, presented women as types of parrots, which squawk antifeminist sentiments like, "The highest mission of a parrot is to minister to the happiness of a private family." The voice of a man identified only as The Master periodically punctuates the parrots' chatter by telling them how pretty they are and that "Polly's place is in the cage." The lone dissenting voice belongs to the Free-Souled Parrot, who protests, "Let me out! I want to be free!" At the end of the play, this parrot begs her fellow birds to follow her, in a passionate call for female solidarity and the vital importance of making the break for freedom, even if it ends in disaster. The image of the bird in its cage, a free creature manacled to its perch within constant sight of a wider world, was scored deep into the rhetoric and belief systems of suffragists and feminists in the early twentieth century—not least for an actress who had played Ibsen's Nora, whose escape from her "doll's house" is likened to a bird taking flight.[39]

Heterodoxy founder Marie Jenney Howe gleefully exposed the absurdity of "anti" arguments in her satirical *Anti-Suffrage Monologue*, voiced by a woman. Inconsistency is built into the monologue's structure: "I have arranged these arguments in couplets. They go together in such a way that if you don't like one you can take the other." Thus women are either "angels" who are above politics, or they are "depraved" and their enfranchisement will "ruin our national life." Women are "cats" who cannot work together or "even be friends"—yet, if they won the vote, "we would have all the women banded together on one side and all the men banded together on the other side, and there would be a sex war which might end in bloody revolution." Women's sole duty is to take care of a man, declares the Anti. And if they are single? "Let them try a little harder and they might find some kind of a man to devote themselves to," she suggests. "What does the Bible say on this subject? It says, 'Seek and ye shall find.' Besides, when I look around me at the men, I feel that God never meant us women to be too particular."[40]

The force behind the humor was that these inconsistencies and absurd generalizations were not simply anti-suffrage arguments. They were the misogynistic water in which all women swam and through which feminists were trying to chart a better course. Another of Mary Shaw's satires, *The Woman of It, or Our Friends, the Anti-Suffragists*, went out of its way to ridicule solemn patriarchal values—in this case, chivalry. The president of

the Anti-Suffrage Club, Mrs. Allright, attempts to win over a
new recruit. Their exchange exposes the vagueness, and incipient
threat, of this cherished value:

MRS. ALLRIGHT: Women were just made to be loved and protected by the strong arm of a loving husband.
MISS BERRY: Protected from what, Mrs. Allright?
MRS. ALLRIGHT: I don't know exactly. But men are very sensitive on that point, Miss Berry. They all say that woman
   needs protection by the strong arm of man . . . Chivalry
   is a very beautiful idea . . . the more inferior to them a
   woman is the greater they feel the chivalry.[41]

Suffragists also embraced the new technology of film. News-
reels across the country spread the visual message of parades and
stunts, and helped bolster the fame of activists. The 1912 film
Votes for Women, featuring Max Eastman and Inez Milholland
alongside suffrage leaders and other well-known progressives,
included footage of a New York parade. The melodrama *Your
Girl and Mine*, now lost, was the fullest treatment of the suffrage
argument on screen, but full-length fiction films were expensive
to produce. The movement had more success latching on to existing celebrity, either by making films featuring famous suffrage
speakers or by inserting suffrage themes into ongoing properties.
What Eighty Million Women Want . . . , a 1913 film that survives
in fragments, features speeches by Emmeline Pankhurst and
Harriot Stanton Blatch. It's unclear how audiences would have
responded to the grainy footage of middle-aged women speaking inaudibly, but presumably the novelty of film, at first, was
enough to draw an audience regardless of the content. People
flocked to see *Our Mutual Girl*, a weekly serial produced by the
Mutual Film Corporation, which featured a heroine traveling
the country being groomed into high society and meeting famous

figures along the way. Among the cameos in the long-running serial was Inez Milholland.

A few days after announcing the formation of her acting company in the spring of 1912, Marie Jenney Howe staged a new kind of suffrage event, at Metropolitan Temple on Seventh Avenue and Fourteenth Street in the West Village. The church had a vast auditorium and was headed by a committed pacifist, so had become a popular venue for suffrage and pro-labor meetings. But the crowd on this evening was so big that only half the audience could squeeze inside, and the performers agreed to repeat their remarks at an overflow event. It was a suffrage meeting, but it didn't look like anything the audience had seen before. It was a performance, an entertainment, a party. Presided over by Marie wielding a blackthorn gavel, and an assistant who rang a cowbell with equal zeal, twenty-five speakers had five minutes each to "knock" an objection to suffrage "into a cocked hat." These objections ranged from "women don't understand politics" to "suffrage makes women less attractive." Most of the men and women on the evening's program came from local Village circles and Heterodoxy: Fola La Follette, Inez Milholland, Charlotte Perkins Gilman, and Inez Haynes Irwin who remembered the atmosphere more than the words—which were recorded and printed as a pamphlet. It was "the most amazing meeting," she gushed. "I have forgotten what I said, but I know I listened to all the others with rapt attention."[42]

There were also speakers from beyond the Village, including Elisabeth Freeman from England, there to answer the charge that militancy, for which the British suffragettes were notorious, "hurts the cause." The audience and the media were particularly taken with Elisabeth. Despite "weighing no more than a hundred pounds," she spoke fiercely in defense of militant tactics, comparing the suffragettes' window breaking and property damage with the American revolutionists' similarly destructive approach to tea. The police, she argued, were the ones escalating the violence. They were not the guardians of law and order but "employees of the British Government who maimed and beat women at the behest of that Government." In other words, they were no better than the mercenary thugs hired by factory owners to attack striking workers. The militants' target, Elisabeth insisted, was not any particular individual. Although she claimed to have been part of a group that had been "so close to [Prime Minister H. H.] Asquith that we could have kidnapped him had we wanted to," she and her friends did not simply want to remove the prime minister or his henchmen, David Lloyd George and Winston Churchill. "We are out, not to rid England of a few men, but to rid her of a system," she said. "And we expect to do it."[43]

Elisabeth Freeman also spoke at another of Marie Jenney Howe's innovative fundraising and audience-building events, an Author's Evening for Suffrage, in January 1914, in which she shared a platform with W. E. B. Du Bois. In a group photograph taken for the event, the *Crisis* editor and civil rights activist is seated—looking somewhat aloof and skeptical—at the end of a row of white journalists, including Inez Haynes Irwin's future husband Will. Marie stands at his right shoulder, alongside Fred and her Heterodoxy friend Paula Jakobi, the coauthor of her suffrage satire. It's hard to know whether such events were truly efforts to persuade audiences who thought differently or—more likely—offered an opportunity for feminists to enjoy the comfort and support of being in a room with those who shared their beliefs. Press attention spread the message further, and helped contribute to the idea that the cause was on the march and that victory was in sight.

Yet despite all the pageantry, energy, and visibility that the new "type" of suffragist brought to her moribund cause in the

1910s, many men and women remained implacably opposed to the idea that women should have a direct voice in government. A powerful ideology held that women's appropriate sphere was private, not public, and that nothing less than the stability and future of the nation depended on keeping those spheres separate. Such a position ignored the realities of industrial capitalism, under which more women than ever were entering the labor force. For working-class women, domestic seclusion was little more than a fantasy. As Inez Milholland argued at Marie's "25 Objections" event, how could women's place be in the home when nine million of them were out at work every day in mills and factories? Why were those numbers rising so fast that "one-fifth of all the women of the world" were working outside the home as she spoke? If those who raised this objection really believed it, what were they planning to do—give those women enough money to allow them to stay home? Or simply let them starve? Her passion made her eloquent, and she was cut off midsentence by the cowbell.

Inez's fervor for the plight of working women was widely shared within her circle of middle-class activists. Indeed, the causes of suffrage and labor rights are impossible to untangle in the 1910s, especially in New York, where protests, fundraisers, rallies, and talks kept both issues in the headlines, with events often featuring the same speakers. The overlap was mirrored in British activism. In 1909, Emmeline Pankhurst, the grande dame of the suffragettes, kicked off her American tour with a speech at Carnegie Hall. "I am what you call a hooligan," the grandmotherly figure announced to her well-heeled audience. A month later, a farewell rally at Cooper Union saw crowds of the newly fired-up faithful spill over and block Fourth Avenue, as Mrs. Pankhurst urged them to support both the suffrage and labor causes. Major suffrage donor Alva Belmont echoed

Mrs. Pankhurst with the declaration: "I was a born rebel!" The rhetoric exposed a fault line—one that the movement would never fully mend—between the wealthy, educated speakers and their audience of overburdened young women who were all too readily classed as "rebels" and "hooligans" and punished, not celebrated, as such. Over the winter of 1909, as suffragists steeled themselves to participate in orderly street parades, tens of thousands of working girls spilled into the streets to demand a voice, vote be damned.

Chapter 3

THE REBEL GIRLS AND
THE MINK BRIGADE

ON THE FIRST MORNING, IT FELT LIKE A PARTY. THOUSANDS of workers stepped away from their sewing machines in hundreds of factories across lower Manhattan and flooded into the streets, wearing their best dresses and their biggest hats. They went out in search of attention. Union bosses begged the girls, in vain, to dress soberly, but they had no interest in garnering sympathy by appearing as waifs. Yelled at by onlookers, they yelled back, jeering at the scabs brought in to keep the machines humming, and hurled rotten eggs at their catcallers.[1] On the picket lines they were determined to prove—to male union leaders as much as to their bosses—that women had just as much stomach and stamina to fight for their rights as men did. Beginning in November 1909 and on through the bitter winter, more than twenty thousand garment workers, most of them young women, staged the largest walkout the industry had ever seen.

In the tenements and the back rooms of shops, in purpose-built factories and converted attics, the garment business fueled the economy around Greenwich Village. It was a grinding, hazardous, and low-paid profession, dominated by women who were often the sole support of their families. By the time of the

1909 strike, just as bohemians and feminists were beginning to gather in the Village, some five hundred garment "shops" in New York employed thirty-five thousand people. They churned out a garment synonymous with the liberated, career-minded "New Woman": the shirtwaist. Also known simply as the "waist," this lightweight collared blouse of cotton or muslin had puffed sleeves, buttoned down the front, and was worn tucked into a long skirt. It could be plain and practical, decorated with pleats and embroidery, or accessorized with a bow tie or decorative "front." By the second decade of the century it was everywhere but starting to go out of fashion, in the way of garments that become ubiquitous, and losing luster as it got cheaper.

As the price of waists fell to barely more than a dollar apiece wholesale, manufacturers needed to sell more to turn the same profits, so they crammed in more sewing machines and ramped up production. The needles pounded from dawn to dusk. Lint filled the air, and doors and windows were blocked. "We worked from sunrise to sunset seven days a week. Saturday till four-thirty o'clock," recalled Clara Lemlich, a young immigrant factory worker from Russia and a ringleader of the strike. "The shops were located in old dilapidated buildings, in the back of stores," she explained. They were gloomy and cramped, lacking electricity, and heated by coal stoves that made the air smoky and posed a constant fire hazard. "The hissing of the machines, the yelling of the Foreman, made life unbearable."[2]

The plight of women factory workers drew many future Heterodites together—partly out of sympathetic horror at the conditions in which these women lived and worked, but partly because of their own complicated yearnings to be self-supporting through their labor. This was the message Charlotte Perkins Gilman hammered home in *Women and Economics*, and especially for women rebelling against an upbringing that groomed them for marriage, it was the powerful connector between their social conscience and their individual self-determination. For Rheta Childe Dorr, a muckraking journalist and one of the older generation of Heterodoxy members, the message was profoundly articulated in Henrik Ibsen's *A Doll's House*, which appeared on Broadway in December 1889, sending shockwaves through late Victorian culture. "We all lived in dolls' houses," wrote Rheta of her peers "and I for one wanted to get out into the world of real things."[3] When fellow Heterodite Edna Kenton published her article extolling the benefits of feminism, she referred to the moment when the central character, Nora, slams the door on her domestic prison and strides out into the unknown as a seismic moment that shook up a generation: "That slammed door reverberated across the roof of the world."[4]

Nora's defection from domesticity was a fantasy, and a privileged one, which left the character's path after leaving her family unexplored. In a similar way, there was a tendency among Heterodites to celebrate work, *any* work, as the path to precious independence. "Our sisters of the poorer class have the most fundamental right for which we are struggling—the right for economic independence, the right to continue their chosen work after marriage," wrote Henrietta Rodman.[5] Ida Rauh, raised in a wealthy secular Jewish household in New York, published a series of short stories exploring the fascination of wealthy progressives with their working-class neighbors. In one, the leisured heroine watches a young woman sewing from her window. "I admired her efficiency, the skill with which she avoided the waste of a second of time," the narrator says, before turning back to her book. Somewhat surprisingly, this intellectual's-eye view of the working poor was published in the evening edition of the socialist newspaper the *New York Call*, which usually prioritized the voices and perspectives of workers. But the push and pull between admiration and sympathy that Ida's narrator expresses toward her working neighbor, and the challenge of solidarity across class boundaries, was widely articulated.[6]

In a previous generation, wealthy and socially progressive women might have understood their role as one of Christian charity, dispensing gifts to the poor without coming close. That was anathema to Heterodoxy women like Rose Pastor Stokes, who told a well-heeled audience of university alumni that she wished to "wipe all philanthropy off the face of the earth," and that charity was "a blind" willfully obscuring the truth of social inequality and deprivation.[7] As a young woman, Rose had been involved in the settlement house movement (it was where she met her rich husband), following a pathway that led many of her fellow Heterodites into social activism. Amid the massive economic inequality of the late nineteenth and early twentieth centuries, settlement houses proliferated in poor urban neighborhoods across the United States and attempted to bridge the gap between worlds.

Settlements provided education, nursing, housing, and social services to poor communities, but sought to transcend charity and create genuine links of friendship and fellowship across the boundaries of class, culture, and gender. Before he married Marie, Fred Howe had lived at Goodrich House in Cleveland, while in New York, at University Settlement on Eldridge Street on the Lower East Side, the Ivy League staff re-created college life in their rooms on the top two floors of the house, dragging their mattresses to the roof on hot nights and exercising in the nude, in homage to the ancient Greeks.[8] The rest of the house contained classrooms, social spaces, offices, and a library, as well as washing facilities—the showers, which most apartments lacked, were used by some eight hundred people a day during the summer and were a deliberate lure to bring members of the local community to the settlement's classes and clubs.[9]

Women, however, were the lifeblood of the movement. The veteran reformer Jane Addams founded the first American settlement, Hull House, in Chicago in 1889, and four years later, nurse Lillian Wald established the influential Henry Street Settlement in New York.[10] Although concentrated in the dense and deprived neighborhoods of the Lower East Side, settlements spread across the city. In the Village, a middle-class Boston woman, Mary Kingsbury, established Greenwich House at 26 Jones Street in 1902, when the street was home to fourteen hundred people speaking twenty-six languages, and no fewer than five saloons. Mary had recently married Vladimir Simkhovitch, a Russian Marxist economics professor at Columbia University,[11] and her young children were useful conversation starters with local women when she took them on walks through the streets.[12] She and Lillian Wald were not Heterodoxy members but were well known, professionally and personally, to many in the club; before moving into College Settlement on Rivington Street, Mary Simkhovitch shared an apartment on Irving Place with journalist and Heterodite Anne O'Hagan (later Shinn), a friend from Boston University.[13]

In 1905, Crystal Eastman, then a student at NYU law school, arrived to live and work at Greenwich House, and found the place and its community exhilarating. She wrote to Max that "sooner or later every really interesting up and doing radical who comes to this country gets down there for a meal." Fourteen years younger than Mary, Crystal was an occasional nanny to the Simkhovitch children and plunged into an intense affair with Vladimir (Mary does not seem to have found out).[14] It was one among many more or less fleeting attachments for Crystal, then in her mid twenties, tall and strikingly attractive, at this restless point in her life. The affair offers an extreme, though not uncommon, example of the way the settlements blurred personal and professional boundaries. Among women, they could offer a haven for same-sex relationships, whether these were stormy, like the brief romance between Lillian Wald and Heterodite Helen Arthur, or settled and long-term, like that between Jane Addams and philanthropist Mary Rozet Smith.[15]

The mission of settlements like Greenwich House was not just to provide services and friendship to their communities but also to understand—by documenting and quantifying—exactly who they were. Residents conducted sociological surveys that were in-depth inquiries into their neighbors' living and working arrangements, going beyond the census to gather a detailed picture of the lives of the poor. This kind of information gathering was a new tool in the fight against poverty, especially in cities, and many Heterodoxy women did this work, through settlements or on behalf of other social reform organizations. They brought to it a feminist consciousness, focusing on the experiences of women as workers in and out of the home.

Crystal Eastman, despite graduating law school second in her class, found firms in the city resolutely opposed to hiring a woman. A Greenwich House contact instead brought her onto a landmark sociological survey being conducted in Pittsburgh. Her job was to study the impact of industrial accidents on workers' families and finances, and her extensive research and interviews, conducted over two years, provided evidence for progressive legislators fighting to introduce workers' compensation laws. Crystal's fellow Heterodite and Greenwich Villager Katharine Anthony, meanwhile, surveyed the lives of women in a German immigrant community on the far west side of Manhattan for her first book, *Mothers Who Must Earn*. These investigations opened feminists' eyes to the complex realities of economic survival for women who lacked the resources, education, and opportunities they themselves enjoyed.

Many Heterodoxy members trained in settlement work shared this faith in the power of sociological research to improve lives. But labor unrest and the evidence of exploitation and deprivation were all around them in New York, and it was becoming increasingly clear that no amount of dance classes and cultural assimilation efforts would compensate for workers' powerlessness in the face of capitalism. Before long, many Heterodites "graduated" from settlement work to trade unionism, mostly via the Women's Trade Union League, an organization dedicated to bringing more women into the American Federation of Labor.[16] Comprising workers and middle-class "allies," whose relationship was often fraught, the WTUL was a national organization, headquartered in Chicago, and headed by a wealthy Brooklyn woman, Margaret Dreier Robins. Her younger sister Mary ran the New York branch, the largest and most active in the league. Though it would see plenty of internal strife over the competing goals of suffrage and trade unionism, and between working women and allies, the WTUL was an important experiment in what an all-female political organization could achieve.

Although the Dreier sisters were not Heterodoxy members, many WTUL allies belonged to the club, including Ida Rauh, Henrietta Rodman, Katharine Anthony, and Mary Heaton Vorse, along with two other writers, Florence Guy Seabury and Rose Emmet Young, a particularly close friend of Marie Jenney Howe.[17] Madeleine Doty offered legal advice to the workers in the league, while Rheta Childe Dorr's journalistic connections helped bring its activities to the press. Rheta was also the only ally who studied Yiddish, to better connect with the majority-Jewish worker contingent.[18] Inez Milholland was inspired to labor activism as an undergraduate at Vassar after speakers from the WTUL visited the campus to ask students to pledge to buy only clothes bearing the union label.[19]

Unionizing New York's female garment workers was a complex task. In contrast to the vast textile factories in northeastern industrial towns, most garment "shops" in the city were small businesses, often owned by Jewish immigrants rather than fat-cat capitalists or corporations. The industry was decentralized, scattered, and seasonal, with a young workforce who moved employers frequently, and saw their work as a stopgap until marriage. The ethnic diversity of the workforce, mostly Russian Jews and Italians, was weaponized to prevent solidarity: bosses actively sought to cultivate mistrust between the different groups and either enforced silence or placed workers next to women who couldn't speak their language. Despite strong traditions of labor organizing in, especially, immigrant Jewish communities, women workers tended to be deeply embedded in their patriarchal cultures and wary of stepping out and standing up for their rights. Quite unlike the romance of self-supporting freedom that their middle-class allies celebrated, their work was usually a contribution to the survival of a whole family.

Despite these challenges, garment workers did sporadically organize for better conditions. One kind of treatment, where the injury was felt deeply and its gendered nature was impossible to ignore, regularly sparked walkouts. Decades before sexual harassment was a legal offense, women knew how it felt to be at the mercy of a sleazy foreman or a handsy boss, and they reacted fiercely. One strike was directed against an employer who insisted that he was showing his workers mere "fatherly affection." If that was how a father behaved, the women said, they would rather be without one, and they nicknamed their walkout the "orphan strike."[20] The WTUL supported these one-off strikes, which could be effective in their small-scale way, although they were often quickly and sometimes violently suppressed by the police and gangsters hired by the bosses.[21]

Gradually, the unrest in the garment industry built to a howl of discontent. Wages slumped with the depression of 1907, and they didn't bounce back as the industry did. Manufacturers were squeezing their workers to the bone with fines for lateness and for mistakes made on the sewing machines, and they even charged them for needles and thread. "Some of us girls who were more class conscious," as Clara Lemlich put it, met together at a building on East Broadway and declared themselves a union: Local 25 of the Waist Makers Union, the beginning of what would become the International Ladies' Garment Workers Union, or ILGWU.[22] Over the summer and fall of 1909, workers struck at several larger factories, and hundreds of women signed up with Local 25. The WTUL ensured that these stories stayed in the press.

In November, the union organized a mass meeting at Cooper Union. Its cavernous, pillared Great Hall was packed with garment workers furious at the abysmal conditions in the factories. They listened to important men make speeches, including Samuel Gompers, head of the American Federation of Labor. "Each one talked about the terrible conditions of the workers in the shops," Clara recalled. "But no [one] gave or made any practical or valid solution." Tired of the talk and hungry for action, Clara demanded the floor and called out in Yiddish for an immediate general strike. "The entire audience rose to its feet," she said. "Men threw their hats in the air, women waved their handkerchiefs." For five minutes, there was chaos. Then she was called up to the stage and the chair of the meeting raised his right hand to her, asking her to recite the traditional Jewish oath, *If I turn traitor to the cause I now pledge, may this hand wither from the arm I now raise.* Hundreds of voices echoed her vow.[23]

At first, things moved quickly. By the end of the first week, more than a hundred small manufacturers had met the strikers' key demands—for a fifty-two-hour week, the abolition of fines, standardized wages and rates for work across the industry, and union recognition. Ten thousand strikers returned to their machines, nearly half the walkout. But the larger factories held out, particularly on the issue of union membership, and by early December, negotiations had stalled. There were plenty of people in need of work in New York, and much of the labor wasn't highly skilled. Manufacturers hired strikebreakers, and the situation on the picket lines grew increasingly violent. Police arrested strikers for disorderly conduct and loitering and began to send them to the Jefferson Market Courthouse in Greenwich Village to await trial alongside sex workers, a deliberate shaming tactic, or directly to the workhouse on Blackwell's Island. The latter policy prompted thousands of strikers and supporters to march on City Hall carrying banners that declared PEACEFUL PICKETING IS THE RIGHT OF EVERY WOMAN.[24] The garment uprising had become a citywide phenomenon.

The WTUL seized on the strike as an opportunity to deepen the connections between workers and middle-class New Women, as well as drive up union membership. In its new headquarters, a townhouse in an elegant district north of the Village, strikers could get a meal and free legal advice; the league provided witnesses, lawyers, and bail funds for those who had been arrested. Heterodoxy's Fola La Follette, at twenty-seven, was already a veteran of the WTUL's supportive efforts. She ensured that the sandwiches fed to Jewish strikers were kosher and gave fundraising speeches in support of the workers. But sometimes the question of how best to help appeared to baffle the allies. During an earlier strike by white-goods workers (those who sewed underwear), Fola was tasked with reading poetry to striking pickets. "As she stood before them, she suddenly felt poetry was not enough" and asked her listeners what she should do instead. A striker called back, "You can go with us on the picket line. If there's a lady with us the police won't beat us up."[25]

Fola became one of several Heterodoxy women to leverage their class status as a guarantor of nonviolence during the strike. Via advertisements in the press and members' social connections, the WTUL recruited society women and students from Barnard, Vassar, and other elite women's colleges to act as "unbiased, impartial observers" of the picket lines. The league hoped, euphemistically, that the "moral effect" of these upper-class observers would guide the protests "in the direction of peace and order"—in other words, restrain the police.[26] After police arrested (and quickly released) the WTUL president Mary Dreier, the league stepped up its efforts to monitor the picket lines. Fola and others accompanied pickets who had been arrested to the police station and to court.

Inez Milholland, a good friend of Fola's, volunteered to lend her support, and her presence helped publicize the strike beyond the neighborhood. The young suffragist was already famous enough that the *New York Times* could title an article simply "Inez Milholland Helping." She was arrested twice: the first time dressed in an evening gown because she planned to go to the opera after her picket-line duty was over. At the end of December, Inez took part in a jubilant socialist reception in the East Village to welcome strikers released from the workhouse. She performed a series of one-woman skits, the WTUL's Leonora O'Reilly (a representative of the workers, rather than a middle-class ally) handed out medals to the freed pickets, and Crystal Eastman led the crowd in a chorus of "La Marseillaise." Inez spent the new year in Elmira, New York, at Crystal and Max's family home (she was dating Max at the time). In January, she was arrested again. This time, she was freed on bail by her father, and her court appearance was delayed until morning so that she didn't have to appear at night court. This consideration,

however, meant that her fellow strikers had to spend the night
in jail. "She didn't lose anything by it," the author of the anonymous "Diary of a Striker" in *The Call* newspaper wrote bitterly.
"[She] had all the excitement she was looking for, posed as a
martyr, had a dozen or more pictures taken free of charge and
was then taken home by her rich pa."[27]

In her speeches, Inez framed the garment workers' strike action in terms of feminist empowerment, the grounds on which
she and other rich women could more easily claim solidarity with
the workers. "I think there comes a point where submission to
unfair treatment becomes abject and slavish . . . and retaliation in
one form or another is indicative of self respect." Many strikers resented the press attention lavished on these glamorous upper-class
activists and suspected—not entirely wrongly—that their cause
was at risk of being co-opted to advance the suffrage agenda. It
was undeniable that the press was fascinated by the rich women
supporting a strike by the women who sewed their clothing and
by the uneasy alliance between the vastly different groups—the
"rebel girls" and the women they dubbed the "mink brigade."

President Taft's daughter Helen, then a college student,
found her way to the picket lines, telling a reporter, "Really, I'll
never put on a shirtwaist again without a shudder," and promising to "speak to papa about the terrible conditions."[28] Mary
Dreier persuaded Anne Morgan, daughter of the millionaire
J. P. Morgan, to appear on the picket line and to make a sizable
donation to the WTUL; in return, Anne was named to the executive board, along with Alva Belmont. These wealthy women
voiced moral outrage at what the strike exposed about the factories: "If we come to fully recognize these conditions, we can't live
our own lives without doing something to help," Anne Morgan
told the *New York Times*. But her help was quickly curtailed: she
quit the WTUL board when she realized that its emphasis was

on political change, not charity, and denounced it as a "socialist organization."[29]

It was, and proudly so. Along with Inez Milholland, the most visible future Heterodite active in the shirtwaist strike was Rose Pastor Stokes, also not yet thirty, outspoken and photogenic. "Her clouds of red-brown curly hair shook loose as she spoke, forming a lovely frame for her large expressive brown eyes and her clear-cut cameo-like features," recalled her friend Elizabeth Gurley Flynn, Heterodoxy's other most prominent labor activist. "She had a tiny scar on the tip of her nose from a cut when she fell as a child, sliding down the banister of her tenement house. It gave her a piquant, retroussé effect."[30]

Rose was a figure of endless fascination to the press, but also to the "girl strikers," because not long ago, she'd been one of them. Born in the Jewish Pale of Settlement in the Russian Empire and raised in the slums of London's Whitechapel neighborhood, Rose had emigrated to America with her family at the age of twelve and went to work rolling cigars in the factories of Cleveland, Ohio. She had just moved to New York to join the staff of the Yiddish *Jewish Daily News* when she was sent to interview James Graham Phelps Stokes at University Settlement on Eldridge Street. Graham, as he was known, was tall, slender, and dark-haired, like a young Abe Lincoln, with a "frank, earnest, and kind expression"—a millionaire's son, alight with sympathy for the poor. Captivated by the petite auburn-haired writer, he invited her to tea at the settlement, then to Thanksgiving dinner. Rose became a regular visitor, content at first to listen to the talk that swirled around the dinner table between the residents and their distinguished guests. Like Crystal Eastman at Greenwich House, she found the settlement stimulating, "a seething center for the exchange of ideas," and before long she was teaching a class there, and getting a rapid education in contemporary sociological theory and practical social change. Much to her surprise, she was also being courted.

Graham had become a friend, a fellow reformer as committed as Rose was to improving the lives of the poorest members of their community. There was no lightning bolt, no grand gesture of devotion. Like many of the activists the couple would come to know in the Village, Graham and Rose wanted to be partners, comrades, friends, and lovers—to redefine marriage as "a union of mind and spirit" as they rearranged society.[31] The couple married on July 18, 1905, Rose's twenty-sixth birthday, and the newspapers went wild for the story of "a child of the ghetto" capturing the heart of a plutocrat, the stuff of sentimental fiction made real. Although they called her Cinderella, Rose did not disappear behind the walls of a Stokes family palace after her marriage. Instead, the newlyweds moved into an ordinary (albeit

Rose Pastor Stokes pictured at her desk, around 1910. Her fame and notoriety grew throughout the 1910s. (*Credit: Library of Congress*)

generously sized) apartment in an East Side tenement building so that they could continue their work among the community. Her marriage made Rose Pastor Stokes the first Jewish woman listed in America's blue-blood almanac, the *Social Register*. She and her husband joined the Socialist Party the same year.[32]

The shirtwaist strike turned Rose from a rich man's wife into a powerful speaker, famous in her own right. She addressed up to ten meetings a day all over the city and was often in court helping to bail out arrested strikers. An illustrated *Collier's* magazine feature on the strike, titled "The Uprising of the Girls," was typical of the coverage, which portrayed Rose as the magnetizing force who could draw the diffident, divided strikers together: "She was on the platform, a score of girls surrounding her, listening rapt." The reporter insisted that it was her person that was powerful, not her message, which they'd heard plenty of times before: "Nothing can be gained unless you hold together." Somehow, until it came from Rose, "it hadn't made the same impression."[33] But her fame could count against her. At a factory on Broadway just below Union Square, Rose challenged a strikebreaker: "What is there in the future for you without the union?" The woman retorted, "I'm in hopes that some rich man will come along and marry me."[34]

The energy and enthusiasm of the strikers and their supporters flagged as the protest dragged on through a bitter winter and into the new year of 1910. The cold was brutal, and the police harassment more so; bail costs kept mounting. When the union finally called an end to the strike in mid-February, organizers could count some victories. They had signed contracts with around 350 smaller shops that agreed to a fifty-two-hour workweek and wage increases of between 12 and 15 percent. The collaboration between middle-class feminists and working-class activists had less concrete but nonetheless important effects, creating a sense of mutual interest and responsibility that would end up bolstering both the suffrage and the ongoing labor fights. If nothing else, the strike made it clear to union men that women were an organizing force to be reckoned with.

Most of the large factories, however, refused to budge on the ILGWU's demands, particularly around worker safety. The firm at the center of the strike, the Triangle Waist Company—which occupied the eighth and ninth floors of the Asch Building just east of Washington Square, in the heart of Greenwich Village—was one of the biggest in the industry, and the most recalcitrant. Its bosses flatly refused the union's urging to install fire escapes and keep exterior doors unlocked. Barely a year later, that refusal would have deadly consequences.

It was a clear day, so you could see the smoke for miles.

On March 25, 1911, Frances Perkins, a friend of Heterodoxy via the WTUL and other channels, was visiting a friend on Washington Square North, in the wealthy Village-adjacent neighborhood where many "mink brigade" women lived. Their afternoon tea was interrupted by sirens and commotion, and from the window they could see people running. The women hurried outside and joined the crowd racing across the park to the building on Washington Place that housed the Triangle Waist Company. They watched helplessly as the fire escapes on the side of the building collapsed like matchsticks under the weight of desperate young workers who had been locked inside the rat-trap factory and now had no way out.

Frances never forgot the scene. Fifty years later, she could still describe it in blunt and brutal detail:

> One by one, the people would fall off. They couldn't hold on any longer—the grip gives way. There began to be panic jumping. People who had their clothes afire would jump. It was a most horrid spectacle. Even when they got the nets up, the nets didn't

hold in a jump from that height. There was no place to go. The fire was between them and any means of exit. There they were. They had gone to the window for air and they jumped. It's that awful choice people talk of—what kind of choice to make?[35]

The horror of the Triangle Fire seared itself into the memory of the crowd of onlookers, and into the soul of New York. Until 9/11, nearly a century later, it was the worst workplace tragedy in the city's history. One hundred forty-six workers, most of them young Jewish and Italian women in their late teens and early twenties, were killed in barely half an hour: choked, crushed, burned, or falling or jumping to their deaths. The firehoses arrived late and couldn't reach the factory floors. The narrow stairwells, when the workers finally forced the locked doors open, became a deadly crush. The elevator worked for a while, thanks to a porter in the basement and operators who, blinded by the smoke, "made desperate, random guesses as to where the floor openings were." But before long, the elevator shaft was blocked by bodies. When people tried jumping into safety nets spread below, they "drove the nets into the sidewalk with such force that the men holding the nets turned somersaults over onto the bodies."[36] Historians' accounts of the day are full of small, chilling details: "One young man assisted three women, one by one, to the ledge and handed them over to their deaths, almost as though he were helping ladies into a carriage. As he brought a fourth girl to the window, she put her arms around him and kissed him. He dropped her into the void. Then he jumped himself, his coat fluttering upward as he fell."[37]

The Triangle Fire was a horrifying spectacle witnessed by thousands and compelling the attention of the world through the media. Although it is possible to convey the horror, it is hard to capture the rage. At the time, the fire was experienced less like a terrorist attack out of the blue and more like a mass shooting today—met with helplessness, fury, exhaustion, paralysis. Not again. Not *again*. Just four months earlier, in Newark, New Jersey, twenty-five factory workers, mostly young women, had died in a fire at the factory where they sewed underwear. "There are buildings in New York where the danger is every bit as great as in the building destroyed in Newark," the New York City fire chief warned on that occasion. "A fire in the daytime would be accompanied by a terrible loss of life."[38]

The WTUL had been working to prevent such a disaster. Ida Rauh, as head of the organization's legislative committee, conducted a survey of factory girls in which they made it clear that fire was their most vivid fear. Ida stressed, therefore, that fire safety should be the league's first priority. She issued her report in March, a matter of days before the Triangle Fire—which occurred in a factory that had in fact passed its safety inspections. The tragedy made it clear that rules were useless if they were not vigilantly enforced.[39]

A week after the fire, on a rainy April morning, the ILGWU staged a vast funeral parade. One hundred twenty thousand people—six times the number who had gone out on strike the previous winter—marched in silence through lower Manhattan behind white horses and a flower-strewn carriage. Their banners declared WE MOURN OUR LOSS, but the mourning was not just for all the Annies and Roses, Benjamins and Teresas killed in the fire. It was because the scale of industrial accidents, capitalism's sheer wastage of human life, was intolerable. As one reformer pointed out, "every year there are 50,000 working men and women killed in the United States—136 a day; almost as many as happened to be killed together on the 25th of March."[40]

After the parade, Rose Schneiderman, one of the figureheads of the shirtwaist strike, took to the stage at a mass rally at the Metropolitan Opera House and filled the hall with her fury. "This is not the first time girls have been burned alive in the city," she told her middle-class audience. "Every week I must learn of the untimely death of one of my sister workers. Every year thousands of us are maimed. The life of men and women is so cheap and property is so sacred." She went on to excoriate the paltry charity of her listeners—"you good people of the public"—who were moved by tragedy to toss a dollar or two to the bereaved, and the police, who had violently cracked down on workers protesting for their rights. "I can't talk fellowship to you who are gathered here," she finished. "Too much blood has been spilled. I know from my experience it is up to the working people to save themselves. The only way they can save themselves is by a strong working-class movement."[41] Among Rose's three and a half thousand listeners that day were Heterodoxy's Mary Heaton Vorse, who tirelessly documented labor struggles across America, and Frances Perkins. According to journalist Will Irwin, "what Frances Perkins saw that day started her on her career."[42]

Nobody watching the fire ever forgot the spectacle, but nobody ever truly paid for the crime. The negligence of the factory owners, the so-called shirtwaist kings Isaac Harris and Max Blanck, was nonetheless readily apparent. In the factory, inner doors had remained locked, against the pleas of the union, so that instead of taking the stairs to leave the building the workers had to take the elevator and pass through a checkpoint where their handbags were searched for any purloined scraps. The workrooms were heated by smoky oil stoves, and the windows fastened closed against fresh air. Cloth fragments and fibers, which hung in the air and choked the workers' lungs, had danced in the fire and fed the flames like kindling. The newspapers called it a holocaust.

The owners' trial, in December, lasted three weeks. The judge heard testimony from more than 150 witnesses, including survivors, firefighters, police officers, and building engineers, as well as the owners themselves.[43] In the end, the shirtwaist kings were found not guilty and collected $65,000 in insurance money. Families who had lost a loved one were paid just $75 each. Before the trial was over, the Triangle Waist Company took out an advertisement "to notify their customers that they are in good working order" at a new headquarters, 9–11 University Place. Inspectors discovered that the building was not fireproof, and the exit to the single fire escape was already blocked by two rows of sewing machines. As Ida Rauh and Rose Schneiderman had predicted, consideration for workers was not something the bosses would give. It was something workers would have to take.

Crystal Eastman's work for the Pittsburgh survey had opened her eyes to the statistical reality and human costs of industrial accidents. "It's rather a gruesome business," she told her mother, of a job that required her to comb through and tabulate death and injury records and interview families.[44] Her sex was an asset, however, giving her entrée with young widows, mothers, and sisters, whose stories helped to humanize what for factory owners was just a mark in the deficit column. One aspect of the experience that struck her forcefully was that working people did not have the "luxury of grief." The urgency of earning a living pushed aside any chance to reflect on a bereavement or come to terms with loss.[45]

The resulting book, despite its unglamorous title, *Work-Accidents and the Law*, brought Crystal a degree of fame in progressive reform circles, and led to New York's governor hiring her onto his new committee investigating the issue of employer liability. A profile of the lone woman commissioner showed an expansion of journalists' small range of fictional referents for female activists, beyond Joan of Arc: Crystal was "Portia Appointed by the Governor," the heroine demanding her pound of flesh. The subject who emerges in the article, however, fiercely resists the (female) interviewer's framing. When it is suggested that what had motivated the shirtwaist strikers was "a love of pretty things . . . beyond their purse-strings," Crystal's response was "vehement." She fought back with the full force of her legal training, becoming "the adversary in every word and gesture."[46]

Crystal argued that worker compensation for injury and death was a humanitarian question. In her book, she clearly showed that factory jobs carried inherent dangers, and accidents usually happened without any obvious fault to be assigned. Injured workers or their families should not have to sue for compensation; instead, she argued, the state ought to compel employers to compensate their workers automatically for injuries and deaths. In September 1910, New York's governor, Charles Evans Hughes, passed groundbreaking legislation to that effect, the first version of a workers' compensation law in the nation—which was immediately challenged in court by private companies. They called it socialistic and unconstitutional, and the day before the Triangle Fire, it was overturned.[47]

Between the bill's passage and the fire, Crystal had been personally devastated by the death of her mother, Annis, from a stroke. Annis, a Unitarian minister and feminist, was a remarkable woman and a powerful influence on Max and Crystal, both of whom were bereft without her. The fire stirred Crystal's still-raw grief to rage. She echoed Rose Schneiderman's fury at the outpouring of donations without real change—the news that a charitable fund had been opened for the victims' families "made my soul sick," she said. "When the dead bodies of girls are found piled up against locked doors leading to the exits after a factory fire . . . who wants to hear about a great relief fund? What we want is to start a revolution." Writing in a social science research journal, she quickly pivots from passionate rhetoric to bald facts, pointing out that in 1909 there were nearly eight hundred accidents on record, but a mere seven prosecutions for labor law violations, out of which two resulted in fines of thirty-five dollars each. In refusing to hold companies accountable for injuries workers suffered on the job, and instead blaming those workers for negligence, the United States stood alone. Gathering and analyzing data did not sound especially revolutionary, but Crystal insisted, "I believe in statistics just as firmly as I believe in revolutions. And what is more, I believe statistics are good stuff to start a revolution with."[48] That conviction would fuel more than the labor movement. Counting the true scale and cost of violence would become an essential strategy for a new organization formed in the same year as the shirtwaist strike, to confront America's growing scourge of racist brutality.

Chapter 4

THE NEW ABOLITIONISTS

In the late summer of 1908, in Springfield, Illinois, a white woman falsely accused a Black man, George Richardson, of rape. In retaliation, a white mob burned Springfield's substantial African American neighborhood to the ground. Black residents fled Springfield in their thousands, and the governor called in the state militia to quell the violence. Racist terror in the streets of Abraham Lincoln's hometown shocked northerners, who had been all too willing to treat lynching and mob violence as a Southern problem. The Springfield violence drew Black and white activists together to create the National Association for the Advancement of Colored People (NAACP) the following year. The coalition of reformers included many activists in Heterodoxy's orbit. The white women on the NAACP masthead—Jane Addams, Lillian Wald, and most importantly Mary White Ovington—were well known to Heterodoxy women via interconnected labor, socialist, peace, and suffrage networks. Inez Milholland was particularly closely connected: her father, John, was the organization's first treasurer, and she, like her mother, contributed to *The Crisis*. (Biographers also speculate that John Milholland and Mary White Ovington, who worked closely together for many years, were lovers.)[1]

The first meeting of the group, in January 1909, was held at the home of William English Walling and Anna Strunsky, a couple who were close friends with Rose and Graham Stokes. English, as he was known, was a writer and socialist descended from slaveholding Kentucky farmers, while Anna was the daughter of Russian Jewish immigrants who had grown up on the Lower East Side and studied at Stanford. They met while covering the first, brutally suppressed Russian Revolution in 1905, and married just a few months after Rose and Graham—it was becoming a trend. Anna's younger sister Rose, who accompanied her to revolutionary Russia, was a member of Heterodoxy, and apparently an anarchist sympathizer; Mary Heaton Vorse remembers her at one point with "a lot of dynamite in her room, that she'd cached for someone." The "Beautiful Strunsky Sisters" and their family were Village fixtures. "Papa Strunsky" ran a bohemian café and was a generous landlord, "who was always willing to hear another tale of woe from his artist and writer roomers."[2]

English Walling's stinging exposé of the events in Springfield were published in the *Independent* magazine on September 3, 1908, under the no-punches-pulled headline "The Race War in the North." He called for a revival of "the spirit of the abolitionists" in an interracial coalition that would compel all Americans to pay attention and understand racist oppression as a moral outrage that it was their duty to fix.[3] The rhetoric of abolition and the figure of Lincoln as the Great Emancipator therefore featured prominently in the NAACP's first public statement, issued on February 12, 1909, Lincoln's birthday. "The Call" imagined how Lincoln might assess race relations in the current moment and was especially aimed at indifferent northerners, insisting that "Silence under these conditions means tacit approval."[4] Written by Oswald Garrison Villard, *New York Evening Post* editor and a descendant of legendary abolitionist William Lloyd Garrison, it was cosigned by sixty prominent reformers, of whom seven were Black, including Mary Church Terrell, Ida B. Wells, and W. E. B. Du Bois, whom the NAACP invited to New York to launch *The Crisis* the following November.

The early NAACP leadership was made up of lawyers, journalists, religious leaders, and politically connected reformers, a majority of whom were white and Jewish men. Their approach to lynching focused on bringing the violence to light, in the pages of *The Crisis* and beyond, and using the negative publicity to pressure sheriffs, mayors, and governors into punishing perpetrators. The work of gathering evidence called for quick action, subterfuge, and guts, as activists infiltrated situations that were often still at boiling point. In May 1916, the NAACP urgently wired the white activist Elisabeth Freeman—who had spoken alongside W. E. B. Du Bois at Marie Jenney Howe's "Authors' Evening for Suffrage" two years earlier—to ask her to travel immediately to Waco, Texas, from Dallas, where she was attending a suffrage convention. The lynching of seventeen-year-old Jesse Washington, in what Du Bois called "The Waco Horror," stood out for its daylight brazenness and the inhuman violence to which the boy's body was subjected. The day after the murder, NAACP secretary Royal Nash tasked Elisabeth with putting together a "confidential report," offering her fifty dollars a week plus expenses. Her information, interviews, and photographs, gathered in conditions of extreme tension and suspicion, formed the basis of an extensive report in *The Crisis* in July. It contributed to the NAACP's strategy of forcing lynching into the public eye in ways that ensured that white leaders could no longer look away and entire towns could be shamed for their complicity.[5] The documenting of violence and counting and classifying of victims were efforts to, as Crystal Eastman had suggested, deploy statistics for revolutionary ends.

The NAACP in its early years, however, had its own blind spots—in particular, it tended to sideline Black women, keeping them out of leadership roles. The trailblazing journalist Ida B. Wells was among the NAACP's founders, but later distanced herself from the organization. She disagreed with its focus on the prosecution of individual acts of violence rather than directly confronting lynching as a system of racist terror by which whites held onto the economic and social power threatened by the Civil War and Reconstruction. Wells also rejected the usual justification for lynchings, that they were punishment for Black men's predatory attacks on white women. Back in 1892, in her investigative pamphlet "Southern Horrors," funded by African American women's groups in New York and Brooklyn, she pointed to the simple fact that women and children, as well as grown men, were regular victims of lynch mobs, and she further demonstrated that the majority of those men had not been convicted of rape. Even consensual sexual contact between Black men and white women was treated as a violation, while assaults by white men on Black women, in contrast, were never treated as violent crimes or punished as rape—proving that there was no "chivalrous" pretext for lynchings. White virtue and Black depravity were unshakable, and race extinguished the privilege of gender.

Unsurprisingly, Ida B. Wells's exposure of white male hypocrisy did not sit well with hypocritical white men. The violent threats she received after the publication of "Southern Horrors" chased her out of Memphis, Tennessee, and she settled in Chicago. With the prominent activist Mary Church Terrell, she helped found the National Association of Colored Women, the most influential network of Black women's clubs, in 1896. Terrell was just as outspoken in her refusal to accept the racist double standard around rape. "Throughout their entire period of bondage colored women were debauched by their masters," she pointed out in 1905, and since emancipation, "prepossessing young colored girls have been considered the rightful prey of white gentleman in the South, and they have been protected neither by public sentiment nor by law." Insofar as those "white gentleman" felt guilty for this quotidian brutality, that guilt was displaced onto Black men and punished at a remove. It was not rape that led to lynchings, Terrell said definitively, but "race hatred."[6]

The club movement led by educated, middle-class Black women in some ways mirrored the activism of contemporary white women's organizations, advocating for suffrage and social reform. But its leaders pushed to link racial justice and women's rights, rather than seeing them as separate issues that had to be pursued one at a time. One New York clubwoman and journalist, Victoria Earle Matthews, cofounded a settlement house to offer training and job placement to young Black women newly arrived and adrift in the city. Unlike the settlements downtown that catered mainly to immigrant families, the White Rose Mission helped young Black women escape sexual exploitation. In one scheme, pretty girls from the rural South were enticed by men posing as employment agents to travel north in expectation of respectable jobs, only to wind up in sex work. As an investigative journalist who could pass for white, Victoria Earle Matthews infiltrated the traffickers and intercepted their victims, meeting them at the docks or the train station and escorting them to the White Rose. In an era luridly obsessed with the menace of "white slavery"—a term that referred to the trafficking of innocent young white women for sex—the very real risks Black girls faced at the hands of predatory men were rarely the subject of scandal and exposé. Black girls were not afforded the privilege of the assumption of innocence.

African Americans moved north in huge numbers in the early twentieth century: 1.6 million left rural communities for northern cities between 1910 and 1930, in pursuit of a freedom that the South simply did not offer.[7] Yet urban life was full of overt and subtle restrictions, and working-class Black women were largely shut out of the forms of labor that allowed their white counterparts a degree of economic and physical freedom. The majority in the 1910s were domestic servants, a far more isolated form of employment than was offered by offices, stores, or even factories, where employees had a community of fellow workers and union activism offered some hope of improving conditions. Cleaning houses or doing laundry for white families also painfully replicated the hierarchies of slavery in making women vulnerable to sexual assault.

The rebellion against conventional marriage that so absorbed the white women of Heterodoxy was less of a preoccupation for Black women's rights activists of the same era, who tended to espouse the philosophy of racial "uplift," which emphasized respectability and conformity with prevailing moral standards. If they supported prevailing patriarchal social structures, it was with the goal of elevating Black men to positions of authority and political influence.[8] By laying claim to feminine virtue through the traditional avenues of marriage and family, "race women" sought respect and power. The feminist language of shared humanity, independence, and equality with men was less relevant to these women, for whom the idea of devoting oneself to the advancement of a husband's career could still be compatible with being a modern, enlightened, "New" woman—assuming, of course, the man was worthy of her support.

ON NEW YEAR'S Day 1913, the *New York Times* marked the fiftieth anniversary of the Emancipation Proclamation with a poem by James Weldon Johnson, who had high hopes for the impact of "Fifty Years" on the world and his own reputation. In the thrill of composition the previous summer, he had written a letter to his wife that displays both the grandiosity of his ambition to be "the first world-acknowledged Aframerican poet" and the intimacy of their relationship, where that poetry could be freely discussed. "To-night I have finished 15 verses of the greatest race poem that has yet been written, and it made me feel like chatting with you about my work—it would be no posing to say, my art, for I know that I am a poet, and with the power to be the first great poet that the race has produced in America."[9]

The half century since the end of slavery had hardly been a triumphant march toward full equality. However, the anniversary—observed with a host of events and commentary throughout the year—offered an opportunity for a widespread reckoning with the current state of race relations and the question of what the future held. For James, that question was, at the time, more cultural than political. As a poet, novelist, and the editor of a poetry column in the *New York Age*, he wrote frequently about the status and future of Black literature and the way in which it was entwined with politics. In late 1916, he was invited to join the NAACP as a field secretary, tasked with traveling across the South to enlist members and open new chapters. In 1920, he would take over as the head of the organization and become one of the country's most visible Black leaders. At his side was his wife Grace, the only Black member of Heterodoxy.

Grace Nail grew up in privileged, sheltered circumstances for a Black woman of her era. Her father was a businessman who ran a hotel, Nail Brothers, on Sixth Avenue in Manhattan, which was boosted and illustrated in Booker T. Washington's 1907 book *The Negro in Business*. In 1904, she met James Weldon Johnson in Brooklyn, after an amateur theatrical evening at the home of one of the neighborhood's wealthy Black families. "She was there with her mother and was taking, it appeared to me, an initiatory peep at life," he remembered. "She was in her middle teens, but carried herself then like a princess."[10] He was fourteen years older and already famous for cowriting, with his brother Rosamond, "Lift Ev'ry Voice and Sing"—initially as a

commission to mark Lincoln's birthday, but swiftly popularized and later adopted by the NAACP as the "Negro National
Anthem."

It was one among many accomplishments. The Johnson
brothers had grown up in Jacksonville, Florida, part of a striving
Black population that, by the turn of the century, was the largest
in the state. The boys excelled at school, and James wound up
the principal of his old school, while Rosamond, a gifted musi-
cian, taught music. James also studied law and became the first
African American admitted to the Florida bar in 1897. Their
hometown success was short-lived, however. In 1901, a massive
fire that started in a mattress factory raged through Jacksonville;
in the interest of protecting a row of houses belonging to the
factory owner, the white fire department allowed the blaze to
decimate the Black quarters of the city.

James's "love for cosmopolitanism" was already drawing
him to New York. Songwriting paid well and expanded his
horizons—in 1905, not long after meeting Grace, he and his
brother left for a European tour, seeing for themselves how the
lives of Black people looked different, freer, and more dignified
in tempting places like Paris. But even the most successful popular musicians and performers were still second class, in James's
view. Music was something whites expected Black people to be
good at, an instinctive talent that would always be subordinate
to the true art of literature, which he had studied at Columbia
University. To cement his literary ambitions and build his brand,
James changed his middle name from "William" to "Weldon,"
to give it "a little distinctiveness," as he explained to a friend, and
to make it "a good deal more of a literary 'trade mark.'"[11]

He chose to conceal that trademark, however, when he published his novel *The Autobiography of an Ex-Colored Man* anonymously in 1912. The title and mystery authorship were designed
to hook readers who wanted to be led, like Dante, into a thrilling

underworld—in this case, the Tenderloin, a lively Black bohemia that flourished along Sixth Avenue, from Twenty-Fourth to Forty-Second Street, in the decade before the Harlem Renaissance.[12] Like the proliferation of novels about Greenwich Village and Harlem, *Autobiography* invites outsiders into the neighborhood's cluster of theaters, gambling dens, interracial black-and-tan dive bars, and brothels, offering what appeared to be unfiltered access to a secret world. The cabaret, to which white "slummers" flocked, is alive with crosscurrents of creative inspiration and desire: performers looking to co-opt "Negro stuff" and women in search of "colored lovers." The novel's protagonist plays ragtime, the Tenderloin's distinctive mashup of classical piano with off-kilter syncopation played with frenetic energy. When he performs at an uptown millionaire's soirée, the audience is captured and enraptured by this sudden eruption of the cabaret into the salon. Denounced as both "musically and morally corrupt," ragtime was banned in New York public schools in 1914 but remained a pop music juggernaut throughout the country from the 1890s to World War I.

Music and literature were not James's only interests or talents—he was also a rising political star. Having helped compose music for Theodore Roosevelt's presidential campaign, he had risen in the ranks of the Republican Party—at the time, the mainstream party more hospitable to African American advancement. In 1906, he began a six-year stint in the diplomatic service, during which he earned excellent money and a national reputation. He was posted to Puerto Cabello, Venezuela, and he and Grace exchanged frequent letters. When his posting moved to Corinto, Nicaragua, James worried whether he "had any sort of right to ask a girl who had lived all her life in New York to come and live in Corinto," a town he found ugly and unappealing. "I tried sincerely to paint Corinto for her in true colors, but, it is probable that, in spite of myself, I threw some splashes

Grace Nail Johnson around the time of her marriage in 1910. (*Credit: James Weldon Johnson Memorial Collection in the Yale Collection of American Literature, Beinecke Rare Book and Manuscript Library*)

of light upon its dull, drab background," he admitted later.[13] Grace was equal to the challenge, however, and the couple married in February 1910, at Grace's family home in Brooklyn. Immediately after their wedding, they left for Corinto, where they stayed two years.

The local people welcomed Grace with the gift of a yellow parrot named LuLu, who became an indulged pet, accompanying the Johnsons when they returned to New York and eventually outliving both of them.[14] Grace studied Spanish and French and threw herself into the role of diplomat's wife, which demanded a balance of political savvy and domestic skill that would serve her well back in New York as a hostess, activist, and arts patron. She toughed it out in Nicaragua, but when the couple were able to visit San José and stay in an upscale hotel, Grace was clearly in her element. "Its air of urbanity, its faultless menu and service, its well-dressed well-mannered patrons, were our first taste of metropolitan life in nearly two years; and it affected Grace like wine," her husband recalled.[15] The picture James drew of his wife in his autobiography was of an intelligent young woman with exacting standards and a love of beauty and elegance.

But the protections of success and status, those cherished American markers of meaning, were fragile for a Black man, even one with James's talents and connections. The inauguration of the overtly racist Wilson administration at the beginning of 1913 spelled the end of James's government career. He resigned before he could be fired, and the couple returned to America, where Grace's brother Jack was beginning to play a part in developing Harlem as an epicenter of Black culture. He worked for the Afro-American Realty company, also featured in *The Negro in Business*, which aimed to counterbalance the mistreatment and discrimination Black tenants faced at the hands of white landlords. Hoping at first to help middle-class African Americans purchase property in the neighborhood, Jack soon realized that the people flocking to the city in their thousands during the Great Migration could not afford to buy. He became a landlord instead, eventually owning around fifty buildings, and a political player both in Harlem and citywide.[16] His company's first purchase was a pair of five-story apartment buildings on 135th Street, with striking curved façades, where Grace and James made their home when they returned to New York. They were close to Jack, who cut a flamboyant figure: photographs from around 1915 show him posing proudly at the wheel of his "first car—a Mercer racing roadster!" and taking his sister out for a spin.[17]

In the sixth year of Heterodoxy's existence, Marie Jenney Howe wrote a letter to Grace, whom she had met several times, to formally invite her into the club. "You were today elected to Heterodoxy with real enthusiasm as many of them know you, so do be a good girl and come regularly and be responsive," Marie wrote. "Heterodoxy is the centre of more real friendliness among women than any group I know. This is its chief recommendation." Clearly, by this point in the club's existence, joining or being "elected" to Heterodoxy was a rare honor, carrying with it the obligation to participate fully. But it's hard to overlook the tone of slightly patronizing affection that Marie adopts to thirty-three-year-old Grace—"be a good girl"—and to wonder how far it reflects simply Marie's fifteen years' seniority, that motherliness for which she was well known, or the unconscious race prejudice of even a progressive white woman of her era. It is also possible that the formality of the "election" felt uncomfortable to Marie, as the invitation tumbles out in a rush, and she immediately follows it up with a more personal note: "I had such a happy time with you two dear people the other evening. I only wish I could be with you oftener."[18]

Marie's letters to Grace, the only side of the correspondence that survives, is a revealing glimpse into the Heterodoxy founder's personality and the women's friendship. Marie uses endearments like "my dearest Grace" and "your old friend," and sends her "love to you and Jim." At one point she tells her, "Your friendship means a lot to me dear Grace, my only regret is that I don't see more of you"—a sentiment she repeats elsewhere. She complains of illness more than once and apologizes for missing social occasions as a result. Although she writes affectionately, there is a sense that she feels hampered by rules of etiquette that seem to belong more to stuffy Victorian drawing rooms than to the rough-and-tumble, candlelight-and-absinthe social world of the Village. In one letter, she begs Grace to tell "Jim" that she (Marie) will have dinner with him "any place he wants to go," so that she can "square [herself] for frustrating his hospitality last winter," a social faux pas she labels "a stupid thing." She adds, "I never make allowance for that hospitality impulse in others and yet I have it so strongly myself that I ought to recognize it in others." The idea that invitations must be reciprocal, and that Marie has offended James by offering one out of turn, seems to strike her with surprising force. It's hard to know, given how few of her letters survive, whether this was habitual anxiety or a sense of delicacy around giving offense to Grace and her husband in particular.

Marie's worries do not seem to have bothered Grace, who, it seems, was a generous and conscientious gift giver, sending her friend a Christmas gift every year, despite Marie's protestations that she doesn't deserve them and will not reciprocate as she does "no Christmasing" herself. Curiously, Marie always insists these are Christmas gifts, although it is equally likely Grace was marking her birthday as well, which fell on December 26. "You are a great little Christmas girl," Marie tells her, thanking her in turn for a yellow pillow ("almost too dainty for use"), a decoration ("I have hung it on my chandelier"), and a tablecloth ("just right for the small dining room table").

In one letter, Marie discusses upcoming plans for Heterodoxy, laying out topics and guest speakers for upcoming weeks. One of these is the regular "men's night." Since "Fred has already been asked," Marie requests Grace's permission to invite James, so that then "you could ask . . . that handsome brother of yours unless you know a still handsomer man." In making this request, Marie makes fun of her own formality and adherence to social nicety: "You see I'm asking your permission first because I want to be proper and conventional and recognize your prior claims." Still more tantalizing than wondering which of Grace's handsome men attended a meeting of Heterodoxy, and how they found the experience, is Marie's exclamation, in one of her Christmas thank-you notes: "I missed you at the Heterodoxy party!"

Grace was unusual, among the gathering of Black cultural elite in Harlem, in involving herself in a Greenwich Village discussion club, and we don't know whether she tried to recruit any uptown friends to join her, although Marie's letters suggest she was open to welcoming Grace's guests. In one undated letter,

likely from the early 1920s, Marie answers a request from Grace
for the names of prominent white activists to serve on a committee organizing a dinner honoring W. E. B. Du Bois. She covers
four pages with a proliferation of names and addresses, mostly
of Heterodoxy women and their husbands, and assures Grace, "I
would not hesitate to ask anyone for so distinguished a man as
Dr. Du Bois. I think anyone would feel privileged to be asked."
The letter demonstrates that cooperation across racial lines was,
at least in Marie's social circles, to be expected.

In 1916, Fred and Marie, along with Henrietta Rodman and
other prominent progressives, launched another organization to
take up issues of discrimination and social improvement in the
city. The Civic Club of New York was intended to be a model
for men and women working together and went so far as to es-
chew the use of the titles "Mr." and "Mrs.," boasting that it was
the first group to fully meet "this modern demand." The organizers also agreed, albeit "after considerable debate," that members would be welcome regardless of race, and they extended
invitations to W. E. B. Du Bois and James Weldon Johnson to
become charter members. It would become one of the few interracial organizations not explicitly or exclusively focused on African American issues. One of its first special committees, on "The
Negro in New York," was chaired by Marie, and it took up (and
won) the case of a female doctor who had been prevented from
taking a position at Bellevue Hospital on the grounds of race.[19]

Heterodoxy women, including Grace Nail Johnson, enjoyed
class and professional privileges that made their experiences of
socializing across the color line and generally moving through
the world as women in the 1910s highly unusual. For most Heterodites, any close personal contact they had with Black women
was with their domestic servants—like Annie, who worked for
Crystal Eastman and her second husband after the birth of their
son.[20] In Inez Haynes Irwin's unpublished autobiography, we see

glimpses of this much more common arrangement. At the end of a chapter in which she names and sketches the various friends and literary luminaries she and her husband hosted in their Greenwich Village house (including Grace), Inez concludes by acknowledging the domestic staff that made her convivial life possible. "To add to the happiness, there was affection, devotion, perfect concord in the kitchen," she writes. "How much I owe to my two beloved negro maids, Mary Mills and Clara Stevens, I cannot put into words."[21] Her handwritten correction to the typescript capitalizes the N to reflect the changing norms around how this word appeared in print.[22] Her autobiography often remarks on the physical appearance of women, rhapsodizing about her friends' beauty, and she mentions her servants again here, adding, "I have always maintained that Negroes are racially much more beautiful than white people."[23] This flattery, like the respectful quoting of the women's full names, is also a form of self-flattery: the white author congratulating herself for her ability to see past society's dehumanizing stereotypes. It does not give the women a voice or a place at the table. We have no record of how Grace felt sharing a place at the Heterodoxy table with established, older writers whose work often traded in unthinking ethnic stereotypes—like Mary Heaton Vorse, whose Village novel *I've Come to Stay* included a stereotypical wise-but-comical Black servant, and Rose Young, the author of a popular series of short stories called the "Miss N—r" stories.[24]

Such demeaning attitudes were widespread at the time and didn't stop Marie from suggesting Rose, Mary, and Inez to Grace as potential sponsors of the Du Bois dinner. But they are a reminder of the distance that loomed between white bohemians and their Black counterparts, despite some shared interests. Both James Weldon Johnson and the Harlem Renaissance writer Claude McKay, who moved to New York in 1914, subscribed to *The Masses*, and McKay later wrote for *The Liberator*,

Max and Crystal Eastman's successor to the magazine, and was close friends with them both. "I liked its slogans, its make-up, and above all, its cartoons," he said of *The Masses*. "And I felt a special interest in its sympathetic and iconoclastic items about the Negro."[25] The Socialist Party, which held more sway in the Village than either mainstream party, was more welcoming to Black members, but even Socialists and anarchists were not automatically inclusive. Acknowledging race—and the many distinct oppressions that it caused—went against some of the most precious tenets of Village leftism. Socialists viewed class as the ultimate unifying force, whereas feminists prioritized gender, so both groups were guilty of downplaying the importance of racial injustice and failing to understand how it intersected with other exclusions.

The question of how best to respond to the social and political inequality of their era preoccupied the women of Heterodoxy and their partners and peers throughout the 1910s. Were the institutions that controlled American life basically sound, in need of modification only, or did the whole edifice need tearing down? By the 1910s, it was increasingly clear that the efforts of reformers through the first decade of the century had been too cautious. Persuasion did not work against the forces of white supremacy or capitalist patriarchy, but mass action did: general strikes, marches, demonstrations that put bodies in the streets and found power in numbers. In the long battle between reformers and revolutionaries, the radicals were about to prevail.

Chapter 5

WHAT WE WANT IS A REVOLUTION

ELIZABETH GURLEY FLYNN WAS PERCHED ON A MUSHROOM stool at the counter of a quick-lunch restaurant in Lawrence, Massachusetts, the first time Mary Heaton Vorse saw her. In the cold winter of 1912, less than a year after the Triangle Fire, Lawrence was a town under siege, "ramparted by prison-like mills before which soldiers with fixed bayonets paced all day long." "Gurley" was barely twenty-one, though she struck Mary as serious and mature, "the picture of a youthful revolutionary girl leader," with classic Irish coloring—pale face, blue eyes, and a cloud of black hair. When she got up to speak in front of crowds of striking mill workers, her energy ran through her audience like "a spurt of flame." She'd been arrested more times than she could count.[1]

Mary was almost twice Elizabeth's age, but their bond was quick and strong, forged in the pressure of the moment in Lawrence, and nurtured over the ensuing years by their shared commitment to the labor cause and their membership in Heterodoxy. Arriving on the midnight train with a fellow journalist, Mary, who had grown up in Amherst, was shocked to see armed troops patrolling the textile mills. "We got breakfast, not talking much, for our familiar New England town had become

Elizabeth Gurley Flynn in her speaking pose, around
the time of the Lawrence strike. (*Credit: Library of
Congress*)

strange and sinister." Elizabeth invited her back to the house
where she was staying, along with her mother, who was taking
care of Elizabeth's baby while she and her fellow leaders coordinated the massive strike. Mary had young children, too, a boy
and a girl, and she knew what it was like to try to balance work
and motherhood, to hold a family together by yourself—her
feckless first husband had died two years earlier, and Elizabeth's
was estranged, somewhere out west. They stuck together. Mary

was covering the strike, while Elizabeth was "speaking, sitting with the strike committee, going to visit the prisoners in jail, and endlessly raising money." The meetings were held in a building a long way from the mills, where a soup kitchen was set up and groceries distributed—the command center for the striking women, who assembled there every morning, waiting eagerly for Gurley or another speaker to put in an appearance. In the evenings, the women dined together in a restaurant in the Syrian quarter or in the homes of the Italian strikers. Off the platform, Elizabeth was different: "calm and tranquil," clearly storing up her "tremendous energy" for her speeches.[2]

"The mills *are* Lawrence," Mary wrote in a substantial and influential exposé in *Harper's*, which caused the American Woolen Company to drop its advertising from the magazine in protest. "You cannot escape them; the smoke of them fills the sky. The great mills of Lawrence make the Lawrence skyline; they dominate and dwarf the churches. From Union Street to Broadway along the canal the mills stretch, a solid wall of brick and wide-paned glass, imposing by their vastness and almost beautiful, as anything is that without pretense is adapted absolutely to its own end."[3] The conditions she describes in those mills, that "strange fortress of industry," are still shocking. According to a medical observer, "a considerable number" of the children who went to work in the mills died within two or three years, and 30 percent of workers were dead by the age of twenty-five.[4] Women were routinely sexually harassed and assaulted by their bosses, lung diseases were rampant, and death or dismemberment by the unsecured machinery was common. As Crystal Eastman was discovering around the same time, with her "gruesome" research into industrial accidents in Pittsburgh, the misery of these conditions was no secret. The challenge lay in forcing bosses, politicians, and the public to care.

At the start of 1912, Massachusetts had enacted a law that cut the hours of women and workers under eighteen years of age to fifty-four hours a week. This was in line with the good intentions of middle-class reformers, often women, who believed in protective legislation—the idea that women and children needed special shielding by the state from capitalist exploitation. (Other feminists argued that women were people, not children, and were capable of doing the same jobs as men—which, not incidentally, were better paid.) In response, the mill owners cut everyone's hours, along with their salaries, and were accused of speeding up output. Workers who already scraped by on two or three dollars a week, most of which went to paying rent in overcrowded slum districts, had nothing more to lose. At the end of January, they walked out.

Elizabeth Gurley Flynn arrived in Lawrence at the beginning of the strike with "Big" Bill Haywood, the brawny and charismatic IWW leader who socialized in the Village, and whom Heterodite Mabel Dodge described waspishly as "a large, soft, overripe Buddha with one eye."[5] They went to work immediately enrolling thousands of workers into the local chapter. True to their vision of cooperation, they enlisted members across racial and ethnic lines, blending them into a remarkably cooperative unit. The IWW's success was owed a great deal to the charisma of its leaders and their skills at public speaking, an art form that would soon lose its dominance with the transition to radio and television. Those technologies, Elizabeth Gurley Flynn noted, "calmed down the approach." In her IWW heyday, public speaking was a full-body business, and contemporary accounts of political leaders discuss the orators' energy, movement, and expression as much as their words. "We gesticulated, we paced the platform, we appealed to the emotions," Elizabeth said. "We provoked arguments and questions. We spoke loudly, passionately. . . . Even when newly-arrived immigrants did not understand our words they shared our spirit."[6] Mary Heaton Vorse vividly described Bill Haywood's communication skills: "When he talked about the children shucking oysters or peeling shrimps he made you see actual children, hands wrinkled with water and painful with salt-water sores."[7] Lawrence was home to workers of twenty-five different nationalities who spoke almost twice as many languages but very little English. Against this singular obstacle to organizing, the IWW managed to fashion a remarkable sense of solidarity and community.

Mary Heaton Vorse's report centered on the death of a nineteen-year-old Syrian striker at the hands of the militia and movingly described the reaction in his community. She and Elizabeth were both struck by the propaganda that had lured workers from across the world to the Massachusetts textile mills with the promise of riches. In places as far-flung as Damascus and Montenegro, posters showed workers in Lawrence "coming out of the mill on one side with bags of money under their arm and going into the bank on the other side."[8] Although the strikers were "of warring nations and warring creeds," they came together spontaneously to protest their exploitation and the strike, Mary claimed, opened their eyes to a world beyond the mill.[9]

The walkout at Lawrence dragged on for nine weeks and became a national scandal. The brutality and arrogance of the mill owners were so blatant that the strike was sympathetically reported and donations flooded in. In New York, where people watched the strike closely, Rose Pastor Stokes and her husband spoke at a fundraising rally where they described scenes of violence. Police and hired militias attacked the nonviolent workers with bayonets: two pregnant Italian women were assaulted and subsequently miscarried. There were farcical elements too: a scheme to plant dynamite was meant to frame workers, but was discovered to be a plot cooked up by the president of the American Woolen Company.

During what came to be known as the Bread and Roses strike, women, who made up more than half the mills' workforce, were on the front lines. The rousing slogan "We deserve bread, and roses too" had been around since before the strike, often attributed to the New York garment strike ringleader Rose Schneiderman, and well enough known that it was incorporated into IWW songs and poems before 1912. Drawing on traditionally feminine iconography to make the point that workers deserve more than mere subsistence, it was an inherently feminist slogan, proclaiming the full humanity of the working woman through her right to pleasure. Elizabeth Gurley Flynn did her best to make clear to the female laborers the weight of their double grievance, as workers and as women. They earned lower pay and were also responsible for the housework and care of children. It was a tough message to put across to traditionally minded women with no interest in feminism. "The old-world attitude of man as 'lord and master' was strong," Elizabeth lamented, but she was an inspiring speaker and managed to rally audiences to her side.[10]

As Lawrence turned into a battleground, the women proved themselves more than equal to the men. They formed human chains in the streets and used concealed scissors to slice soldiers' uniforms to ribbons. Police attacked them with truncheons, targeting arms and breasts, and killed one striker, a woman named Anna LoPizzo. Newspapers blamed "unruly and undisciplined female elements" and described Elizabeth Gurley Flynn as "a reincarnation of the militant and maddened woman who led the march of the Commune from Paris to Versailles"—apparently confusing the anarchist Louise Michel, one of the leaders of the Commune uprising in 1871, with the infamous market women who marched on Versailles at the start of the French Revolution a century before.[11] It scarcely mattered—the specter of militant, unruly women was chilling to men who were used to unchallenged power.

Early in February, nurse and birth control campaigner Margaret Sanger, who had recently moved to New York City and joined the Socialist Party's women's committee, organized an effort to send hundreds of strikers' children to friends, relatives, and sympathetic strangers in New York and Vermont for safety. However, she turned down Alva Belmont's offer of help, sniffing that the heiress was a mere "publicity seeker." Elizabeth went along on the train, which was greeted at Grand Central Station by a crowd of five thousand people singing the Socialist anthem, "The Internationale," and waving red banners.[12]

The mill owners and city authorities knew bad publicity when they saw it, and intervened to try to stop a second transport of children. Unfortunately, they chose to do it by arresting and locking up mothers and children, taking the situation from bad to unconscionable. As Mary wrote in her *Harper's* article, the "forcible detention" of children was, surely, the rare event that Americans all over the country would rise up to protest. Along with furious editorials, nationwide attention, and massive fundraising for the strikers and their children, a congressional investigation was organized. First Lady Nellie Taft was among the audience members who heard devastating eyewitness testimony about the strike and working conditions in the mills, including from a young woman who had lost part of her scalp when a machine trapped her hair.[13] In mid-March, the mill owners capitulated. The American Woolen Company acceded to every demand, sending wages up throughout the New England textile industry for nearly a quarter of a million workers. It then promptly raised prices on wool and cotton products to pay for it.

The Lawrence strike was a turning point for many members of the Women's Trade Union League who had been involved with the shirtwaist strike in New York two winters before.

Having eyed the radical IWW with trepidation, they could not now deny the union's momentum, which dovetailed with their own group's disillusionment at the conservative attitudes of their longtime ally, the American Federation of Labor (AFL). The WTUL had firmly supported the powerful union, which distinguished between "skilled" and "unskilled" workers and drew boundaries along racial and gender lines. But when the AFL pushed for an early end to the strike at Lawrence and pressured the Boston branch of the WTUL to stay out of the fight, WTUL women were furious.[14] As the New York leader Mary Dreier wrote to Leonora O'Reilly, one of the workers who increasingly held power in the group: "The attitude of the labor men to the working women has changed me from being an ardent supporter of labor to a somewhat rabid supporter of women and to feel that the enfranchisement of women and especially my working-class sisters is the supreme issue." The challenge now was to find a way to fight for labor and women together.

Elizabeth Gurley Flynn had long declared the causes of women's equality and workers' empowerment to be intimately, inextricably linked.[15] She had read her Charlotte Perkins Gilman but challenged her central thesis, that economic independence was the best way to liberate women. Perhaps earning their own living would allow privileged, middle-class women to free themselves from the dominance of men, but for millions of their sisters who couldn't access professional jobs, life would still be unequal. Women were paid less than men in all industries, and most working women couldn't support themselves, let alone a family, on their salary alone. Pay inequality was there by design, part of the social structure of gendered dependence.

Elizabeth's feminist and socialist—later communist—political beliefs were rooted in her upbringing and her Irish identity. Her mother had insisted on using female doctors, then a rarity, to deliver all four of her babies, and Elizabeth, the eldest, was named after the woman who brought her into the world in 1890. The children, according to Elizabeth, "drew in a burning hatred of British rule with our mother's milk" and, from this early anti-imperial nourishment, developed sympathy and solidarity with oppressed people around the world. She and her siblings grew up in poverty in the Bronx but inhabited a rich intellectual world. She excelled at school, especially in debating, and regularly crossed the bridge into Harlem to have the run of the 125th Street library. She assembled her worldview through the writing of Mary Wollstonecraft, Henry David Thoreau, Karl Marx, Ralph Waldo Emerson, and the plays of Henrik Ibsen and George Bernard Shaw, which ripped the veneer off Victorian fantasies of femininity and domesticity.

At the age of twelve, Elizabeth discovered socialism at an event organized by some German neighbors. The talks, she said, lit "a flame within me"—and fired up her parents just as strongly. The Flynns took home as many pamphlets and papers as they could afford, and her father Tom, in particular, immersed himself so deeply in reading and learning about this new political theory that it interfered with his ability (or willingness) to work. He took the enthusiastic Elizabeth to endless meetings and coached her as she grew into a precocious speaker. Elizabeth gave her first public speech, "What Socialism Will Do for Women," in January 1906 to a small meeting in Harlem. Her energy and youth, as much as her innovative feminist take on the new egalitarian politics, quickly made her a star.[16]

American socialism in the early twentieth century developed out of theories stretching back to the dawn of industrialization, when the supposedly benign, paternalistic relationship between rural laborers and landowners gave way to the anonymity of urban factory work and opened up a massive disparity in numbers and power between workers and bosses. Wealth gathered in the hands of those bosses until it concentrated and stagnated, corrupting democracy. The only way to get it flowing down to ordinary workers, it seemed to many, would be with force. The sentiments Elizabeth encountered in the meeting halls and on the streets of New York City were reverberating globally. On the Lower East Side, she encountered a livelier scene than the stuffy meetings she'd attended uptown, as refugee Russian Jews infused politics with music, art, stories, and dancing. This was socialism as culture, a way of life. "As a matter of theory many Socialists give joy its place in the scheme of things," wrote Grace Potter, a writer and psychoanalyst whom Elizabeth later came to know in Heterodoxy. "We know it is the aim of existence."[17] That radical joy would become the guiding spirit of bohemian Greenwich Village in the next two decades.

Elizabeth soon found her political home with the Industrial Workers of the World, the newest and most radical socialist organization in America. "The working class and the employing class have nothing in common," declared the group's founding manifesto. "There can be no peace so long as hunger and want are found among millions of working people and the few, who make up the employing class, have all the good things of life." The IWW was a new vision of an activist movement. Youthful and militant, its members—known as Wobblies—rejected the middle-class, middle-aged stodginess of existing leftists, and it welcomed women, immigrants, and Black workers equally. Its goal was to enlist everyone in a particular industry into the same union and eventually—so the vision went—to merge into a single union, the basis for a worker-controlled socialist state. The IWW harnessed a spirit of joy and optimism that was infectious, even romantic. They were famous for their music. "There is no period in all the labor history of America that is more picturesque, that has in it more gaiety and heroism than the early days of the singing [W]obblies," wrote Mary Heaton Vorse in the mid-1920s.[18] Teenage Elizabeth was an organizer within the year. Exceptionally talented at inspiring her listeners, she was immortalized in song as the "Rebel Girl" by famed IWW activist and songwriter Joe Hill.

Elizabeth's first action was in Bridgeport, Connecticut, where more than a thousand steel-tube manufacturers were on strike. There, she organized street meetings in English and the workers' native Hungarian, and the novelty of her youth and gender once again drew crowds in to listen. She also helped coordinate stop-work protests, a new strategy in which workers sat idle at their machines rather than walking off the job, thereby preventing scabs from taking their places, and avoiding lockouts. Such protests dramatized the power of the worker's body and will, both in themselves and collectively, and drove home the point that people were not machines. Elizabeth was uncompromising in her belief that American capitalism was fundamentally opposed to workers' liberation, and that the route to freedom and power could not lie through compromise and negotiation, cutting deals with the bosses to make life better in tiny increments. Workers didn't need to settle for scraps from the master's table when it was their labor that paid for the feast. If they took a stand together, they could jam up the gears of the economy with work stoppages, sit-ins, and strikes—they could take back the power that was rightfully theirs. She took to the podium, again and again, to tell them so.

Late in the summer of 1906, Elizabeth was arrested for the first time, at the age of fifteen, while giving a speech from a makeshift platform at the corner of Broadway and Thirty-Eighth Street in the Tenderloin district. The crowd was captivated by the contrast between her appearance and the fire of her argument:

a schoolgirl with long black braids, railing against American capitalism. Journalists dubbed her the "East Side Joan of Arc," mistakenly assuming that she lived among the downtown Jewish socialists and deploying their go-to nickname for young female activists. Women as diverse as Inez Milholland and the shirtwaist strike leaders Clara Lemlich and Rose Schneiderman were called Joan of Arc, as was Rose Pastor Stokes—when she wasn't the "East Side Cinderella." These nicknames were at once celebratory and belittling, turning committed young organizers into mythical figures. They also implied, quite wrongly, that the women stood alone.

Elizabeth first met Marie Jenney Howe in Cleveland in 1907, before Fred and Marie moved to New York. The seventeen-year-old organizer was visiting the city on her circuitous way home from Chicago after a big IWW convention and gave a talk on socialism in the public square. Fred and Marie attended the talk with the city's liberal mayor Tom Johnson, a close associate of Fred's. According to Elizabeth, she allowed the mayor to escort her to lunch at his mansion—swallowing her qualms about associating with capitalists—and there she met the Howes for the first time. "I'm glad you liked my little talk," Elizabeth said to Marie, as the women clasped hands, beginning a friendship that would last for decades.[19]

That same year, Elizabeth dropped out of high school to become a full-time organizer. Later in her life she would regret her loss of education, but at the time, nothing seemed more urgent than the life-or-death struggle between workers and capitalists. She packed up and left her parents' Bronx apartment for the Mesabi Iron Range in Minnesota to support a strike by the miners there. It was a vastly different environment from the dense, smoky cities where Elizabeth had grown up and cut her teeth as an organizer—thrilling, wild, and romantic. She fell in love with the place, and the men who seemed to embody that wildness and freedom, so intensely that she "married the first one she met," according to her friend and IWW leader Vincent St. John.[20] The relationship was stormy and short-lived, made harder by Elizabeth's demanding schedule as a speaker and organizer.

In May 1910, as suffragists marched in the streets of New York, nineteen-year-old Elizabeth gave birth to her son, Fred, whom she nicknamed "Buster." He was her second child, following a baby who had died after just a few hours. Rose Pastor Stokes, who knew Elizabeth through their shared IWW and socialist networks, invited the new mother and baby to stay with her on Caritas, a three-acre private island in Long Island Sound that she and Graham had received as a wedding gift from her mother-in-law. The summer months on the island, reading in the sun while two-month-old Fred slept, were a valuable respite for Elizabeth and the basis for a lifelong friendship with Rose. The latter's fourteen-room mansion—which she and Graham built to be both a home and a gathering place for fellow leftists, including W. E. B. Du Bois and Charlotte Perkins Gilman—was a far cry from the Flynn family's cramped Bronx tenement.[21] But despite Rose's newfound wealth, and the difference of religion, she and Elizabeth had a lot in common. Their shared working-class backgrounds made them unusual within Heterodoxy, as did their close, enduring bonds with their mothers and younger siblings. Whereas many middle-class feminists sought an escape from their origins in pursuit of independence, both Elizabeth and Rose continued to live with and financially support their family members well into adulthood.

Elizabeth's commitment to the IWW meant that she was soon on the move again, however. "In those days no traveling Socialist or IWW speaker went to a hotel," Elizabeth recalled. "It was customary to stay at a local comrade's house. This was partly a matter of economy. . . . But, more than all else, it was a comradeship, even if you slept with one of the children or on a couch in the dining room. It would have been considered cold and unfriendly to allow a speaker to go off alone to a hotel."[22] Once her son was weaned, Elizabeth entrusted him to her family, though when a strike was a long, drawn-out affair, as in Lawrence, she brought Fred and her mother with her.

By the time of the Lawrence strike, Elizabeth's marriage to Fred's father was over, and she began a relationship with Carlo Tresca, a charismatic anarchist and fiery IWW speaker who had been exiled from his native Italy some years before. "He was then a tall, slender, handsome man in his mid-thirties and I was deeply in love with him," she said. The two worked and lived together until 1925, throwing themselves into strikes and labor battles across the country. Carlo's antics made Elizabeth's brushes with the law look tame and earnest by comparison: he was once jailed for "shouting '*Viva Socialismo*' in a cop's face," arrested dozens more times, shot, bombed, kidnapped, and attacked by a hired assassin. "A beard covered a bad scar on the side of his face, where one of his innumerable enemies had attacked him in Pittsburgh," Elizabeth offered casually, in describing him. They did not marry, because both were still legally attached to previous spouses, and besides, their "code," Elizabeth said, was "not to remain with someone you did not love, but to honestly and openly avow a real attachment." It was a thoroughly modern, bohemian, feminist code, except that Carlo was a compulsive womanizer. As Elizabeth put it, he "had a roving eye that roved in my direction in Lawrence and now, some ten years later, was roving elsewhere."[23] Unfortunately for her, it didn't rove very far. The couple finally broke up when Elizabeth discovered he had been having an affair with her younger sister and had fathered her child while they were all living together in the Flynn family home.

Although she remained skeptical of gendered groups like the WTUL that tried to work for labor rights across class lines, her personal experiences with male socialists may have softened Elizabeth toward female support networks. She later called her membership in Heterodoxy "an experience of unbroken delight to me!" and added that, "I treasure the friendships and stimulating association it has given me. It has been a glimpse of the women of the future, big spirited, intellectually alert, devoid of the old 'femininity' which has been replaced by a wonderful free-masonry of women." Friendship, if not politics, could cross class lines. Her invocation of "freemasonry" is also telling in its implication of secrecy and enduring loyalty. For women as visible as Elizabeth and Rose Pastor Stokes, the freedom of that closed door, a space for talking without reporters or restraint, must have been a relief. In her autobiography, Elizabeth credits Heterodoxy with making her "conscious of women and their many accomplishments." It crystallized an awareness of women's solidarity that reconnected her with her fiercely feminist mother. "My mother, who had great pride in women, was very pleased by my association with them," she wrote.[24]

For Mary Heaton Vorse, the Lawrence strike symbolized the power of worker solidarity and community, as she witnessed a disparate collection of downtrodden people create something quite new and beautiful under the pressure of the moment. "A strike like this makes people think," she wrote hopefully—perhaps projecting a little, or betraying some of the enormous impact that the events were having on her personally. "We knew now where we belonged," she wrote. "On the side of the workers, and not with the comfortable people among whom we were born."[25] For the rest of her long career as a journalist, the fight for labor rights would be the consuming focus. She did not, however, want to become an organizer herself, believing that she could not do the role justice, or perhaps that she was not quite as idealistic as she needed to be, as Elizabeth was. Instead, in Lawrence, she inaugurated a new kind of on-the-ground, sympathetic labor reporting. "I wanted to see wages go up and the babies' death rate go down," she wrote quite simply. "There must be thousands like myself who are not indifferent, but only ignorant." Bringing attention to labor issues, making people notice and making them care, would now become a consuming challenge for the Village bohemians.

Chapter 6

TO DYNAMITE NEW YORK

BY 1913, THE REVOLUTION THAT CRYSTAL EASTMAN HAD called for seemed imminent, in multiple political and cultural arenas. The new year in New York was marked by mass walk-outs of waiters, chefs, and busboys from the city's grandest mid-town hotels and restaurants—the Astor, the Knickerbocker, the Waldorf-Astoria, and the massive Belmont, on Forty-Second and Park, owned by the family of suffrage benefactor Alva Belmont's late husband. The action hit wealthy New Yorkers squarely in their vulnerable pocketbooks and stomachs. Strike organizers were arrested for sabotage for allegedly tampering with diners' food, but waiters also struck against their bosses with the opposite of sabotage, pouring wine at full strength that they'd been ordered to water down. Picketers massed outside the city's most stylish eateries, while in the dining rooms, activists in evening dress would blow a whistle on a signal to cause a mass walkout. Rose Pastor Stokes's photograph was circulated among hotel managers, who feared that she might check in disguised in her millionaire's-wife finery and start signing up their staff to the union.

Once again, Elizabeth Gurley Flynn was at the forefront of the action. The strikers met in a hall that also housed rehearsals for Broadway musicals, and the "choruses of beautiful singing and dancing girls" created a lively, festive atmosphere that contrasted with the wintry brutality the IWW had left behind in Lawrence. She and Carlo Tresca were in the first heat of their affair, which went public when Carlo was caught up in a fight with police and dropped a book from his coat pocket—a copy of Elizabeth Barrett Browning's *Sonnets from the Portuguese*, which Elizabeth had inscribed with an "affectionate greeting." The next day, their "secret IWW romance" was all over the papers, a sure sign of Elizabeth's growing fame and the persistent fascination of the press with the love lives of prominent women.[1]

The waiters' walkout faced similar challenges to the shirtwaist strike: a patchwork of disconnected employers, and a multilingual, precarious, and easily threatened workforce, whose skills were sorely undervalued (when restaurants brought in college boys to replace the waiters, diners complained that they were useless). Elizabeth proposed an end to tipping, replacing the ad hoc system with a steady living wage for waiters and busboys. "No independent man likes to take a tip," she told her all-male audience. The men worried that their wives wouldn't support their strike, fearing that waiters' jobs were too precarious to risk, so Elizabeth promised to organize a dance, at which wives would be "gently converted to unionism by competent speakers." She vowed, "We'll make them like the women of Lawrence."[2]

Before long, however, a much larger industrial walkout again summoned Elizabeth away from New York. In nearby Paterson, New Jersey, where the Passaic River crashes almost eighty feet over the Great Falls, the enormous energy of the water powered more than three hundred factories. They formed the heart of America's booming silk industry, producing roughly half the country's supply. To weave and dye the threads extracted from silkworm cocoons into fabric and ribbons, the industry needed manpower to rival the power of the water, and found it in thousands of immigrant laborers who worked fifty-five hours a week, six days out of seven, from the age of nine.[3] In the eyes of the mill owners—growing fabulously wealthy off the shimmering output of their looms—the water and the workers were similar forms of power: irrational, inarticulate, and inexhaustible.

But the price per yard of fabric was falling, eating into the owners' profits. In January 1913, the Doherty mill tried to crank up its output by forcing its weavers to run four looms at once instead of two. This would have put hundreds of people out of work and made the workload unbearable for those who remained, who were already barely surviving on wages that were stagnant or declining. If a mistake damaged the cloth, the employee had to pay for it, but didn't get to take the flawed cloth home. The Doherty workers organized a strike, a small and desperate action that seemed likely to fizzle, until the IWW arrived.

The crucial factor, as the organizers knew from other strikes, was how interlinked the various parts of the Paterson silk industry were: the dyers and weavers in the multiple factories were all part of the same system. If one mill succeeded in speeding up output, firing workers and pressurizing those who remained, the others would follow. Conditions in the dye factories were especially brutal; working in rooms filled with acrid steam, workers' hands and mouths were stained with dye, which they had to taste to check the level of acid. Ten-hour days were the norm across the industry. Paterson's problems were a result of both capitalism and technology. As ribbon-weaving machines, for example, improved in capacity and became easier to operate, they needed fewer and less-skilled workers. This meant that experienced and higher-paid men could be pushed out in favor of more easily exploited young women.[4]

Despite the union's reputation for confrontation, the IWW's most powerful weapon was refusal. Refusal to work to make the factory owners rich, refusal to react to provocation, refusal to quit or stand down. "Your power is in your folded arms," Bill Haywood told the strikers. But to achieve anything, the local walkout needed to become a general strike, with all the workers—weavers, dyers, winders, quilters, pickers, bockers—demanding an eight-hour day and a 25 percent pay rise across the board. No such action had been taken before, and it would cripple an entire industry.

Elizabeth arrived in Paterson in late January and was promptly thrown into jail, along with the other IWW leaders—among them Carlo and Big Bill Haywood. The police, effectively working for the manufacturers, had several elastic charges to choose from: incitement to riot, unlawful assemblage, disorderly conduct. These were the legacy of earlier industrial actions, after which "practically anything said from a strike platform" in New Jersey could be construed as "inciting to riot" or "preaching anarchy."[5] Now, when the strikers gathered in meeting halls to listen to IWW speeches, the police had a playbook: they sent hecklers to disrupt and interrupt, in the hope of provoking violence. When strikers kicked out the intruders, the authorities called it "an assault upon the police" and the press called it a riot. The next day, strikers found the hall doors barred and guarded. As tensions increased, Elizabeth urged the young women in her audience to practice their own form of refusal, by boycotting a ball put on by the police. "I don't believe a woman in the working class wants to put her hand in the bloody hand of a policeman," she said, encouraging them to picket the dance hall instead. "Don't let any girls go in to dance if you can help it. I think the right-minded girls will join in your protest against police brutality."[6]

John Reed went to Paterson in early 1913 to report for *The Masses* on the strike and the prison conditions. Despite the uncomfortable ethnic stereotyping that runs through his article, he demonstrates how easy it was to be arrested under any provocation and credits the bravery of the Jewish and Italian strikers. The IWW believed incarceration was a "devise [*sic*] of capitalism to terrorize the working class," and that familiarity would neutralize the terror, breeding contempt and empowering resistance. Arrest therefore became part of IWW's strategy, to overwhelm the system by flooding it with prisoners and to demystify prison itself, to destroy the "fear and respect" in which the institution was held. It would no longer be shameful to go to jail, but a badge of honor.[7] Back in New York on May 7, billed as a "poet-observer," John Reed related his experiences in Paterson to a large, politically diverse audience at a debate on socialism, sponsored by *The Masses* and chaired by Inez Milholland.[8]

Despite the rough treatment meted out to the strikers under arrest, the Paterson strike as a whole was relatively peaceful, certainly by the standards of other IWW actions of the period. There was only one death, an Italian father named Valentino Modestino, shot on his doorstep by a pair of private detectives employed by a mill owner who were drunk and waving guns in order to disperse a crowd of strikers. His heavily pregnant wife went into premature labor, which almost killed her, and she was left a widow with three other children to support. The strikers rallied round to support the family and used their plight to generate sympathy for the cause.

As Rose Pastor Stokes had done from her bully pulpit during the garment workers' strike, Elizabeth Gurley Flynn specifically called out the exploitation of working women in Paterson, drawing connections between gender and class oppression. She exposed the plight of the teenage girls who worked in the silk industry and the system of "contract slavery" that kept them barely surviving. In a typical factory, the owner withheld half the girls' wages as security, and later returned them without interest. "But if the girl quits voluntarily," she wrote in outrage, the owner "coolly POCKETS ALL THE MONEY HE HAS

HELD BACK." Even if the girl served out her agreed term, her pay was docked for all kinds of reasons, and the fines added up, so that many girls took home less than $2.00 out of an already paltry $6.50 wage. Girls worked ten hours a day and were not allowed to sit. "If a girl sits on the steam pipe she is summarily fired." There was no ventilation, but they were fined for opening windows. On Saturdays, the workers had to clean the factory, "including the floor upon which the masculine bosses have been spitting great wads of tobacco all week."

Elizabeth also described the routine sexual harassment the girls endured, from fellow workers and from bosses. Their toilets were adjacent to the men's, separated only by flimsy partitions that were easily cut through, so that "the girls are subjected to all sorts of indecent and obscene remarks from the other side." Bosses veered between "slave-driving" moods, in which girls were "sworn at, pushed and shoved around," and, perhaps worse, "affectionate" ones, which meant he "put his arm around them indiscriminately." Given the economic pressure and the helplessness of the girls under the contract system, no doubt this delicate phrasing implied much worse. Elizabeth knew that there was no use appealing to the bosses' supposed respect for the fairer sex, or to the promises of protective legislation. It was only through economic justice, the fair and equal distribution of wages, that the girls could protect themselves. "We want to make it impossible for this 'Christian gentleman' to say: 'Bring our children to me; let me weave their soft bodies, their rosy cheeks, the light of their eyes, into cheap ribbon,'" Elizabeth wrote with passion. Only money, not morals, would make it impossible.[9]

But the IWW's fight in Paterson was not only about workers' struggles. It was about the larger injustice of an industry that had grown 800 percent in forty years, with no benefit to the workers who created that growth. The union railed against "absentee capitalists"—the wealthy owners who extracted riches from Paterson but spent their money in New York City so the community could not benefit even indirectly from their wealth. The only people working, living, and spending money in Paterson were the workers, who couldn't afford to build up the town's cultural assets. Despite their proximity to New York, for instance, Italian workers never got to hear visiting opera singers: "Whenever were Caruso or Tetrazzini in Paterson, though there are thousands of their countrymen who would go without food to hear them once?" The right of workers, just as much as social elites, to art, to culture, and to beauty was fundamental to the IWW's beliefs, to the guiding ethos of bread and roses.

As IWW-LED STRIKE activity lit up industries across the country, modern American artists were increasingly consumed with questions of access and display: not only who got to see art but who chose what art there was to see. It was almost impossible to get homegrown work exhibited in New York in the early twentieth century. Prestige, renown, and collector dollars clustered around European artists and the lodestar of Paris. American painters complained that New York gallerists were allergic to abstraction and sniffy about impressionism; meanwhile, in Europe, they were already on to postimpressionism. The Macbeth Gallery in midtown was the first in New York devoted to American art and had made waves, in 1908, with a group show of eight artists, including Robert Henri and John Sloan, who drew cartoons and covers for *The Masses* and socialized in the Village. "The Eight" formed the core of the Ashcan School, a label denoting their focus on scenes of gritty urban realism, which stuck despite most of them hating it. In January 1912, as millworkers were walking off the job in Lawrence, several of the same artists founded the Association of American Painters and Sculptors (AAPS), declaring that they would "lead the public taste in art, rather than follow it."[10] Groups like this were springing up all over the city at the time, upstart radicals seeking to wrest power from their conservative elders. Their concerns mirrored the issues of political inclusion and representation that were consuming labor organizers, suffragists, and civil rights advocates at the same time.

Shortly after the AAPS was born, two of its central organizers traveled to Europe to view, borrow, and purchase work for a planned international exhibition. They picked up works by Brancusi and Duchamp in Paris, and Van Gogh, Cézanne, and Matisse in London, many of them on display as part of the second Post-Impressionist Exhibition at the Grafton Galleries. Curated in the fall of 1912 by the Bloomsbury Group art critic Roger Fry, the exhibition was the second iteration of a show that, two years before, had inspired Fry's friend Virginia Woolf's famous claim that "on or about December 1910, human character changed."[11] The seismic impact of that earlier show convinced the Americans that they would have a similar blockbuster on their hands in New York, and they planned an ambitious exhibition of modern art for early 1913. It would take one of Heterodoxy's most dynamic and complicated members to make it happen.

As a child, Mabel Dodge had "yearned for a life ennobled by Poetry and Beauty."[12] What she got was Buffalo, and an upbringing that groomed her for a life of stifled, purely decorative domesticity. Like Marie Jenney Howe and the Heterodite sisters Grace and Mabel Potter, Mabel was born into a wealthy family in upstate New York at the dawn of the Gilded Age, but her grooming as an obedient society wife was no match in the end for that artistic yearning. She was sent to elite schools for girls, then spent time in Europe on the feminine "finishing" tour that was popular at the time for making American girls just cultured enough to be marriageable. Her family perhaps reckoned without her befriending Natalie Barney, from Dayton, Ohio, who would soon come into her inheritance, settle in Paris, and begin hosting legendary artistic salons at her home at 20 Rue Jacob.

The openly lesbian Barney was a prolific writer and equally prolific lover, and several members of Heterodoxy came into her
orbit, including Fola La Follette and Marie Jenney Howe, who
lived with Barney in the 1920s when she moved to Paris to write
a biography of the feminist writer George Sand.[13]

In her teens, Mabel Dodge had a few intense but fleeting
romances with women, which she wrote about in her autobiography. But in 1900, when she turned twenty-one, she asserted
her independence by secretly becoming engaged to Karl Evans,
an outdoorsy young man who was part of her country-club set
in Buffalo and the fiancé of one of her friends. Even though
the engagement enraged her father, Mabel was following the
rules in some ways: she kept her passion for art and writing (and
women) a secret from Karl. When he convinced her to accom-
pany him on a trip out of town that ended at a small country
church, minister at the ready, she went along with his plan. "I
was married—the passive, truly female experience," as she described it. A few weeks later, her family, conceding defeat, staged
a big society wedding in Buffalo. Mabel was pregnant within
the year—another of those experiences that she thought of as
happening *to* her, allowing her to sink into the blissful passivity
of the wife and mother. "It was so wonderful to give up—to lose
completely my sense of individual life."[14]

That passive absorption into family life vanished quickly,
however, after the arrival of her son John in 1903, when Mabel's
"individual life" came back with a vengeance. She was already
embroiled in a secret affair with her gynecologist, also named
John and possibly the father of her child. While she was recov-
ering from surgery after the birth, her father died, and a few
months later, Karl was accidentally shot in the back while out
hunting and did not recover. He died the day before Mabel's
twenty-fifth birthday, in February 1904.[15] To escape the loom-
ing scandal of her affair with the doctor, Mabel's family sent her

to Europe. On the ship over, she met an American architect named Edwin Dodge. The couple married in Paris in November and settled in Florence the following year. There, for the first time in her life, Mabel was free to indulge her yearning for art and for those who created it. She devoted herself to creating a haven for herself and visiting artistic friends, including the avant-garde writers Mina Loy and Djuna Barnes.

The Villa Curonia was a sixteenth-century Medici palazzo outside the city, a glorious money pit where Mabel began her second act as a salonnière, a hostess and patron of the arts, amid fin de siècle decor and Italian antiques. It was a role enabled by money and sustained by Mabel's determination, artistic appreciation, and genius for social organizing. In eighteenth- and nineteenth-century France, wealthy women who could not wield power in the public sphere exerted behind-the-scenes influence at their exclusive gatherings of the artistic and political elite. In Mabel's time, it was American expatriates in Paris who were reviving the salon tradition. Along with her scandalous old friend Natalie Barney, whose Friday evenings combined party and performance, and later Sylvia Beach, the owner of the Shakespeare and Company bookstore that was a hub of Anglophone literary mingling, there was Gertrude Stein, who, first with her brother Leo and then with her partner Alice B. Toklas, dedicated herself to promoting modern art and artists.

In 1911, Mabel attended one of the Steins' salons. Once a week, on Saturday evenings, they would open the shutters on the gallery space next door to their shared apartment on Rue de Fleurus, which had originally been intended as a studio for Leo, before he discovered he had far more talent as a collector than a creator of art. These salons were somewhat austere, at least by Mabel's standards: there was no food or drink, and the evenings were devoted to viewing and learning (from Leo, who held court) about the cubist and postimpressionist art stacked high on the walls.[16] Mabel was entranced, nonetheless, and invited Gertrude and Alice to stay at the Villa Curonia, sending "several urgent telegrams" to press them. When they visited, in the fall of 1911, they had "a very amusing time," Gertrude reported, describing Mabel in *The Autobiography of Alice B. Toklas* as "a stoutish woman with a very sturdy fringe of heavy hair over her forehead, heavy long lashes and very pretty eyes and a very old fashioned coquetry."[17]

Like many rich, restless, artistically inclined women, Mabel often found her generosity repaid in unflattering caricatures. But Gertrude Stein took her seriously. Her short prose, "Portrait of Mabel Dodge at the Villa Curonia" was at once a tribute to her hostess and an experiment in applying the visual techniques of cubism—its collages, unexpected juxtapositions, and resistance to representation—to literature. The result was a short, rhythmically dense, mostly abstract composition, less identifiably about Mabel than about the space she created at her villa. Opening with the deceptively simple line, "The days are wonderful and the nights are wonderful and the life is pleasant," the portrait unfolds with repeated invocations of what "there is" and what "there is not" and, later, what "there can be." Objects appear every now and then—blankets, paper, a bottle, a "little raw potato," a vase—offering anchors for a reader grasping for figurative certainty; they are the kind of objects that appear frequently in contemporary cubist collages by Braque or Picasso, with their newspapers and bottles layered on tilting tabletops. At the Villa Curonia, there are walls and doors, floors, a house, a garden, but also something intangible that is more important than these solid boundaries: "The particular space is not beguiling. There is that participation." A creative community is born in the interplay between place and people.[18] The portrait's obscurity was not always well received, and Leo Stein was among several people who attempted a parody; his begins, "Mabel Dodge/Hodge podge."[19] Mabel was immensely proud of the tribute, however, and paid to have three hundred copies printed and bound in intricately patterned Florentine paper, which she gave away as gifts: promoting both Gertrude Stein as an artist and herself as a muse.

When Mabel returned to New York in 1912, after almost a decade in Italy, she went resentfully and reluctantly. She and her "wet blanket" of a husband, Edwin, had made the move largely for the sake of her son John's schooling, and Mabel didn't think she had much of a place in her native country, among people for whom progress and the almighty dollar outshone the guiding lights of her life, Art and Beauty (and beautiful artists). She hated that her son was becoming an all-American boy, eagerly attending baseball games with his stepfather, and that the sensitive Italian in him was fading away. Alone in her Fifth Avenue apartment, she had nothing to do and "lay listless on the pale French gray couch, dangling a languid arm," surrounded by antiques—in the midst of a striving, booming modern city.[20] She blamed Edwin. The already strained marriage wouldn't last the year.

The energy of Greenwich Village gradually pierced Mabel's gloom. Gertrude Stein sent over her friend Hutchins Hapgood, the well-connected journalist married to the writer Neith Boyce, a close friend of several Heterodites.[21] "Hutch" listened patiently to Mabel's litany of discontents about her marriage, while Edwin escaped across the street to the Brevoort Hotel, "the locale where most anything from Europe might be picked up," and met the up-and-coming sculptor Jo Davidson, who brought other people, "like a child trailing strange bright rags of seaweed gathered on some shore whose waters spread to far neighborhoods." The city's tides kept turning up new people: artists and actors, activists and "earnest naive anarchists," including Heterodites Mary Heaton Vorse and Ida Rauh. But to Mabel, the assemblage lacked coherence, like a broken jigsaw puzzle;

Mabel Dodge hosted weekly salons at her elegant home at 23 Fifth Avenue, on the wealthy northern edge of Washington Square. (*Credit: Mabel Dodge Luhan Collection, Yale Collection of American Literature, Beinecke Rare Book and Manuscript Library*)

"though they were all part of one picture, they were so jumbled and scattered that they never made a discernible pattern."[22] It would be up to her to put the pieces in order.

At the suggestion of one of her many influential male friends, the journalist Lincoln Steffens, in early 1913 Mabel began to "have Evenings!" in her apartment at 23 Fifth Avenue. Instead of merely letting people wash up, she went out in pursuit of "Important People" and brought them together at salons that were as tightly curated as any gallery show. "I became a species of Head Hunter," she said, laying claim to a dizzying diversity of guests: "Socialists, Trade-Unionists, Anarchists, Suffragists, Poets, Relations, Lawyers, Murderers, 'Old Friends,' Psychoanalysts, IWWs, Single Taxers, Birth Controlists, Newspapermen, Artists, Modern Artists, Clubwomen, Place-is-in-the-home Women, Clergymen, and just plain men."[23] Like Heterodoxy,

named for the diversity of its guests (at least as far as professions
and opinions went), Mabel's salon was based on the idea that
stimulating conversation and new ideas sprang from difference,
from the surprise of an unfamiliar person. But unlike Marie Jenney Howe's determinedly egalitarian club, a salon necessarily had
a host (or more usually, a hostess) who set the tone and the terms
of the evening—the more idiosyncratic, the better.

As Gertrude Stein suggested, and Mabel herself intuited, her
true artistic talent lay in creating "an *ambiente*," bringing people
together and generating a sort of social magic. She began with
the setting. Guests walked in up a red-carpeted staircase and arrived in the apartment that she had painted entirely white, with
white linen curtains and a white bearskin rug: an empty gallery
in which she would gradually build up a discerning collection
of artwork and "*People!*" whom she assembled like sculptures:
"Never, for fifty years, have I left off pursuing, fusing, speculat-
ing, identifying, grouping, devouring and rejecting!"[24] Once she
had assembled her guests, she admired them like a connoisseur,
sitting to one side in a low-cut gown and letting the conversation unfold around her. Her Italian manservant, Vittorio, kept
the guests well supplied with Scotch. Gorgonzola sandwiches
and Virginia ham were served on incongruously ornate platters
from the Florentine ceramicist Cantagalli. Disapproving journalists reported that women as well as men helped themselves
from the bowls full of gold-tipped cigarettes. At the end of the
night, "Vittorio opened the dining-room doors to reveal a re-
fectory table spread with ham and olives, cold salads and beef;
a side table held siphon bottles, rye, lemonade, and kümmel in
bottles shaped like Russian bears."[25]

The lavishness of Mabel's hospitality was no doubt part of
the appeal, and the incongruity of guests and setting was part
of the fun. The agitators of the IWW like Big Bill Haywood
looked thrillingly out of place eating her fancy sandwiches and

leaning against her medieval tapestries. But not everyone met as equals. At one early gathering, Mabel's friend Carl Van Vechten, a complicated figure who was among the most important white boosters of the Harlem Renaissance, brought a pair of Black entertainers to perform for a small audience—including Hutch, Neith, and the svelte, dark-haired Heterodoxy actress Helen Westley (whom her hostess compared to "a good-natured lizard"). Even for Mabel, whose pungent descriptions often border on the surreal, the portrayal is dehumanizing—she calls the "Negress" appalling and unrestrained, and adds, "They both leered and rolled their suggestive eyes and made me feel first hot and then cold." Carl's enthusiasm for the performance strikes her as almost more horrifying, as he rolls his eyes and gives "little shrieks" that make him "resemble the clattering Negroes."[26] Mabel's palpable, sweaty embarrassment at this transgression of racial boundaries is a reminder that although she could welcome anarchists, artists, and even "murderers" as equals, there were still categories that couldn't be accommodated, even at the most avant-garde gatherings. With the exception of the tiny intellectual-reformer class connected to the NAACP, Black people in New York in the 1910s who mixed with bohemians were most often part of the spectacle, not the conversation.

Conversation, however, was what Mabel most prized— "Enmities fade away as soon as people talk," she claimed.[27] Her salons had a more formal structure than Heterodoxy meetings, although a lot of the same women were regulars at both. A designated discussion leader would kick things off with a speech on a prearranged topic, and two hours of discussion would follow. The ubiquitous Margaret Sanger addressed the group on birth control, and the young IWW leader Frank Tannenbaum, who led a contingent of jobless men to occupy New York City churches in the winter of 1914, spoke on unemployment. In theory, the organized structure of Mabel's evenings was an attempt to rein in what she

called "these young cocksure boys"—the recent Harvard graduates and energetic young writers like John Reed, who addressed
the salon about his trip to Mexico reporting on Pancho Villa's
exploits.[28] But she was also enthralled by dominant men, and they
left their mark on her gatherings and her life. Not long after her
salon came into being, he and Mabel began an intense affair.

A typical Greenwich Village chain of connections led a man
named James Gregg into Mabel Dodge's front room one day
in late 1912, introduced by her friend Clara Davidge, who was
married to the head of the new Association of American Painters and Sculptors. "You know Gertrude Stein," the visitor announced. He then suggested that Mabel write an article about
her friend for the photographer and gallerist Alfred Stieglitz's
journal *Camera Work*. The magazine was to be sold at the vast
exhibition the AAPS was planning as their answer to the post-
impressionist spectacles in London, to show New York what
modern art, American and European, really looked like. Stein's
"Portrait of Mabel Dodge" was to be the only nonpictorial
work of modern art exhibited. Mabel accepted the challenge of
explaining the piece, and its relation to cubism, in her article
"Speculations, or Post-Impressionism in Prose."

Mabel's essay compared Gertrude Stein to Picasso and
connected cubism to a larger spirit of revolution brewing in
American and European society. "Nearly every thinking person nowadays is in revolt against something," she wrote. She
challenged the usual detractors of cubism, who called it ugly, by
asking "how does one know" that it is in fact ugly and not simply
unfamiliar? "Each time that beauty has been reborn in the world
it has needed complete readjustment of sense perceptions," she
argued. In a rousing conclusion in praise of the new, she chose
a pointedly maternal metaphor: "Is it so difficult to remember
that life at birth is always painful and rarely lovely?"[29] Gertrude

was delighted with the article and wrote to Mabel, "Really it is awfully well done and I am as proud as punch."[30]

Of course, the exhibition's organizers did not come to the wealthy and generous Mabel purely for her insights into cubism. But she accepted the role of benefactor quite happily—as she put it, "I had an automobile, with a smug chauffeur named Albert driving it in bearskins, and I had a small bank account with nothing much to buy except flowers and cigarettes." She wrote a check for $500 to the committee and began gathering art from private collections around the city. It made her feel "as though the Exhibition were mine. *I* would upset America . . . *I* was going to dynamite New York and nothing would stop me."[31]

When it opened on February 17, 1913, in the cavernous 69th Regiment Armory on Lexington Avenue and Twenty-Fifth Street, the International Exhibition of Modern Art was a sensation. With well over a thousand works on display, including paintings, sculpture, and decorative arts, it challenged and galvanized its audience, exposing most of them for the first time to artists who were pushing the boundaries of representation and restructuring the age-old relationship of the viewer, the work, and the world. The Armory Show, as it was known, fitted into a larger story of modernity arriving in New York, opening just after the new Grand Central Station and just before the Woolworth Building, the tallest in the city, blazed into electrified life.

Nearly ninety thousand people saw the show in New York and more than twice as many when it traveled to Chicago, where outraged students set fire to paintings by Matisse in effigy. A flood of newspaper articles and cartoons praised, pilloried, and parodied the show. On the day of Woodrow Wilson's inauguration, on March 4, one of the candidates he defeated, former President Theodore Roosevelt, visited the exhibition and wrote dismissively about it, comparing Duchamp's *Nude Descending a*

Staircase unfavorably to "a Navajo rug in his bathroom."[32] And Mabel Dodge was at the heart of it all. "I suddenly found myself in a whirlpool of new, unfamiliar life," she wrote. "If Gertrude Stein was born at the Armory show, so was 'Mabel Dodge.'"[33]

As an event that would "dynamite" New York and its conservative artistic establishment, the Armory Show was something of a self-fulfilling prophecy: enough people said it was a rupture with the past that people accepted and remembered it that way—just as Virginia Woolf's claim about "human character chang[ing]" as a result of a previous art exhibition had been both a joke about hyperbolic cultural-historical claims and one of the most influential of such claims. It was a revolution, in other words, because people said it would be. Mabel's friend Hutch Hapgood, who wrote a front-page feature for his newspaper, announced that he was treating the exhibition "as I would a great fire, an earthquake or a political revolution."[34] America felt poised for an explosion. When it came, however, just over a year later with the outbreak of World War I in Europe, it did not herald the overthrow of the old order. Dynamite could only do so much.

For women, the art world was yet another arena in which the promised explosion failed to blast open the doors. Although the Armory Show welcomed a remarkable fifty female artists, there were five times as many men on display, and women's contributions were concentrated in less prestigious areas like applied arts (embroidery, ceramics) and illustration. One of the most prominent women participants was Katherine Dreier, the artist sister of WTUL leaders Margaret and Mary, who had studied in Paris and was a protégée of Marcel Duchamp. Marguerite Zorach, whose contribution to the exhibition is lost, had a more clearly modern style, influenced by the Fauvists; she was already a Greenwich Villager and would come to know members of Heterodoxy through her work as a set designer for the Provincetown

Players theater company, to which many of them belonged as actors, writers, and managers.

Although women struggled to compete with men for recognition and success as artists, many American feminists of this era found the study of art—especially in Paris—opened the door to personal liberation. Within Heterodoxy, the path from Montparnasse atelier to Greenwich Village studio was well trodden, even if the women eventually left art behind. When Mary Heaton (later Vorse) was nineteen, she begged her wealthy family to let her go to Paris, where she managed to enjoy the romance and freedom of the fin de siècle Left Bank even with her mother there as a chaperone. Back in America, she moved to New York alone to continue her art studies, but eventually decided she couldn't paint well enough to keep going. Instead, she attached herself to the male-dominated literary scene, drinking and pontificating in downtown cafés. "I am part of the avant-garde," she wrote exultantly. "I have overstepped the bounds!"[35] Mary embraced the persona of the "Bachelor Girl," made fashionable in a column by her friend Neith Boyce in a new high-society weekly called *Vogue*. At the turn of the century, both girls gave up their bachelor roles to marry fellow writers, and both would struggle in the ensuing decades to balance family obligations with their own creative work.[36]

Mary Ware Dennett, born two years before Mary Heaton Vorse in Massachusetts, also had a youthful adventure in Paris. She stayed longer in the art world, however, becoming an art teacher and, with her sister, reviving the medieval Spanish craft of guadamaçiles, a form of tooled and gilded leather wall hanging. She also married on the cusp of the new century, and with her husband, Hartley, a devotee of the Arts and Crafts movement, set up an interior design business. The marriage did not last, however, since Hartley's artistic pretensions apparently led him to think more freely than Mary did about his vows. After he opted to establish a ménage à trois with a couple whose home he was decorating, Mary declined his offer to make a fourth in the arrangement and suffered through a scandalous public divorce. The experience redirected her life, leading her away from art down a more urgent feminist path. The mother of two sons, she would become a leading advocate for frank, honest sex education, as well as for access to birth control and improved maternal healthcare.[37]

For the practicing Heterodoxy artists, feminist activism and creative work were intertwined. Ida Sedgwick Proper, one of the club's original twenty-five charter members, was born within a year of both Marys and also trained in Paris as a young woman, but she differed in pursuing painting as a career. Her style showed the influence of the French postimpressionists and an eye trained on women's worlds. At the Salon d'Automne in 1910, which revealed Matisse's *La Danse*, Ida exhibited a depiction of an afternoon tea. She painted white-gowned nursemaids and babies in Paris parks, and groups of women sewing and gossiping together under the curve of big hats: lively, light-dappled scenes rendered in loose brushstrokes.

When she returned to New York in 1911, Ida found herself looking for a way to circumvent the strict authority of the New York gallery system, just as the male artists of the AAPS were. In December 1912, she and her studio mate, the sculptor Malvina Hoffman, rented the first floor of a brownstone on East Thirty-Seventh Street to display their work. The *New York Times* framed their decision as a broader political act: "When you are a suffragette artist you do not depend upon the good graces of an agent or gallery to get your wares before the public," observed the reporter, "but you strike right out for yourself." Three years later, Ida struck out for herself and her fellow "suffragette" artists by curating a major exhibition of American women's art at the Macbeth Gallery. The exhibition served as a suffrage fundraiser and a declaration of women artists' right to occupy gallery space on an equal footing with men—some ninety women contributed their work across a wide range of styles and approaches. In contrast to the Armory Show, it was not a declaration of modernity or a gesture to the future but an attempt to redress the past, by demonstrating that women, and their talent, had been there all along.

Ida's 1915 suffrage exhibition was the product of a network of female friendships and professional associations reflecting the tight-knit New York art scene, and the still tighter circles of women within it. Many of the artists had studied at the Art Students' League in New York, and nearly all of them had apprenticed in Paris. Their art reflected these influences, showcasing plenty of urban realism and impressionistic verve. But there were also more traditional pieces, such as decorative figurines and paintings heavy with classical allusion. Despite the suffrage theme, only a few works directly referenced the fight, including a dramatic watercolor of a nighttime suffrage meeting in which an elegant speaker on a street-corner podium declaims to a crowd. Most of the artists made their political stance more obliquely. One popular tactic among "suffragette artists" was to reclaim the visual rhetoric of motherhood from traditionalists, who insisted that the vote was a threat to family values, and to instead celebrate the bond between mother and child as something women could have *as well as* political rights. "Babies, Babies Everywhere!" proclaimed one newspaper in response to the number of artists who exhibited intimate portraits of motherhood.[38] The overt femininity and beauty of these images were a riposte to the cartoon images of ugly, mannish suffragettes and part of the glamorous makeover of the women's movement in the 1910s.

AFTER THE THRILL of the Armory Show abated, Mabel Dodge wanted a break from artists, publicity wrangling, and New York. Her romantic life continued to be turbulent. After Edwin "flowed out" of her life, several others flowed in. "As soon as the winter of the armoury show [sic] was over Mabel Dodge came back to Europe and she brought with her . . . her collection des jeunes gens assortis, a mixed assortment of young men," wrote Gertrude Stein. "In the lot were Carl Van Vechten, Robert Jones and John [Jack] Reed. . . . I remember the evening they all came. Picasso was there too. He looked at John Reed critically and said, *le genre de Braque mais beaucoup moins rigolo*, [Georges] Braque's kind but much less diverting."[39] He might not have amused Picasso, but Jack had plenty of other admirers, including, most enthusiastically, Mabel. Their affair lasted through most of 1913, on and dramatically off, and is inextricably connected with Mabel's other major creative undertaking of that year, the Paterson Pageant.

According to Mabel Dodge, the idea for the Paterson Pageant came from Mabel Dodge—or, rather, from an ineffable force below her conscious mind that had bubbled up unbidden as she sat amid a crowd of radicals in a Greenwich Village apartment. It was a Friday night after she had returned from Europe, and she'd hosted Hutch Hapgood and Neith Boyce for dinner. As they sat by candlelight drinking wine (Neith "fingered the stem of her glass, saying nothing," as her husband and his newly single confidante chattered away), Hutch suggested they go on to a new party. Different white walls, different candles, and the enormous difference a few blocks made between an heiress and an ordinary working woman—in this case, a schoolteacher who was IWW leader Bill Haywood's current lover.[40]

The discussion turned to the plight of the silk workers in Paterson, twenty miles and a world away from Greenwich Village, who had been on strike since before the Armory Show. The problem, as always, with labor actions was how to make outsiders care, how to make them look at the events differently. Everyone knew, in some way, that conditions were terrible and Something

Must Be Done. But how did you move rich people past head-shaking and regrets to actual purse-opening support? And how did you make yet another strike matter, especially when it took place outside New York City and the strikers couldn't be easily drafted to march in the streets and make their presence felt? The answer, it seemed to Mabel and Jack Reed, who enthusiastically took up her suggestion, would be to harness the Village's greatest asset, its creative talent. They would bring the strikers in, not for a demonstration, but for a dramatization of their fight that would rivet the city.

The strikers in Paterson only heard about the pageant three weeks before it was due to be staged, but they threw themselves into developing scenes with Jack Reed, who was directing the project with the help of a megaphone to get himself heard in the vast rehearsal space. In the Village, the project became a collective creative endeavor, with Heterodoxy women including Inez Haynes Irwin, Henrietta Rodman, Rose Pastor Stokes, and especially Mabel Dodge whipping up support, painting scenery, and publicizing the pageant across the city. A substantial contingent of Heterodites, including the playwright Susan Glaspell, newly arrived in New York, attended. The audience numbered fifteen thousand and the line for tickets stretched twenty-eight blocks.[41] The creative and logistical demands of the pageant drove Jack Reed almost to collapse; Mabel, characteristically, declared that "he couldn't have done it without me."[42]

On June 7, a thousand strikers marched up Fifth Avenue to Madison Square Garden, then a large theatrical venue at Twenty-Sixth Street. It was a populist venue and an ambitious one—the phrase about *selling out Madison Square Garden* derives from this era, not from its modern incarnation as a sports arena perched atop the churning bowels of Penn Station. It hosted political rallies and boxing matches, events that went for big energy, big spectacle, and big crowds. A boisterous place, not a bohemian one, but perfect for a pageant that would become emblematic of the overlap between art and politics. At the last possible moment, as the marchers approached, the organizers pulled a switch to illuminate the letters *IWW*, picked out in ten-foot-high red lights on top of the building.[43]

The huge spectacle of the pageant brought Paterson to life in the middle of New York City. Arriving at the Garden and marching onto the stage, the strikers sang and reenacted scenes from their ongoing strike. According to one reporter, flexing his up-to-the-minute vocabulary, the event was infused with "a startling touch of ultra modernity—or rather of Futurism." The writer Randolph Bourne noted that the pageant represented "a new social art . . . in the American world, something genuinely and excitingly new."[44] It was made up of six "episodes" against a backdrop of "dead" mills—a mural of the factory painted by *Masses* artist John Sloan. "Only the return of the workers to the mills can give the dead things life," the pageant program explained. "The mills remain dead throughout the enactment of the following episodes."

The evening began with a vivid recreation of the mill in operation just before the strike, early on a February morning. Heterodoxy's Grace Potter described the scene: "First we saw the mill, stretching its black stories menacing to the sky. Its windows were lit, its whistles blowing. . . . Then the unending whirr of iron-hearted machinery began."[45] The workers sang "La Marseillaise," and the audience was encouraged to join in, with the help of words printed in the program. As the strike unfolded through subsequent episodes, the audience witnessed mass picketing, the violence of the police as they clubbed and arrested strikers, and a reenactment of the death and funeral of Valentino Modestino: "The strikers passing drop red carnations and ribbons upon the coffin until it is buried beneath the crimson symbol of the workers' blood." After the funeral, a mass IWW meeting was staged, with speeches and songs, followed by a May Day parade, with bands and flag-waving, celebrating "the international revolutionary Labor Day" and connecting the strike to the wider socialist agenda. Scenes showed strikers' children being handed over to "strike mothers" from other cities for safety during "the war in the silk industry."[46] Star leaders, including Elizabeth Gurley Flynn, appeared onstage. Finally, the pageant showed victory: a law passed to achieve the eight-hour day. "They wave their hands, they shout, they dance, they embrace each other in a social passion that pales individual feeling to nothing," wrote Grace Potter of the performers. The audience responded with a similar surge of collective feeling, as from the boxes and balconies came "the sound of sobbing that was drowned in singing."[47] That triumphant ending was a painful deviation from the reality of the strike, which yielded hardly any of the workers' demands.

An avant-garde pageant reenacting a labor strike was about the most 1913 idea Jack and Mabel could have had. Twenty-first-century sensibilities might well revolt against the idea of shipping in more than a thousand impoverished factory workers to reenact their suffering at the direction of a crew of Harvard-educated amateur dramatists, for an audience of well-heeled New Yorkers—even as a fundraiser. But in 1913, pageants were a theatrical and political phenomenon. Although they are most familiar to us now in the form of beauty pageants, the pageant at the time of Paterson was a multilayered visual spectacle, incorporating elaborate costumes and painted backdrops, music and movement. Whereas a Shakespeare play or contemporary drawing-room comedy was an elitist phenomenon, expensive to access and often requiring a level of advanced education to appreciate, the tools of pageantry were democratic. A "vigorous pageant renaissance" was underway across America, dramatizing well-known stories from the national past and reaffirming the audience's sense of community and national pride.[48] Pageant organizers believed fervently in the power of a theatrical spectacle to reach an audience emotionally and unite them in sympathy with one another and with the performers. A pageant audience was not supposed to forget itself, but to participate, to shape the event.

Pageants were popular with suffrage organizers, who often kicked off or ended their parades with some form of pageant. Well-known activists like Inez Milholland would appear as symbolic figures—gowned in suffrage gold, green, and purple as "The Future" of the American woman, for example, or in a tableau with children, representing "Woman Enfranchised."[49] Unlike a realistic play, in which the audience was meant to enter like flies on the wall of a human drama, a pageant did not rely on narrative or the suspension of disbelief. A series of set pieces represented particular themes or events, often a march through history ending with a better, brighter vision of the future. Through spectacle rather than argument, pageants were designed to dazzle, amuse, and ultimately convince the audience of a political idea.

In the fall of 1913, W. E. B. Du Bois showed himself a man of his time by writing and staging an enormous pageant of Black history, which he called "The People of Peoples and Their Gift to Man" (later renamed "The Star of Ethiopia"). It formed part of New York's ten-day Emancipation Exposition, held to celebrate the fiftieth anniversary of the Emancipation Proclamation. The event was attended by more than thirty thousand people in what *The Crisis* called "perhaps the largest single celebration which colored people have had in the North." With a cast of more than a thousand, Du Bois's three-hour, six-episode pageant told the story of Black Americans from prehistory through ancient Egypt, the Atlantic slave trade, and the Civil War. It was staged six months after the Paterson Pageant, on October 22, 1913, at the 12th Regiment Armory, a hulking structure on

Columbus Avenue and Sixty-Third Street that was demolished in the late 1950s to make way for Lincoln Center. The "Star of Ethiopia" shows a striking and unusual overlap of the work of the NAACP with the avant-garde theatrical experiments of the Greenwich Villagers. Activists in multiple arenas, however, recognized the power of narrative and spectacle to influence audiences' understandings of history and affect the political future.

Mabel Dodge, in her description of the Paterson Pageant, leaned into the art form's power to transcend the stark differences of class and experience, evoking a fantasy of solidarity achieved through theater: "For a few electric moments there was a terrible unity between all those people. They were one: the workers who had come to show their comrades what was happening across the river, and the workers who had come to see it. I have never felt such a high pulsing vibration in any gathering before or since."[50] That "terrible unity," that mystical oneness of audience and performers, was an effect that powerfully inspired theatrical innovators across Europe and America. Susan Glaspell recalled sitting up late with Jack Reed after the performance, talking "of what the theater might be," how the performers "forgot they were on a stage," and the "feeling of oneness" the pageant achieved. Its larger achievements, however, were doubtful. Generally judged effective as theater, the pageant was viewed by many as a distraction from the politics of the strike, and it was an abject failure as a fundraiser. In its aftermath, radicals and creatives raked over the vanished illusion in search of a lesson.

The strike in Paterson stumbled on but lost momentum after the high of the pageant. Over the summer, several employers offered deals to entice workers back, and higher-paid skilled workers in particular wanted to settle. The IWW organizers tried to hold them together—their whole philosophy depended on solidarity among all workers—but by the end of July, most employees were back at work.[51] Elizabeth Gurley Flynn was bitterly disappointed. According to her friend Mary Heaton Vorse, she had considered the pageant beautiful as art, but believed it "had much to do with the failure of the strike."[52] That failure spelled the end of the IWW's major actions in the industrial Northeast and the beginning of the end of its dominance in American labor activism. Elizabeth's work was far from over, but it was a serious setback for her dreams of revolution.

Chapter 7

FEMI-*WHAT?*

IN LESS THAN TWO YEARS SINCE HETERODOXY HAD BEGUN TO meet, the term *feminism* had moved rapidly from curiosity to ubiquity. As feminists would be driven to do repeatedly over the years, Marie Jenney Howe wanted to clear up the myriad misconceptions around the meaning of the word. In February 1914, she organized a pair of public forums at Cooper Union for that purpose. Unlike her similar events for suffrage, which took a pickax to a fifty-year buildup of cliché and assumptions around the issue of women's right to vote, these "feminist mass meetings" were about the discovery and discussion of a new idea. Posters for the event announced, "What Is Feminism? Come and Find Out." The events were not about preaching to the converted, still less about recruiting for Heterodoxy, a group that was already in danger of growing unmanageably large. Instead, they were an opportunity for famous feminists to define themselves in front of a curious, skeptical audience.

The two meetings offer a revealing way of understanding the principles that united the women of Heterodoxy and hint at the currents of conflict that already pulsed through the inchoate theory of feminism. The first meeting took as its subject "What Feminism Means to Me" and showcased short personal histories

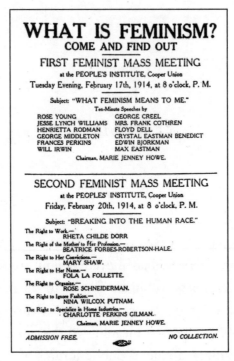

WHAT IS FEMINISM?
COME AND FIND OUT

FIRST FEMINIST MASS MEETING
at the PEOPLE'S INSTITUTE, Cooper Union
Tuesday Evening, February 17th, 1914, at 8 o'clock, P. M.

Subject: "WHAT FEMINISM MEANS TO ME."

Ten-Minute Speeches by

ROSE YOUNG	GEORGE CREEL
JESSE LYNCH WILLIAMS	MRS. FRANK COTHREN
HENRIETTA RODMAN	FLOYD DELL
GEORGE MIDDLETON	CRYSTAL EASTMAN BENEDICT
FRANCES PERKINS	EDWIN BJORKMAN
WILL IRWIN	MAX EASTMAN

Chairman, MARIE JENNEY HOWE.

SECOND FEMINIST MASS MEETING
at the PEOPLES' INSTITUTE, Cooper Union
Friday, February 20th, 1914, at 8 o'clock, P. M.

Subject: "BREAKING INTO THE HUMAN RACE."

The Right to Work.—
RHETA CHILDE DORR

The Right of the Mother to Her Profession.—
BEATRICE FORBES-ROBERTSON-HALE.

The Right to Her Convictions.—
MARY SHAW.

The Right to Her Name.—
FOLA LA FOLLETTE.

The Right to Organize.—
ROSE SCHNEIDERMAN.

The Right to Ignore Fashion.—
NINA WILCOX PUTNAM.

The Right to Specialize in Home Industries.—
CHARLOTTE PERKINS GILMAN.

Chairman, MARIE JENNEY HOWE.

ADMISSION FREE.   NO COLLECTION.

Marie Jenney Howe's 1914 public meetings invited the audience to discover what the new term *feminism* was all about. (*Credit: New-York Historical Society*)

from twelve local bohemian writers and activists, six men and six women. The *New York Times* attended the event and reported that the auditorium was filled almost to capacity with an audience made up of more men than women: an important detail that shows how far men felt themselves to be implicated and invested in the question of women's social position. This first mass meeting emphasized that feminism was, in some irreducible way, *personal*, that its meaning was malleable according to individual experience and beliefs. The second meeting, featuring only women speakers, focused instead on a series of social and political rights that feminists claimed for themselves. So, from the first, Marie Jenney Howe and her Heterodoxy friends considered feminism to be both a personal, psychological experience and a question of political rights.

The speakers at the first mass meeting agreed that the central question of feminism was "freedom for women," but they defined that in different ways. Given ten-minute slots, they aimed for pith over profundity. Most of the male speakers were the partners of Heterodoxy members, including Max Eastman and George Middleton, married to Fola La Follette. Like several other speakers, George focused on men's and women's shared humanity, claiming both sexes were "made of the same soul stuff," a truth that was far more important than "biological bosh." He made his points by belaboring metaphors of fashion and clothing in a way that a female speaker might have resisted. "Feminism is not a femaleness with fewer petticoats; it does not seek to crinoline men," he declared. Instead, "It asks a new fashion in the social garments of each." Max quipped that feminism was "the name for the newly discovered and highly surprising fact that it is just as important for a woman to be happy as a man."[1] Strikingly attractive and increasingly sought after as a social and political commentator, Max used his virile image and his loudly proclaimed feminism to counteract the stereotypes anti-suffragists circulated, which presented the husbands of feminists as pathetic, abused creatures forced to don aprons and care for babies while their wives took over the public sphere.

Feminism was thoroughly in vogue among the young male radicals of the Village. The previous year, Max's friend Floyd Dell had published *Women as World-Builders: Studies in Modern Feminism*, which profiled a wide range of contemporary luminaries, including Charlotte Perkins Gilman, Isadora Duncan, Emma Goldman, and Emmeline Pankhurst. Explaining why he, a man, should care enough to write such profiles, Floyd declared, "Men are tired of subservient women"—or, rather, of the stealthy "pretty slave" who only pretends to subservience long enough to dupe a man into marriage. In "Confessions of a Feminist Man," which he wrote for *The Masses* the month after Marie's first Cooper Union event, he echoed Max in his argument that men wanted "a comrade and an equal" because it was right, but also because it promised to be "more fun." He returned to the rhetoric of enslavement in his claim that no man had a right to enjoy his own freedom while "a woman-slave" languished in a dungeon underneath his feet. White progressives of this time, especially suffragists, frequently used the language of slavery to refer to women's lack of rights in politics and marriage. They generally failed to make any connection to the plight of African Americans, either historically or in their own day.[2]

Writer Rose Young supplied more f-words in her own definition of feminism: "some fight, some fate, and some fun." Frances Perkins, who had been working since the Triangle Fire to improve industrial workers' safety, declared most memorably of all, "Feminism means revolution, and I am a revolutionist."[3] The *New-York Tribune*, while taking a rather patronizing tone toward "these exhilarating evenings," voiced a concern that would be a common one over the years: that feminism was too broad an idea to count as a coherent philosophy. "It goes tripping on its own sweet way regardless of definitions"—and it was capacious enough to sweep along both anti-suffragists and militant suffragettes as part of its "very wide stream."[4]

Perhaps in order to head off this kind of critique, the speakers at Marie's second event, "Breaking into the Human Race," laid aside personal doctrines in favor of outlining a series of rights feminists claimed for themselves, including the "Right to Work," the "Right to Her Convictions," and the "Right to Organize." This time, the speakers were all women, and in Marie's words, each was "a practical liver of her own feminist theories." Heterodoxy member Nina Wilcox Putnam, a prolific novelist and screenwriter, spoke on the "Right to Ignore Fashion." She wore "a flowing yellow kimono . . . a string of big green, red, white, and yellow beads around her neck, and a wide silver hair-band around her forehead"—a "startling" getup, according to a reporter in the audience. Ignoring fashion, to Nina, was clearly not about dressing unobtrusively. It was part of a larger movement to free women from the physical restraint of corsets and long, heavy skirts. But where Victorian dress reformers were happy to proceed by (literal) inches, pushing for women's skirts to be shortened to mere ankle-grazing length, Nina was far more radical, embodying George Middleton's idea about feminism requiring a whole "new fashion in the social garments" of men and women. Her "kimono" indicates that she adopted the bohemian costume of a draped tunic or jacket over loose pants, an outfit that advertised its wearer's rejection of the much-prized hourglass figure and the corset that made it possible. Fashion, Nina told the journalist Ida Tarbell in the familiar terminology of the day, was an issue that called for "revolt, not reform."[5]

Journalist Rheta Childe Dorr spoke about the "Right to Work" in terms that sound strikingly contemporary, passionate about women's access to not only good jobs but also opportunities to advance within them and to be paid the same as their male colleagues. Describing how it took her three years to land a job on a newspaper that did not involve writing "Advice to the Lovelorn," Rheta also noted that her twenty-five-dollar-a-week salary had not been raised in four years: "That's what I mean when I say women haven't got the same right as men to work for promotion." But Rose Schneiderman immediately struck back at Rheta's class privilege. The labor leader pointed out that "among the women of the real working class there was not and never had been any question as to their right to work" and, further, that the right to "stay home a bit" might be welcomed. She, like many in the labor movement, saw "industrial solidarity" as the only true path to emancipation for working-class women. Marie Jenney

Howe, speaking for the "Right to Vote," argued that there were different types of women just as there were different types of men, and the fact that some women did not want equality was no reason to deny the vote to those who did. But it was left to Margaret Hinchey, a vocal Irish labor organizer connected with the Heterodoxy women via the WTUL, to put forward the most innovative scheme for winning the vote. She called on women to take brooms with them when they went out dancing so that when a man asked them to dance, they could "see whether he is wearing a suffrage button, and if he is not, get up and dance with the broom. If you do this in this present day of tango mania half the men in New York City will be converted before 1915."[6]

Heterodoxy members were in the vanguard of defining feminism for the American public in print as well as in person. When the prominent monthly news magazine *McClure's* gave Inez Milholland a platform as the "conductor" of its new Department for Women, it declared, "No movement of this century is more significant or more deep rooted than the movement to readjust the social position of women," distinguishing between feminism—the broad general aspect of the movement—and suffrage, "its immediate political aspects." Inez was a leader who could speak to both.[7] Rose Young's substantial essay in *Good Housekeeping* magazine called "What Is Feminism?" further demonstrated that, for the magazine's middle-class, decidedly not radical female audience, the question was still a new one. "Has the question reached your home town yet?" she began, before going on to hazard an answer. "'Femi-what?' Your average citizen will venture."

The confusion was quite real. Was feminism about women's freedom, rights, or interests? Was it a struggle or a revolt? A doctrine, an assertion, or a feeling? Distinguishing between feminism and suffrage, Rose suggested that all specific political goals were "parts of something greater, vaster"—namely, the development of the woman as individual. In this, the feminist was simply a product of her time: "In art, in philosophy, in business, the twentieth-century demand is for the man who 'thinks for himself,'" she declared. In child development, the same was true; in place of rote learning, and in line with the much-in-vogue Montessori method, the aim now was to help children discover their own personalities. Yet society was much less tolerant of women who pursued their individualism, Rose noted, than men or children. The essay builds to an optimistic, if extremely vague, assessment that this individual growth is inextricable from social or "racial" improvement (meaning, here, the human race)—a utopianism that was also very much of its time.[8]

The seriousness with which Heterodoxy members took their roles as ambassadors of feminism did not mean they could not laugh at the trappings of their own rebellion. Just as it did in the Village and in the suffrage movement, satire served to bond the club into a stronger sense of its own identity. Club member Florence Guy Woolston's pseudoscientific survey, "Marriage Customs and Taboos Among the Heterodites," is a fascinating insight into both the club's feminist principles and the sexual conventions of the wider culture with which they were in conflict. The essay, a mock taxonomy of the club's proudly unorthodox romantic affairs, spoofs the work of fellow member Elsie Clews Parsons, a sociologist and anthropologist who wrote extensively about gender and the family. Claiming to be a reprint from the *Scientific Monthly*, Florence's essay jokingly examines the dwellings, clothing, ornaments, marriage customs, fecundity, and taboos of the Heterodites, "a tribe of women living on the Island of Manhattan in the North Seas."[9]

Florence, one of Heterodoxy's many journalists, divided her friends into three groups. First there were the "monotonists," who "mated young" and remained attached to their partners, "by pressure of habit and circumstance" or out of "sheer inertia."

Monotonists were also kept together by society, by the "diffi-culty of unmating," that is, divorce, which was still expensive, scandalous, and punitive. The rest of Heterodoxy fell into the categories of "varietists" and "resistants." Varietists preferred "a succession of matings" with a series of partners—a choice that took determination, discretion, and reliable access to birth con-trol. A varietist who married did not automatically become a monotonist, however. Despite wearing wedding rings, outward tokens that marked them out as "nominally the exclusive pos-session of some male," Florence hinted that several Heterodoxy monotonists "practiced variety secretly." Under her own schema, Florence might be called a monotonist-varietist: she was married and divorced twice: first to Howard B. Woolston, a sociologist and a suffragist who had spoken at Marie Jenney Howe's "25 An-swers to Antis" event in 1912, and then to a psychologist named David Seabury. Her comic essays appeared in a volume called *The Delicatessen Husband*, in 1926, and a decade later, she published a relationship guide with the frank title *Love Is a Challenge*.

Florence noted that many would-be varietists married for practical purposes, "because the marriage union label is useful in some lines of professional work." She might have been thinking of Ida Rauh, who freely admitted when she married Max East-man that she would have preferred to live with him unmarried, but for her fear that the scandal would interfere with her ability to continue her activism. The final category, "resistants," rejected heterosexual marriage or partnership altogether. Florence wrote that "true resistants" were rare, despite the sizable number of Heterodites who did not marry. These women maintained the public appearance of spinsterhood, but within the club it was well known that the lack of a marriage band did not mean the absence of romantic commitment, often to another woman.

A keen suffragist, Florence edited the *Woman Voter* magazine, which prominently featured club members on its masthead. Like

Crystal Eastman, Florence had studied sociology at Columbia University and followed a path well trodden by her Heterodoxy friends, from work in a settlement house to carrying out social science research at the Russell Sage Foundation. Progressive young Heterodites flocked to this new institution, founded in 1907 by the widow of a railroad magnate: alongside Florence were Katharine Anthony; Crystal Eastman, whose Pittsburgh survey was underwritten by the foundation; and Madeleine Doty, who was secretary of the foundation's committee on children's courts. Florence teased that the foundation was supporting her survey of Heterodoxy customs, and that "Other data concerning Totems, Ceremonial Gatherings, Education and Sex Ideals of the Early Heterodites will be published in book form by the Russell Sage Foundation in 1920."

THE SPEAKERS AT Marie's feminist meetings voiced an overarching concern with how to make feminist theories apply in everyday life, particularly within marriage, which, they believed, might be reformed if partners could be placed on a more equal footing. They drew on the model of less historically fraught relationships, calling the ideal partnership a "companionate" or "sibling" marriage. Inez Milholland chose in one of her first columns for *McClure's* to tackle this issue under the rubric of "the changing home." She began by declaring, "No one, of course,— least of all the advanced feminist thinkers,—questions the imperative beauty and value of romantic love. Indeed, the hope is that marriage, far from being undermined or destroyed, can be made real and lasting." What that meant in theory was that marriage should be disentangled from the economic constraints that reduced it to legalized prostitution. What it meant in practice was anyone's guess. Feminist writers like Inez were eloquent on what marriage ought not to be—"It is as easy to make a dead rose-bush blossom by a court order as to breathe life into a sex-relationship that is not a real marriage in the hearts of the persons concerned"—yet faltered into lofty vagueness when describing the modern ideal: "a fine, healthy, continuous companionship and sharing of burdens, permitting the rearing of healthy children under the continuous intelligent and loving care of the parents." The stress on *continuous* reveals the tautology. An enduring marriage endures; a successful marriage is one that succeeds.[10]

Within Heterodoxy, several of the most successful "monotonist" marriages involved women who were professionally active, often working with their husbands, and who did not have children. For instance, Leta and Harry Hollingworth, both psychologists, met and married in their native Nebraska in 1908 and trained at Columbia University. Each remained associated with that institution and its related schools, Barnard and Teachers College, throughout their careers. An experienced teacher, and one of several in Heterodoxy who promoted Montessori education, Leta became interested in "exceptional" children, and in the 1920s launched the first program to study and teach gifted children. After she died, in her early fifties, in 1939, Harry wrote a biography of Leta, in which he wrote that early in their marriage when she was forced to be a housewife, unable to work due to New York's ban on married teachers, she "stifled her own eager longing for intellectual activity like that of her husband."[11] Grace and James Weldon Johnson had a similarly enduring marriage, rooted in shared work, in their case in civil rights activism. When it was cut tragically short by James's death in a car accident in 1938—Grace was behind the wheel, and profoundly traumatized—she dedicated the rest of her life to his legacy. Her Heterodoxy friend Fola La Follette cabled from Washington, DC, with a note that testifies to the depth of friendship forged in the club: "My love and deep sympathy to you dear Grace stop this blow falls hardest on you but all who knew and loved Jim experience a deep personal loss in his death he was one of the wise and great men of his time and a rare and precious friend."[12]

In many other relationships founded on shared goals and shared activist work, like Max Eastman and Ida Rauh's, the arrival of a baby upset the balance irrevocably. Even feminist men, having grown up immersed in the cultural glorification of women as domestic creatures and natural mothers, often found their political ideals faltering when faced with the prospect of shared parenting. As Charlotte Perkins Gilman and others pointed out, that revered myth of the "angel in the house" was a cultural sleight of hand to obscure their financial and legal dependency on men. But that didn't make it any less powerful.

Not all Heterodoxy's monotonists were straight. Several of the club's lesbian couples enjoyed long, supportive, and nurturing partnerships, although they could not declare them legally. Elisabeth Irwin and Katharine Anthony were acknowledged and treated as a couple by their friends. "They kept house together," wrote Inez Haynes Irwin (no relation to Elisabeth). "Katharine was the author of a generous line of brilliant biographies; a wise woman with a philosophic outlook and a delicious sense of humor," she went on. "Elisabeth was a live, warm earthy type with the fine trained mind of an educator. She was an iconoclast."[13] It wasn't just their bohemian friends who knew of their relationship, however—in her letters to her family, Katharine passed on Elisabeth's love and wrote of "we" rather than "I." They lived together for thirty years, adopted children together, and owned a New York City home and a Connecticut country house in a hamlet called Gaylordsville, jokingly calling themselves "the Gay Ladies of Gaylordsville."[14] When Elisabeth died of cancer in 1942, she left "all of my estate whatsoever its nature or kind" to Katharine. In her grief, Katharine, who lived into her late eighties, turned to her close friend, Congresswoman Jeannette

Rankin, whom she had also met at Patchin Place. She described how she had drawn strength and support from her partner: "Elisabeth manufactured optimism for me for thirty years."[15]

Dr. Jo Baker, four years older than Katharine Anthony, had several committed relationships with women. When she first qualified as a physician, she shared a home and a medical practice with Dr. Florence M. Laighton. After World War I, she met the novelist Ida "I. A. R." Wylie, an adventurous and outgoing English Australian woman who was active in the British suffrage fight before moving to New York and joining Heterodoxy. She later moved with Dr. Jo to Princeton, where they shared a home with another doctor, Louise Pearce. The women published autobiographies back-to-back in 1939 and 1940, though neither discusses their relationship. In *Fighting for Life*, Jo describes a dramatic trip through Soviet Russia in the early 1920s in the company of her "friend" Ida, in which they share hotel rooms and transportation, but the focus is on adventure rather than intimacy.

Ida, for her part, hints at her sexuality but explains it in terms that would have made sense to any Heterodoxy woman, with an emphasis on friendship and equality. "I have always liked women better than men," she writes. "I am more at ease with them and more amused by them. I too am rather bored by a conventional relationship which seems to involve either my playing up to someone or playing down to someone." She goes on to suggest that the kind of equal companionship with men that feminists were seeking is only possible once sexual desire, and the prospect of marriage, have been overcome or left behind: "Here and there and especially in my latter years when there should be no further danger of my trying to ensnare one of them I have established some real friendships with men in which we meet and like each other on equal terms as human beings." Fortunately, she says, she has never wanted to marry any of them, "nor with the

Dr. Jo Baker adopted "masculine drag" at work, for practical and personal reasons. (*Credit: Schlesinger Library, Harvard Radcliffe Institute*)

exception of that one misguided German Grenadier, have any of them wanted to marry me."[16]

Other confirmed or very likely lesbian partnerships among Heterodites and their circle included suffragist and playwright Paula Jakobi's long relationship with Carl Van Vechten's first wife, Anna (Carl had a number of affairs with men). Helen Hull, a novelist and English professor at Wellesley and Columbia, had a lifelong relationship with her fellow professor and children's author Mable Louise Robinson, while radical cartoonist Lou Rogers and prison-reform activist Elizabeth Watson were likely partners for a time, although Lou later married, declaring, "Love is good wherever it comes from."[17] Other club members had relationships with both men and women. After the implosion of her relationship with Carlo Tresca and her temporary retirement from activism in the mid-1920s, Elizabeth Gurley Flynn spent a decade living in Portland with Dr. Marie Equi. Mabel Dodge and Charlotte Perkins Gilman both had intense and important relationships with women during their teens and early twenties, and Marie Jenney Howe had, at the very least, an intensely emotional connection with Rose Young, to whom she dedicated her biography of the scandalous bisexual writer George Sand. Second-wave feminist historians have expressed astonishment that the lesbians and straight women within the club were able to form strong friendships, and that differences in sexuality didn't get in the way of their working together—which may say more about the tensions among feminists of the late twentieth century than it does about Heterodoxy.[18] At the time, it seems that for both queer and straight Heterodites—whether they were monotonists, varietists, or resistants—sexuality was less important than shared feminist ideals.

The relationships between women within Heterodoxy occurred at a time of transition in American understandings of female same-sex intimacy. During Katharine Anthony and Elisabeth Irwin's heyday as the "gay ladies," the blithe assumption of innocence in women's close friendships was giving way to suspicion. The language of "inversion" arrived with the European sexologists in the late nineteenth century to denote same-sex attraction and, often, to categorize it as a form of perversion or deviance. When members of the avant-garde began to embrace psychoanalysis, they also took on board the distinction between "normal" or "healthy" sexual development and its opposite. During the 1910s and, especially, the 1920s, it became more socially acceptable to discuss women's sexual desire openly and to wonder—and worry—aloud about where it might lead.

The state, however, was wary of criminalizing sexual behavior between women. Instead, laws attacked how women presented themselves in public. Like most of the country, New York in the early twentieth century had laws on the books against cross-dressing and face painting, but these were generally meant to punish the act of disguising one's appearance in order to commit *another* crime. Gradually, however, these "masquerade laws" came to be used to police gender nonconformity. In 1913, a male-presenting person was arrested in a Brooklyn bar despite not committing any other crime; after one magistrate released him, he was rearrested and found guilty of "associating with idle and vicious persons" and given a three-year sentence at a reformatory. Newspaper reports made it clear that the sentence was a pretext for the real crime of gender nonconformity. "No girl would dress in men's clothing unless she is twisted in her moral viewpoint," the magistrate decreed.[19]

Several Heterodoxy members experimented with gender-nonconforming clothing, but their class and professional status generally protected them from similar abuse. Those who worked in male-dominated fields saw men's clothing as useful professional drag or, as Dr. Jo Baker called it, "protective coloring." Another Heterodite, Kathleen de Vere Taylor, who was a suffrage activist, Greenwich Villager, and, unusually, a stockbroker, cuts a dapper figure in a photograph from the mid-1910s, in a houndstooth jacket, white shirt, and plaid tie, with no jewelry save a tie pin. Dr. Jo emphasized the practicality of her similar look: "My man-tailored suits and shirtwaists and stiff collars and four-in-hand ties were a trifle expensive, but they more than paid their way as buffer. They were also very little trouble. I could order a suit and another dozen shirtwaists and collars with hardly a tenth of the time and energy that buying a single new frock would have required." She was at pains to clarify that her masculine attire was not a political statement, nor even a personal preference. "Dr. Mary Walker wore trousers to startle men into recognizing that a woman was demanding men's rights," she wrote, referencing a trailblazing Civil War surgeon. Jo insisted, at a length that begins to sound like she is protesting too much, that her clothes are not making a statement:

> I wore a standard costume—almost a uniform—because the last thing I wanted was to be conspicuously feminine when working with men. . . . At home, of course, I kept a certain amount of conventional and thoroughly feminine attire for these rare occasions when I could allow myself a social holiday. And yet, I am sure that there are today a great number of my old-time friends who never saw me dressed in any other way, for I wore that costume in my daily work for over twenty-five years.[20]

Florence Woolston, in her "Marriage Customs" survey, observes, "Some of the Heterodites affect male attire for the upper story and would go further were it not forbidden by law."[21] Even among the avant-garde Village feminists, trousers represented a line that was far too socially risky to cross. For Christmas in 1914, Henrietta Rodman, the Heterodite infamous for "stirring things up," organized a ball at the Leslie, a hall for dances and social events on the Upper West Side of Manhattan. Several Heterodoxy friends were among the partygoers, including Mary Ware Dennett, Inez Haynes Irwin, and Marie Jenney Howe, whose husband danced with Henrietta's adopted daughter Alice.[22] Reporters attended the ball hoping to glimpse "fair dancers in trouserettes"—apparently, Henrietta had planned a pageant displaying women's dress "from the primitivists to the futurists," but her busy schedule and the absence of one of the models meant the plan was abandoned. Still, there were plenty of women in "Turkish trousers," and a reporter lavished description on the two women whose clothing was more transgressive. Alice, an out lesbian, "looked like a pretty boy with her short-cropped hair, loose blouse, golf stockings, and sandals."[23] Another woman, "in very becoming overalls," was a writer, Florence King, who would go on to marry Villager Carl Zigrosser, the journalist who attended Patchin Place gatherings with Katharine Anthony and Elisabeth Irwin. Carl described his wife as "a modern emancipated woman—athletic, efficient, priding herself on economic independence"; the paper called her a "Futurist Maud Muller," a blend of ultramodern and rural-nostalgic.[24]

In both cases, the reporters stressed that the young women in male attire were still undeniably feminine, even that their boyish dress made them even more attractive. Henrietta herself wore a simple classical costume, although she said that (like many Village feminists) her ideal "Futurist" outfit would be Chinese-inspired and gender-ambiguous, with "loose trousers and a long coat coming to the knees."[25] Many Heterodites were no doubt drawn to Charlotte Perkins Gilman's humanist feminism in part because it downplayed the gender binary. Marie Jenney Howe and Katharine Anthony, in their feminist biographies, chose subjects whose gender presentation blended traditionally masculine and feminine traits. Beyond avant-garde circles, however, there was vanishingly little cultural space to acknowledge the longing that anthropologist Elsie Clews Parsons expressed in her journal, of an external appearance that could change and reflect a shifting internal gender identity. "This morning perhaps I may feel like a male; let me act like one," she wrote. "This afternoon I may feel like a female. Let me act like one. At midday or at midnight I may feel sexless; let me therefore act sexlessly."[26] Questions that linked gender presentation, sexual orientation, and women's psychological development were not ones that the women of Heterodoxy would have grown up asking. But by the time the club began to meet, the Village milieu was consumed with them. The direction of Heterodites' individual feminist journeys was diverted into a new and irresistible channel, carved by a controversial doctor in Vienna.

Chapter 8

DOES MR. FREUD LIVE
IN THE VILLAGE?

SIGMUND FREUD MADE ONLY ONE VISIT TO AMERICA, IN SEP-
tember 1909, to Clark University in Worcester, Massachusetts,
in the company of Carl Jung; allegedly, as his ship arrived in
New York Harbor, he delivered the movie villain line: "They
don't realize that we are bringing them the plague." He'd been
invited for an occasion marking the college's twentieth anniversary; everyone involved seems to have been rather surprised that
he said yes. His five lectures were delivered in German, the lin-
gua franca of the American academy, and went untranslated.
Nevertheless, his visit was an event, received by many in the
intellectual avant-garde not as a sickness but as its cure. It did
not matter that a great deal of what passed for Freudian theory in the 1910s, especially around female sexuality, was only
loosely connected to his actual writings, which did not deal in
a significant way with women's development until much later.
The bohemians' broad-strokes understanding of psychoanalysis
supported everything they had been grasping toward in their intimate relationships: frankness about sexuality, recognition that
men and women shared equally intense desires, and rejection of
the tight trammeling force of traditional marriage.

Mabel Dodge was among the most enthusiastic early pro-
moters of Freud's ideas. Her tumultuous affair with Jack Reed
had finally ended in late 1913. "I cannot live with you," he told
her in a note. "You smother me. You crush me. You want to kill
my spirit." In her grief, Mabel took an overdose of veronal—a
barbiturate commonly used as a sleep aid—while Jack left for
Mexico, on assignment to cover Pancho Villa's attempted revolution.[1] After Mabel recovered, she began with renewed vigor to
seek answers to the dilemma of how to balance her sexual desires
with her own mental health and happiness. It was a quest she
had been on for some time, perhaps her whole adult life. At her
salon in December, she introduced A. A. Brill, Freud's translator and America's first practitioner of the new magical mind
cure, psychoanalysis. It didn't take long for Freudian ideas to
spread like wildfire through the Village.

Psychoanalytic practice dovetailed with a particular interest
of Heterodoxy: the members' reexamination of their own personal development through a feminist lens, looking to childhood, and especially their relationships with their mothers,
to locate specifically female experiences of oppression and the
moment when they discovered things could be different. Most
Heterodoxy women regarded themselves and their friends as
important and unusual, and many of them wrote extensively
about their own lives in the effort to both understand themselves
and communicate their forward-thinking ideas. In addition to
numerous memoirs and autobiographical novels, several Heterodites contributed to a series assembled in the mid-1920s by
Freda Kirchwey, a young editor at *The Nation* closely connected
to the group. Under the cover of anonymity, seventeen "Modern
Women"—including Heterodoxy's Inez Haynes Irwin, Crystal
Eastman, the cartoonist Lou Rogers, social worker and librar-
ian Alice Mary Kimball, journalist Ruth Pickering, and novelist
Mary Hunter Austin—analyzed the sources of their feminism in

the pages of the magazine, which hoped to "discover the origin of their modern point of view toward men, marriage, children, and jobs." Was it "spirited ancestors"? "Thwarted ambition"? "Distaste for domestic drudgery"? Three psychologists—one of whom was also a Heterodoxy member, Beatrice M. Hinkle—responded with their own interpretations.[2]

No member of the group, however, was as exhaustive in her process of self-examination and self-explanation as Mabel Dodge, who had plenty to say and the time to say it. In all, she wrote some twenty-five volumes of autobiography, of which four were published in the 1930s as *Intimate Memories*. Such a voluminous record is both helpful and not—it is hard to disentangle what Mabel says about herself and her world, especially at a distance, from other people's perspectives or competing truths, especially since women who talk a great deal about themselves are rarely listened to as patiently as men who do the same. But a few solid truths do emerge. Mabel was always attracted to those who "did things," as she characterized Heterodoxy women, and wanted to "do things" herself, but that creative doing was always at odds with the temptation to let a man take the lead, to, as she put it, "lie back and float in the dominating decisive current of an all-knowing, all-understanding man."[3] Mabel learned through psychoanalysis to see her sexual desires as a "Power" that controlled her and to see heterosexual love as her ultimate feminine raison d'être. As one historian puts it, the fact that, "despite an enormous self-absorption beyond the means or energy of most women," Mabel remained confused and dissatisfied by her inability to reconcile these competing passions for art and for men "is evidence of how badly women were served by the Freudian view that love was their true destiny."[4]

Freud's focus on sexuality, especially child sexual development, made his theories taboo in all but the most rebellious intellectual circles in America. Freud himself worried about this, writing to Jung that "once they discover the sexual core of our psychological theories they will drop us."[5] But this "sexual core" was a central reason why these theories were so popular, especially among radical feminists—a surprising alliance, given that in later decades feminists would be some of Freud's fiercest critics. But his frankness, at the time, was revelatory in a culture that could barely articulate how babies were made. "We ought not to aim so high that we completely neglect the original animality of our nature," he told his audience at Clark. Cultural high-mindedness, the effort to "sublimate" sexual desires into creative or professional work, was unsustainable in the long term.

Freud's call for honesty and openness around sex was revolutionary to the Village feminists in the 1910s. It was not until later, when his theories enjoyed a wide popular resurgence in the wake of his death and the end of World War II, that they were seized on by so-called experts in order to pathologize and punish social deviance—homosexuality, in particular, but also feminism and "permissive" parenting. The rigid gender policing of 1950s America justified itself by reference to these cutting-edge psychological theories—it was not, as is sometimes assumed, simply the return of repressed "tradition." But in Heterodoxy's heyday, this popular understanding of Freudian theory, and its apparent reinforcement of traditional gender roles, was still a long way off.

Mabel Dodge's analyst A. A. Brill, an Austrian immigrant, returned to Europe to study the new science of psychoanalysis shortly after qualifying as a doctor. He met Freud and studied with Carl Jung before returning to America. In 1909, the year of Freud's visit to Clark, he published the first translation of his fellow Austrian's work, *Some Papers on Hysteria*. Brill was tireless in his promotion of psychoanalysis, advocating for its recognition in the academy, teaching at New York University, and founding the New York Psychoanalytic Society, the first organization promoting the practice in his adopted home. Yet until the mid-1920s, A. A. Brill insisted that psychoanalysis be practiced only by qualified medical doctors. That restriction was just one reason why psychoanalysis was, at first, an enormously male-dominated field. Its scandalous reputation further discouraged aspiring women practitioners. It took a bold woman to undergo psychoanalysis, and a bolder one still to study and practice it. It should not be surprising by now that the most prominent female psychoanalysts in America in the 1910s and 1920s belonged to Heterodoxy.

Grace Potter joined the club along with her sister Mabel Potter Daggett, a prominent journalist and suffrage advocate. The Potter sisters were born in Syracuse in the early 1870s, making them contemporaries of young Marie Jenney Howe. Grace had some medical training at Syracuse University, but moved to New York City in 1902 and began to work as a journalist. In 1904, at the age of thirty, she traveled to Vienna and befriended Sigmund Freud and his daughter Anna. She studied under psychoanalysts Otto Rank and Carl Jung and spent a year in Berlin teaching in the Freudian clinic there. Back in the United States, she became enmeshed in the nascent cultural scene of Greenwich Village. Along with her husband, Ernest Holcombe, whom she divorced in 1920, she was one of the founders of the Liberal Club, the early venue for Heterodoxy meetings and all manner of legendary Village lectures, parties, and dances. Grace was active in the suffrage movement, and in 1911, in the wake of the Triangle Fire, she joined the state's factory investigation commission alongside Frances Perkins.

As a psychoanalyst, Grace established a practice in New York, operating out of the National Arts Club in Gramercy Park, and worked to promote Freudian theories in the press. Through Heterodoxy, she had access to a network of journalists and was interviewed or published by her friends throughout the

1920s and 1930s. Grace's psychoanalytical approach was classical. She identified adult problems as the result of repressed early childhood experiences, meaning emotional conflicts before the age of seven that the child couldn't resolve or absorb. To cope, the child's mind retreated from the conflict and walled it off in the psyche. Buried deep, this denied experience continued to pulse through the consciousness, damaging the patient's adult relationships and marring her happiness. "The wishes in the Unconscious clamor for freedom and pleasure," Grace explained to a journalist in the mid-1920s, even though their bearers had no idea where those feelings originated. It was only through analysis, the working of the unconscious mind, that the sufferer could identify the origin of her pain and overcome it.

For Grace Potter, psychoanalysis was also creatively liberating because it allowed patients to recognize the entwining of libidinal and artistic energies. "[Sex] has to do with other creation than that of new human beings," she argued. "It has to do with every kind of creation—a new state, a poem, a picture, a great bridge, a happier world."[6] Her own chosen medium was drama, and when the Provincetown Players established their theater in the heart of Greenwich Village in 1916, she was involved as a writer and director. Although she was no great talent as a playwright, her psychoanalytic practice and reputation grew throughout the 1920s.

At the same time as Grace was establishing herself as a Freudian analyst, her fellow Heterodite Beatrice Hinkle was challenging Freud's approach to women and female psychosexual development. The two women had a lot in common nonetheless: they were almost the same age, both married and mothers, although Beatrice had been born and raised across the country, in San Francisco. The daughter of a doctor, she entered medical school in 1895, despite the mockery and bafflement of her husband. He lived long enough to see her graduate, four years later, but then Beatrice found herself, on the cusp of the new century, widowed with two young children to provide for. Her qualifications led her to become San Francisco's first female city physician, and in 1905, she decided to move to New York.

Beatrice's growing interest in psychology and the intertwining of physical and mental health led her, like Grace Potter, to Europe, where she studied Freudianism and underwent analysis. But in contrast to Grace, Beatrice found Freud's theories of infant development reductive and particularly lacking when it came to women. She considered the castration theory to be "far-fetched." When she met Carl Jung, however, she felt she had "found the key." The way that Jung understood the libido more broadly than Freud appealed to her. Libido was not a purely sexual drive but what she called an "energetic concept of life." Furthermore, she liked that Jung allowed the possibility that the circumstances of a person's current life—not just her distant childhood—were causing her problems. For women operating under patriarchy, such an observation seemed undeniable, and Beatrice was convinced. Her translation of Jung, in 1916, would be the Swiss psychoanalyst's first introduction to the English-speaking world.[7]

For both Grace Potter and Beatrice Hinkle, and for Heterodoxy as a whole, psychoanalysis offered an irresistible solution for a problem in feminism that political liberation could not solve: the internalized sense of inferiority to men that held women back from achieving their human potential. Even the very successful, very privileged women in the club grappled with the sense that no matter how much they achieved, they would never be seen as men's equals, and they were wearing themselves out playing a game that was rigged against them. In 1915, Katharine Anthony wrote a study of German and Scandinavian feminism that was astute on the psychological challenges of women's liberation. She argued that the goal of feminism was

"the restoration of women's self-respect" and the removal of the
"psychological residue of subjection" to men.[8] Beatrice Hinkle
concurred, believing that even professional, liberated women
were still in "psychic bondage" to men. For the rest of her career, she would devote herself to understanding and easing the
psychological burdens of women's emancipation, in the interest
of furthering the cause of feminism.

Beatrice's psychoanalytic practice was at 10 Gramercy Park,
practically next door to Grace Potter in her office at the National
Arts Club. It was a well-heeled but still bohemian-spirited enclave, and Beatrice's clients were often artists and writers "seeking help in releasing their creative energies." They included a
young Max Eastman, and later the writer Kahlil Gibran, and the
poet and literary editor James Oppenheim, author of the poem
"Bread and Roses" that helped popularize the quintessential
women's labor slogan. Within Heterodoxy, Fola La Follette was
a longtime patient. In the mid-1920s, Fola wrote to her husband
that "I am getting something out of it that is very vital." But she
stopped herself going further, breaking off with "enough of this.
I know the subject irritates you." Given how much of Fola's analyst's practice focused on helping women free themselves from
the weight of male judgment, it's jarring to see a moment that
looks so much like self-censoring.[9]

Both of Heterodoxy's psychoanalysts framed gender in essentialist terms, speaking of a universal "masculine mind" and
a "woman's psychology." In common with most psychoanalytic
writers of their era, whether they were treating patients or popu-
larizing Freudian or Jungian theories in the press, neither Grace
nor Beatrice took race or class distinctions into account when
considering how individuals interacted with the world. Instead,
they spoke to an implicitly white and middle-class reader. Beatrice Hinkle was distinctive, however, in her interest in how
masculine psychology developed and how it affected women.

She examined how the conflict between men's worship of their mothers conflicted with their deep-seated "fear and dread of woman," onto whom they projected all their own feelings of inferiority. By contrast, she argued, women feared the opposite sex because of "definite acts of injustice and discrimination . . . forced upon her" by men. Beatrice believed that the supportive company of other women was vital for the process of overcoming the sense of gendered inferiority that patriarchy instilled so ruthlessly; as she wrote in 1932, "unless woman recognizes the inherent value of other women, she cannot really respect herself."[10]

This insight of Beatrice's pointed to another fraught question that Heterodoxy feminists faced in considering their own psychological development. Beyond the family, and the potent formative experiences of early childhood, it was surely society that most profoundly shaped how a woman thought and behaved. The intense grooming for marriage, the general lack of intellectual development, the fierce taboos around sex, and everywhere a culture of subservience to men and suspicious rivalry with other women—these might be reinforced in the family, or in some cases challenged, but they were powerful forces nonetheless. Where did *they* originate? Could *they* be fought?

Heterodoxy's Elsie Clews Parsons studied sociology, anthropology, and ethnography in order to explore and challenge these dominant societal assumptions governing and limiting women's lives. Like many of her friends in the club, she located the root of her feminist ideas in her upbringing and her conflicts with her mother. Elsie was born into wealth and privilege in New York in 1875, the daughter of an English banker and an American heiress, and raised to be a society wife. In her teens, she shut herself in her bedroom for two days rather than put on stays (a kind of corset); Elsie considered this an act of feminist principle, while her mother dismissed it as a silly act of rebellion.[11] It was a revealing conflict. Elsie was preoccupied with the kinds of psychological restriction that shaped women's lives just as firmly, and invisibly, as boning in a corset compressed their bodies. She went on to earn a PhD in sociology from Columbia University's pioneering School of Social Work, which helped shape the political and scientific thinking of her fellow Heterodites Elisabeth Irwin, Crystal Eastman, and Leta Hollingworth, and her thinking pushed especially at women's internalized patriarchal and misogynist ideas. "Hitherto feminists have been so impressed by the institutional bondage of woman . . . that questions of inner freedom have rarely occurred to them," she wrote, arguing—as many of her Heterodoxy friends agreed—that suffrage was only a small part of the larger issue of women's emancipation.[12]

In 1900, Elsie married Herbert Parsons, a progressive Republican who served three terms in Congress, became a political

Elsie Clews Parsons was a wealthy feminist anthropologist, pictured here in the New Mexico desert, where she undertook fieldwork. (*Credit: Schlesinger Library, Harvard Radcliffe Institute*)

ally of Theodore Roosevelt, and was a strong supporter of women's suffrage. Elsie's 1906 book *The Family* advocated, among other things, for birth control and trial marriage, after which a couple could easily separate if the marriage "proved unsuccessful and in the absence of offspring without suffering any great degree of public condemnation." Although Elsie published the book under a male pseudonym, she was identified and excoriated in the press, which caused an embarrassing controversy for her politician husband. But she was quite serious about the need to rethink the functioning of marriage. Although she believed in the principle of monogamy, she and Herbert both had affairs, and she was able to rationalize and accept this less-than-ideal situation within her larger belief system. For Elsie, a mother of four, a truly rational system would separate sex from parenthood. Love between adults was a private issue, and a couple ought to be free to end a sexual relationship at any time, with no obligation. The welfare of children, however, was a public matter, so she argued that parents should be required to sign a contract with the state laying out their responsibilities.

During the early years of Heterodoxy, after the birth of her last child, Elsie picked up her pen again and wrote prolifically. She was a regular contributor to *The Masses* and published four widely praised books in quick succession—*Religious Chastity*, *Fear and Conventionality*, *Social Freedom*, and *Social Rule*. Running through all her writing was an overriding concern with the internal and external forces that held individuals back from fully expressing themselves and that held societies back from change. She drew on her study of other cultures chiefly to illuminate her own, and in her later anthropological work, she was certainly guilty of a reductive and patronizing attitude to cultures she considered more "primitive" than her own. But she also found points of connection that she used to challenge her readers' assumptions about their cultural superiority—especially when it came to the treatment of women. She showed that menstruation taboos remained powerful even in the "civilized" West, which pressured women to conceal their condition, never mentioning it or letting it interfere with their activities, even if it meant they had to "endure extraordinary discomfort and pain" in the process. Similarly, the veneer of "chivalry"—as Mary Shaw had neatly observed in her suffrage satire—disguised a form of oppression that was used to keep women of all classes "most rigorously and most subtly in their place."[13]

Leta Hollingworth was another Heterodoxy member acutely interested in the connection between women's bodies and their place in society. Her dissertation at Columbia, "Functional Periodicity," is an interesting complement to Elsie's writing on period taboos. Leta set out to overturn the deep-rooted prejudice that periods rendered a woman mentally and physically incapacitated—a myth that provided cover for their exclusion from many professional careers. Although of course some women suffered pain and discomfort during their period, she argued that this did not affect their mental abilities and that women were perfectly capable of rational thought during their monthly cycle. Her later research continued to challenge the supposed links between sex differences and gender hierarchies. Through an examination of infant anatomy, she struck down the idea that it was men's physical "variability" (versus women's less varied biology) that explained, and allowed, their superiority in society. Rheta Childe Dorr popularized Leta's research in a major feature in 1915 in the *New York Times Magazine*, "Is Woman Biologically Barred from Success?" No, was the clear message, but Leta acknowledged the psychological impact of sex discrimination, which she said made women "timid, unambitious, and self-distrustful."[14]

Whether in print or through their actions, most of the women of Heterodoxy were advocates for "free love"—a broad set of ideas that had been swirling in avant-garde circles since the late nineteenth century about how to place intimate relationships on fairer, franker, and more rational grounds. Though the name was daring, and helped toward scandal by figures like the notorious Victoria Woodhull, free lovers usually put more emphasis on the *free* than the *love*. Infused with socialist and abolitionist sentiment, the emphasis was on "owning or possessing oneself," which "struck a specifically gendered chord" at the time.[15] Through practical measures like sex education, birth control, and easier divorce, and guided by new psychological theories about human development, free lovers hoped to liberate men and women from the obligation of "monotony." By talking about love and sex openly, they challenged repressive Victorian morals and tangled directly with their self-appointed guardians—represented since 1873 by Anthony Comstock, postal inspector, anti-vice crusader, and architect of sweeping obscenity laws for which his name became a shorthand.

Other freethinkers of the time, in Britain and America, called themselves "sex radicals" and advocated for a more enlightened approach to the natural human experience of sex, raising such unmentionable topics as masturbation, female orgasms, marital rape, and "inversion," or queer desire. In the United States, Emma Goldman incorporated sex radical and free love rhetoric into her speeches and wrote publicly and privately about women's sexual pleasure. The figure of Goldman—a fierce, stoutly built, middle-aged anarchist—as the face of free love did not help its image, though her speeches and writing did underscore the link feminists were beginning to discern between bodily autonomy and social justice. In 1905, a teenage Elizabeth Gurley Flynn was inspired by hearing Goldman speak, just as she was beginning to make connections between socialist and feminist thinking, between women's right to earn their living and their need to understand and control their own bodies.

Part of the problem with the discourse of free love was the severe taboos on what could be said and imagined and the need to always pay lip service to certain types of conformity—marriage, for one, and heterosexuality, as another—despite what individuals actually did. The popular press was all too eager to portray free love as sexual anarchy (again, Goldman's association didn't help), and so the idea took hold that a free lover was simply a woman who slept around, outside marriage, just like a man. According to Carl Zigrosser, the Patchin Place discussion group once welcomed as a guest a local madam, who denounced free lovers as scabs on the honest labor of sex workers.[16]

On some late nights, the Patchin group would "adjourn to the Women's Night Court at Jefferson Market...to watch a poor unfortunate who had been accosted by a detective in plain clothes and then arrested by him, being arraigned."[17] This "poor unfortunate" would have been a sex worker trapped in a sting operation, a routine practice of the police in the area. Since 1910, the ornate courthouse that backed onto Patchin Place had tried only women's cases, and then only after eight in the evening. The intent was to quickly process crimes and misdemeanors committed after normal court hours (mainly prostitution) so that women did not have to spend the night in jail. By 1918, however, the public spectacle—the Patchin group were not unusual in treating it as entertainment—had grown so unruly that it was converted to a day court. Many feminists saw prostitution through an economic lens, as a woman's act of desperation, and believed that it ought to be curbed through alleviating poverty rather than criminalizing women.

The vociferous opposition to free love and birth control in this era had as much to do with white supremacy as it did with sexual morals. The frequently invoked specter of "race suicide" was the fear that educated, middle-class, native-born white women were having fewer children, while Black and immigrant women were mothers many times over. In a sly article for *The Masses*, Elsie Clews Parsons made a series of logical, if counterintuitive, arguments to spell out the implications of what "those conservative and alarmist moralists" were saying. She begins by suggesting that a modern, feminist woman has children "as an expression of herself"—or of her love for another—rather than because of "sentimentality," "powerlessness," or "ignorance." Yet, the only way this elite, educated "desirable" mother can have the professionally fulfilling life for which she's been trained is to limit the number of children she has, which angers "the race-suicide croakers."[18]

The solutions Elsie offers to this dilemma would require a fundamental reforming of society. Would the moralists be willing to make those changes, she asks? To eliminate the distinction between legitimate and illegitimate offspring, say? Rather than blaming college-educated women for having fewer children, society ought to find ways to widen "the narrow limits within which love and maternity are open to her." The "peasant education" of immigrants, so deplored by the eugenicists croaking about race suicide, in fact matches the ignorance being pushed by "the Board of Education that excludes the teacher-mother or by the State Legislature that makes the control of conception illegal." In other words, the policymakers attacking feminists were in fact allied with the backward, "peasant" ideologies and cultures they claimed to fear.

Some Heterodites, however, vigorously fought the association between women's sexual and social liberation, notably the ardent suffragist Beatrice Forbes-Robertson Hale. The daughter of an illustrious English stage family who had moved to New York in 1907, at age twenty-three, Beatrice published a book offering her own interpretation of feminism, *What Women Want*, in 1914. In it, she argues in favor of romantic monogamy (she was recently married herself, to the journalist Swinburne Hale) and suggests that free love misunderstood the inevitable emotional entanglements of sex. "By the very nature of love, it can never be free," she argues. "Indifference can be free, but not love." Even without the laws of marriage or the tie of children, she believed, "the very fact that two people love and give themselves to each other creates instantly a host of subtleties of consideration, obligation, pity, tenderness, mutual interest, and habit, harder to break than the stoutest chain." To counter the common claim that feminists were seeking the same unfettered sexual freedom that men enjoyed, and that this ought to be praised on the grounds of equality, she instead insisted that rather than stooping to men's level, women ought to be raising them up: "Women are almost entirely united in their belief in the single standard of morals between the sexes, and there are very few who believe that this standard should be other than the purest." Defending monogamy against charges of boredom, she insisted that the depth of emotional experience that came from years of marriage was far superior to the shallow variety that was all the "free lance" woman could gather.[19]

Beatrice's beliefs were not unusual in the feminist movement, or in Heterodoxy, especially in later years. In the more conservative atmosphere of the late 1920s, Leta Hollingworth argued to the group, apparently without pushback, that the "perfect feminist" was both happily married and a mother.[20] Leta did not have children herself, but she seems to have had one of the happier Heterodoxy marriages, the "result of a romance remarkable for its modernity," according to Rheta Childe Dorr (who was divorced).[21] Beatrice Hale had three daughters but likewise divorced her unfaithful and mentally unstable husband in 1920, after a decade of marriage. Whereas connecting their own lives and histories to the theories of feminism was integral to the way Heterodoxy members formulated their theories, the inevitable problem of personal bias went underexamined, especially when it came to the most intimate relationships. It remained difficult for women to talk honestly about what they really wanted—even to find the words. Shortly after Beatrice Hale published her defense of monogamy, the poet Edna St. Vincent Millay and her younger sister Norma, new arrivals in the Village and rising literary and theatrical stars, were working valiantly to get comfortable with the bohemians' sexual openness. "We sat darning socks on Waverly Place and practiced the use of profanity as we stitched," Norma remembered. "Needle in, shit. Needle out, piss. Needle in, fuck. Needle out, cunt. Until we were easy with the words."[22]

But words were not deeds. For heterosexual women, what passed in the Village for liberation could end up simply reinforcing male desires and male control. Floyd Dell, one of Edna St. Vincent Millay's first lovers, left her for a woman who was content to give him marriage and children. By the early 1930s, he felt comfortable admitting, "I did not want to be married to a girl artist; I wanted to be married to a girl who would not put her career before children—or even before me, hideously reactionary as the thought would have seemed a few years ago."[23] As Mabel Dodge wrote to Neith Boyce—whose husband frequently indulged the modernity of his marriage by straying outside it—it often looked as though free love was just an excuse for men to behave the way they always had, yet patting themselves on the back as modern and feminist in the process.[24]

Mabel, however, did not blame men so much as the intractable power imbalance that, for her, lay at the heart of heterosexual relationships. In *The Masses* in 1916, her anonymously published stories "A Quarrel" and "The Parting" offer a searing picture of the pattern she kept repeating with men, most recently in her relationship with the painter Maurice Sterne, who would soon become her third husband. The unnamed wife sees her husband as the "source of her life," and she hates him for it; he, meanwhile, escapes into his work but is choked by the guilt she induces in him as a result.

The vocabulary of psychoanalysis was a strange new taste in the early 1910s, a piquant, complex sauce for earthy profanity. But the combination, of science and sex, was thrilling to bohemian feminists. Bursting free of stifled, repressed upbringings, they fervently believed that if things could only be *said*, and said honestly and plainly, if new feelings and emotional states could be identified and named, surely the world—or at least the world of men and women together—could change? It was a challenge that so preoccupied Heterodoxy women in this era that their creative works, their poetry, fiction, and especially plays, are dominated by characters who are trying to talk themselves, and each other, into the future.

Chapter 9

SUPPRESSED DESIRES

THE VILLAGE RADICALS DECAMPED IN THE SUMMER MONTHS. Heterodoxy stopped meeting in the city, and its members followed each other like migrating birds to wherever was cheap and inspiring and just this side of fashionable. Croton-on-Hudson, north of the city, was one enclave, where Max and Crystal Eastman, Jack Reed, and Mabel Dodge spent time, while Marie Jenney Howe's summer home was in neighboring Harmon. Provincetown, farther afield, was another. There, Mary Heaton Vorse was a pioneer. Since marrying Joe O'Brien after the dramatic weeks in Lawrence, she had begun to make the rough, remote Massachusetts fishing village her summer getaway. The couple quickly turned it into the summer "colony" of their Greenwich Village friends, but Mary's house there was an anchor for her throughout her life. At first it was Mary and Joe plus her old friend, the former "Bachelor Girl" Neith Boyce, with Hutch Hapgood and their children. In 1913, a pair of Village newcomers joined them: midwestern transplants Susan Glaspell and her husband George Cram Cook, whom everyone called "Jig." They spent the summers drinking a great deal of whiskey and talking together, late into the night, about theater and themselves and the future of each.

In the summer of 1914, the three women were all in their late thirties or early forties: Neith the eldest, and Susan, at thirty-seven, the youngest. This was an age when they were considering where they were and where they wanted to go. All three had been successful since their early twenties as journalists and fiction writers. They shared long, intimate experiences with the struggle to forge loving, sustainable relationships with men who were also writers, against the twin monsters of sexual and professional jealousy. Mary's first husband and Neith's current one were both openly unfaithful, believing it part of the natural and irrepressible instinct of male sexuality but also an expression of rebellion against bourgeois convention. This second line of argument stymied feminist wives—after all, weren't they, too, engaged in just that rebellion? How could they forbid a husband's philandering without becoming the oppressor?

Labor journalist Mary Heaton Vorse was one of the first Greenwich Villagers to buy a summer home in the fishing village of Provincetown. (*Credit: Schlesinger Library, Harvard Radcliffe Institute*)

Bert Vorse, unfaithful and unemployable, had always been jealous of Mary's ease and success as a writer. The couple were estranged by the time he died suddenly of a cerebral hemorrhage, alone in a hotel on Staten Island in 1910. The next day, Mary's mother died of heart failure. After these back-to-back blows, it is hardly surprising that the direction of Mary's life and writing changed. Yet it was not the losses of 1910 but the 1912 strike in Lawrence that she would always identify as the turning point. Her marriage to Joe O'Brien, not long afterward, was a revelation. A gregarious and loving man, he enjoyed fixing up her Provincetown house and taking care of her children, freeing Mary to write, which she was doing prolifically and profitably. Not long after they met, she wrote to him in some astonishment: "Dear, in this little piece of time you have made yourself more a part of my life than anyone else ever has. And you come into an inner piece of my spirit that I have kept closed always." Joe was even more effusive, telling her, "This is daytime in my soul. The dawn and the singing in my soul and my melted listening heart all belong to you." They married in April 1912, and Mary joked that both her children "promptly [came] down with measles to celebrate."[1] In early 1914, she gave birth to her third child, a red-haired boy they named Joel. The only shadow was Joe's bouts of unexplained illness.

Susan Glaspell took a path to Heterodoxy and the Village that mirrored many others' in the club. She was born and raised in rural Iowa, outside Davenport, before joining the small but growing cohort of college women. After graduating from Drake University in Des Moines in 1899, Susan took a reporting job with a local newspaper, making her one of the many Heterodites whose professional training—and feminist awakening—came through journalism. Having embarked on a career, women journalists soon faced a growing sense of frustration about how hard it was for them to advance in a male-dominated profession. Getting a foot in the door was one thing, and not easy in itself, but shouldering the rest of the way into the room could take a lifetime.

Depending on who was present, some Heterodoxy meetings must have felt—and probably acted—like a blend of journalism networking event and professional support group. In addition to those women who wrote for *The Masses* and other socialist and suffrage magazines out of conviction rather than for pay, the journalists in the club included Mabel Potter Daggett, California transplant Bessie Beatty, and Katherine Leckie, who was an editor for the leading women's magazine *The Delineator*, which published many club members. Gertrude B. Kelley, a longstanding contributor to the *Pittsburgh Press*, was nicknamed "Pittsburgh's first sob sister."[2] They were the lucky ones. Male editors were reluctant to give staff jobs or regular work to women, in part because reporting was seen as unladylike and dangerous, but also because it would take coveted jobs from men. Rheta Childe Dorr described how she was turned down at the *New York Sun* by "a young man in pink shirt-sleeves and nose-glasses" who "informed [her] in tones of finality that the 'Sun' had no women on its staff and never expected to have." After spending a fruitless series of mornings and afternoons visiting "every newspaper . . . in New York," she concluded that "Park Row was a masculine monopoly" and that the women she knew who had broken in must have used "burglar's tools." The women's departments, known as Hen Coops, were often a female journalist's best hope of a staff position. Rheta landed a job on the woman's page of the *New York Evening Post* in 1900 after an "insistent siege" of the city's many papers.[3] Owned by suffragist, pacifist, and NAACP cofounder Oswald Garrison Villard, the *Post* was more welcoming to women: Heterodoxy's Rose Young also worked there.

Other club members sold stories at "space rates"—that is, freelance—where the money was meager but at least male and female writers were treated equally. The reviews section was also an option: club member and Villager Nell P. Dawson was the longtime literary critic at the *New York Globe*. Madeleine Doty, who snuck into Harvard Law classes disguised as a man before earning her law degree from NYU, answered the *New York Times's* call for a "man" to write book reviews. She said she would be happy to publish under a male pen name, and the paper hired her as "Otis Notman," which she used as a byline for hundreds of reviews, essays, and author interviews without anyone apparently realizing the name meant "O, 'tis not [a] man."[4]

Susan Glaspell, therefore, was unusual, as a woman, in getting assigned at a Des Moines newspaper to cover politics and crime. The experience provided plenty of material for her fiction—and her feminism, after in-depth exposure to the law's discriminatory treatment of women. But it was a grueling job: her Heterodoxy contemporary Anne O'Hagan Shinn estimated that a newspaperwoman in the early twentieth century "must be willing to wade through snow, to swim, if need be, overflowing gutters, to face cutting winds, to tramp in dog day heat, and at the end to write as sparklingly as nature and education permit."[5]

Susan didn't last long, and at age twenty-four returned to Davenport to focus on writing fiction, soon getting involved in the close-knit literary scene. At its center were Jig Cook, a married professor of English and classics at the University of Iowa, and Floyd Dell, an up-and-coming writer and literary editor who was about ten years younger but had been working as a reporter in the city since the age of seventeen. Susan's burgeoning relationship with Jig attracted unpleasant scrutiny in the small community—he was already on his second marriage, and his wife was pregnant.[6] Jig left for Chicago, followed by Susan, who paid her way with the prize money for one of her short stories. There, he and Floyd Dell worked together on the *Chicago Literary Review* showcasing modernist writers. In 1909 Susan published her first novel, *The Glory of the Conquered*, which became a best seller, and put out a second before she and Jig relocated to Greenwich Village in 1913. Jig arrived in time for the closing night of the Armory Show, in March, when the venue was crammed with ten thousand spectators; Susan got there in April, just in time to plunge into the preparations for the Paterson Pageant. Floyd Dell joined them in October.[7]

Playwright and novelist Susan Glaspell moved to the Village in 1913 and became a founder of the Provincetown Players. The painting is by her friend William L'Engle. "That is why I look so nice and refined," she explained, adding that she would have looked happier if she'd known this image would be shared with Marie Jenney Howe. (*Credit: Schlesinger Library, Harvard Radcliffe Institute*)

There, Susan was invited to join Heterodoxy, although she was ambivalent about the value of all-women societies and depicted women's clubs with a sardonic eye in her plays and stories. In her papers, there is only one reference to a club meeting, a diary entry for Saturday, March 19, 1921, that reads "Heterodoxy at one"—the regularity of the meetings, however, likely meant it wasn't always necessary to write a reminder.[8]

In common with her Heterodoxy peers, Susan was intrigued by feminism for the way it constantly needed to be worked on, worked out, and worked over. A questing curiosity about love, fidelity, and gender roles pulses through all her literary work. She returned again and again to the theme of women's liberation and its limits, writing and directing a series of rich and fascinating plays in which formal experimentation and the subject matter of experiments in living fed each other. Her best-known play, *Trifles*, has its roots in a homicide case she covered as a reporter in Iowa. It is a murder mystery in which the details of the dead man's domestic life, overlooked by the male detectives, turn out to hold clues to a history of marital abuse and, therefore, the answer to the riddle of who killed him. The women who uncover it, however, choose to guard the wife's secret, knowing that there would be no justice for her, no compassion, under the law. The play exposes the gulf between men's and women's systems of knowledge and understanding that even the best intentions could not truly bridge.

The Villagers who gathered in Provincetown in the summer had long been intrigued by the possibilities of a new, modern theater to reflect and dramatize the new, modern thinkers who were upending the conventions of their upbringing. The urge to break with the past was everywhere—in visual art, music, dance, and literature, in physics and philosophy and psychology. Common-sense norms like perspective and tonality, art that looked like the world and harmonized with it, were being trampled. Friedrich

Nietzsche, who first appeared in translation in America around 1910, championed self-determination without guilt. He "saved my soul from Tolstoi, Jesus, and Mr. and Mrs. Browning," according to Jig Cook—that is, from both religious faith and literary realism.[9] Jig was in thrall to the mythos of ancient Greece, with its pagan rituals and its thrillingly nonrepresentational theater, which offered an escape from the well-grooved, moralizing narratives of the Victorian era. The Paterson Pageant had been an exhilarating experiment in drama that was both ancient and modern: collective and formally ritualistic in ways that collapsed the distance between centuries and yet, in content, ripped from headlines still being written.

Then, of course, there was Freud. His writings and his method, inherently dramatic, were compared to detective fiction, which was enjoying a popular contemporary boom—the analyst peeling back layers of deception and obfuscation to reveal the truth: ugly but undeniable. The fallout from the revelation was not the psychoanalyst's concern, any more than it was Poirot's job to prosecute the murderer. In published case studies, as in detective stories, the fascination for the reader lay in following the trail of clues, putting together and discarding her own theories, and enjoying the diabolical cleverness of the detective. For those actually undergoing analysis, the revelation, the connection between behavior and cause, was rarely neat or singular, and understanding did not instantly spell freedom. But most Villagers were not in treatment, they were simply in thrall to the *idea* of uncovering some kind of truth, some kind of new path. Unsurprisingly, those trying to move drama beyond familiar plots and predictable moral lessons seized on psychoanalysis as a rich new vein of storytelling.

They also needed, and could create, new venues. The "little theaters" springing up everywhere in the early twentieth century were easy enough to set up; the bareness of the set and the immediacy of the action were the point: a reaction against Broadway's style, its lavish sets, mannered acting, star players, and general air of overstuffed complacency. They were also a revolt against the psychological shallowness that all that decoration obscured. Victorian stage drama, even when it was not quite melodrama, preferred to present unambiguously good or bad characters caught in situations with social as well as personal consequences. Popular Broadway plays showed a clear connection between thought and action, characters whose reasoning was transparent to themselves. Even when plays explored marriage, as many did, the drama tended to coalesce around the basic moral question of fidelity, which was also—in a patriarchal world—a drama of social stability. Plays featured cheating women, illegitimate children, divorce, and contested inheritances to examine not their emotional impact on the people involved but the risk they posed to the social order. The little theaters, instead, made psychological questions themselves the crux of the action.[10]

European theatrical innovators were already starting to upset stage convention. Modern, satirical, "cynical" playwrights created dramas that placed self over society and that cared about how women (in particular) *felt* as well as how they behaved. In 1911, a group of actors from the Abbey Theatre in Dublin toured American theaters. This group, especially its founder, the poet W. B. Yeats, had a powerful impact on the Village's performing artists, and most of them made the trip to the Maxine Elliott Theatre in midtown during the group's six-week residency. "Quite possibly there would have been no Provincetown Players had there not been the Irish Players," Susan Glaspell said. Their realistic depictions of daily life, modern life, honestly told, particularly inspired Jig Cook. "What he saw done for Irish life he wanted for American life—no stage conventions in the way of projecting with the humility of true feeling."[11] The following year, several future Villagers launched the Chicago Little

Theatre, including Jig, Floyd, and Edna Kenton, a member of Heterodoxy who would become the unofficial historian of the Provincetown Players.

From its earliest days, bohemian Greenwich Village had been a hub of theatrical experimentation. Ida Rauh, often named as the most talented actress among the various local theatrical troupes, was growing impatient with the "absurd" amateurs at the Liberal Club.[12] Along with several other writers and performers who wanted to take theater more seriously, she planned a new group called the Washington Square Players, which began to take shape over the winter of 1914. They limited themselves to one-act plays and prided themselves on high standards. Ida's fellow Heterodoxy actress Helen Westley, who would go on to have a long career in the cinema, was a cofounder and a regular on the Washington Square Players stage, which staged work by Heterodoxy members, including Rose Pastor Stokes.[13] Unlike the Provincetown Players, which would be strictly devoted to developing new "native" drama, the Washington Square Players staged several modernist European plays, though they also showcased Americans, including Susan Glaspell, John Reed, and Eugene O'Neill. Their most important criterion was "artistic merit," which meant the work had to speak to more than its immediate coterie. The group rejected several plays that would go on to be mounted by the Provincetown Players, including its debut *Suppressed Desires*, which was judged "too special."[14]

Not far from Washington Square, the Neighborhood Playhouse opened in 1915 as a creative offshoot of Lillian Wald's long-established Henry Street Settlement. Two philanthropist sisters, Alice and Irene Lewisohn, who were major funders of the WTUL and had been working at the settlement for several years, were keenly interested in the theater. They built a three-story, red-brick theater at the corner of Pitt and Grand Streets on the Lower East Side, where they showed films and mounted productions that were notably avant-garde, incorporating music, poetry, and especially dance. The choreographer Martha Graham and Heterodoxy dancer Agnes de Mille both performed at the playhouse and taught at its school in the early 1920s. The Neighborhood Playhouse led Heterodite Helen Arthur, a lawyer, to a new career as a theatrical agent and manager. She had lived at Henry Street when she was in her late twenties, and had an intense relationship with Lillian Wald, who was twelve years older. Lillian "coaxed Arthur out of repeated depressions, encouraged her law practice, managed her finances, and kept her bankbook so that she would not overspend." In return, Helen offered her a childlike loyalty, writing as the "son" to her "mommy."[15] The affair was intense but short-lived, and after its implosion, Helen's passion was redirected toward the theater. She began writing reviews and working however she could, doing administrative work, managing actors, and writing her own plays.

Helen's legal background, love of the theater, and connection with Henry Street made her an obvious choice to help the Lewisohn sisters get the Neighborhood Playhouse off the ground, and she became the theater manager. Through her work at the playhouse, she met Agnes Morgan, who was her own age and would become the in-house director for the theater until it closed in 1927. Helen, "lithe, shirt-waisted, and stiff-collared," was known for her masculine clothing and described by Alice Lewisohn as "dapper, bright-eyed, keen" and by a performer as "quite a pixie, bright as a whistle, and a little devilish too." This was in contrast to "her friend, the quiet, serious, watchful Agnes Morgan."[16] Despite Alice's euphemism, the relationship between the two women was well known in the theater and among the Heterodites, and lasted until Helen's death in 1939.

These other Village theatrical experiments, however, were soon overshadowed by the Provincetown Players. Over the course of seven years, from a scrappy experiment on the edge of the ocean to a slightly less scrappy institution at the heart of the Village, the "players" revolutionized American theater. "It all began in 'talk' of course, in the summer of 1915, at Provincetown, that then-primitive, faraway little fishing town on the tip of Cape Cod where for a number of years a group of people who 'did things' had spent quiet summers together."[17] The words are Edna Kenton's, the Heterodoxy member who was a stalwart organizer of the group, and her perhaps unconscious echo of Mabel Dodge's phrase—*women who did things*—is a hint of how integral Heterodoxy was to the theater's operations.

The first performance, on July 15, 1915, was a double bill staged in Neith Boyce and Hutch Hapgood's rented cottage, which had "a great living room large enough to hold a few players and fair audience." As described by Edna Kenton, the first play was staged on the veranda, lit by candles, with "the backdrop of the moving ocean with its anchored ships and twinkling lights."[18] This was Neith's play *Constancy*, a riff on the recently ended affair between Mabel and John Reed—both of whom were in the audience. Although its approach was satirical, *Constancy* grappled with questions that were serious concerns for Heterodoxy and Village women: how to achieve intimacy within a relationship without sacrificing independence, and how to balance men's and women's expectations for what a "modern" love affair looked like. "The colors were orange and yellow against the sea," Neith wrote to her father-in-law, pride bursting through her modesty. "We gave it at 10 o'clock at night and really it was lovely—the scene, I mean. I have been mightily complimented on my acting!!!" She played the wife, Moira, opposite Joe O'Brien, Mary Heaton Vorse's husband.

The second play on the bill, for which the audience turned their chairs around and faced inward, was cowritten and performed by Susan and Jig. *Suppressed Desires* spoofed another all-consuming Village passion, psychoanalysis. As in *Constancy*, its lightness of touch belies the seriousness of the question at the play's heart: How important is self-knowledge to happiness? The play is rife with in-joke humor and up-to-the-minute cultural references. "You could not go out to buy a bun without hearing about some one's complex," Susan recalled, of her first months in the Village. She and Jig "thought psychoanalysis would be amusing in a play," so set out to capture it, in all its excitement and absurdity. Sitting in front of the fire at home in Milligan Place, a tucked-away street around the corner from Patchin Place, "we tossed the lines back and forth at one another and wondered if anyone else would ever have as much fun with it as we were having."

In the play, a married couple, Stephen and Henrietta Brewster are bickering over breakfast about Henrietta's newfound passion for psychoanalysis. Stephen is an architect, and Henrietta, an intellectual; their tiny Greenwich Village flat and its environs form a small, distinct, recognizable world. Henrietta's sister, Mabel, has arrived for a visit from Chicago, where she lives with her dentist husband. The backwardness of the Midwest, which Jig and Susan had recently left, is one of many in-jokes: "I don't think we have them in Chicago," Mabel says, of the suppressed desires Henrietta insists she must be harboring. The dull stability of the dentist husband may have been a jab at Louise Bryant, a new star in the Provincetown orbit who had abandoned a dentist husband in Portland, Oregon, before moving to the Village and starting an affair with (among others) Jack Reed, whom she eventually married. The names "Henrietta" and "Mabel," likewise, were synonymous with flamboyant Heterodoxy feminists whom everyone knew in person or by reputation.

The plot is simple and silly, but the conflict it pinpoints is a serious one, between bourgeois convention and individual freedom, complicated by the question of whether the entrapped bourgeoisie even know that they need to be free. Henrietta's sister Mabel, plump and conventional, dreams that she is a hen, being hurried along with the command to "step, hen!" When she undergoes analysis at Henrietta's urging, the analyst ("A. E. Russell") enlightens her to her own dissatisfaction. The secret lies in the ridiculous pun: "Step Hen" is Stephen, while "Hen" alone is her sister's nickname: she wishes to be her sister and to run away with her sister's husband. In vain, Henrietta tries to persuade her that the hen clue reveals a secret passion for Lyman Eggleston ("Egg"), an intellectual of Mabel's acquaintance whom her husband dislikes. Mabel protests that she isn't unhappy or in love with Stephen, but she is terrified of what Henrietta has told her, that unacknowledged desires can land their sufferers in the insane asylum.

In the meantime, Stephen himself has gone for analysis, after a dream in which he has found himself in a field, with the walls of a building falling away. The analyst suggests that the vision is not rooted in his professional anxiety as an architect, but his suppressed desire to escape the confines of marriage. Henrietta, devastated, flings her psychoanalytic journals and textbooks to the floor, Mabel declares herself happy in her marriage, and Stephen in his, and the ending is a triumph of the status quo over the dubious freedom of burning it all down. Suppressing unspoken desires, the play suggests heretically, may sometimes be both necessary and wise. Despite its glancing and rather disparaging treatment of the subject, the play did effectively show why psychoanalysis was so influential: it truly seemed to offer a route to liberation not only from the external trappings of convention but also from the internalized conformity that made rebellion even more difficult. To know yourself was to free yourself. The challenge was how to get to that knowledge without falling into a new trap, a bear pit of narcissism from which the only escape was laughter.

Suppressed Desires was far from the only Provincetown or little theater production to comment on psychoanalysis, which was as tightly bound up with the new drama as it was with the new feminism. Psychoanalyst Grace Potter was part of the Provincetown Players from its early days, contributing as a writer who—in keeping with the collaborative ethos of the group—was closely involved with the production of her own plays. In early 1918, one of her one-act plays, *About Six*, was performed by the company as part of a triple bill that included a work of Floyd Dell's. Grace directed it herself, as many Provincetown writers did (with varying degrees of success), but the script is lost. According to Edna Kenton, the play, set in "A Disorderly Flat in New York," was one of several to focus on "New York's underworld" and was "written with realism and understanding."[19] A reviewer, however, suggests it was not a particularly searching analysis of the new psychology, sniffing that there was little in either Floyd's or Grace's contribution that would help distinguish the Players "from popular vaudeville."[20]

The audience in Provincetown on that first summer evening was delighted, however, encouraging the little band of actors and writers to add two more one-act plays for a full evening's entertainment, for which they could charge admission. Needing a space bigger than their friends' living room, Mary Heaton Vorse offered up a building she owned on a fishing wharf by the ocean, a space big enough to house an audience of a hundred or so. The players emptied the space of fish and rigged up a makeshift stage. Throughout August and September, they again staged *Constancy* and *Suppressed Desires*, along with one or two other one-acts. As their reputation and ambitions grew, the theater group issued a manifesto in which they described the plays they wanted to stage—true American plays that had "real artistic, literary, and dramatic merit," in contrast to "Broadway merit"—shorthand for the sentimental commercialism that dominated the mainstream theater.

Located on a wharf owned by Mary Heaton Vorse, the first Provincetown Playhouse was a ramshackle storage building that became an iconic
site in American theater history. (*Credit: Courtesy of Pilgrim Monument
and Provincetown Museum, Provincetown, MA, Salvador R. Vasques III
Collection*)

The following summer, the players returned with renewed
zeal. This time, they rigged up the theater on the wharf with electricity, circus-style seating, a fresh coat of paint, and a movable
stage. The opening bill, on July 13, 1916, included a revival of
Suppressed Desires and new plays by Neith Boyce and Jack Reed;
the second included *The Game* by Louise Bryant and *Bound East
for Cardiff* by a writer who had recently been introduced to the
group and would become its most celebrated contributor, Eugene O'Neill. According to Susan, "Gene" simply showed up
with "a whole trunk full of plays" and joined the group; before
long he had started an affair with Louise Bryant.[21]

That November, back in the Village, the Provincetown Players established a performance space on MacDougal Street, in
the building next door to the Liberal Club, once again with
Suppressed Desires on the bill. Until 1922, when the fame of the
theater and the lure of Broadway had ended its run as a true
"little" theater, it operated a season from the fall to the spring,

staging works that ranged from realistic domestic dramas to visual and formal experiments set anywhere from ancient Greece to the distant future. Experimental modernist Djuna Barnes was a part of the group and remembered it with nostalgia: "We used to sit on the most uncomfortable benches imaginable . . . glad to suffer partial paralysis of the upper leg and an entire stoppage of the spinal juices, just to hear Ida Rauh come out of the wings and say, 'Life, bring me a fresh rose!'"[22]

Ida was particularly important to the group, as an actress, director, and guiding light. Although Djuna Barnes's memory implies a certain florid staginess, Ida and the rest of the players were struggling to achieve a style of acting that broke from the stiff, declamatory style that dominated Broadway (and that Eugene O'Neill's actor father, incidentally, was famous for). "I am looking for something simpler in the theater, something which is more natural," Ida told an interviewer in 1920.[23] We don't know whether it was her commitment to naturalness or her familiarity with the burgeoning Harlem cultural scene, but in her preparations to direct Eugene O'Neill's *The Dreamy Kid*, a play with an African American cast, she refused outright to put white actors in blackface, as was then standard practice on Broadway. Instead, she assembled a cast of unknowns by visiting, as she explained, "the YMCA, the library, the churches, and everywhere else in Harlem."[24] James Weldon Johnson would later praise the Provincetown Players as the "initial and greatest force in opening up the way for the Negro on the dramatic stage."[25] Ida's leading man would go on to appear on Broadway.

Ida Rauh, Susan Glaspell, Edna Kenton, and Mary Heaton Vorse were the central Heterodites in the Players, but there were many more, including Edna's sister Mabel Reber, who joined her in Greenwich Village after working as a society reporter on the *Chicago Tribune*. Mabel created costumes for the theater, including geometric shapes built out of pasteboard boxes for the futuristic fantasy *5050*, while her husband helped build the company's sets.[26] Daisy Thompson, Inez Haynes Irwin's creative sister, lent props from her "quaint and curious" Village shop, and Eleanor Fitzgerald, a red-haired anarchist, joined Kenton in running the theater a few seasons in. "Fitzie," as she was known, was apparently enough of a devotee of Freud to put her pet collie under analysis, a detail that feels ripped from a discarded draft of *Suppressed Desires*.[27] She was not the only anarchist in the ranks, either: performer Stella Ballantine, whose husband Teddy was an actor and director with the Players, was the "niece and adoring partisan" of Emma Goldman, and described growing up in her "fiery shadow" in a background talk at one of Heterodoxy's meetings.[28]

The professional Heterodite actresses Helen Westley and Margaret Wycherly also lent their talents, the latter in Susan Glaspell's controversial play *The Verge*, in 1921. This play, which took feminist convictions to murderous extremes, was cherished among Heterodoxy, amounting, according to one member, to a sacred text. Elsie Dufour, a dancer who founded a school teaching her signature form of rhythmic, expressive movement in the 1920s, experienced the club's discussion of *The Verge* as though "they were worshiping at some holy shrine; their voices and their eyes were full of religious excitement." Claiming that she was "the only woman not under the spell," Elsie's attempts at "ordinary dramatic criticism" were quickly silenced: "they all glared upon me, as if they thought I should be excommunicated."[29] This take on Heterodoxy as an ecstatic church certainly gets at one kind of truth: feminism often, to these women, constituted a kind of religious identity.[30] But there are caveats: Elsie was younger than the core of the group, and the anecdote was reported by Hutch Hapgood several years later, in a cultural atmosphere that was much more hostile to feminism (and by an author who had definitely soured on it). It may be that a spirit of sisterhood made the Heterodites close ranks around the play, but it seems unfair to suggest they did so unthinkingly. Heterodoxy Journalist Ruth Hale defended it in print, while *New York Globe* drama critic Maida Castellun argued that it was Susan Glaspell's violation of gender norms that had caused the furor. She declared approvingly, "Miss Glaspell has left the conventions of the stage behind" by daring to choose "a woman instead of a man to incarnate the restless audacious, creative spirit that goes beyond the verge of human experience and social conventions."[31]

   As the absorbing project of Provincetown got underway in the Village, however, it left behind one of its core members: Mary Heaton Vorse, who had provided not only the original theater building but also a vital spirit, according to Susan Glaspell, of hospitality in her "rambling, endless, wonderful house" in Provincetown.[32] In the late summer of 1915, Joe O'Brien's off-and-on stomach pain returned, badly enough that Mary and Neith cut their theatrical experimentation short to take him back to New York, where he went into hospital. Mary went to stay with her friend Frances Perkins and nursed him as best she could, but the illness turned out to be an aggressive stomach cancer. Joe died that October, after he and Mary had been married just three and a half years. Susan Glaspell turned the friends' shock and grief into a poetic eulogy for *The Masses* that begins, "It's strange without you, I do not like it." The poem dwells in the contradictions of a personality that combined "graceful levity" and "fiery dissatisfactions," a person who was both "The life of the party" and "a tree way off by itself." A vivid picture emerges of the swirl of political, creative, and domestic passions that bound the Villagers and the Provincetown friends:

> I want to sit over a drink with you and talk about the
> IWW and the damned magazines and the Germans; I
> want to argue with you about building bookshelves and
> planting bulbs.

I want awfully to tell you about a joke I heard yesterday.
And now that you are gone, I want intensely to find you.[33]

Mary's loss was paralyzing for some time. She was unable
to leave her bed and was treated with veronal and morphine,
the latter of which became a source of addiction for her. Hutch
Hapgood wrote to Neith that Mary's friends were visiting her
often and that she seemed "very weak and very soft and lovely."
Unable to write and sell her lighthearted fiction, and running
through her savings, Mary suffered through a bleak winter. Her
young children were ill with whooping cough and the toddler,
Joel, contracted pneumonia.[34] Joe's death threw a shadow over
the playful experiments of the Villagers and their romantic dramas, revealing the fragility of even the strongest relationships
and their exposure to forces quite outside the reach of any psychologist. No matter the extent of a woman's independence,
tragedies like Mary's made clear how vital a network of supportive, loving friends truly was, for both emotional and practical
reasons.

Heterodoxy members regularly came together over the years
to provide financial assistance to members going through tough
times, which happened with increasing frequency as the women
aged, and especially as the Depression of the 1930s began to
bite.[35] Their personal lives and their sociological investigations
over the years both drove home the precarity of women in a society structured for dependence on male providers. Many of them
had known experiences like Dr. Jo Baker's, whose father's death
wiped out the family's financial security when she was in her
teens. But even without undergoing tragedy, modern feminists
knew that their own liberation would be incomplete until it was
possible for women to combine fulfilling work in the world with
the joys and comforts of whatever private life they chose.

Chapter 10

"THE BABY IS THE GREAT PROBLEM"

Rose Young's 1914 article "What Is Feminism?" carried a full-page photograph of the very beautiful Beatrice Forbes-Robertson Hale with her baby daughters, and a caption that ends: "Feminism means for Mrs. Hale merely adapting herself to the twentieth century—work *and* babies." That same year, Beatrice dedicated her book *What Women Want* to her girls, Sanchia, and twins Rosemary and Clemency, calling them "Daughters of the New Age." How, though, to balance "work *and* babies"? An outwardly conventional family life, with husband and children, *and* important public work? Seeking the solution to this challenge, which eludes many feminists to this day, split Heterodites into different camps and drove them to embrace a range of differing ideological positions and practical strategies.

For followers of Charlotte Perkins Gilman, and devotees of her progressive woman's bible *Women and Economics*, the dream of equality in marriage was impossible so long as women's choices to leave a relationship or stay were constrained by the need to survive. Charlotte's feminist theories focused on restructuring society rather than retraining male hearts and minds, and the logical extension was an overriding concern with women's right to support themselves out of recognition of their shared humanity with men. By contrast, Charlotte's great rival, the Swedish feminist Ellen Key, believed that maternity was the root of female exceptionality and female power, and therefore the state should provide for women based on their capacity as mothers. Although irreducibly essentialist, her thinking diverged from traditional Victorian separate-spheres ideology in its disregard for marriage and for men in general. These "humanist" and "motherist" approaches to feminism often conflicted, and women in Heterodoxy argued them endlessly and found their own ways to reconcile them. Marie Jenney Howe, for instance, a firm believer in men's and women's equal humanity, coauthored a detailed article with her husband in support of "motherhood pensions," a form of state benefit gaining traction around the country that amounted to state-funded maternity leave.[1]

During the spring of 1914, not long after Marie Jenney Howe's mass meetings explaining the concept of feminism, Henrietta Rodman invited a group of local activist men and women to her apartment on East Seventeenth Street, near Second Avenue, for the launch of a new organization, the Feminist Alliance. The group would be a more politically engaged and public corollary to Heterodoxy, including many of the same members but open equally to men. Heading it up were Henrietta and her husband, Herman de Fremery, a Columbia professor whom Henrietta had met at the Liberal Club. Leta Hollingworth was on the board, along with figures from the overlapping activist circles of the city and those who worked at the Russell Sage Foundation and the Women's Trade Union League. The Feminist Alliance's membership of fifty was drawn from those same circles: middle- and upper-class reformers and political leaders who knew one another socially and professionally and were increasingly known to the public as well.

The Feminist Alliance defined feminism as a movement demanding "the removal of all social, political, economic, and

Henrietta Rodman was a teacher and feminist activist determined to find creative ways for women to balance family and career. (*Credit: Library of Congress*)

other discriminations which are based upon sex, and the award of all rights and duties in all fields on the basis of individual capacity alone." It further distilled that definition in its proposed amendment to the US Constitution: "No civil or political right shall be refused any person on account of sex."[2] To Henrietta Rodman, the alliance's political demands were hardly radical, but she knew that mainstream thought was very far from recognizing gender equality in this way. One had to start somewhere.

That spring, the alliance announced a practical scheme to "relieve modern women from the physical drudgery of housework and bringing up children and leave them time and opportunity to do useful work," as Henrietta put it.[3] She and Heterodoxy friends had been trying to find a way to do this for years: to escape the traditional family home, the symbolically loaded site that many women experienced as one of drudgery, at best, and find an alternative way to set up a home. They experimented with collectives like the settlement houses and A Club, as well as more idiosyncratic arrangements. Crystal Eastman, in an essay called "Marriage Under Two Roofs," celebrated the independence and romance of living a few streets away from her husband—although she painted a rather rosier picture than the reality, since the arrangement left her with the bulk of the child-care and her husband much more freedom to do as he chose.[4] At the age of thirty, the Heterodite novelist Fannie Hurst secretly married a Russian-born pianist, kept her unmarried name, and maintained separate homes—a choice that caused a scandal when the *New York Times* revealed her marriage five years later, at the height of a housing shortage.[5] In the wake of the publicity, similarly independent marital arrangements were known as "Fannie Hurst marriages."

Very few women, however, had the means for such an indulgence. Housing for financially independent women was desperately scarce. In New York, those who dwelt between the extremes of Fifth Avenue mansions and downtown slums had to compete with thousands of other workers for affordable housing. Many women who could not live with their families had to brave the strict rules of women-only boarding houses and apartment buildings, giving up the nominal social independence that was a large part of the purpose of their work. For women who wanted less conventional arrangements, or for women who loved other women, housing shortages could create opportunities for shared living situations that nobody would question and allowed the formation of alternative communities. But the realities of running a private home in an era before conveniences like washing machines, vacuum cleaners, and dishwashers meant that any woman who wanted to marry, have children, and hold onto her career needed an understanding husband and money to pay for help.

The Feminist Alliance proposed a solution that, it hoped, could be more widely beneficial. Their scheme was a dedicated apartment complex, accommodating 250 families, in which cleaning, cooking, and childcare were organized communally and undertaken by trained professionals. The building would have a laundry and a kitchen in the basement, where a dedicated nutritionist would plan meals to be prepared and delivered to individual apartments via dumbwaiter in insulated containers. The apartments would have tiny "kitchen-closets," but otherwise, food preparation wouldn't take up space, mental or physical, in working women's lives. Such luxuries weren't unknown in fancy, purpose-built New York apartment buildings, where renters were lured, much as they are today, by amenities that would off-set the inevitable lack of space.

What set the feminist apartment concept apart was the twenty-four-hour child nursery, Montessori school, and play-ground on the roof. Up above the choked, polluted streets, the children would cultivate their own garden plots and play on swings and in sandboxes—at one point, the Feminist Alliance lobbied for a state law requiring similar playgrounds on all New York apartment rooftops. All these amenities, Henrietta argued, would free up women to go out of the home and earn a living, enjoying both independence and—in the hours outside work—a more concentrated, pleasurable, and enriched version of mother-hood. The scheme was inspired by Charlotte Perkins Gilman, in both her established economic theories and her new turn to utopian fiction. Charlotte's 1910 novel, *What Diantha Did*, seri-alized in her magazine *The Forerunner*, tells the story of Diantha Bell, a young woman in California who leaves her family and fiancé to start a business providing domestic services to pro-fessional women. Quite different to traditional live-in service, a system rife with abuse and exploitation, Diantha's business

trains and provides for working girls and eventually builds to
the creation of a feminist apartment building—all guided by an
entirely modern spirit of expertise and efficiency.

For feminists who believed deeply in the importance of earning a living, any reliance on men and money, and the labor of
exploited women, was anathema. Henrietta Rodman, like Charlotte Perkins Gilman, also believed that the "industrially isolated
home" was bad for men and women alike, because it put undue
pressure on the marriage and turned a space that ought to be devoted to rest and pleasure into a workplace for women—where
the labor was physically exhausting, lonely, endless, and paid
worse than any factory. Private servants were not the answer either, even when they could be afforded: young, primarily white
women were abandoning live-in domestic service in huge numbers in this era, choosing the higher wages and greater freedom
offered by work in shops, offices, and factories. Black women
did not have the same opportunities, and so domestic service,
especially the hard labor of cleaning and laundry, increasingly
fell to them. Yet Henrietta's earnest goal was to find a way to
professionalize the care of home and children, improving the
status and situation of domestic workers, and offsetting the costs
of training and higher wages by sharing the work among multiple households.

Inevitably, the cost of the project soared beyond the means of
the middle-class workers it was intended for. Even though more
than a hundred families applied for spaces after the building was
announced, the up-front costs of constructing on the chosen
site, in the heart of Greenwich Village at the corner of Waverly
Place and Eleventh Street, would require wealthy investors. This
led to disputes within the alliance, and between Henrietta and
her husband—she remained committed to a democratic sharing
of costs, while he urged her to accept the backing of a handful
of sympathetic philanthropists. Even so, the monthly rent for a

family of four using all the services on offer, including the nursery and school, would have amounted to nearly six thousand dollars in modern rates—far beyond the reach of a teacher, except one in a rich dual-income household, although not that far beyond the cost of similar luxury elevator buildings in the city, where childcare was not included. Of course, costs might have been lowered if Henrietta would compromise on her goal of employing professionally trained and well paid workers to run the building and instead fell back on an underpaid staff of young women who lived out of sight in the basement, as other apartment buildings did. But she truly believed there was a way to infuse domestic work with dignity and elevate its status, leaving "a home that is no one's workshop," as Charlotte Perkins Gilman put it.[6]

The idea that childcare, in particular, might be outsourced to experts drew the ire of critics from a range of ideological backgrounds. The Feminist Alliance's focus on professional, collective child-rearing ran deeply counter to American society's assumptions about motherhood as a natural gift. One critic likened the proposed apartment system to a Southern plantation under slavery: the communal care of children being a marker of how little society valued them. Yet the Feminist Alliance's plan turned on the idea, gaining ground in intellectual circles in the early twentieth century, that expertise and study mattered at least as much as nature when it came to raising children well—indeed, engaging expert care was a sign of how much, not how little, parents valued their children's development. Part of what made Charlotte Perkins Gilman so controversial was her willingness to admit simply that many parents were not good at raising their children, and that mothers did not know best or instinctively what was right—even that society was failing children by leaving their upbringing to the chance of birth.

Yet even those who scorned her theories were beginning to frame the question in similar terms, talking of knowledge rather than nurture. One of Charlotte's most implacable ideological enemies, Alice Hill Chittenden, the president of the New York State Association Opposed to Woman Suffrage, challenged the communal-care proposal with the question "Why should not the mother be the expert and specialist for her own child?"[7] To which Henrietta Rodman would have countered, Well, why *should* she be? Henrietta's feminist vision imagined a society in which all people were free to pursue their natural talents. "The mother will not be forced to give up her skilled work to enter the field of baby tending in which she is unskilled," she said. Children would not be left with "untrained nursery maid[s]" but instead with "highly efficient, scientifically educated, young women whose career will be child culture." Optimistically, she concluded, "And self-respect will be preserved all around."[8]

In a vicious rebuttal in the *New York Times*, a writer named Laura Fay-Smith exaggerated and mocked Henrietta's scheme as "that feminist paradise palace": evidence of the "monstrous egotism" at the heart of the feminist movement, which aimed to "buy immunity from all that is disagreeable drudgery."[9] In some ways, her critique was not entirely wide of the mark—a system in which professional women went out to work and left other women to do housework and childcare, even where those women were elevated with the tag "professional" or "expert," was not in the end so different from what privileged, educated women were doing anyway, or from what rich women had always done, even if their goals were not traditionally to advance their careers. The writer's pointing out the dearth of good professional jobs for women, arguing that they would be abandoning their babies for the unfulfilling life of a stenographer, say, was also a somewhat sore point for feminists, though they would probably have argued that the problem lay with professions that didn't allow women to advance rather than with the women who nevertheless wanted to work outside the home.

The combination of expense, bad publicity, and internal dis-
agreements led the Feminist Alliance to abandon its apartment
scheme in October 1914, with the outbreak of war in Europe a
further contributing factor. Despite the ever-increasing urgency
of housing needs and the crisis in the cost of living in New York,
which doubled between 1915 and 1920, the feminist apartment
scheme fell apart. Its legacy, however, lay in its important challenge to the stereotype that feminists were not interested in family life. Rather, feminists within Heterodoxy wanted to figure
out how to keep what they valued from the family—love, support, children, a comfortable home—but reshape it to fit their
own desires rather than contorting themselves to fit a single
pattern.

In most jobs open to women in the 1910s, pregnancy was at
best an inconvenience, and barely any accommodation was made
for expectant or new mothers in the workplace, mostly because
they were not supposed to be there. As Henrietta Rodman put
it, "The baby is the great problem of the woman who attempts
to carry the responsibilities of wage-earning and citizenship."[10]
And it was very much assumed to be *her* problem. The broad cultural expectation was that a woman would give up her job upon
getting married and disappear from public notice; Elsie Clews
Parsons noted that in 1913, a pregnant woman dining out was a
scandal.[11] Concealing her condition and shifting her attention to
the home were simply what was done, and for a pregnant unmarried woman, invisibility was even more of an imperative. Some
jobs made it easier than others, and domestic settings were especially fraught with anxiety. The scenario of a middle-class woman
thrown into turmoil by an unmarried servant's pregnancy caught
the imagination of a surprising number of women writers at this
time, including several in the pages of *The Masses*.

In several older, melodramatic versions of this story, the maid
who won't reveal the name of her baby's father turns out to be

pregnant by her employer's husband—given the power dynamics of domestic service, a situation that was no doubt common in real life. But *Masses* writers used this scenario to explore knottier questions of moral and economic responsibility between women of different classes. Heterodoxy's Helen Hull, in her story "Usury," explores the relationship between an elderly spinster, Miss Cora, and her young servant Lizzie, who has lost a pregnancy by one man and now is engaged to another. When the first man returns and wants to marry her, Miss Cora pressures her to accept him, assuming that this course of action will serve to "remedy" her "mistake." But witnessing how sincerely Lizzie and her new fiancé love one another shakes the employer's certainty that she has the right to interfere or indeed has any monopoly on moral behavior. The title of Dorothy Weil's "A New Woman?" meanwhile, referring to the trammeled life of an unmarried mother working as a servant, shows how class, patriarchy, and biology combine to make a mockery of the fantasy of modern female liberation.[12]

The question of how women were to balance work and family was a widespread social preoccupation, and the women in Heterodoxy discussed it, wrote about it, and, in their different ways, lived it. Katharine Anthony, who would go on to become an influential biographer of famous and notorious women, based her first book, *Mothers Who Must Earn*, on a research project she had undertaken for the Russell Sage Foundation. The study examined the economics of family life in a neglected industrial area on the far west side of midtown Manhattan, which was home to a working-class German and Irish community. Having studied in Germany, Katharine not only had the language skills to communicate with the immigrant families in the area, but also was well versed in German feminist theories—influenced by Ellen Key—that foregrounded motherhood as the central issue of women's liberation. She was deeply interested in psychology and family dynamics, so was able to imbue her fact-heavy study with "genuine human sympathy," according to one reviewer, who also noted that Katharine "chose to live in the milieu of her work" in contrast to "your average society 'slummer' who descends among the poor from the heights of Riverside or upper Fifth Avenue and vanishes thence again to tango or bridge."[13] Village documentarian and photojournalist Jessie Tarbox Beals worked alongside Katharine to capture the West Side neighborhood and its inhabitants.

Katharine was not one of the Heterodites born to wealth. She was raised in hardscrabble rural Arkansas and had found her way to the Village via jobs in teaching, in high school and college, and the booming field of social science research. Her study vehemently defended the motives of the working women in her book against accusations that they were neglectful or selfish, lacking in maternal instinct. In fact, she argued, the very opposite was true: "It is for the sake of their children that they work, as mothers have done from time immemorial. The last penny of their earnings is absorbed by their homes."

In the first three decades of the twentieth century, the number of married women in the workforce doubled, and they made up around 30 percent of the total number of working women. But it is impossible to tell from census data alone how many of those women were supporting children on their sole income. Katharine's book gives a detailed snapshot of a fairly typical working-class neighborhood and suggests that, contrary to common assumptions at the time, many families needed both parents to work in order to survive. Of the 370 employed mothers she studied, nearly half had husbands who also worked. Around a third were widowed, a tenth had been deserted, and nearly another tenth had husbands who were either incapacitated or "idle." Only a tiny fraction were separated, and Katharine claimed that "divorce is unknown on the West Side."[14] The expense and scandal ensured that the deliberate ending of a marriage was all but impossible, except for the most privileged, and even they needed to be able to prove adultery or abandonment, often at a trial. The much-divorced feminists of Heterodoxy really were unusual.

Many of them, however, followed a professional path that was widely shared with less prominent or unorthodox women: teaching. In the early twentieth century, the vast majority of both Black and white women who had access to higher education and sought a professional career worked in schools and colleges. Women made up around 90 percent of the twenty thousand teachers in New York in the early twentieth century, and many members of Heterodoxy who weren't independently wealthy had done stints in the classroom, including Katharine Anthony, Henrietta Rodman, and the journalist Florence Woolston. They were keenly aware of the power of the role but also of its drudgery, poor pay, strict rules, and all-powerful school boards, which were generally run by conservative men. Henrietta Rodman, who taught English at Wadleigh High, the first public high school for girls in New York City, was especially aware of the constraint of those rules. Unlike other Heterodites whose teaching experience was brief, or carried out in elite college spaces, Henrietta taught English as a career and saw her role as introducing a new generation to feminism, with classes that amounted to a proto-Women's Studies curriculum.[15] She was therefore particularly well placed, in 1914, to challenge the school board on its sexism.

Five years earlier, New York's school board had formalized the ad hoc, unwritten policies that governed teachers across the recently unified city.[16] These included an outright ban on the hiring of any married woman, unless she could prove her husband was physically or mentally incapacitated or had abandoned her at least three years before. Married women who already had jobs had to keep those marriages secret or risk being fired. Rheta Childe Dorr put the moral stakes plainly: "Aside from the injustice and the undesirability of dooming a large body of superior women to celibacy, the system inevitably leads to deceit and hypocrisy."[17] Rules against married women teaching were, ostensibly, about the belief that they ought to be devoting their energies to home and hearth. But under the surface lurked the fear of their sexual knowledge. Might not married women, let alone pregnant ones, corrupt their young charges by their mere presence?

The married teacher issue was part of the larger, fractious debate between radical feminists and moderate progressives over protective labor legislation. In a world convinced of deep and essential physical differences between men and women, it seemed to many people like common sense to put limits on the hours the "weaker sex" could work and the bodily strain they could endure. Similar theories governed the thinking around child labor, underscoring the connection Progressive Era society saw between women and children: neither group able to stand alone or to advocate for themselves. The problem with protective labor laws was that the jobs and hours coded male were barred to women, and men were routinely paid better, so legislation meaning to carve out a safe space for women ended up keeping them in their place. It also meant that protections for men were overlooked, a serious problem given the shocking rate of industrial accidents Crystal Eastman had uncovered in Pittsburgh. When it came to a female-dominated profession like teaching, it seemed less that women were being protected than that their life choices were being policed. To Henrietta Rodman and her friends, it was clear that the true target of laws restricting *how* women should work was their right to work at all.

Of course, among nearly twenty thousand working female teachers, plenty were already married. But the school board could turn a blind eye—unless someone like Henrietta poked them in it. Her first jab was to present a mass meeting of influential women's club members with a petition asking the state to ban discrimination against married and mother-teachers. "A life of work should not deprive women of the joy of motherhood, nor should motherhood deprive the world of her work," it averred. Next, the veteran teacher got married herself, without disclosing her new status to the board. It wasn't long before the secret was revealed (most likely by Henrietta herself) and covered prominently in the city's five daily newspapers, which spread the false but salacious rumor that she and Herman de Fremery lived in a ménage à trois with his first wife. Her public marriage, followed by her refusal to take her husband's name, deliberately exposed the school board's don't-ask-don't-tell strategy regarding married women. This policy already deeply troubled some members, one of whom declared it was "not only inhuman but uncivilized, and uncultured as well," to require women to hide the fact that they were married. Another, who favored banning married teachers entirely, scoffed at the problem: "Women can't keep a secret twenty-four hours."[18]

Even if a married woman managed to bite her tongue and keep her husband out of sight, she couldn't hide an advanced pregnancy. The argument against married teachers quickly became a fight about *mother*-teachers. Under the auspices of yet another feminist organization, the League for the Civic Service of Women, Henrietta Rodman began publicizing the cases of women fired after becoming pregnant—cases that the school board understandably did not want circulating widely in the press. In October 1914, after the outbreak of war in Europe and the shelving of her feminist housing project, Henrietta announced that she would introduce a bill into the state legislature banning employers from refusing to hire married women or mothers. Shortly afterward, the league took up the case of a

Bronx teacher named Bridgett Peixotto, who had taken a leave of absence in order to give birth, only to find herself dismissed for "neglect of duty" and "gross misconduct" when her secret was given away to the board. Those accusations would have prevented her from ever getting another teaching position. Her treatment, according to the state Supreme Court justice who found in her favor, was "repugnant to the law and good morals," and he compelled the board to reinstate her and to allow established teachers to marry.

The board did not give up gracefully, but immediately appealed against the court's decision, and Peixotto's case dragged on. Meanwhile, the board declared it would no longer hire married women and that its newest employees would not be allowed to keep teaching after marriage. Those who had been in their positions since before the rules changed could stay on but had to report their marriages. At the same time, the board drew up a list of teachers it believed might be pregnant, and at least one member urged the immediate dismissal of all the married teachers. The situation remained at this fierce standoff for a few weeks, until a young pregnant teacher who had defied the board by remaining in the classroom finally gave birth—barely twelve hours after leaving the classroom on Friday afternoon.

The case was sensational and divisive, pitting those who saw the young teacher, Lora M. Wagner, as a feminist heroine against those who judged her a reckless, unfit mother, who had endangered her baby "under the advice of women agitators." In the corridor outside Lora's hospital room, Henrietta guarded mother and baby and faced down a crowd of journalists. A group of supporters, members of both Heterodoxy and the League for the Civic Service of Women—including Crystal Eastman, Charlotte Perkins Gilman, and lawyer and suffragist Marion Cothren—wrote to the state commissioner of education in support of the young mother and to highlight the urgent need for a maternity leave policy. They published an open letter to Lora, in which they declared, "We are heartily in sympathy with you in your struggle for the most fundamental rights of women—to work and bear children." The feminists had some support on the school board (one member called them "a body of persons with 16th-century ideas"), yet only five voted to give Lora maternity leave, and the rest to dismiss her. Of the five women on the board, only the two unmarried women voted in Lora's favor, demonstrating that women who likely had families themselves were less sanguine about a woman's ability to combine work and motherhood than those who did not.

It was not simply a question of the individual babies and their care. Motherhood was a profoundly, inescapably political question in this era, across the ideological spectrum. Protecting the health and welfare of babies—and by extension, policing the behavior of their mothers—was a central tenet of eugenics, the theory underlying everything from fights for clean water to campaigns against immigration. The term "race suicide" was as capacious as it was dramatic, applied to anything that threatened white supremacy and the health of white mothers and babies. The vitriolic attacks on feminism and its white, middle-class figureheads were energized by fears about the declining white Protestant birth rate versus the high numbers of babies born to Catholics, Jews, immigrants, and other "undesirable" groups coded as foreign. According to New York school board member John Martin and his wife, Prestonia Mann Martin, who cowrote several denunciations of feminism and particularly attacked the Feminist Alliance's communal living scheme, the women's movement was akin to "national suicide."[19]

Yet as Heterodoxy feminists in the mother-teacher fight adroitly pointed out, the school board's actions were entirely backward if it wanted to promote motherhood among educated, middle-class white women. Its actions against married teachers were "penalizing maternity," Beatrice Forbes-Robertson Hale argued to Mayor Mitchel. Furthermore, in threatening pregnant teachers with dismissal, wasn't the board tacitly endorsing birth control—which, as feminists well knew, was illegal? But pointing out the hypocrisy and inconsistency in their opponents' arguments did not work to convince the board to change its tactics. Nor did it convince the mayor to intervene and reinstate mother-teachers like Lora Wagner who had been dismissed in disgrace for the "gross misconduct" of having children within wedlock.

Infuriated and frustrated, Henrietta wrote a savage satirical letter, published in the *New York Tribune*, describing the new game of "mother-baiting" that was being used to kick mothers out of teaching roles. "The game is rather rough," she wrote, "but like wife-beating, which used to be so popular, it is played for the benefit of women." The board, unamused, charged her with insubordination. A few days before her feminist ball at the end of 1914, they suspended her without pay from her job at Wadleigh High School for Girls in South Harlem, where she had taught for ten years. "I don't mind a fight," Henrietta told the press, citing her Revolutionary great-grandfather and abolitionist grandfather. "There is fighting blood in me." In her magazine *The Forerunner*, Charlotte Perkins Gilman celebrated her friend in forceful terms. "Heroes are often inconvenient, and quite generally unwise," she wrote. "Martyrs are almost always a nuisance."[20]

In the end, Henrietta wasn't exactly heroine or martyr, victor or outcast. She was removed from the school she loved and placed in a less academic institution, but during the period of her suspension, most of 1915, she worked as an education writer for the *New-York Tribune*, reporting almost daily about education in the city and her foes on the school board. Her articles explored alternative educational theories, vocational training, and curriculum experiments. She interviewed Dr. Maria Montessori during her much-heralded American tour and for a while cherished a hope of opening her own Montessori school in Greenwich Village. Making that dream a reality would fall to her fellow Heterodite Elisabeth Irwin, who launched the progressive Little Red Schoolhouse on Bleecker Street in 1921.

The United States was gripped by Montessori fever in the early 1910s, and Heterodoxy women shared fully in the fascination with the new pedagogy, with its guiding principle of allowing children's innate personalities to "flower up into *themselves*," as Rose Young had put it, rather than imposing rigid rote learning.[21] The theory dovetailed with their interest in Freudianism as a means for women, a similarly disempowered class of person, to develop their inner spiritual selves. The Heterodites' role in spreading the gospel in the press no doubt generated some lively club discussions, especially with Leta Hollingworth's research to draw on. Stella Ballantine, Emma Goldman's niece, had two sons and was a "fervent Montessorian."[22] In February 1913, as New York was consumed with the Armory Show, Mary Heaton Vorse was in Europe working on a commission from *Woman's Home Companion* to write a series of articles about Maria Montessori and her methods. For working mothers of young children like Mary, the idea that children did not need constant attention and discipline to thrive held an obvious appeal, even if it was shot through with guilt. The popular notion that the Italian doctor's much-lauded "method" was just an excuse to give up on discipline was hard to shake; even Joe, by all accounts an attentive and loving stepfather, wrote a story poking fun at it. "You may have a Montessori mother," he has the little boy in the story tell his sister, "but you've got a mighty sore father!"[23]

In early January 1915, Bridgett Peixotto was restored to her teaching job at PS 14 in the Bronx, with back pay. She lived close to the school and was able to hire a nurse and go home at lunchtime to feed her baby. The February issue of the *Woman Voter*, edited by Florence Woolston, reported on her reinstatement and the commissioner of education's judgment that no woman ought to be penalized for "the lawful, natural consequence of marriage." As the suffrage magazine argued, cases like Bridgett Peixotto's "epitomize the whole question of equal civic rights for women (no men teachers having been dismissed for fatherhood)" as well as women's right to economic independence, and any worker's right to be judged by her work "rather than by the opinions of others as to the regulation of her private life."[24] For teachers, that meant the right to continue with a job that many deeply loved.[25]

To avoid further embarrassing conflicts, the school board eventually enacted a maternity leave policy. The League for the Civic Service of Women protested its terms—two years, mandatory, without pay—but the very existence of the policy was an important concession to the idea that women could be both workers and mothers. The battle, however, only underscored how important it was for women to have a voice, and a vote, in public policy negotiations.

Chapter 11

HOW LONG MUST WE WAIT?

On a sunny October day in 1915, a young, newly famous woman was walking alone in the city, enjoying "the wonderful anonymity that New York affords." All of a sudden her solitude exploded in the blare of a marching band and the "soprano din" of women's voices. From a side street she watched as "phalanxes of women swung up the street . . . young, old, blonde, dark, grey, fat." She observed the contrast between the "older zealots"—dowagers with determined faces, easily captured by caricaturists—and the younger women, the new types, with their "long-stemmed casual quality," their "modish bobs" and "simple sporty clothes." Although she was the same age as this younger cohort, the observer felt distant from them, unable to speak their "language of lobbies, pressure groups, hearings, resolutions, chairmen, and delegations." All of a sudden, apparently without a conscious decision, she found herself among them, succumbing to what Heterodoxy's Dr. Jo Baker called "psychological suction" into the suffrage movement.[1] And there she was, "in formation," marching up Fifth Avenue, helping the woman at her side to hold up the heavy pole of a banner reading Move Over, Gentlemen. We Have Come to Stay.

Her neighbor, "a brilliant-eyed, dark-haired mite," introduced herself as Marie Jenney Howe (this new recruit made the
common mistake of assuming that her maiden name, Jenney,
was a middle name, Jenny). Marie explained that her husband
Fred was also marching farther back in the parade, amid the
cluster of male supporters who were "grinning and a little sheep-
ish" in their public role. But although Marie's warm embrace of
this onlooker seemed accidental, she and Fred, a "pair of fiery
liberals," knew perfectly well who she was. They'd been reading
one of her stories together just the night before.[2]

Fannie Hurst, a middle-class German-Jewish girl from St.
Louis, had moved to New York five years earlier, in 1910, with
ambitions to become a writer. Her first few months saw her
struggling against a tide of rejections, until gradually it turned,
and then "success came in torrents."[3] Not yet thirty, she had
made her name as a chronicler of the lives, loves, and heartbreak
of young, downtrodden women. Soon after she got to know
the Howes, Fred let her into Ellis Island to talk to the immigrants arriving from Europe and use their unfiltered stories as
the raw material of her fiction. Marie, meanwhile, invited her
to join Heterodoxy, where several members made a living writing woman-centered stories that hovered in the lucrative space
between sentimental, realist, and feminist. During that first suffrage march, Fannie was embarrassed to spot in the crowd an
editor of her acquaintance. There was still something exposing
about marching to demand her rights as a professional woman
who was dependent on men's approval for her living. But the
next day, he sent over a handwritten note inviting her to write
a story for his magazine, proposing the title "Gentlemen, Move
Over."

The suffrage parade that drew in Fannie Hurst, in October
1915, was the high-water mark of the movement's optimism,
pomp, and spectacle, and Heterodoxy women were out in force.

The parade drew twenty-five thousand marchers, mostly dressed in white, with yellow sashes and banners. There were women on horseback, a contingent of flag-draped automobiles, and more than fifty bands. The parade was led by "Disenfranchised Woman" chained to men dressed in black, representing Ignorance, Prejudice, and Vice. "The whole thing was a grand show in the bright sunshine of early fall . . . the air just a little crisp, the bands playing and thousands on thousands of determined and disciplined women steadily marching from Union Square to 59th Street in a demonstration of solidarity that made each individual in the line of march feel like a giantess in her own right," recalled Dr. Jo Baker, proudly in line with the professional women. "What a thrill we did get out of it!"[4]

Throughout the fall, New York feminists and suffragists, middle-class allies and working women, Heterodites and conservatives joined hands in a temporary alliance in the run-up to a vital state referendum at the beginning of November. Under the umbrella of the Empire State Campaign Committee, led by Carrie Chapman Catt of the Woman Suffrage Party, it would be the first serious chance at women's enfranchisement in the state in years, and with campaigns running simultaneously in New Jersey, Pennsylvania, and Massachusetts, women were confident that 1915 would be the year that a major eastern state finally granted them the vote.

The city was blanketed in propaganda. Leaflets, handbills, and posters went up all over, and on the subway, "lap board ladies" who had been banned from posting billboards instead rode the trains for hours on end holding placards in their laps. The "sandwichettes" took up their posts on street corners, with buglers to attract attention, and a Suffrage Baby Truck gave out toys to children.[5] There were dances in the streets of the Lower East Side and concerts in midtown, and by the last two weeks of the campaign it was estimated that more than a hundred speeches a night entertained, cajoled, persuaded, and begged men to give women the recognition they could get no other way. Broadway turned into a suffrage epicenter. On October 27, less than a week before the vote, there was a coordinated takeover of the theaters, which were decked out in bunting, flags, and posters. Matchbooks sold at intermission were emblazoned with the message VOTE YES ON WOMAN SUFFRAGE NOVEMBER 2, and suffragists gave speeches between the acts. A young aspiring actress, Dorothy Newell, appeared on the front cover of newspapers nationwide dressed in a backless evening gown, with VOTES FOR WOMEN painted in block letters across her bare skin.[6]

In the years since the garment strike and the Triangle Fire, activists of the Women's Trade Union League had grown increasingly disillusioned with the male labor leaders, who still refused to take their demands seriously. They committed themselves more and more fully to the suffrage cause, believing that without the vote, their power would always be limited and their status secondary. Ida Rauh, along with WTUL director Mary Dreier, coordinated the league's efforts with the suffrage leadership and made daily speeches. They deployed their star speaker, the blunt Irish laundrywoman Margaret Hinchey, who had spoken at Marie Jenney Howe's suffrage events, to persuade—or intimidate—her working-class male audiences into supporting suffrage.[7]

The Woman Suffrage Party's magazine, the *Woman Voter*, was by now a Heterodoxy production, edited by Florence Woolston, with the painter Ida Sedgwick Proper serving as art editor and journalist Anne O'Hagan Shinn as campaign editor collating news and event listings for the different districts across the state. Alongside advertisements for "Votes for Women" chocolate, Karo syrup, and Swift's Premium Oleomargarine, the magazine carried editorials from women in the labor movement as well as from elite suffragists, and it provided an important source of announcements about publications and events in support of the cause. Beatrice Forbes-Robertson Hale, Marie Jenney Howe, Fola La Follette, and Mary Shaw were among the many club members who contributed; in some issues, fully half the masthead was made up of women who also attended Heterodoxy's Saturday meetings.

"She is small, positive, energetic and I think a Southerner," wrote *Masses* artist and Armory Show exhibitor John Sloan, accurate on all but the last count (she was from Maine), when Lou Rogers paid him a visit to ask him to take on some illustration work. Lou had only recently arrived in New York, in 1908, "without a cent and without knowing a soul," but knowing that she wanted to earn her living with her drawings. Born Annie Lucasta Rogers, Lou found her career boosted when she adopted her gender-ambiguous first name, bypassing editors' prejudices against women artists. It suited her own gender-rebellious life, as well—like Dr. Jo Baker, she adopted masculine clothing and had relationships with women. With Ami Mali Hicks and Ida Sedgwick Proper, she was a member of Heterodoxy's small contingent of professional artists, and her medium of cartooning showed the range of visual creativity even in that small group.[8]

Lou's art wasn't a gallery affair. In its way, it was just as much a performance as the skits, plays, and speeches that enlivened the suffrage movement. At times, it was a literal performance. Lou would set up a folding easel on a street corner or in Times Square and, dressed in an artist's smock, risking hecklers and ridicule, she attracted a crowd eager to see a cartoon emerge from the blank paper. It was a nerve-wracking undertaking in which "the drawing had to be swift and telling and the talk as straight cut as the picture." As she explained in 1913, "It is not art as art that I am interested in. It's art as a chance to help women see their own problems."[9] Feeling strongly that the "other side" in the suffrage fight had taken the lead in visual persuasion, with their cowering men and battle-ax suffragette wives, she experimented with symbolic representations of the fight, similar to the Republican elephant and Democratic donkey created in the 1870s by Thomas Nast. She tried the camel for woman suffrage, "On account of its endurance [and] its age-old reputation for carrying enormous burdens," and the slow-moving turtle for its opponents. But her most powerful cartoons feature human figures: strong, slender women struggling against the burdens of male oppression.[10]

One of her most striking illustrations, "Tearing Off the Bonds," depicts a figure tightly wrapped in ropes that read "Politics is no place for women." Wearing a look of grim determination, the woman wrenches the ropes apart to free herself.[11] Another shows a woman in a cell out of which she's clawed one window—"education"—and is almost finished with a second, "suffrage," which casts bright light on her upturned, triumphant face. The cartoon, published in late 1911, had the same title that Marie Jenney Howe would later adopt for taking Heterodoxy's feminist ideas to the public: "Breaking into the Human Race."

Ida Sedgwick Proper, who showcased Lou's cartoons in the *Woman Voter*, was energetic in bringing together suffrage and the art world in the fall of 1915. In addition to the fundraising exhibition of women's art that she curated at the Macbeth Gallery, she spearheaded an art contest to design an election poster, inviting submissions to her home, just off Union Square to the north of the Village. Ida helped publicize the contest by posing with her fellow organizers in *Illustrated Milliner* modeling "stylish hats"—yet another instance of the merging of suffrage with the fashion world at the time. Posing along with Ida was the contest's judge, Rose O'Neill, an illustrator and well-known Village bohemian, although not a known Heterodoxy member. Rose wore elegant Chinese-inspired tunics and robes she designed herself, and in 1915 also judged another suffrage-related

BREAKING INTO THE HUMAN RACE

Heterodoxy's Lou Rogers was a political cartoonist influential in the suffrage and birth control movements. This cartoon was published in the *Woman's Journal*, the newspaper of the National American Woman Suffrage Association, December 2, 1911. (*Credit: Schlesinger Library, Harvard Radcliffe Institute*)

contest, this time to design a universal style of dress, which its organizers hoped might be the practical equivalent of a man's suit. Although they wouldn't go so far as to endorse an outfit with trousers, the organizers were adamant they wanted a design with *pockets*.[12] Originally from Missouri, Rose became famous thanks to her cartoon Kewpies ("cutie-pies"), babies with big eyes, pointed bonnets, frilled knickers, and chubby naked legs, which were wildly popular as illustrations. They made Rose a millionaire when they were licensed and mass-produced as (eternally creepy) dolls. During the suffrage movement, she harnessed their mass appeal by putting placards in the hands of marching toddlers to demand the vote "for our mothers." The real-life parades also prominently featured women pushing their babies in banner-draped carriages, at once playing into fears that fighting for suffrage would take women out of the domestic realm and suggesting that the realm could stretch to accommodate politics.

On November 3, despite the optimism, pageantry, and money (much of which flowed out of Alva Belmont's deep pockets), suffragists woke up to a crushing defeat. The men of New York reasserted their authority with an unignorable margin of nearly two hundred thousand votes against allowing women to participate in the democratic process as full citizens. In the city, where it was hoped the progressives might have an edge, the pro side lost by eighty-nine thousand votes, or almost two to one. Some suffragists, Harriot Stanton Blatch among them, turned on working-class immigrants in their search for a scapegoat, even though those men did not vote against the measure in markedly greater numbers than other groups, and one of the two districts (of thirty-one) that did pass the measure was the heavily Jewish Lower East Side. "I am glad that they are free," Harriot declared, "but I call it tyranny and license for them to have power to pass upon me and upon the native-born women of America and a disgrace that the men of our country will force us to submit to it."[13] The language here, of forcible submission, carries ugly echoes of the rhetoric around lynching, another contemporary lightning-rod issue that pitted the power and status of white women against that of nonwhite men.

The bitterness of the defeat and the search for blame fractured the alliances among the different suffrage groups in New York, and two main rivals emerged: the more politically conservative National American Woman Suffrage Association (NAWSA), which still clung to its state-by-state strategy, and the more radical Congressional Union, soon to become the National Woman's Party. Led from Washington, DC, by the Quaker troublemaker Alice Paul, the CU was pushing for a federal amendment to win the vote and pressuring President Wilson directly.

But there were other sources of fracture and dismay among feminists and suffragists. Increasingly, the activists of Heterodoxy were being pulled in different directions, arguing among themselves over where their energies were best spent. Throughout 1915 and into 1916, the threat of America's involvement in the carnage of World War I hung in the air, a tangible terror that drove many women to organize for peace. There were strong connections between the movements for suffrage and for peace, both urging a voice for women in government to counteract destructive masculine forces. But as the 1916 presidential election approached, that alliance faltered. Wilson's campaign promise was simple: to continue to keep America out of the war. Republican Charles Evans Hughes, however, promised the federal suffrage amendment that Wilson refused to consider. Trade unionists traditionally were pro-Democratic, but Wilson's racist policies and beliefs were anathema to activists for racial justice. Those divisions would only deepen in the coming months.

Meanwhile, the social round of life in Greenwich Village continued. Just two days after the defeat of the suffrage referendum, a female journalist issued a detailed, illustrated dispatch from a recent trip to "the Bohemia of America." Visiting the Liberal Club, the latest incarnation of Polly's, and the restaurant run by Polly's brother Louis, she notes that "Greenwich Villagers gather on such terms of intimacy that the onlooker feels rather forlorn." The outsider, the "person who is merely seeing the process," can never fully enter into the spirit of the place or make sense of the "rather unintelligible pattern" that is being woven by "conversation and food and cigarettes." This yearning would characterize reports on the Village for the next few years, as the area became more of a draw for tourists and slummers. The "real" Village is always just out of reach, not quite what is expected, not visible on this one night. In the Liberal Club, the visitors' disappointment is palpable, beginning when they are let in despite the sign promising access only to members, and continuing when they find "everybody singing and dancing and nobody waving a red flag or shouting 'Down with everything!'" They quickly decide, "This club was too tame that night." Such reports were all part of building the mythology of the Village. This one is full of names (and caricatures) of local luminaries the reader is supposed to have heard of; at Polly's, which is also familiar ("Oh, yes, the restaurant with the bare, unpainted tables and the green walls and gaslight and high ceilings"), the author watches them flit from table to table. One kisses Polly, then goes over "to talk to pictorial Crystal Eastman Benedict in a coral colored gown." Another has just come from a sitting with Crystal's sister-in-law Ida Rauh, who—in between her acting roles and her speaking engagements with the WTUL—is trying her hand at sculpture.[14] Social pleasures and the company of friends offset the disappointments of the world outside the charmed circle of the Village and the club.

WHEREAS THE SUFFRAGE fight in 1915 was a vibrant public spectacle, a different feminist fight was ongoing in a much less visible register. The battle over birth control was not a matter of pageants and parades; it was, in large part, the battle to raise the issue in public at all. As discussions of sexuality became less taboo, the hypocrisy and misery around the restrictions on contraception were becoming harder to ignore, and the issue became increasingly important for the women of Heterodoxy. For those immersed in the labor movement, the issue was one of inequality: rich women had always been able to control the size of their families and discreetly obtain contraceptives or abortions. It was working-class women whose health and futures were at risk in a culture that kept secret even the most basic sexual knowledge. Activists like Elizabeth Gurley Flynn agreed with Emma Goldman that birth control was "above all, a workingwoman's question."[15] Inez Milholland concurred, pointing out that keeping this knowledge a secret was rank hypocrisy. "Very often the people who oppose the teaching of birth control are people who practice it themselves, but object to the extension of such knowledge to others."[16]

Crystal Eastman was unusual in connecting the birth control fight to women's larger right to sexual pleasure. Women might not agree that economic justice was fundamental to feminism, she acknowledged, but surely they could see that birth control *was*, on the grounds that, bluntly speaking, "Feminists are not nuns." She outlined a simple yet heartfelt vision of a future in which women's freedom, joy, and control of their bodies were inextricably linked: "We want to love and to be loved, and most of us want children, one or two at least," she said. "But we want our love to be joyous and free—not clouded with ignorance and fear." She insisted that "this precious sex knowledge" ought to belong not just to the educated, socially enlightened "conscious feminists" who made up her readership but equally to "all the millions of unconscious feminists that swarm the earth."[17] All women deserved to know how their bodies worked, and poor women had as much right to plan their families and love freely and joyfully as rich women did.

It remained scandalous, however, even to imply that unmarried women might be able to have sex without consequences. In defiance of biological reality, but in deference to cultural necessity, most birth control activists treated marriage as a fundamental condition for sexual activity. Framing the idea as a matter of free speech and social equality could be a way of dodging the issue, allowing the assumption of marriage to go unspoken. To suggest that a woman had the right to make her bodily decisions herself, without the guidance of a husband or a doctor, and to pursue sexual pleasure simply for its own sake was a radical stance. Unsurprisingly, it was the one voiced by Emma Goldman, who regarded love—"the strongest and deepest element in all life" and "the freest, the most powerful moulder of human destiny"—as the antithesis of "that poor State-and-Church begotten weed, marriage." Here, Goldman echoed feminist theorist Ellen Key, who considered marriage irrelevant to maternity. Within Heterodoxy, Katharine Anthony, a lesbian who did not give birth to children, ardently endorsed Key, arguing that birth control represented "the direct effort of the maternal instinct to find its own way between compulsory sterility and enforced over-breeding." Contraception was a way of working with, not against, motherhood.[18]

Florence Woolston's survey of Heterodoxy marriage customs noted that twenty members out of seventy-five (in 1919) were mothers, a rate of "fecundity" that was well below average for the time. When they did have children, their families were notably small, and only a handful of members had three or more children. Several members adopted children, including Henrietta Rodman, who adopted three daughters between 1910 and 1913, before and after her marriage, and the novelist Zona Gale, who married at age fifty-three. In 1916, Katharine Anthony returned from a trip to find in her apartment "a perfect little flower of a girl aged four," one of several adopted children she would raise with Elisabeth Irwin, apparently the more enthusiastically maternal of the two women. "She is one of the most charming babies that I have ever seen," Katharine wrote to a friend. "She came from the Municipal Lodging House, I am told, and her mother is a prostitute."[19] The casualness of this report is striking, with no hint of how the child, or her mother, felt about the arrangement.

Heterodites who had children themselves often gave birth considerably later in life than their less radical peers: Crystal Eastman, for example, gave birth to her son and daughter at the ages of thirty-six and forty. Florence's "Marriage Customs" survey credited the low birth rate in the club to the members' familiarity with "Neo-Malthusianism" (population control via contraception) and "Sangerism" (education-based birth control). Even taken lightly, the survey makes clear that the women of Heterodoxy were able to lead their unconventional lives, to combine their important work with "one or two children," and to time the children's arrival because they had the money and knowledge to control their reproduction. But the wider access of women to birth control, especially overburdened working-class mothers, became an important, and contentious, focus of Heterodoxy's activism in the late 1910s.

Margaret Sanger settled with her husband William in uptown Manhattan in 1910 and quickly became part of the citywide radical scene. She was inspired to take up the birth control fight by her work as a nurse, in which she witnessed the bloody impact of too much childbearing on women's overburdened bodies, and by the experience of her mother, who died young after enduring eighteen pregnancies. In 1912, the editor of the woman's page of the Socialist newspaper *The Call* asked Margaret to publish and respond to the letters she got from women desperate to prevent pregnancy. This led to a series, "What Every Young Girl Should Know," which ran in the weekend edition of the paper—until one Sunday readers were confronted with only the words "Nothing! By order of the U.S. Post Office" running down the page. An unlikely arbiter of public morality, the post office had long played an outsized role in shaping American sex lives, thanks to its head, Anthony Comstock, whose namesake laws banned the circulation of any material deemed by his officials to be obscene, which included all information about sex and contraception. Because magazines and newspapers relied on the mail for distribution, this censorship had a far-reaching, chilling effect.

Margaret Sanger had worked with members of Heterodoxy during the Lawrence textile strike, when she and Elizabeth Gurley Flynn oversaw the transportation of workers' children to New York. In late 1914, she decided to start a magazine, the *Woman Rebel*, to challenge "Comstockery" and sexual ignorance together. She approached Heterodoxy to ask for their support. The group was, apparently, "not responsive" to her plan, and accordingly her first issue was "dominated by [her] bitterness at other women activists."[20] Mabel Dodge did offer the magazine financial support, but it remains unclear why others in Heterodoxy didn't support the *Woman Rebel*. It's possible members were simply stretched thin—there were so many avant-garde little magazines to support, and perhaps they thought that between *The Masses*, Emma Goldman's *Mother Earth*, and Charlotte Perkins Gilman's *The Forerunner*, the "woman rebel" ground was already adequately covered. It's been suggested that she was too politically radical for the group, or that she lacked the education and refinement they looked for in a figurehead.[21] But those charges seem unlikely, given the diversity of opinions in Heterodoxy and the fearlessness with which members published and proclaimed them. It might simply have been that the group was unwilling to commit single-mindedly to the birth control cause, with fierce battles ongoing for suffrage, labor rights, and against the war. One anonymous Heterodite noted publicly that "cranks" on a single subject would not be happy at their meetings—perhaps it was a remark with a target in mind.[22]

Margaret Sanger further complained that Heterodoxy was preoccupied with what she saw as trivialities, like whether women should change their names upon marriage or wear wedding rings. As the objects of feminist organizing, those fights certainly had lower stakes than the often life-or-death question of reproductive autonomy. But Heterodoxy was never truly a political club, with concrete objectives in the advancement of women's rights. In their lively, social, meandering meetings, members were far more interested in discussing the links between their various causes, believing that a society that treated women as the legal possessions of men could not be reformed one piece at a time. Ida Rauh, for example, embodied the interconnections between feminist fights. Already famous for refusing to become "Mrs. Eastman" and making a name for herself with the Provincetown Players, she provoked her own arrest for birth control activism in 1916 by tossing pamphlets from the window of a rented limousine as she drove through Union Square.[23]

Several Heterodoxy members did nonetheless work closely with Margaret Sanger. In the pages of her *Birth Control Review*, the successor to the *Woman Rebel*, Crystal Eastman was a contributor and Lou Rogers worked as art editor. Lou's blunt cartooning style skewered the hypocrisy of male moralists who liked nothing better than to chastise women for transgressions they eagerly committed themselves. *The Masses* was also deeply invested in the cause, printing cartoons and articles that denounced the restrictions on birth control information and the harassment of activists for sharing it, and framed the issue as one of patriarchal oppression. Short stories and poems entered into the emotional side of the question. Heterodoxy's Helen Hull published a story, "Till Death," that depicts a sympathetic doctor unable to help a patient who begs her for a way to prevent having any more children.[24] It sets up Comstock as the chief adversary, although interestingly, he agreed to an interview with the magazine in February 1914.[25] Titled "Anthony and the Devil," the piece presents Comstock initially as a "harmless old gentleman," who is transformed into a fanatic as soon as the interviewer, a woman named Gertrude Marvin, asks him about teaching "sex-hygiene" in schools. He fulminates that "there is a personal Devil sitting in a real Hell tempting young and innocent children to look at obscene pictures and books," and argues that one glimpse of a "vile" picture can cause an indelible trauma. The interviewer asks, incredulously:

"You believe in a real personal Devil?"

"Most emphatically I do! Don't you?"

"No, sir."

The exchange lays bare the impossibility of rational connection over the fault line of deep, unquestioned dogma.[26]

In August 1914, Margaret Sanger was charged under the Comstock Act with "circulating obscene literature." She escaped to Europe, which left her husband, William, who worked with her, to face the charges and serve the thirty-day sentence. Throughout the following year, *The Masses* published editorials by Floyd Dell and Max Eastman and letters in support of the Sangers. Their arguments made it clear that this primarily was a battle over knowledge. Douches, condoms, and diaphragms could be lifesaving, but only if they were used correctly, which required a basic understanding of anatomy and reproductive function. It was this information that most preoccupied Heterodoxy's Mary Ware Dennett, as a birth control campaigner and a sex educator.

Mary had given birth to three sons, one of whom died at three weeks old. Her experience with childbirth was traumatic and put her life at risk, and she was not alone in looking for a way to make it safer and less painful. Decades before the epidural became available, Mary was an enthusiastic promoter of a childbirth process known as "twilight sleep," in which a cocktail of morphine and scopolamine, an amnesia drug, was injected at the start of labor, allowing women to enter a semiconscious state and emerge from childbirth with no memory of the experience. Scopolamine, however, was not an anesthetic, and women could still experience severe pain, especially if the delicate dosage balance was incorrect. Despite the risks and novelty, the procedure was extremely popular with women in the areas of Germany where it was being developed and tested.

In 1912, an American woman returned from giving birth in Freiburg and described her experience as a "fairy tale." Two female journalists from *McClure's Magazine*, enlisting a pregnant woman as an undercover informant, promptly traveled to the women's clinic at the University of Baden to investigate, and concluded that the practice was beneficial and ought to be adopted in the United States. A storm of attention followed, and a woman who had given birth under twilight sleep was invited to share her experience at Heterodoxy, after which Mabel Dodge lent her financial support to the Twilight Sleep Association.[27] New York's Jewish Maternity Hospital tested the practice, and obstetricians inundated with requests warned sternly of the dangers of one-sided magazine articles.

After one of the practice's leading American advocates died in childbirth, however, twilight sleep rapidly lost popularity, although it wasn't clear whether the practice was to blame for her death. As the United States lurched toward war with Germany, magazines turned against stories of German medical miracles. Although it remained a niche treatment that few women received, twilight sleep nevertheless permitted a public conversation about women's suffering during childbirth and the possibility that it might be eased or eliminated. Perhaps ironically, its longer legacy was to further tilt the control of childbirth toward hospitals and mostly male doctors.

In 1915, when her son Carleton was fourteen and his brother Devon ten, Mary Ware Dennett confronted the challenge of teaching them about sex. As a single mother, she felt all the more keenly the need to find a way to give them honest, accurate information without embarrassment. She accordingly composed a short, twenty-page pamphlet that she called *The Sex Side of Life*, which covered its subject with surprising frankness, including detailed, labeled anatomical diagrams. "I believe we owe it to children to be specific if we talk about the subject at all," she wrote in her introduction. Even more strikingly, she made it clear that the pamphlet would emphasize the pleasures of sex, making "the frank, unashamed declaration that the climax of sex emotion is an unsurpassed joy, something which rightly belongs to every moral human being, a joy to be proudly and serenely experienced." The pamphlet rejected "all mention of 'brute' or 'animal' passion" on the grounds that such talk was "an aspersion on the brutes" and sent the harmful message "that there is an essential baseness in the sex relation." It's striking that this language is so carefully gender neutral—sexual passion and sexual pleasure belong to men and women alike, which was far from an accepted cultural standard at the time.

Gender-specific advice is kept to a minimum throughout. Mary advised girls to "be quieter than usual and avoid cold baths and getting their feet wet" during menstruation, while boys were told that sexual urges and nighttime "seminal emissions" were the equivalent, for them, of a girl's period. Her approach to masturbation (aka "auto-erotism" or "self-abuse," a term she rejected) was forthright and equal opportunity. "Boys and girls sometimes get the habit of handling their sex organs so as to get them excited," she told her readers plainly, before going on to reassure them that, although "for generations this habit has been considered wrong and dangerous," there was now scientific evidence that "the chief harm has come from the worry caused by doing it." Instead, she advised, "the thing to do is to keep as calm as possible and keep very busy and very healthy," and not dwell on sex "till the excitement grows unnatural."[28]

It is likely the pamphlet's refusal to shame teenagers for their curiosity or to moralize their desires away was what made it eventually fall foul of government censors. After circulating the guide privately for some time, Mary found a medical journal open to publishing it, and she received so many requests that she began to sell copies for twenty-five cents apiece: first to individuals at home and abroad, and then, in bulk, to public schools, health departments, and the YMCA and YWCA. In 1922, however, the pamphlet was judged to be obscene and was subsequently suppressed. The censors refused to tell Mary why or to give her the opportunity to make edits—not then, and not when she challenged the ban again in 1925. Her defense of the pamphlet eventually triggered a high-profile court case that had

Birth control activist Mary Ware Dennett raised her sons as a single mother and became notorious when she published the frank sex education pamphlet she had written for them as boys. (*Credit: Schlesinger Library, Harvard Radcliffe Institute*)

a domino effect in striking down America's stubbornly lingering obscenity laws. James Joyce has this Boston grandmother indirectly to thank for allowing *Ulysses* to circulate in print.[29]

Believing that there was space, and need, for more than a single voice on the issue of birth control, Mary Ware Dennett founded the National Birth Control League in 1915, while Margaret Sanger was overseas. The league tapped the generosity of wealthy women and deployed the rhetoric of science to make its arguments. Mary became one of Margaret Sanger's most influential supporters, rivals, and eventually, antagonists. The two differed ideologically, and Margaret hated to share the limelight. At the helm of her new organization, the American Birth Control League, Margaret focused on changing the law so that sex information and contraceptives could be supplied to married women via their doctors. Mary, however, attacked that approach as "circuitous, undignified, [and] impracticable," for the obvious reason that it would restrict the information to those who could afford medical care, but also because it would unjustly exclude single women.[30] Mary also objected to Margaret's efforts to get prominent eugenicists on board with her campaign and thus cede authority to powerful men instead of fighting for women's rights. The intersection of the birth control movement and eugenic thinking in this era is unavoidable. The basic principle that society should work to ensure mothers and babies were as healthy as possible, carried to term and with a good chance of living past the age of five, was deeply tainted by racist notions of "fitness," "quality," and other loaded terms.

Mary's organization downplayed questions of maternal and societal health, instead focusing narrowly on the law and free speech. It pushed for a simple repeal of the statutes banning the mailing of birth control information, and in 1926 Mary published a book on the subject, *Birth Control Laws*. A few years later, she wrote to Margaret Sanger, hoping to reconcile and enlist her support. Her letter reminisced about "a day back in 1915 when you lunched with me at my apartment, and the shine in your eye when you talked of your determination not to rest till the people had the knowledge and the help they needed and birth control was rescued from indecency."[31] Margaret refused.

In January 1916, Margaret Sanger's obscenity case came to trial. Mary Heaton Vorse, emerging from her grief at Joe's death and throwing herself back into the fray, helped organize a "Women's Emergency Committee" to coordinate supporters. Rose Pastor Stokes and Elsie Clews Parsons spoke at a dinner at the Brevoort, during which Elsie proposed that women who had used birth control stand up and say so. Unfortunately, this feminist "Spartacus" moment did not come off, as only one woman volunteered to take part. A few months later, the same women organized an event at Carnegie Hall to support Emma Goldman, who had recently been arrested for distributing contraceptive information. Rose Pastor Stokes went up onstage to denounce the secrecy around birth control as a capitalist plot. "Capitalism needs human lives to keep the wheels of industry humming," she declared. "It doesn't care about quality. Its incessant cry is for quantity."[32] When she handed out a booklet on birth control to her working-class audience, Rose "had her hair ripped from its fastenings and her shirtwaist almost torn off" by women desperate to get their hands on the information.[33] It's worth noting that the contraceptive method being shared at such cost was as ineffective as it was onerous. "Just before you take the risk," Rose wrote carefully, a woman should inject glycerin into the vagina, and then "IMMEDIATELY AFTER" douche thoroughly with a solution of peroxide and warm water.[34] Despite its dubious reliability, douching was one of the most popular forms of birth control, because unlike condoms, it was within a woman's control.

Other methods were becoming available, however. When Margaret Sanger set up the country's first birth control clinic in the immigrant neighborhood of Brownsville, Brooklyn, in October 1916, things were rather more medically sound. Working with her sister, Ethel Byrne, and a Yiddish-speaking nurse, Fania Mindell, the clinic fitted women with diaphragms and gave out comprehensive healthcare advice in English, Hungarian, Italian, and Yiddish. The clinic saw four hundred women in the ten days it was in operation, a stark illustration of how desperately it was needed. All three organizers were duly arrested, and members of Heterodoxy organized another fundraising rally at Carnegie Hall in their defense. Mary Ware Dennett and a "committee of 100," including Elsie Clews Parsons, Mary Heaton Vorse, Rose Pastor Stokes, and Crystal Eastman, raised a thousand dollars in support and secured the governor's pardon for Ethel Byrne, who had gone on hunger strike during her imprisonment.

As a fight over free speech—as it was understood by Village radicals—the birth control fight connected to larger questions of citizenship and the vote, raising the question of who had a right to protest unjust laws, and shone an unflattering light on who made those laws, why, and with what authority. The closely fought election of 1916 and its aftermath would see a dramatic coalescence of the fights with which Heterodoxy women and their peers had been engaged, around the central question of the individual's relationship with the state. The notion of "full humanity," so vital for the club's spiritual and psychological feminism, was beginning to feel the pressure of national politics, under which it shifted into the legalistic realm of citizenship. Who was a citizen, and what were his, or her, rights? How were those rights to be claimed, exercised, and guaranteed?

Chapter 12

A WOMAN'S WAR AGAINST WAR

THROUGHOUT THE SUMMER OF 1914, FROM THE ASSASSINA-
tion of Archduke Franz Ferdinand in Sarajevo on June 28,
through the frantic jostling of alliances and treaties that eventually led to war, Americans kept an anxious eye on events in
Europe. In Provincetown, Mary Heaton Vorse, Susan Glaspell,
and a growing cohort of Villagers—big enough for Polly Holladay to relocate her restaurant temporarily to the seaside village—
spent the summer in a tense, belligerent, boozy haze, more
preoccupied with sexual jealousy than military maneuvering (or
perhaps, channeling political fears into personal ones). The day
after war was declared, a chaotic scene unfolded that featured a
case of whiskey, the drafting of a statement of socialist opposition to war, a nude party on the beach, one or two unsuccessful
attempts at suicide by drowning, a violent fight between Polly
and her jealous lover, Hippolyte Havel, and the next day a hasty
departure of the rowdy so-called intellectuals from the village.[1]

Back in New York, fearful that pro-war voices would tum-
ble the United States into the conflict in those first fever-pitch
days, a group of female pacifists organized a parade against the
war at the end of August. Dubbed the March of Mourners, it
borrowed from the established visual tactics of the labor and

suffrage movements, overlaid with the dignity of silence. Thirteen hundred women wearing black, or white with a black armband, marched down Fifth Avenue from Fifty-Ninth Street to Union Square, undeterred by the rain. "There were no bands; there was dead silence and the crowds watched the parade in the spirit of the marchers, with sympathy and approval," wrote *New York Evening Post* editor Oswald Garrison Villard, whose mother, seventy-year-old suffrage stalwart Fanny Garrison Villard, was an organizer of the march. A local police captain estimated that there were around twenty thousand spectators and compared it to the most recent suffrage parade—an indication of how quickly these events had entered the lifeblood of the city.

At the head of the parade, two Heterodoxy journalists dressed in white, Rose Young and Florence Woolston, supported a large white pennant emblazoned with a dove and the word PEACE. Their fellow club member and journalist Katharine Leckie, who acted as a publicist for pacifist causes, was among the executive committee members just behind, and photographs show Marie Jenney Howe in the procession as well. Further back, behind the muffled drums and the Boy Scouts, appeared Charlotte Perkins Gilman, Mary Ware Dennett, and Mary Shaw, among other prominent women, several of them suffrage leaders. A group of socialist women broke the organizers' promise to keep the parade nonpartisan and turned out with red badges and armbands. An African American poet and contributor to *The Crisis*, Rosalie Jonas, "led a brigade of thirty negro [*sic*] women she had gathered from 'Hell's Kitchen,'" while an automobile carried a Chinese and an Indian woman in "native costume." There were several children in the parade, including a four-year-old drummer. "Irving Macabee Berger, a Brooklyn baby, who was propelled in a carriage by his mother, was not as game as Edward [another baby, who slept throughout]," a reporter noted. "At 26th st. he set up a howl, and was hastily removed to the sidewalk." While there was no concluding rally, the parade was intended to be "the starting point of a definite movement."[2]

Pacifism, in the early twentieth century, was not cleanly aligned with any political party. In New York, a city that was home to thousands of immigrants from different parts of Europe, the authorities swiftly restricted parades or demonstrations for particular nationalities. Prior to World War I, some of the most powerful voices for peace were industrialists, who promoted internationalism—another word for pacifism in this era—in the name of global trade. Preventing war was a matter of high-level, closed-door negotiation among a few powerful men, not a democratic or populist movement. Capitalists like Andrew Carnegie and, especially, Henry Ford were vocal in their opposition to American intervention in foreign wars on economic grounds rather than humanitarian. When war broke out in Europe, and especially when graphic reports arrived of German atrocities during the invasion of Belgium, former president Theodore Roosevelt led the chorus baying for enemy blood. More moderate progressives saw an opportunity for the United States to cement its global power by brokering peace between the combatants. Socialists and radicals were more skeptical, declaring that working men were being sacrificed in an industrial slaughter that would enrich capitalists and liberate nobody.

A few months after the March of Mourners, the Woman's Peace Party was formally established at a convention in Washington, DC. Its goals and tactics contrasted sharply with industrialists' efforts, and not only because of the gender of the participants. The WPP was headed by conservative leaders of the suffrage movement, national progressive figures like Jane Addams, and women who had been involved with the much older American Peace Society, including Mary Ware Dennett's aunt, Lucia Ames Mead, who became the organization's national secretary. Most of these organizers were in their mid fifties or older and deployed the gender-essentialist rhetoric of an earlier generation, contrasting women's moral purity and maternal instincts with the equally instinctive male lust for violence and power. Even women who were opposed to suffrage could be reached through sentimental appeals on these grounds. Peace was one area of politics that could always make rhetorical space for women through motherhood, as the ubiquitous anti-war ballad "I Didn't Raise My Boy to Be a Soldier" made clear. The WPP's platform demanded that the government consult "the mother half of humanity" in making its war policies—a demand that President Wilson and Congress flatly ignored.

In New York, however, younger, more radical women formulated their objections to war in quite different terms, seeing militarism and nationalism as evils inextricable from the sexism, racism, and classism that they had been fighting for most of their adult lives. Crystal Eastman led the New York City Woman's Peace Party (NYC-WPP) in its efforts against military buildup, xenophobia, and conscription. She believed that women were crucial voices in the opposition to war, not because they were (or could be) mothers but because they were citizens who deserved a say in their government's decisions. With her idealism shaped in the settlement house, Crystal shared Jane Addams's vision of "global human kinship"—essentially, its values of neighborliness and mutual care writ large around the world.[3] But her vision of pacifism included an explicit, socialist condemnation of the business-oriented, profit-driven "internationalism" of men like Carnegie. If there was to be a woman's peace effort at all, it had to make clear that war was something men created from which women and children suffered. Such an argument was also essentialist, but only because war itself, more starkly than any other human activity, divided the world by gender and forced women to accept a role of passive endurance.

Crystal Eastman was active in many causes, and during WWI became a leader in the women's peace movement. (*Credit: Library of Congress*)

Crystal was far from alone in trying to wrest a feminist, activist ideology from the war's complex matrices of gender, suffering, and responsibility. She enlisted a significant number of Heterodoxy members into the NYC-WPP, including her close friends Madeleine Doty, Ida Rauh, and Inez Milholland, along with Marie Jenney Howe, the novelist Mary Austin, Mary Shaw, Katharine Anthony and Elisabeth Irwin, and Rose Pastor Stokes. The women found creative ways to use their authority in other areas to argue for pacifism; Heterodoxy anthropologist, Elsie Clews Parsons, for instance, took to the pages of the *Scientific Monthly* to repudiate the myth that war was a "natural" male instinct and that women had no involvement in it—and that this social organization was visible everywhere, even in prehistoric and "primitive" cultures. This was an argument that anti-suffragists frequently deployed to justify denying women the vote: if the essence of politics is war, then women, who do not fight, have no right to a say in it. "Let the militarist anti-suffragist assert his belief in government by force if he likes," Elsie said, "but let him not try to justify it by the precedents of primitive life."[4]

Fola La Follette's situation, meanwhile, was complicated by her national profile as the daughter of Robert "Fighting Bob" La Follette, the progressive Republican senator from Wisconsin who was one of the most prominent anti-war voices in Congress. More than a quarter of his state's population had German or Austrian ancestry, and its industrial cities harbored important pockets of socialist influence: Milwaukee sent the first Socialist, Victor Berger, to the US Congress in 1910. Wisconsin had a special significance for Crystal Eastman, too, who had been recruited to lead its drive for a suffrage amendment in 1912, where she was helped by Fola and her father, a staunch suffrage advocate. Fellow Heterodite Zona Gale, a native daughter and successful novelist and playwright, also advised her on the best way to reach out to the state's rural voters. The referendum failed, faced with dirty tricks and counter-propaganda from the powerful brewers' associations, which feared that women's suffrage spelled temperance. Crystal had even married a Wisconsinite, an insurance agent named Wallace Benedict, in May 1911—the day after her brother Max married Ida. She briefly tried a life as a rich man's wife in Milwaukee before she persuaded "Bennie" to move back with her to Greenwich Village in the summer of 1913.

In the fall of 1914 and into the new year, the war in Europe hung as an anxious cloud over the activities of the Village and Heterodoxy. Mabel Dodge wrote in *The Masses* about scenes she'd witnessed in France and England and argued that "the only hope of a permanent peace lies in a woman's war against war."[5] Henrietta Rodman abandoned her scheme for a feminist apartment house once the war put a stop to all nonmilitary construction projects and instead threw herself into peace work. The Heterodites grappled with how to balance their personal identities as feminists with their public roles and responsibilities as activists—and, of course, worried about their jobs, homes, and families. Max Eastman moved out of the home he shared with Ida and their son, Daniel, after an affair with the baby's nanny; Crystal's marriage, too, was breaking up over her husband's infidelity. Ida's energy went into founding the Washington Square Players, while Crystal was working with Alice Paul and Lucy Burns in Washington on their push to turn suffrage from a state-by-state to a federal question. By the 1914 midterms, there were nearly four million women in the western states who had the right to vote. The Congressional Union's strategy was to force Wilson and the Democrats to act by persuading those women to vote against them. "It is impossible to give in a few words any adequate picture of the anger of Democratic leaders at our entrance into the campaign," recalled Heterodoxy member and core CU campaigner Doris Stevens.[6]

Crystal Eastman and Mary Heaton Vorse had first met in the spring of 1913 in Budapest, where both were attending a meeting of the International Woman Suffrage Alliance. There, Mary had been "stirred and thrilled to the depths" by the vision of solidarity among women from twenty-six countries, not unlike the feeling of hope she had derived from the international spirit at Lawrence. When they met, both women were recently married and taking trips that combined work with the pleasures of a delayed honeymoon. But their meeting was not a success—Crystal reported to Max that Mary, almost forty to her thirty-two, clashed with Crystal's husband, Bennie, and that having started the evening in "mild dislike" the two proceeded to "violent antipathy." Crystal, siding with her husband, said firmly, "She is awful."[7] It seems unsurprising that the serious Mary would have clashed with Crystal's wealthy, socially polished (and socialistically uncommitted) husband; probably Joe O'Brien's dominant presence didn't help smooth over the four-way clash of sizable egos. In writing to Max, who was working closely with Mary at *The Masses*, Crystal might have been poking a little at her own jealousy and uncertainty in her marriage to Bennie, whom Max disliked. Whatever the precise cause of this first failed meeting, Mary's and Crystal's overlapping work and social lives would eventually build an intimacy and shared sense of purpose that outlasted either of their marriages.

In April 1915, they met again at a similar international gathering of women, but in a wholly different atmosphere, as members of the American delegation to the International Congress of Women, held in neutral Holland (after rescheduling from Berlin). With great difficulty, the convention brought together 1,136 participants, from both neutral and combatant countries, and adopted a platform very similar to the WPP's. Before the departure of the Americans, the feverishly pro-war Theodore Roosevelt had whipped up abuse against the delegates, calling their cause "silly and base" and the women themselves, cowards. Yet they still made the slow and dangerous crossing—on a Dutch liner, under a blue-and-white banner that simply read PEACE.[8] Katherine Leckie was also there, in her capacity as a press agent for the Hungarian pacifist Rosika Schwimmer, a star speaker who had been touring the United States.

The radical-minded Heterodites felt out of place among the suffrage veterans and senior reformers, whom Mary judged to be inhibited and reserved, "women who had walked decorously all their days hedged in by the 'thou shall nots' of middle-class life." Those decorous exteriors hid a whole spectrum of ideologies and theories about peace, however, and Mary's description of the forty-plus women in the American delegation shows her to be impressed and amused by the variety: "Cranks, women with nostrums for ending war, and women who had come for the ride, New Thought cranks with Christian Science smiles and blue ribbons in their hair, hard-working Hull House women, little half-baked enthusiasts, elderly war horses of peace, riding furious hobbies." Mary was nonetheless impressed by the women's dedication and daring, and moved by the suffering of the women from the combatant nations. During a moment of silence held for the victims of the war, she was struck by the wave of "awful, silent, hopeless frozen grief" that swept over the audience.[9]

Barely two weeks after the women's conference in The Hague, the danger of the crossing to Europe was made horrifyingly clear in the German U-boat attack on the British ocean liner *Lusitania*. The deaths of 128 Americans, among more than a thousand casualties, turned public opinion decisively against Germany. The US government stepped up its strategy of war "preparedness," which allowed for a massive increase in military spending and weapons production. The hawks insisted that they could build up an arsenal, conscript and train troops, without being drawn inexorably into the war. But as more radical pacifists pointed out, all those new guns built in the first act were bound to go off in the second. "The national genius cannot be directed to war preparation and genuine peace at the same time," Crystal Eastman argued.[10] Prospects for the United States brokering a lasting peace deal were looking increasingly remote.

At the end of the year, Crystal was invited to join another international peace effort, this time the pet project of the industrialist Henry Ford. She declined, as did many other prominent reformers, skeptical of the millionaire's rather vague and self-aggrandizing project to end the war by himself. But others agreed to give the peace ship a chance, including Inez Milholland. Katherine Leckie was hired as public relations manager for what became known as the Ford Peace Expedition, and she helped select guests and journalists for the trip. Heterodoxy suffrage cartoonist Lou Rogers and her close friend, and possibly partner, Elizabeth Watson, a WTUL member, were also on board. A huge crowd watched the *Oscar II* depart from the port at Hoboken, New Jersey, while a band played the pacifist anthem "I Didn't Raise My Boy to Be a Soldier." There were more than forty journalists on board whose skepticism about the mission was reflected in their coverage. They described endless conflict between the would-be peacemakers, as well as a serious outbreak of flu that confined Ford to his cabin. Once the ship arrived in Norway, the delegates found that neutral nation to be far more enthusiastically pro-war than they had hoped, and before long Ford abandoned the trip and returned to America.[11]

THROUGHOUT 1915, THE NAACP was fighting a new battle, on the new terrain of technology and entertainment: one that challenged the Village radicals' commitment to free speech as a fundamental moral value. Released in the spring, D. W. Griffiths's racist epic of Southern pride, *The Birth of a Nation*, had proven wildly popular with white audiences across the country. The film was doing its part to revive the moribund Ku Klux Klan, which it portrayed as heroic saviors of a civilization under threat from emancipated Black people. Jane Addams did not mince words in her opinion of the "unjust and untrue" film, and cautioned that "history is easy to misuse. . . . You can use history to demonstrate anything, when you take certain of its facts and emphasize them to the exclusion of the rest." She described the film's portrayal of the KKK, in the role of "the melodrama hero," as "perfectly ridiculous" and condemned as "revolting" the scenes that showed white women being sexually menaced by Black men. "At every turn the Klan is made to appeal to the enthusiasm of the spectator as the heroic defender of a victimized people. None of the outrageous, vicious, misguided outrages, which it certainly committed, are shown." She expressed hope that the film might be suppressed, concluding that "as an appeal to race prejudice, it is full of danger." Rabbi Stephen Wise, another prominent cofounder of the NAACP, called it "an indescribably foul and loathsome libel on a race of human beings."[12]

At the time, however, there was no central process for approving a movie for nationwide distribution, so it was up to local film boards—made up almost exclusively of white people—to decide which audiences saw what. The boards could demand significant edits before they would approve a film, and local theater owners and religious lobby groups wielded considerable power, so there might be a significant difference in what audiences saw between, say, New York and Alabama, and local protests could make a concrete difference. The NAACP mobilized its support nationwide to ask film boards to censor the film, and mounted public education campaigns to counter its most damaging story lines. But after "six weeks of constant effort," NAACP secretary

Mary Childs Nerney wrote in exasperation to a member of the executive committee in Chicago, they had "gotten nowhere." In Boston, William Monroe Trotter, a prominent radical Black leader, grew impatient with the indirect condemnations in the press. He stormed the box office at the Tremont Theater with a group of fellow Black activists after they were refused tickets, and his arrest spurred the NAACP to organize a huge demonstration the following day at Faneuil Hall. Elsewhere in the country, especially in Philadelphia and Chicago, *Birth of a Nation* prompted protests from Black citizens and outbursts of violence from white gangs, who murdered a Black teenager in Lafayette, Indiana, in April—supposedly inspired by the film, although it was unclear whether they had actually seen it.

Director Griffiths and Thomas Dixon Jr., the author of the novel on which the film was based, were unrepentant in the face of moral outrage. Griffiths decried "censorship," but he freely admitted that his film was intended to be "an influence against the intermarriage of blacks and whites." Dixon went further, disparaging the NAACP as "the Negro Intermarriage Society." Their comments betrayed the sexual paranoia that undergirded the film's racism and was also, notoriously, a pretext for lynchings and mob violence. The controversy rolled on for months after the film's initial release. Actual violence, or disturbances of the peace, gave authorities cover to ban the film, and it was eventually banned in three states and several cities. The NAACP organized a boycott, although this didn't do much to dent its robust profits.

Not everyone was comfortable with the approach of censoring or suppressing Griffiths's version of history, however, no matter how distorted and damaging it might be. An eloquent defense of *Birth of a Nation* on free speech grounds appeared, surprisingly, in *The Crisis*, written by Inez Milholland and published almost two years after the film first appeared, demonstrating the longevity of the issues it raised. Inez opposed the suppression of *Birth of a Nation* on the grounds that "to suppress evil is to drive it underground, not to exterminate it," and, further, that suppression only made evil things (or good ones) stronger. She laid out her position in terms that repeatedly opposed evil—secret, underground, festering, and hard to combat—to moral goodness, rooted in truth and gilded in light. Following the principle that people ought to be free to judge for themselves, the essay was full of faith in the power of education to correctly shape those judgments—and of the belief that moral judgments and aesthetic ones were basically equivalent. "I protest against 'The Birth of a Nation' as vigorously as my neighbor," Inez wrote. "I find it historically false, untrue to life, bad art, melodramatic, and meretricious, caddish, dull, and exaggerated, but I would not suppress it for all that, just because it does not happen to suit my taste or morals."

Despite the very real danger of a resurgent KKK, Inez insisted that censorship could do more harm than a film ever could. Furthermore, she suggested, the controversy over the film had clarified things. "Points of view have been crystallized, prejudices cleared away. . . . Those who have faith in the Negro race and its capacities know better the reasons for their faith; while the belittlers of the Negro have had a stamp given to their opposition which shows its true colors. We all know now where we are at, at heart." A Black reader, among those who made up nearly 80 percent of *The Crisis*'s audience, might point out that she had always known where she was, and that her right to exist, and to have her history told accurately, was hardly a matter of a white person's point of view.[13]

As the controversy over the film rolled on, the dominance of white leadership in racial justice causes in the North was beginning to be openly challenged. Marcus Garvey, the Jamaican founder of the United Negro Improvement Association, a pan-African advocacy organization, moved to the United States in 1916. When he visited W. E. B. Du Bois in New York, he was shocked to discover that the staff of *The Crisis* and the leadership of the NAACP were mostly white.[14] Garvey might have confronted Du Bois more forcefully than some, but he was not alone in his skepticism about the whiteness of the NAACP. In August, the white leader Joel Spingarn hosted a conference of fifty activists at his country estate, Amenia, in Troutbeck, New York. The three-day event was intended to hammer out the differences among and between Black activists and their white supporters, and it generated a "Unity Platform" focused on education and political rights. As Du Bois wrote, "The time has come for Americans of Negro descent and all those who believed in a democracy wide enough to include such Americans to get into close and sympathetic conference." Garvey was not there, still being new to the country and the cause, but W. E. B. Du Bois and James Weldon Johnson were both there, along with Grace's brother Jack Nail and, most likely, Grace herself, although she does not appear in the surviving photographs. Veteran women's rights activists Mary Church Terrell and Addie Hunton were also present, as was Elsie Clews Parsons's husband, Herbert, a prominent politician. "Miss Inez Milholland," one of the featured speakers, stuck out as a woman and for her youth.

IN 1916, THE annual suffrage parade in New York City was subsumed into a vast parade for war preparedness. In early May, just days after Jesse Washington was lynched in Waco, Texas, and Rose Pastor Stokes's distribution of birth control pamphlets provoked a near riot at Carnegie Hall, 135,000 people marched through the city in one of the largest demonstrations New York had ever seen. It dwarfed even the previous year's suffrage extravaganza by orders of magnitude.[15] Many suffragists affiliated with the moderate NAWSA proudly marched in the parade, showing their support for a policy that their more radical peers, in Heterodoxy, the Woman's Peace Party, and Alice Paul's National Woman's Party, deplored. Although later events made preparedness seem like an inexorable slide, there remained serious opposition to the war. In July, in San Francisco, a similarly enormous preparedness parade was bombed, killing ten people and wounding dozens more. Two radical labor leaders associated with the IWW were arrested, and in a brazen display of perjury and bias, sentenced to life imprisonment—despite high-profile campaigns for their release, both served more than twenty years in prison, and the true culprits were never caught. That same summer, in a New Jersey warehouse, German saboteurs ignited two million pounds of explosives destined for the Allied front, resulting in an apocalyptic blast that lasted twenty minutes, killed seven people, shattered windows across lower Manhattan, and must have felt like the end of the world.[16]

Crystal Eastman stepped up her anti-war activities by working full-time with another peace organization, the American Union Against Militarism (AUAM), a mixed-gender group that was less radical than her New York WPP but more politically influential. She wrote a manifesto, "A Platform of Real Preparedness," that inverted the militarist euphemism and instead imagined preparedness as international solidarity, celebrating multiculturalism and denouncing imperialism and war profiteering. Thanks to Crystal, the AUAM could also boast the only truly successful example of peaceful mediation in this tense era: it sent a small committee to negotiate with Pancho Villa in Mexico after the Mexican Army clashed with US troops at Carrizal in July, and averted a full-scale war. According to her biographer, "Crystal had led the way to a radical internationalist scheme that demonstrated that citizen diplomacy can successfully prevent war."[17]

Amid the heat of preparedness, the AUAM hired a publicist to help it mount an engaging campaign against what felt like an impossible target. Walter Fuller was an Englishman who managed the press relations for his sisters' folk-singing trio, the Fuller Sisters, who had come to America on a successful tour and performed twice for President Wilson. When Walter met Crystal, the AUAM's general secretary, he reported to one of his sisters that she was "very American—in the New York sense of the word—no respecter of persons—no sentimentality—no Europeanized refinements." That was a good thing in his eyes—Walter and Crystal married in September, after she finalized her divorce from Bennie (she was already pregnant with their son, Jeffrey). Together, they wrote a script for a satirical anti-war film and devised the AUAM's Truth About Preparedness campaign, which involved a traveling exhibit called War Against War. Because no cause was complete without a parade, they came up with a stunt to catch the eye of even the most protest-jaded reporter: a seventeen-foot-tall dinosaur named Jingo, built out of papier-mâché and painted gold. ALL ARMOR PLATES AND NO BRAINS read an explanatory sign. "This animal believed in 'Preparedness' and is now extinct."[18]

As the November 1916 presidential election approached, the national mood was in flux. The European conflict was locked, on the Western Front, in a muddy, bloody stalemate, and Wilson's policy direction was unclear and tentative, in contrast to Teddy Roosevelt's constant drumbeat for war. Meanwhile, labor unrest continued. Although preparedness ramped up industrial production and generated massive profits for factory owners, workers still had to claw out the most basic wage raises and protections. In New York, a walkout of workers on the subways, trolleys, and elevated trains paralyzed the city and grew violent.[19]

Elizabeth Gurley Flynn and the IWW were in Minnesota, meanwhile, another effort to organize miners on the iron-rich

Range. Elizabeth called on her old friend Mary Heaton Vorse to join her and write about the tense standoff, in which a miner's wife had been accused of murdering a sheriff's deputy and was arrested with her baby. Several IWW organizers, unsurprisingly including Carlo Tresca, had also been arrested. The situation struck at the core of Elizabeth's organizing and Mary's reporting sympathies, in the unjust treatment of a young mother and the trumped-up charges being used to suppress IWW activities. The call pulled Mary out of her lingering grief, and she wrote her only piece of *Masses* labor reportage, "Accessories Before the Fact," about the strike. She also brought the case to public notice in the pages of mainstream magazines like *Harper's*, in which her Lawrence reporting had had such an impact. Mary made no secret in her reporting of her activist goals, and no pretense of neutrality. Although she was not employed by the unions, she donated to relief funds and was open about her sympathy for the workers, believing that "the line between journalistic coverage of a strike and active involvement in it was fluid."[20]

The 1916 election drove a wedge between activists in different battles. The AUAM supported Woodrow Wilson, who had refused to endorse a suffrage amendment but had kept America out of the war—his so far unanswerable slogan. His challenger, Republican Charles Evans Hughes, was the progressive, moderate former governor of New York, with whom Crystal had worked on the Employers' Liability Commission in 1909. Hughes had promised to bring the constitutional amendment to a vote—"My view is that the proposed amendment should be submitted and ratified and the subject removed from political discussion"—while Wilson repeatedly told the women they could afford to wait.

However, Alice Paul's group had reduced the Democrats' majority in the midterms by encouraging western women to enter protest votes against the party, political leaders were scrambling to influence their strategy. Young Heterodoxy suffragist Doris Stevens, the political director of the campaign in Washington, DC, reported sardonically on the change in tone from the representatives of the Democratic and Republican National Committees. "No more questions on mother and home! No swan song on the passing of charm and womanly loveliness! Only agile scrambling by each committee member to ask with eagerness and some heat, 'Well, if this amendment has not passed Congress by then, what will you do in the elections of 1916?'"[21] Undeniably, though, the loudest belligerent voices belonged to Republicans, and Wilson was running on the promise of peace. The agonizing choice seemed to be suffrage and war, or no suffrage and no war.

The close friendship between Inez Milholland and Crystal Eastman faltered over the competing claims of peace and suffrage activism. Despite her attendance on the Ford peace mission and her work with the WPP, under the influence of the DC-based radicals, Inez had become convinced that suffrage had to be their primary focus and that every other hoped-for reform would flow from the breaking loose of women's political chains. "Do not let anyone convince you that there is any more important issue in the country today than votes for women," she said in 1916, aiming her words pointedly, it seemed, at Crystal and the other Heterodoxy women who were concentrating on peace.[22]

Ahead of the election, Alice Paul enlisted Inez for a lightning tour of the western, enfranchised states to whip up support for Hughes, exploiting the star power and energy that were invaluable assets to the cause. But the statuesque Inez was not as robust as she looked. Supported emotionally and physically by her younger sister Vida, also a committed suffragist, Inez made stops in more than twenty-five cities across Wyoming, Oregon, Washington, Montana, Utah, Nevada, and California, in two months. The schedule would have been tiring even had air travel been available: by train, it was debilitating. She addressed enormous crowds, and after one event shook hands with more than five hundred people, while barely able to stand up. Before leaving on the tour, she wrote to her husband, Eugen Boissevain, that a doctor in Chicago had diagnosed her with tonsilitis, telling her the infection had been "draining into [her] system a slow poison for at least two years."[23] In Seattle, she saw another doctor, who agreed that she had tonsilitis, which cheered her up, since it seemed easily curable. In letters to Eugen, she strenuously tried to reason away her full-body aches and pains, physical weakness, and the "great black and blue bruises" all over her body as merely symptoms of blood poisoning or perhaps, as the doctor had suggested, a lack of calcium. She was looking forward to their upcoming trip to her husband's native Holland, where she decided she would have her tonsils removed at once.[24]

In Los Angeles on October 23, Inez collapsed at the podium during her speech and was admitted to the Good Samaritan hospital. She was hemorrhaging blood, was diagnosed with severe anemia, and had a dangerously low level of red blood cells. But still, her condition didn't strike Alice Paul as serious enough to curtail her grueling schedule. Cabling her, "Calamity for you abandon tour" (*sic*), Alice planned to send her on to Chicago and then New York as soon as she recovered.[25] Her plans to continue capitalizing on Inez's presence reveal her star speaker's importance as a vote-getter and fundraiser but also the impossibility of imagining that such a vibrant young woman could be fatally ill. Yet on November 25, after more than a month in hospital, during which she endured ice baths to lower her temperature and multiple blood transfusions, Inez Milholland died, at the age of just thirty. As one of Heterodoxy's youngest, most famous, and most active members, it was barely conceivable that she should be its first casualty.

The club was devastated by Inez's death and members has-
tened to pay tribute to the remarkable range of her interests and
political commitments. Crystal, who was heavily pregnant, organized a huge memorial service at Cooper Union on December
21. "Her whole aspiration was for fuller liberty," she declared, in
a tribute that bore witness to the capaciousness of her friend's
commitments, as a "socialist-trade unionist-prison reformer-
feminist-suffragist-pacifist." She declared it "very wonderful"
that Inez could be claimed by so many movements. "All our great
movements at which the dull world laughs—are one at heart,"
Crystal insisted. "They are phases of the struggle for liberty."[26]

For those who knew the outspoken, frequently outrageous
Inez personally, the rapidity with which she was turned into a
plaster saint by the leaders of the suffrage movement must have
been chilling. Her image, useful in life, became ubiquitous in
death. Mounted on her white horse, she graced banners and
posters, and her words became slogans: "Forward into Light,"
and her appeal to Wilson: "Mr. President, How Long Must We
Wait for Liberty?" Four days after the memorial in Inez's spiritual home of Greenwich Village, Alice Paul staged an elaborate
service in Statuary Hall in the US Capitol: Inez was the first
woman to be honored in such a way. There were hymns, a ren-
dition of the suffrage anthem known as the "Women's Marseillaise," and an address by the suffragist Maud Younger. Activists
hoped that Inez's death might move Wilson to support woman
suffrage in her honor, but he rejected their request outright. It
was a sign that the tactics of persuasion, even seduction, which
had seemed so potent earlier in the decade, were no match for
the cold reality of politics, especially as war approached. The suffragists would have to take the fight to the president's doorstep.

Chapter 13

PACIFISM VERSUS PATRIOTISM

In January, days after Inez Milholland's Christmas memorial service, a delegation of suffragists presented President Wilson with a simple demand, that he exert his influence to bring the suffrage amendment to an immediate vote. "It plainly irritates him to be so plainly spoken to," noted Heterodoxy member Doris Stevens, who was in the room. Now in her late twenties, Doris first became active in the suffrage movement at Oberlin College and had been working closely for the past four years with Alice Paul—a leader whom she compared to Lenin, for their similar "cool, practical, rational" qualities. Wilson would continue to rebuff the suffragists for most of his second term, insisting that he supported their cause in private but could not compel his party to take up the issue.

By 1917, it was no longer a question of making anyone "like the idea," as Max Eastman had put it, but of making them move on their approval. The suffrage movement was "languishing," as Doris put it, precisely *because* so many people believed its victory was inevitable.[1] They needed a visual reminder that the business was still unfinished. Inez Haynes Irwin, who would later write a history of the National Woman's Party, claimed to have given Alice Paul the idea, inspired by her recent experience working

on behalf of arrested IWW radicals in San Francisco. "Fresh
from California and the labor fights I saw there, I said instantly,
'Why don't you picket him?'"[2]

The "Silent Sentinels," as they called themselves, were no
more than a curiosity at first. Through the bitterly cold months
of January and February, women stood silently, in shifts, holding banners demanding the president's action on suffrage. "Their
reactions were those of any human beings called upon to set
their teeth doggedly and hang on to an unpleasant job," Doris
Stevens wrote. As such, they were far more likely to be heard
asking, "When will that woman come to relieve me? I have stood
here an hour and a half and my feet are like blocks of ice," than
extolling the glory of their action. Month after month, women
from across the country arrived to volunteer and to offer warm
clothing, "hot bricks to stand on [and] coffee in thermos bottles."[3] The veteran Black suffrage leader Mary Church Terrell,
who lived in Washington, and her adult daughter Phyllis, joined
the protest several times at Alice Paul's request.[4] But during the
winter and spring, the pickets barely distracted the government
from the "sporting prospect" of entry into the war.[5]

In February, the *New York Times* announced "Pacifists Drop
Suffrage." More accurately, it was the other way around. In New
York, Vira Boarman Whitehouse, the socially elite head of the
state's Woman Suffrage Party, pledged the service of half a million suffragists if the United States entered the war. Many of the
party members were outraged. They wrote a letter denouncing
her plan and followed it up with a mass meeting on February 10
to "discuss war as it relates to the interests of women."[6] Katharine Anthony, a staunch pacifist, was among the attendees. Vira
Whitehouse and other conservative suffragists saw the war as an
opportunity for women to "earn" the vote through overt displays
of patriotism; NAWSA's magazine had been running regular
advertisements that presented war service as a quid pro quo. This

was the same calculation the British suffragettes had made when they agreed to suspend their campaigning for the duration of the war.[7] Distancing herself both from the Silent Sentinels and from the feminists in the Village, the conservative leader Carrie Chapman Catt proclaimed that suffrage was a "bourgeois movement with nothing radical about it."[8]

The split over suffrage tactics was just one of a pattern of fractures that threatened to shatter Heterodoxy's charmed life in 1917. By its very nature, war demanded that people take sides: pacifist or patriot. There was no room for nuance or the complex balance of different priorities and commitments that had made the club such a vibrant place for discussion in its early years. There was no more room, it seemed, for Heterodoxy.

Elizabeth Gurley Flynn remembered a formal standoff: "A few super-patriots were shocked at the anti-war sentiments freely expressed at our meetings," she wrote. "They demanded the expulsion of Rose Pastor Stokes and myself," the most visible radicals in the group. "When the club refused, they resigned."[9] Elizabeth did not name names, so it's unclear exactly who resigned in this way, but both Charlotte Perkins Gilman and Rheta Childe Dorr were vocal supporters of the war. In later years, both framed their decision to quit the club as one of changing priorities and interests rather than a crisis as Elizabeth describes. Charlotte, who was deeply skeptical of Freudianism, later said she left when "all the heresies seemed to center on sex psychology and pacifism."[10] Yet there is evidence she addressed the club in 1921, and she continued to be close with many members, including the novelist Zona Gale, who wrote the introduction to her autobiography.[11]

Rheta, by contrast, framed her departure as the casting off of a trivial social obligation. "I remained an ardent and devoted member of Heterodoxy until the World War came to shake mankind as nothing else has done for two thousand years," she recalled. "It shook me to such a degree that alternate Saturday luncheons had no more attractions for me." She went on to take a position that rather self-servingly reframed the club's approach to the war by reference to American history. "I know that Heterodoxy in 1917 was just about what the American Colonies were, according to John Quincy Adams, when the Revolutionary War was at its height—one-third fighting, one-third indifferent, and one-third Tory. But when the Revolutionary War was at its height I should have been just where I was in 1917, in the fighting one-third."[12] Rheta traveled to the front as a war reporter as well as to Russia after the revolution, and her fighting spirit was hardly in question. But her attitude to her pacifist friends in the club seems sadly dismissive. To oppose the war while America was fighting was hardly indifference: it was to take an increasingly risky and isolated stance as the country cracked down on radicalism.

Several more conservative members of Heterodoxy found a path between war fervor and feminist principles through charitable efforts on behalf of refugees and wounded soldiers, which had proliferated rapidly in New York since 1914. Beatrice Forbes-Robertson Hale had been running the British War Relief Association since the beginning of the conflict, collecting money and medical supplies for hospitals on the front and in her native England. The association also supplied patterns for women wanting to knit socks, scarves, and underwear for soldiers.[13] Mary Shaw, her fellow actress, created a new, less radical women's club in 1917 that she called the Gamut Club, which she envisaged as a meeting place for "professional women from diverse fields" that could take place in a residential clubhouse along the lines of the well-established, elite institution of the gentleman's club. While she never managed to raise funds to build this permanent space, the Gamut Club in its temporary home opened its doors to servicemen, providing a canteen and social activities for them. And despite her leadership of the conservative suffrage faction, her opposition to pacifism and to picketing the White House, Vira Boarman Whitehouse was herself a member of Heterodoxy, likely brought in through her shared suffrage background with Marie Jenney Howe. She was one of the club's few members on the Social Register—besides, of course, Rose Pastor Stokes.

By far the strongest impulse in the club, however, was defiant opposition to militarism. Beginning in January 1917, the biweekly magazine *Four Lights* was largely a Heterodoxy production, intended to "voice the young, uncompromising women's peace movement" as embodied in the New York branch of the Woman's Peace Party. The youngest *Four Lights* contributor, future *Nation* editor Freda Kirchwey, was just twenty-four in 1917, and most of the staff were in their thirties and early forties; the oldest contributor was NAACP stalwart Mary White Ovington, fifty-two. The majority were Heterodoxy members: Crystal Eastman, Madeleine Doty, Anne Herendeen, Edna Kenton, Fola La Follette, Marjorie Benton Cooke, Katharine Anthony, and Elisabeth Irwin. Named after lines in a poem about the sixteenth-century explorer Ferdinand Magellan, the magazine's logo was a sailboat at sea and its motto, "An Adventure in Internationalism." In the first issue, editors Anne Herendeen and Edna Kenton announced a distinctive editorial policy. "Four Lights will not give any of its lustre to the jewel of consistency," they wrote, explaining that each issue would have a new team of three editors from a rotating volunteer staff. "If you do not like this number, be sure to get the next!"

The journal's pacifism was considerably more radical than the platform of the national WPP. As well as arguing for international cooperation and an end to the current war, its articles underscored the connections between militarism and racism, imperialism, capitalism, and antifeminism. In keeping with the spirit of the Village's other creative projects, particularly theater, *Four Lights* deployed satire and irony as weapons, exposing the cardinal sin of hypocrisy wherever it could. The editors joked about the way gender was grist for the propaganda mill: at one point they reprinted a news item about the Red Cross that called it "the big brother of the Army and Navy," under the headline WE THOUGHT IT WAS A GIRL—a pointed joke about the way wartime propaganda endlessly recycled images of women as nurses and caregivers. The journal drily pointed out the sexist assumptions underlying both pro- and anti-war stories. Editors took aim at a *Nation* report about soldiers sexually assaulting enemy women, which contended that the victims, both in their own eyes and the judgment of society, "had better in the majority of cases be dead." *Four Lights* pointed out that it was only men who took this "better dead than dishonored" claim to be "self-evident" and that "It would be enlightening to learn what proportion of women agree." To expose readers to the kinds of stories they couldn't easily see, the journal also shared stories from foreign newspapers, which were not always pro-war. In its first months of operation, the journal wrote approvingly of President Wilson and expressed the cherished hope of American progressives, that the country could stand as a beacon, "the hope of the world."[14]

It did not last. Three days before Wilson's second inauguration, the controversy over the "Zimmermann telegram" erupted. The British intercepted a telegram from the German foreign minister, Arthur Zimmermann, to his country's ambassador in Mexico, outlining a plan to draw that nation into the war on Germany's side by promising to restore its lost territory in Texas, Arizona, and New Mexico. There were whisperings that the telegram was a hoax by the British to pull the United States into the war, until Zimmermann confessed to sending it. It scarcely mattered. Like it or not, the Americans were already implicated in a war with a global reach. The Germans had recently engaged in a policy of unrestricted submarine warfare targeting officially neutral as well as enemy ships; since the sinking of the *Lusita-nia*, the horror of U-boat attacks had been a point of particular sensitivity even among anti-war Americans. Even some in the Socialist Party, revolted by this "international crime," drafted a statement of support for the government and the war. Graham Stokes and English Walling helped write this "Socialist protest," and Charlotte Perkins Gilman was among the signatories. Rose Pastor Stokes, however, was not. Her feelings on the war were evolving. She resigned from the Woman's Peace Party around this time, refusing both the labels "pacifist" and "patriot." But a nuanced position, one that valued human life and international solidarity while also holding warmongers to account, was increasingly impossible to hold.[15]

That was underscored in a matter of days, while fallout from the telegram was still front-page news, when a massive worker uprising in Russia launched the first phase of the Bolshevik Revolution. By the middle of the month, the czar would be overthrown and, as John Reed jubilantly wrote in *The Masses*, "The cumbersome medieval tyranny that ruled Russia has vanished like smoke before the wind."[16] Indeed, the provisional government set up in Russia swiftly passed measures that feminists and radicals in America only dreamed about. The death penalty was abolished, political prisoners freed, and women granted the right to vote. The provisional government swept away the czarist regime's cobweb of antisemitic laws, including the Pale of Settlement into which Jews had been herded—where Rose, the Strunsky sisters, Clara Lemlich, and hundreds of thousands of other Jewish immigrants in New York were born.[17]

The events in Russia, and the terror that the country would now withdraw from the conflict, spurred the Allies to pressure the United States further. No amount of protest from anti-war voices was able to slow the country's march toward intervention. On April 2, President Wilson asked Congress for a declaration of war. On the same day, the first woman to serve in the House of Representatives, Jeanette Rankin of Montana, was sworn into office—before launching her political career, she had been a Greenwich Villager, suffrage worker, and Heterodoxy friend, who studied social work at Columbia University with Katharine Anthony. She was one among fifty when she voted against the war; Robert La Follette, in the Senate, was one of six in opposition. Such a tiny protest made no difference. Four days later, the United States officially entered World War I.

The next few weeks chillingly demonstrated how quickly the value Heterodoxy held most dear—the right to speak one's mind—would come under assault in the war years. Crystal Eastman and the members of the NYC-WPP held a meeting to clarify their opposition to the war in this new climate. Their primary targets for protest were conscription and the crackdown on free speech, which began immediately. As early as April 22, Katharine Anthony was arrested for "pasting placards on windows along Broadway between Eleventh and Thirteenth Streets and giving away buttons. On the placards was printed: 'No Conscription! Thou Shalt Not Kill!' The buttons bore the inscription: 'Not a Man for War!'" Along with a social worker friend who had helped her, Katharine was charged with disorderly conduct and held on $200 bail.[18]

New York City, the site of destructive riots against the Civil War draft, cracked down hard and early on anti-war sentiment. The mayor quickly set up a committee to issue loyalty oaths to all city workers, including public school teachers like Henrietta Rodman, who refused to sign. The five Socialists in the state government, assumed to be anti-war, were expelled from office; the party's literature was destroyed and officials arrested.[19] Civilian vigilante groups sprang up as an outlet for the xenophobia and bloodlust that coursed through the country. Those who could not, or would not, join the fight themselves enlisted in the American Protective League. The government put a fifty-dollar bounty on the heads of "draft-dodgers," licensing these self-appointed patriots to break up anti-war meetings and harass and beat up anyone they disliked—trade unionists, immigrants, Black people, radicals—in the name of rooting out spies and protecting democracy. Registration for universal conscription began in June 1917, for the first time in American history. In a wave of parades, banners, flags, bands, and bunting, nearly ten million men showed up to put their names down for the fight.

Four Lights became steadily more savage about Wilson's hypocrisy and the way that war rhetoric twisted progressive values into martial ones. "A war instigated in the name of national vengeance is now declared to be a fight for 'Democracy,'" seethed a writer named Olivia Howard Dunbar. "The slaughter, starvation and utter humiliation of a foreign people is urged as a means of converting it to 'Democracy.'" The journal argued against conscription in the strongest possible terms and—along with the NYC-WPP—mobilized against the forced enlisting of women's support. In July, the New York governor ordered a census of all women available for war work, and though men could note their objection to military service, women could not. The national Woman's Peace Party "heartily endorsed" volunteer war work, but the New York branch saw it as capitulation to military force and argued that women should "enter into no sort of war work direct or indirect." Katharine Anthony's short story, "Sister Susie's Peril," castigated the volunteer women's war effort, arguing that one of the most popular, apparently innocuous forms of relief work, knitting socks for soldiers, was an act of class warfare that attacked the livelihoods of women garment workers. Furthermore, she said, it was absurd, "a peculiarly infantile form of patriotism." Of course a government that had handed out billions of dollars in contracts to build tanks, guns, and destroyers could afford socks for the army's feet. The story made uncomfortable reading even for many pacifists.

The Espionage Act, a Revolutionary-era piece of legislation that suppressed dissent, was revived in mid-June 1917, with far-reaching, chilling effects. A few days after *Four Lights* published what became known as its "Sister Susie Number," it was accused of violating the act. Editor and Heterodoxy member Margaret Lane wrote with strained levity that they were "being honored by an investigation from the Department of Justice" on July 20. "An agent from that department spent an hour in our office the other day—especially wishing to know whether any alien enemies are helping to edit FOUR LIGHTS."[20]

The atmosphere for radical politics darkened quickly, because the law now made it a felony to print anything that might "cause insubordination, disloyalty, mutiny or refusal of [military] duty."[21] The new postmaster general, Comstock's successor Albert Sidney Burleson, had sweeping powers to enforce the crackdown on dissent. Burleson was a wealthy Texan who had pushed Wilson, in the first month of his administration, to introduce segregation into the postal service and, quietly, through the rest of the federal workforce.[22] In his role as spy catcher, he targeted *The Masses* and the *New York Call*, along with *Four Lights*. Emma Goldman's *Mother Earth* was shut down and her list of subscribers seized, and all IWW mailings were banned. The Liberal Club, that bastion of playful debate and socialist theater, "disintegrated."[23]

At twenty-five years' distance, Dr. Jo Baker took the whole situation lightly. Despite being "no pacifist whatever," she recalled that she "had the privilege, shared with a great many other women, of being suspected of mildly radical sympathies which during the war were, of course, synonymous with giving aid and comfort to the enemy." She implied, however, that the "war hysteria" that placed Heterodoxy under suspicion had originated within the group's own ranks. According to club legend, she said, "a worried member of Heterodoxy had written a letter calling on the Secret Service men to keep an eye on the club's weekly meetings because its rolls contained so many pacifists and radicals." The "fantastic result" was intensive surveillance. "We really did have to shift our meeting-place every week to keep from being watched," the doctor said. "It was just like an E. Phillips Oppenheim novel. All except the characters, that is. My colleagues in treason were not sloe-eyed countesses with small pearl-handled revolvers in their pocketbooks but people like Crystal Eastman, Fannie Hurst, Rose Pastor Stokes, Inez Haynes Irwin, Fola La Follette and Mabel Dodge Luhan."[24]

For those in the club who were actively engaged in anti-war activities, the surveillance felt a great deal more threatening. Women were arrested and questioned, had their phones tapped and telegrams intercepted. Fola La Follette was persecuted for her father's outspoken opposition to the war, for which he received death threats and nooses in the mail and was burned in effigy.[25] In New York, "People snubbed her, cut her and behaved like idiot barbarians," wrote Mabel Dodge, perceiving that Heterodoxy offered a "safe refuge" from the pressure. "Everyone was glad to see her, no one there paid any attention to war hysteria, Fola was Fola, as she had always been. She would come in looking somewhat pale and pinched, but after an hour in that warm fellowship her face flushed and her muscles relaxed. It must have been a comfort to come there."[26]

Shortly after the passage of the Espionage Act, Mary Heaton Vorse and Elizabeth Gurley Flynn went to the theater together. Mary reported on their meeting: "'If I were in the IWW now,' [Elizabeth] said, 'whether I opened my mouth or didn't I would surely be arrested. It's rather nice to draw a long breath.' Next day she was arrested just the same. She was one of 166 associated with the IWW indicted for conspiracy." In September, federal agents made a sweep of all the IWW's nearly fifty offices nationwide, as well as the homes of many members. Strikes and boycotts, which had long been essential weapons in the unions' arsenal, were now reconfigured as threats to the war effort; undermining capitalist profits was now undermining democracy. The IWW, on a steep decline since the high of the Paterson Pageant, was defanged by the Espionage Act and all but inactive by the end of the war. From 1918, Elizabeth's energies were focused on "getting political prisoners out of jail."[27]

This aspect of labor work, the defense of those spuriously arrested for their organizing, had been one of Elizabeth's main concerns for some years now. She devoted considerable time and energy to the Workers' Defense Union, a group that brought together lawyers and radicals to fight these free speech battles. Some in the IWW viewed it as a distraction, targeting the wrong enemy by taking on "the Bull [the police] and not the boss." But Elizabeth's experiences on the strike front lines had shown her how often those enemies were one and the same. In Lawrence, the battle to free her colleagues Joe Ettor and Arturo Giovannitti had turned on their right to speak freely from the podium, and not be charged with inciting violence simply because violence happened somewhere in the same city at the same time.

The Espionage Act freed the government from the need to come up with excuses to crack down on dissent—voicing opposition to the war was enough. During the war, conspiracy and espionage charges were brought against Jeannette Rankin, Emma Goldman, and Rose Pastor Stokes. Elizabeth was active in their defense and frank about the toll the work took on her. "It is hard to re-create a picture of the long years of intense brutal reaction which lasted from 1917–1927 . . . it seemed then like a hideous nightmare amidst the hum and horror of it all, working day and night in a defense office." Over one Christmas she should have been spending at home "filling my child's stockings," she was holed up in an office in the back room of the socialist Rand School working to defend a group of Russian deportees.[28]

As Mary noted, it didn't take long for Elizabeth herself to be indicted for anti-war propaganda, along with 165 male IWW members. The pretext was a pamphlet she'd written for the Paterson strike, *Sabotage*. Although she hadn't wanted the pamphlet published, and it had appeared long before the passage of the Espionage Act and in fact argued *against* sabotage, she was facing forty years in prison and a $4,000 fine. She refused to give in without a fight but also had no interest in martyrdom. Several of the other Wobblies wanted to stand together—solidarity forever—but Elizabeth moved for severance, intending to force the government into footing the bill for a stack of separate trials. It was a risky but ultimately successful strategy, but she was not proud of it, still less of the personal plea that she wrote to President Wilson claiming she had all but severed her ties with the IWW and was trying to support her family. Elizabeth was freed, and the charges against her dropped in 1922, but her comrades went to prison for several years.[29] It was not as though she had their support, anyway—Big Bill Haywood fled to the Soviet Union after the revolution, leaving Elizabeth in a state of deep disillusionment with both the IWW and the Village liberals who had abandoned radicalism when it got too dangerous.

With the war underway, the divisions with the suffrage movement deepened, yet the push for the vote had never felt more urgent to women left on the sidelines as their government made life-or-death decisions. Conservative suffragists allied with NAWSA stepped forward to form a government body that would coordinate women's war service, in a bid to prove their patriotism. In August, a *Masses* editorial denounced NAWSA's complicity, attacking their maneuvering "to gain a political privilege" as an intense disappointment to "those who regard the political emancipation of women as part and parcel of human emancipation."[30] By contrast, it praised the White House pickets. Most Heterodites agreed with this position, and many supported or worked with Alice Paul. Her National Woman's Party was officially neutral on the war, insisting that it was open to members of all political opinions, who could be "united on no other subject" but suffrage.[31] Rheta Childe Dorr, who left Heterodoxy in high dudgeon over its anti-war stance, was at the same time a prominent figure in the NWP and the first editor of its magazine, *The Suffragist*, positions that kept her in close working contact with, among others, leading pacifist Crystal Eastman. Charlotte Perkins Gilman, too, served on the NWP's executive committee.

In June 1917, the government finally took notice of the NWP pickets who had been installed outside its gates since the winter, when they unfurled a banner in front of a visiting Russian delegation accusing the president of deceiving his guests by claiming the United States was a democracy. The deliberate inversion of the rhetoric of patriotism, publicly on display in the heart of the capital, enraged a watching crowd, who destroyed the banner and attacked the pickets. The government, desperate to keep Russia from pulling out of the war, was furious with the protesters for turning Wilson's fine speeches in praise of democracy against him. Two days later, the arrests began.

Doris Stevens was one among many NWP picketers to spend time in the city jail and Occoquan Workhouse in Virginia. Her account of the suffragists' prison ordeal makes it clear that class privilege and connections did not protect them from abuse. Another Heterodite, a wealthy and well-connected suffragist from New Jersey named Alison Turnbull Hopkins, served time with Doris. Her husband, John A. H. Hopkins, had run Wilson's reelection campaign in New Jersey (while Alison worked against him, for Hughes and suffrage). He bluntly confronted the president after he had visited her: "How would you like to have your wife sleep in a dirty workhouse next to prostitutes?" The couple had recently been Wilson's dinner guests, celebrating his reelection. "Now Mrs. Hopkins had been arrested at his gate and thrown into prison."[32] Doris bore witness to conditions and treatment that were so shocking that prison reform briefly threatened to supplant suffrage as an area of focus for activists. But the dismissive response from the authorities reinforced Alice Paul's conviction that women had to win citizenship before they could exert any power over their society.

Doris's account of imprisonment focuses on the small, psychological torments that demoralize and dehumanize inmates. "Prisoners are punished for speaking to one another at table," she observes. "They cannot even whisper, much less smile or laugh. They must be conscious always of their 'guilt.'" The "sour soup" and stale, worm-infested bread is inedible, despite their hunger. The women have to beg for toilet paper and share slivers of dirty soap. "It is enough to imprison people. Why seek to degrade them utterly?"[33] The exposure of the brutal and unsanitary conditions at the Occoquan Workhouse, as endured by society ladies, frail grandmothers, and attractive young militants, kept the media spotlight on prisons, as well as on Wilson's prevaricating on the suffrage issue.

The well-connected inmates of the National Woman's Party smuggled out details of their treatment on scraps of paper, and their reputations stood for them: Lavinia Dock, then aged sixty, had a national profile as secretary of the American Federation of Nurses and had worked for twenty years as a visiting nurse at the Henry Street Settlement with Lillian Wald. When she told people "I really thought . . . that I could eat everything, but here I have hard work choking down enough food to keep the life in

Heterodoxy members Doris Stevens, Alison Turnbull Hopkins, and another elite suffragist, Eunice Dana Brannan, dressed in their prison uniforms, photographed during their detention at Occoquan Workhouse, Virginia. (*Credit: Library of Congress*)

me," they listened. They listened, too, to a matron discharged for showing kindness to inmates, who testified that blankets were washed just once a year and that prisoners with contagious diseases were not isolated. These details, along with stories of beatings and isolation punishments, prompted Jeannette Rankin to introduce a resolution in Congress that called for an investigation of conditions in the workhouse.

Within Heterodoxy, Doris was not alone in her interest in prison reform. In 1913, lawyer and journalist Madeleine Doty had adopted the alias "Maggie Martin" and committed herself to a week in a women's prison in Auburn, New York, to investigate the conditions, accompanied by her good friend, "my companion in misery," fellow Heterodite Elizabeth Watson.

Madeleine's 1916 book *Society's Misfits* was based on her imprisonment and the accounts of it she wrote for *Century* and *Good Housekeeping* magazines. The experience prompted her to advocate for change, and she was soon appointed to the state's new Prison Reform Commission, where she fought for basic standards such as edible food, reliable sanitation, and some measure of self-government for prisoners. Her book, however, goes much further, declaring: "Our whole penal system, the criminal law, the courts, reformatories and prisons, stand on the eve of a great revolution."[34]

In her political imprisonment, Doris Stevens was especially shocked by the systemic, deep-rooted racism. Black prisoners were given worse clothing, housing, and medical care, and racial difference was deliberately used to compound the humiliation of the white, middle-class detainees. Doris notes that after dinner, "we went back to our cots to try to sleep side by side with negro prostitutes." She quickly clarifies: "Not that we shrank from these women on account of their color, but how terrible to know that the institution had gone out of its way to bring these prisoners from their own wing to the white wing in an attempt to humiliate us." Elsewhere, she described how the authorities whipped up "race hatred" between the prisoners. "It was not infrequent that the jail officers summoned black girls to attack white women, if the latter disobeyed," she wrote and gave details of one incident involving the white suffragists, who were protesting against the removal of one of their number to an unknown location. "Black girls were called and commanded to physically attack the suffragists," and after they refused, were "goaded to deliver blows" by the warden's threats.[35]

Doris's account is sympathetic and class conscious but uses the language conventions of her day to report the speech of the suffragists' "dusky comrades" in the cells—she records one young Black woman's speech in heavy dialect, a common device in fiction at the time. The conversation demonstrates that the "negress" understands the suffrage movement but doesn't herself feel connected to it. To the white suffragist's explanation of their protest, she responds, "'O—Yass'm, I know. I seen yo' parades, an' meetin's, an' everythin'. . . . You's alright. I hopes yo' git it." Clearly, the vote is something for "you," in this woman's understanding, not "me." Doris did note, however, that many of the inmates they got to know in the workhouse came to NWP headquarters after their release in search of money, jobs, or simply "spiritual encouragement to face life after the wrecking experience of imprisonment."

Shortly after this exchange, she gives the young Black woman a chance to explain her own grievance with the system of crime and punishment, and particularly with laws targeting the poor.

> They sen' yo' down here once, an' then yo' come out without a cent, and try to look fo' a job, an' befo' yo' can fin' one a cop walks up an' asks yo' whah yo' live, an' ef yo' haven't got a place yet, becaus' yo' ain' got a cent to ren' one with, he says, "Come with me, I'll fin' yo' a home," an' hustles yo' off to the p'lice station an' down heah again, an' you're called a 'vag' (vagrant).

Vagrancy laws were notorious for their misuse, as a way to target poor communities of color and criminalize people for poverty.[36] It is only a glimpse, but this exchange indicates that the suffragists' class privilege did not blind them to the larger injustices of a system they knew would not trap them as it did Black women.[37]

IN LATE JUNE and early July, as the first suffragists were being transferred to Occoquan Workhouse, racist violence tore through the streets of East St. Louis, just over the Illinois border from the Missouri metropolis. African Americans had been moving to St. Louis in the thousands in pursuit of jobs in the city's booming factories—most of which were located over the river to escape city and state regulations. The years of "prepared-ness" and now the outbreak of war massively boosted factory out-put, but tensions were growing. When the white labor unions called a strike for better wages, the abundance of Black workers, who were barred from joining the unions, constituted a replace-ment workforce with no particular incentive to respect the picket line. The tension worsened over the course of the summer, with sporadic outbreaks of violence and retaliation culminating in a white mob storming through the city's Black neighborhoods, setting fire to buildings and shooting, beating, and hanging peo-ple indiscriminately—violence that, the *St. Louis Post-Dispatch* reported, the police either ignored or joined in. Ida B. Wells, re-porting for the *Chicago Defender*, put the Black death toll between 40 and 150 people, and several thousand people lost their homes.

In New York, the NAACP sought a new way to demonstrate that racist violence could not simply go unnoticed or unpunished. Grace and James Weldon Johnson, along with Grace's brother Jack, were among the organizers of what they called the Negro Silent Protest Parade, a mass street demonstration that has been called the first civil rights march, which took place a block from the Nail family's restaurant. Taking cues from the suffrage, la-bor, and peace marches that had become a familiar sight in the activist city, the Silent March was nevertheless something new, not least because it was made up exclusively of Black New York-ers. On July 28, some ten thousand smartly dressed people—women and children in white, and men in dark suits—marched down Fifth Avenue accompanied by only muffled drumbeats and carrying banners that said things like RACE PREJUDICE IS THE OFFSPRING OF IGNORANCE AND THE MOTHER OF LYNCHING. The NAACP flyer calling participants to the march framed their participation as an obligation, a demonstration of solidarity: "Be in line on Saturday and show that you have not become callous to the sorrows of your race."

The protest included a petition that sought a "redress of grievances" from the president and Congress. In the name of the Black population of New York as well as "the sentiment of the people of Negro descent throughout this land," the petitioners made their case bluntly: 2,867 men and women had been "lynched by mobs without trial" since 1886, and only a handful of people punished at all, none for murder. Moreover, violent mobs "have harried and murdered colored citizens time and time again with impunity," culminating in the East St. Louis atrocity. The NAACP insisted this was not just a Black problem but that "this spirit of lawlessness is doing untold injury to our country," and it demanded that lynching and mob violence be made federal crimes. Finally, drawing a bold connection to the hypocrisy of a nation fighting a war for democracy overseas while refusing to prosecute injustice at home, the petitioners declared that "no nation that seeks to fight the battles of civilization can afford to march in blood-smeared garments."[38]

The delegation that went to deliver the petition to Washington, DC, included James Weldon Johnson and Jack Nail, along with ten other prominent Black leaders, including Madam C. J. Walker, the cosmetics mogul. They put their demands in the hands of J. P. Tumulty, the president's secretary, acerbically noting that Wilson himself apparently "was 'too busy' to receive the Delegation of Negroes from New York." In the pages of Four Lights, meanwhile, Mary White Ovington excoriated Wilson for his silence in the wake of the violence. She explicitly accused white American soldiers of instigating the riot, an accurate charge that was, nonetheless, not made in any other white publication.

In October 1917, another push for the vote gained force in New York, with little of the pageantry and unity of two years earlier. Vira Boarman Whitehouse, the elite Heterodite at the helm of the Woman Suffrage Party, once again emphatically linked the demand for suffrage to the war effort, declaring that "love of country and a desire to serve are the basis of the overwhelming demand for suffrage on the part of the women of New York State."[39] The banners pushed for suffrage on the grounds of women's maternal sacrifice: OUR SONS ARE FIGHTING FOR DEMOCRACY. The marchers and organizers distanced themselves from the radicals in Washington by insisting on their loyalty to the president. NWP members refused to join the march, instead distributing copies of their magazine praising the picketing. On November 6, a majority of eighty thousand voters carried the referendum to an easy victory and granted women the vote, in a landmark decision that nevertheless stopped short of full inclusion by denying suffrage to Native Americans. The victory was immediately eclipsed, however, by a second revolutionary convulsion in Russia the very next day.

At the end of the war, the ratification of a federal amendment for suffrage was still almost two years away. Would women be able to vote in the next presidential election? Would either their war service—or their refusal of it—be rewarded with citizenship? Throughout the fall of 1917, the suffragists imprisoned in Washington, DC, demanded to be treated as political prisoners and went on hunger strike when that was refused. Although they happened behind the barred doors of prison cells, hunger strikes were as much of a spectacle, in their way, as were the parades, as the British suffragettes had learned. Even in refusing them the status of political prisoner, the government was forced to acknowledge the women as political agents—making their exclusion from the arena of electoral politics all the more jarring. In late November, Doris Stevens wrote the NWP had "thirty determined women on hunger strike, of whom eight were in a state of almost total collapse." The government realized that "it could not afford to feed thirty women forcibly and risk the social and political consequences; nor could it let thirty women starve themselves to death, and likewise take the consequences," and "capitulated," releasing all the prisoners shortly after Thanksgiving.

The House voted to allow women the vote on January 10, 1918, after a debate that exposed the gendered paranoia of its opponents, which Doris recorded at some length. According to a Republican from New Jersey, not only the outcome of the war but also the fate of the nation was at stake. "A nation will endure just so long as its men are virile," the congressman declared. "History, physiology, and psychology all show that giving woman equal political rights with man makes ultimately for the deterioration of manhood." Including these comments might have entertained Doris's readers, safe on the other side of their victory. But they also indicate how deeply gender differences were ingrained in the culture, and how much work there would still be to achieve genuine equality.[40]

For most of the final year of the war, the NWP members turned to other means of persuasion, ceasing the picket protest while they pressed the Senate to take up the suffrage issue. On the late Inez Milholland's birthday, August 6, they organized a protest in Lafayette Park, opposite the White House, during which almost fifty speakers were arrested and held until charges were finally issued for "holding a meeting" and, in a few cases, "climbing on a statue." As Doris put it, "the familiar farce ensued," although in this case, the women were taken to a disused former men's workhouse in the grounds of a nearby prison, which had been declared unfit for human habitation almost ten years earlier. The conditions, and the smells, can be imagined. The women immediately went on hunger strike. In September, the suffrage amendment failed to pass the Senate by two votes.

Outside the prison walls, the women once again began to turn the president's declarations about democracy and freedom against him. In early 1919, while Wilson was overseas at the Paris peace talks, women set fire to fragments of his speeches in an urn just outside the White House gates. When he rejected a plea from a delegation of French women to include women's suffrage as part of his "Fourteen Points" plan for lasting international peace, it was a dispiriting sign that the connection the suffragists had been trying to make for years, between women's participation in government and a fairer and more stable society, had not been heard. Still more frustratingly, during the same month as the NWP members were burning Wilson's speeches, the state of Nebraska became the thirty-sixth state to ratify a different amendment, once intimately entwined with suffrage and now, to most young radicals, an irrelevance. The Eighteenth Amendment banning the manufacture, sale, or transportation of alcohol would go into effect in a year, proving that politicians were willing to radically restructure both the Constitution and American society at the urging of dedicated lobbyists.[41]

Finally, still dogged by Alice Paul while his attention was focused on the Versailles peace treaty, President Wilson scheduled a special session of Congress during which women's suffrage quickly and decisively passed the House and the Senate. It would take another year before sufficient states had ratified the Nineteenth Amendment for it to pass into law. The slog for ratification eventually came down to Tennessee, a state where racist opposition to suffrage was open and potent, based on the fear that Black women would rush to the polls while white women would "disdain to mingle" with a multiracial, mixed-gender crowd.[42] After an eleventh-hour push to include the word *white* in the text of the Nineteenth Amendment was defeated, it was signed into law during the early hours of August 26. Native American women, however, were excluded from citizenship until 1924 and continued to face state-level discrimination.[43] Although her implacable opponent, President Wilson, gave her no credit for the victory, Alice Paul raised a (nonalcoholic) glass in celebration, and immediately began strategizing for what was next. Crystal Eastman, likewise, hailed ratification as "a day to begin with, not a day to end with." Ida B. Wells, speaking to a local Republican group in Rochester, New York, called the vote "a benefit to the race as a whole" and wished both Frederick Douglass and Susan B. Anthony could have been there to see it.[44]

With nine weeks to go before the next presidential election, there was a rush to register women to vote. Republicans had a strong lead, for their suffrage support and their record of greater racial cooperation, but already, across the South, the same literacy requirements that kept Black men from voting were being applied "with discriminatory vigor" to their sisters.[45] A very loose estimate—just the first in a century-long effort to try to make sense of the "women's vote"—held that only a third to a half of eligible women exercised their new right compared to two-thirds of men, across region, party, race, and class lines. Republican Warren G. Harding was elected in a landslide. It was the beginning of a decade that would see his party sharply diverge from its "Party of Lincoln" roots and embrace increasingly conservative policies and rhetoric.

Chapter 14

RED SCARE, RED SUMMER

VILLAGE RADICALS WERE EMBOLDENED AND INSPIRED BY THE
victory of the Bolsheviks, who seized power in St. Petersburg on
November 7, 1917—an event Katharine Anthony called "nothing less than the great rainbow after the world flood."[1] Her fellow Heterodite, the young journalist Bessie Beatty, concurred:
"To have failed to see the hope in the Russian Revolution is to
be as a blind man looking at a sunrise."[2] *Hope* was the note that
sounded and resounded through American liberals' accounts in
these early months. For feminists, that hope lay especially in
the Bolsheviks' astoundingly progressive Family Code, passed
in 1918. It liberalized divorce laws, allowed access to abortion,
and offered paid maternity leave before and after birth to married and unmarried women alike, abolishing also the category
of illegitimacy. To watching American feminists, it was a heady
moment. What could it possibly look and feel like, to win all
your battles at once?

Madeleine Doty was in the midst of a journalistic world tour
investigating the impact of the Great War on women, when she
arrived in St. Petersburg (then called Petrograd) in November
1917. She had traveled from China, across Siberia, to find a city
convulsed in revolution. It was "thrillingly interesting," especially

in the early days, when the Bolsheviks were issuing new decrees every day, each more liberating than the last. "One day all titles were abolished; the next, judges and lawyers were eliminated," she reported for *The Atlantic*, confessing to "a wicked delight on that occasion"—as a lawyer herself, she said, she was well aware "how little justice there often is in the law."[3] With her in the city, among the throng of foreign journalists, were two younger writers and Heterodoxy associates, Bessie Beatty and Louise Bryant, who was traveling with Jack Reed, her new husband.

Louise had only lived in the Village for a little over a year before she and Jack left for Petrograd. In her previous home of Portland, Oregon, she had been friends with Sara Bard Field, a suffragist, poet, and social activist who'd gotten to know Marie Jenney Howe during her time in Cleveland. In 1915, Alice Paul had deputized Sara to gather half a million signatures in favor of suffrage at the Panama-Pacific Exposition in San Francisco and drive them cross-country to the White House—an extraordinary two-month odyssey that received extensive press coverage. After her trip, Sara was staying in New York with her friend Ida Rauh, and the women took the newly arrived Louise as a guest to a Heterodoxy meeting. Through the club, Louise became friends with several of its regular members, including Madeleine Doty, Inez Milholland, and Stella Ballantine.[4]

Bessie Beatty was working as a columnist on the *San Francisco Bulletin* at the time of her trip to Russia. In San Francisco, she had covered labor strikes and, most recently, the framing of radicals Thomas Mooney and Warren K. Billings as culprits in the deadly Preparedness Day bombing in July 1916. After the war, she would move to New York to become an editor at the women's magazine *McCall's* and eventually make her name as a radio commentator. In Russia, Bessie was one of the first civilians to enter the Winter Palace after the fall of the provisional government. She interviewed Leon Trotsky and the women soldiers of

Bessie Beatty was one of several Heterodoxy
journalists to report from the war zone and
the Russian Revolution. (*Credit: Schlesinger
Library, Harvard Radcliffe Institute*)

the notorious all-female "Battalion of Death." Inspired by them,
she wrote that women could and would fight in wars, that they
were "potential soldiers . . . and will continue to be until the
muddled old world is remade upon a basis of human freedom
and safety."[5]

Rheta Childe Dorr had traveled to Russia at the beginning of
1917, but over the course of the year grew increasingly critical
of the Bolsheviks and wary of the increasing violence, and had
left by the time Madeleine arrived. Her book *Inside the Russian
Revolution*, published well before the October Revolution that
toppled Alexander Kerensky's moderate provisional government, ends on a note of cautious optimism. "Man must hope,"

she writes, before explaining that what she's witnessed in Russia has neither softened her own socialist beliefs nor hardened them into anarchy. "I believe that the next economic development will be socialism, that is coöperation, common ownership of the principal means of production, and the administration of all departments of government for the collective good of all the people." She cautions that Russia has placed too much power in the hands of a small governing class, but that its people are "developing"—in industry, skills, and economics—at a remarkable rate. "The lesson of Russia to America is patient, intelligent, clear-sighted preparation for the next economic development," she concludes, stressing the importance of universal education. It was a vain hope: "patient" was the last possible adjective to describe the events of the next few months.[6]

All four women wrote books about their experiences in Russia, showing different levels of sympathy with the Bolsheviks and optimism for the revolution, but all foregrounding an interest in women and the potential of the Bolshevik program for reinventing their place in society. Louise Bryant's *Six Red Months in Russia* and Bessie Beatty's *The Red Heart of Russia* both focused fully on the revolutionary nation, demonstrating the appetite of publishers for firsthand accounts. Madeleine's experiences in Russia, meanwhile, formed the basis of several chapters of her book *Behind Battle Lines: Around the World in 1918*. Optimistic as they were—Bessie's declaration in her book "I had been alive at a great moment, and knew it was great" was typical—these feminist observers of the new order in Russia were not entirely starry-eyed. Overthrowing an autocratic leader did not extinguish the habits of deference, hierarchy, and patriarchy that kept men and women in their place the world over. At a major political convention in St. Petersburg, Bessie counted just twenty-three women among sixteen hundred delegates. "Many other women were in evidence, but they were behind the samovars, serving tea and caviar and sausage sandwiches," she noted. "Some wore red armbands, ushered the men to their seats, took stenographic reports of proceedings, and counted ballots. It was so natural that it almost made me homesick."[7]

Back in Greenwich Village, the Russian Revolution was celebrated by many as a harbinger of the glorious global socialist future. But even within the bohemians' precious oasis, the dream was under threat. The evolution of the Village in the 1910s was dizzyingly fast. Gentrification and urban planning were changing the physical character of the neighborhood just as surely as the radical backlash was targeting its central cast of characters. The time that had elapsed from the era when it was rather a daring thing for a middle-class New Yorker to visit the neighborhood, let alone move there, to the moment when its tearooms and artists' studios had become tourist attractions, was only about five years. In her postcard snapshots of bohemia, most taken around 1917, Jessie Tarbox Beals captured a world on the cusp of vanishing into cliché: cobbled alleys and basement drinking dens; young men in spectacles flirting with bobbed-haired young women in smocks; tearooms with bare floorboards, kitted out with ikat wall hangings, repurposed church pews, and wooden tables with white cloth runners; basement shops filled with antiques and tat; Polly Holladay forking servings of spaghetti out of a communal bowl; Romany Marie in front of her samovar in her Russian-themed tavern; a smiling young woman in an oversized beret at the door of her art gallery, who made a living as a tour guide to the neighborhood. In one, Jessie poses in front of her own art gallery, which she established in 1917. Local guidebooks included a who's who of local characters—Henrietta Rodman, "who bearded the Board of Education"; Susan Glaspell, "who writes all the best plays"; and "The Old Masses Crowd"—and carried advertisements for cafés, shops, and bohemian dressmakers. Fania Mindell, Margaret Sanger's translator at the Brownsville birth control clinic, ran "Little Russia," selling "copper and brass articles" as well as hats, scarves, and handbags "embroidered in true Russian fashion," while the Washington Square Bookshop boasted, "We have a complete shelf of Psychoanalysis and the Psychology of Sex."[8]

Floyd Dell lamented as bitterly as any New Yorker ever has when their neighborhood gets discovered and the rents go up. "Fabulous prices were charged for anything with a roof over it," he complained. "Then the show-places, with imbecile names, began to be opened—'picturesque' (ie, unsanitary) places where the Uptowners pay two dollars for a bad sandwich and a thimbleful of coffee, and look at each other and think they are seeing life."[9] The irony, that Floyd himself had been instrumental in promoting the Village as a haven for free thinking and free loving since his arrival just a few years earlier, was apparently lost on him.

The influx of outsiders and the rising rents were the visible tip of a more aggressive destruction: as construction and transportation projects opened up the neighborhood, so an official cleanup targeted the nonconformist and transgressive elements whose behavior and haunts were not so "picturesque." The Village had always been a queer haven, but there was an almost eightfold increase in the number of men convicted in Manhattan for "homosexual solicitation" between 1916 and 1920.[10] Homophobic cultural panics targeted dance halls and cabarets, in particular, along with the anything-goes artists' balls and "pagan routs" that the Village had been known for. In 1917, Djuna Barnes, in a piece called "How the Villagers Amuse Themselves," reported from a dance at Webster Hall, already scrubbed of its most subversive elements. She quotes a young trans man, Alexis, who channels Oscar Wilde as he complains, "These days, one can sit in the gutter of Manhattan and arise covered with nothing worse than the shadow of a star." Even in "its most corrupt sewers," one finds "nothing but a lot of castoff ethics."[11]

The linking of a wide range of pursuits in the name of liberty and *the new*—suffrage, birth control, socialism, art, theater, psychology—was what gave Heterodoxy and the Village their energy. One could talk about anything, *anything*! Now, that sparkling web was tightening into a net. One could be convicted for anything (*anything!*), too. The Russian Revolution lent urgency to the government's crackdown on the constitutional liberties that middle-class radicals had largely taken for granted. The freewheeling welter of people who rubbed shoulders in the Village—free lovers and anarchists, socialists and feminists, suffragists and civil rights activists, artists and social workers, journalists and poets—were the same individuals and publications targeted during and after World War I.

The first of the two trials of the editorial staff of *The Masses* took place in the spring of 1918, after the authorities finally identified "treasonous material" in the pages of the August 1917 issue—guest-edited by the future Catholic radical Dorothy Day, although she was not charged alongside Max Eastman, Floyd Dell, John Reed, and the other editors. The only woman arraigned was a new contributor, Josephine Bell, who had never met any of her alleged coconspirators before and was dismissed by Judge Learned Hand before the trial began. The judge also dismissed the charge of "conspiracy to cause mutiny and refusal of duty" (i.e., conscription) before the jury began its deliberations. But the judge's support, and the generally confident, even carnivalesque atmosphere of the trial, could not quite overcome the unease of the situation. The jury's actions, especially, made it clear that the Red Scare was not just a top-down, official phenomenon. Despite being reminded by the judge that the defendants had a right to hold whatever political views they chose, the majority were eager to convict. When the single dissenting voice on the twelve-man jury was revealed to be a Socialist, the other jurors attempted to have him charged as a conspirator as well, and when that failed, to drag him out into the street and physically attack him. A hasty mistrial was declared. At the second trial, in September, there was still no unanimous decision against the magazine—which was, in any case, defunct.

Max had already moved on—he and Crystal launched *The Liberator* in March 1918. The new magazine was less provocative than its predecessor, its editors painfully aware that the world had changed profoundly, and that a magazine that was constantly silenced was not much use to anyone. When Max passed major responsibility to Floyd Dell in 1922, art and poetry became more of a focus than international news reporting. The Harlem Renaissance poet Claude McKay was closely involved with the magazine after meeting Crystal in 1919—in his autobiography he described her as "the most beautiful white woman I ever knew," who embodied "all that was fundamentally fine, noble and genuine in American democracy."[12] Many *Masses* editors and contributors were featured in the new magazine's pages, which were thin and fragile to keep costs down. Inez Haynes Irwin reported on her experiences in wartime France, and Louise Bryant from Russia; Crystal herself wrote a dispatch from revolutionary Hungary and invited Mary Heaton Vorse by telegram to cover a strike at the end of 1919. She wrote praising Mary's gift for finding the "vivid human story," indicating that her initial dislike had warmed into, at least, professional respect.[13]

In May 1918, the Sedition Act had widened the already broad scope of the Espionage Act to target anti-war and anti-government sentiments in speech as well as writing. Already, in March, Rose Pastor Stokes was facing serious charges after making an anti-war speech to a women's club in Kansas City, then writing in to the *Kansas City Star* to clarify its report of her remarks, declaring that she had certainly *not* suggested that every citizen ought to support the government unquestioningly: "No government which is for the profiteers can also be for the people, while the government is for the profiteers."[14] The Bureau of Investigation arrested her a few days later in Missouri, and Graham traveled out by train to pay her $10,000 bail. At her trial, the prosecutor attacked her as an inherently treacherous "foreign-born woman" whose advocacy of birth control was further proof of her degeneracy. She was given a ten-year prison sentence, which she appealed and which was ultimately dismissed in 1920. A note to Marie Jenney Howe around this time makes her caution and defiance quite clear. "What I would inscribe myself, I dare not, lest (should this be found by the D[epartment] of J[ustice]) you too, be rendered 'hors de la loi'! But—you know the bond."[15]

In the final months of the war, a battle opened on a new and unexpected front. Beginning in the spring, a virulent new strain of influenza arrived in the United States. Appearing first in a military camp in Kansas, it spread rapidly among soldiers as they massed and mobilized around the country and traveled to ports to ship out overseas. Nicknamed "Spanish" for no loftier reason than that Spain had remained neutral during the Great War, the flu caused far more deaths than bullets and bayonets in the two years that it raged, killing tens of millions worldwide. The deaths were clustered disproportionately among young people in their late twenties and early thirties—researchers now believe this was because they missed exposure to a similar strain of the flu as children, while older and younger people had been exposed and thus had antibodies to fight it.

In New York, the flu appeared in August on a ship arriving from Europe, but by the time the health commissioner placed the port under quarantine a month later, it had spread throughout the city. Randolph Bourne, the thirty-two-year-old journalist and radical who had been a Village fixture and friend to many in Heterodoxy, died on Christmas Day of complications from the virus. Neith Boyce and Hutch Hapgood's eldest son,

Boyce, nicknamed Harry, was another victim of the epidemic, and Neith devoted herself to writing a biography of him.

That same fall, in New York, women were lining up to exercise their hard-won right to vote for the first time in their lives. Katharine Anthony described "the satisfaction of registering for my first vote . . . at the little tailor-shop across the street. It was the first day and half the line were women." By the time registration for the midterm elections ended in October, women made up more than a third of 648,000 registered voters in New York City—and the city recorded more than four thousand new flu cases.[16] In the elections on November 5, despite Wilson's efforts, Republicans won a majority in the House and the Senate. A week later, the Armistice signaled the end, at last, of nearly five years of unrelenting war that had killed and displaced millions of people and redrawn the political map of the world.

The end of the war did not end the government suppression of free speech and leftist activism—far from it. Despite the government harassment, the labor movement was more active and confrontational than ever. In the last year of the war, several thousand wildcat strikes sparked across the country; it's been estimated that by the end of 1919, one in five American workers, from miners to stage actors, had walked out on strike.[17] IWW activists in California were convicted of violating the Espionage Act two months after the Armistice, an event Katharine Anthony saw as evidence that "the measures of suppression" would "continue unchanged."

In January 1919, Marie Jenney Howe was taken into custody outside her Village apartment by "Secret Service hounds" and questioned about her activities and her radical friends. She was not allowed to contact her husband or a lawyer while she was grilled about her suffrage work and socialist and pacifist convictions, which were now treasonous.[18] There were increasingly ominous signs that radicalism was the government's new enemy, and it would fight this war just as fiercely as it had Germany. In New York, the Lusk Committee—the Joint Legislative Committee to Investigate Radical Activities—set its sights on Elizabeth Gurley Flynn, for her work with the IWW and, more recently, on behalf of Black activists, who were also directly targeted. Attorney General Mitchell A. Palmer's raids began in October 1919, targeting hundreds of immigrants, particularly Russians, for attack, imprisonment, and deportation. Elizabeth and the Workers' Defense Union scrambled to help where they could, and Henrietta Rodman turned the Feminist Alliance over to her "as a support committee."[19] But the pace was simply too much. Emma Goldman was deported to her native Russia on December 21, 1919; two weeks later, almost five and a half thousand people were arrested for suspected radical activities in a single day.[20]

In 1920, the Socialist Party once again nominated as its candidate for president the veteran leader Eugene Debs, who was sixty-four years old and incarcerated in federal prison in Atlanta. He had been arrested during the summer of 1918 and charged under the Sedition Act for speaking against the military draft; he was sentenced and imprisoned the following spring, with Rose Pastor Stokes at his side. Unable to traverse the country in his train carriage dubbed the "Red Special," as he had done during previous campaigns, Debs nonetheless won just over 900,000 votes, or 3.4 percent of the electorate—almost as many as he had won eight years earlier, when he'd garnered 6 percent of the vote, at the high point of his own and his party's popularity. But the backlash was thorough. In the early 1920s, the moderate American Federation of Labor lost more than a million members, many of whom flocked to the ascendant Ku Klux Klan, and more than thirty states outlawed the display of red flags. Civil war and violence in Russia soured American optimism around the Russian Revolution, the more so after the Bolsheviks won the war and outlawed all opposition parties. In 1921, Emma Goldman published her book *My Disillusionment in Russia* and left the country for good.

Her defection enraged Rose Pastor Stokes, who said she ought to be "burned in effigy."[21] Rose remained a true believer. In November 1922, she and Max Eastman were among the American delegation in Moscow for the celebration of the revolution's fifth anniversary; Max would soon renounce his former left-wing beliefs, while Rose would cling and harden hers. In the period of her arrest and trial, she became a founder of the group that would become the American Communist Party. She was particularly involved with recruiting Black left-wing leaders, several of whom she hosted for dinner at her Greenwich Village apartment in 1919, including Claude McKay. Her activities began to divide her from Graham (and even more so, his family) both personally and politically, and he filed for divorce in 1925. Her commitment to the cause deepened, even as she disappeared from the public eye—Cinderella turned out of the palace. Some years later, a reporter tracked Rose down to a small apartment in the East Village where she was living with her second husband, a Communist Party member some seventeen years her junior, and writing her unfinished autobiography. She was diagnosed with breast cancer in 1930, and her old friends, including Elizabeth Gurley Flynn and Langston Hughes, held a fundraiser to help her travel to Germany for an experimental treatment. Despite their efforts, she died in Frankfurt in 1933, aged just fifty-four.[22]

Shortly after Rose's divorce, in 1926, Elizabeth Gurley Flynn was toasted at a testimonial dinner, sponsored by a roster of famous names from the American Left, who paid tribute to her years of tireless work in the IWW and beyond. Her personal life, however, was falling apart. Having just discovered the true identity of her sister's child, and thus living proof of Carlo's infidelity under her own roof, she turned to Mary Heaton Vorse, who rushed from Provincetown to New York to comfort her. Mary was moved to see "her terrific will crashing against circumstance" and horrified by the way her grief diminished her to a feminine stereotype—"her talking like some girl, a jealous pitifully unbalanced creature."[23] In poor health and in need of rest and nurture, Elizabeth moved to Portland, Oregon, to live with Marie Equi, a doctor and IWW supporter who was notorious for performing abortions and dispensing birth control information.

In the mid-1930s, Elizabeth returned to New York and resumed her activities but in a very different climate for left-wing activism. She, too, embraced Communism and would be imprisoned for her activities during the Cold War. The shadow of that second, still more paralyzing Red Scare makes it difficult to assess the contributions of radicals in the early twentieth century and to recover the optimism they once felt, on the verge of revolution. Within Heterodoxy, however, both Rose and Elizabeth—along with Rose Strunsky and Mary Heaton Vorse—helped push the club's feminist thinking further to the left, to embed socialism within suffrage activism, and to challenge the club to consider the full spectrum of exclusion and oppression in American society.

Over the summer and fall of 1919, the violence against Black Americans convulsed the country, in what James Weldon Johnson dubbed the "Red Summer." The aftermath of the return of soldiers from the Great War, battle-scarred and jobless, coupled with ongoing strikes and perceptions that Black workers were being brought in as scabs, led to more than twenty-five white outbursts of violence against Black citizens and property in cities and towns across the country. Some of the worst was in Chicago, where violence raged on the South Side for nearly two weeks after a Black boy swimming in a supposedly white section of Lake Michigan was stoned and drowned. In rural Elaine, Arkansas, it is estimated that well over two hundred people were massacred in the wake of an effort by Black sharecroppers to unionize. The Elaine Massacre made it clear that the crackdown on political radicals and the racist violence of the Red Summer were inextricably linked. In July 1919, *The Liberator* published Claude McKay's poem "If We Must Die," a powerful rallying cry that became known as a "manifesto" of the Harlem Renaissance. Often paired on the program of Black public events with James Weldon Johnson's "Lift Ev'ry Voice," the poem encapsulates the fatalism and fury of the moment, building to its closing lines: "Like men we'll face the murderous, cowardly pack, / Pressed to the wall, dying, but fighting back!"[24]

In September 1919, Marie Jenney Howe replied to a letter from Grace Nail Johnson, assuring her, "Indeed I did read all about the race riots," and noting that "the liberal weeklies and the Call straightened out the newspaper misrepresentations." But her tone is far from optimistic. "The public is more callous than ever to horrors and injustice," she continues. "The war has made us insensitive, and the number and extent of injustices make one despair." It's clear from the letter that Marie was highly conscious of the importance of press coverage to spur political action, and of the inaccurate way that the white mainstream press reported on racist violence. She refers to the recent attack on John Shillady, a white NAACP activist, as "almost a good thing if it wasn't too hard on him," as it spurred a congressional investigation into lynching.[25]

Since the Amenia Conference in 1916, James Weldon Johnson had been tireless in his work for the NAACP, traveling, lecturing, and opening branches across the South. Within three years, there were more than 150 branches in the South, and the white membership had almost entirely ceded power to Black leaders.[26] As the organization's leader from 1920, James began the practice of flying an enormous black flag from the window of its office in Greenwich Village that announced A MAN WAS

LYNCHED YESTERDAY. This kind of street protest—provocative, unavoidable, motionless, and silent—bears some comparison with the way other activists, like the White House suffrage pickets had been using bodies and billboards to make themselves seen and heard. But as those movements had already seen, spectacle alone did not make change. The NAACP had recently published a detailed report on lynching over the past thirty years, demonstrating yet again that it was a national problem, that its victims included women and children, and that the alleged rape of white women was no more than a shallow pretext. But under Woodrow Wilson, who had overseen a steady increase in racial segregation in the federal government, Black leaders had little hope of their concerns reaching the highest levels of power.

Some therefore placed their hope in a different political approach. Not long after the violence in East St. Louis in 1917, Leonidas Dyer, a Republican congressman from that city, introduced legislation to make lynching and mob violence a federal felony. The Dyer Bill was intended to counter the local prejudices and power dynamics that let white defendants off the hook, and it included sentencing guidelines: a minimum of five years in prison for anyone who participated in a lynching, and fines to be paid to victims and their families, as well as fines and prison time for anyone who failed to protect a victim or to prosecute the perpetrators. After being introduced several times, the Dyer Bill finally passed the House of Representatives in January 1922, after another powerful silent protest in Washington, DC. The Senate, however, dominated by a powerful bloc of segregationist Southern Democrats, filibustered the bill, and the NAACP stepped up its campaign. Flexing their political power in the wake of the Nineteenth Amendment, Black women took up the fight energetically on the ground, pressuring Republican senators and congressmen who, at the time, worked in the party most supportive of civil rights. In Delaware, for instance,

Grace Nail Johnson's friend Alice Dunbar Nelson—writer, teacher, and widow of the highly respected poet Paul Laurence Dunbar—led a group of African American women to defeat their local congressman, who had opposed the Dyer Bill.[27]

In early 1922, Grace Nail Johnson, who rarely took an independent lead as an activist, became the New York representative of a new women's group calling itself the Anti-Lynching Crusaders. Drawing attention to violence against Black women in particular, the group brought together members of the NAACP and the National Association of Colored Women (NACW), headed by Mary Church Terrell. Marie Jenney Howe promptly requested that Grace address Heterodoxy on the issue. According to Marie, Grace "modestly hesitated, partly because of the harrowing nature of the subject," but the club pressed Marie to invite her again: "Several expressed themselves as strongly in favor of hearing all about it and you were strongly urged to speak. So now I hope you will accept and will know that everybody wants you and your subject."[28]

Although the Anti-Lynching Crusaders continued to argue that rape was not a true pretext for lynching, they no longer focused on the concurrent sexual victimization of Black women. Instead, they concentrated on stories of victims who had been hanged and burned alive, of mutilated pregnant women and murdered children. It was a tactic calculated to capture the support of white women, especially those with roots in the abolitionist movement, where horror was also used as a tactic to move powerful people to action. Announcing their intention to enroll a million women nationwide in their movement, and to raise a dollar from each of them before January 1, 1923, Grace described the Crusaders simply as "a band of women united to stop lynching." Sharing a list of eighty-three women lynched between 1889 and 1921, organized by state, Grace pressed the appeal as a nationwide call that would enlist every club and organization for women in the country. But she also appealed specifically to white women, naming Consumers' League head Florence Kelley as "an active and interested supporter" and her fellow Heterodite, the novelist Zona Gale, as a volunteer.[29]

Zona Gale was also mentioned by the national leader of the Anti-Lynching Crusaders, the clubwoman Mary Talbert, in a letter to Mary White Ovington in October, asking for her endorsement. "This is the first time in the history of the colored women that they have turned to their sister white organizations and asked for moral and financial support," she wrote, "and as we have never failed you in any cause that has come to US, we do not believe that YOU will fail us now." Grace Johnson cited the efforts of white women who had protested—and in some cases, prevented—lynchings in Texas, Georgia, Alabama, and Tennessee and suggested that the new group would be "following [their] lead." By appealing to gender solidarity and, in the wake of WWI, patriotic pride, the Anti-Lynching Crusaders emphasized inclusiveness. "American women are realizing that until this crime is ended, no home is sacred from violence, no part of the country from race clashes, and the fair name of our country is soiled throughout the civilized world," Grace said.[30] It is worth noting that a hundred years later, despite repeated efforts by legislators, lynching is still not recognized as a federal hate crime. The most recent effort, the Emmett Till Anti-lynching Act, was passed 410–4 in the House in February 2020, but as of this writing remains stalled in the Senate due to Senator Rand Paul's objections.

During the 1920s, partly as a result of the NAACP's tireless efforts to keep the issue in the press and to prosecute perpetrators, the overall number of lynchings nationwide declined. But intimidation and violence against Black people continued with the rise of the KKK, thousands of whom marched in white robes in front of the US capitol after the end of the war. Elizabeth Gurley Flynn and the Workers' Defense Union mobilized to protest the organization and to counter its racist messaging. In June 1921, after the massacre and destruction of the Black community in Tulsa, Oklahoma, five hundred people attended a WDU meeting in Harlem to discuss the events and plan protests.[31] Black activists and white leftist organizations were increasingly recognizing common cause in the 1920s, as the conservative tide turned against them both.

To many freethinking New Yorkers, the arrival of Prohibition at the dawn of the new decade was much more than a cramp in style. It symbolized the defeat of Heterodoxy's, and the Village's, most cherished values: cosmopolitanism and the exchange of ideas across borders, women's rights, tolerance of difference, socialism, and freedom of speech. Like later drug laws, Prohibition disproportionately targeted poor communities and people of color, and ushered in a new, far-reaching, national law enforcement structure. It was a symbol of the triumph of white Christian nativism, a tide that would only increase in power throughout the decade. Yet the same decade would witness an unprecedented visibility for Black Americans in the literature and culture of New York and the nation.

Harlem was coming into its own as a center of cultural as well as political power for Black Americans when Grace Johnson's real estate developer brother Jack helped build the YMCA next door to the Johnsons' apartment on 135th Street. It opened in 1919 as a cultural center and home base for new transplants to the neighborhood, including Claude McKay, Langston Hughes, and Richard Wright. Around the corner on 136th was the townhouse owned by the heiress A'lelia Walker, daughter of the millionaire Madame C. J. Walker, who was nicknamed the "joy-goddess of 1920s Harlem" by Langston Hughes and who hosted a salon every bit as thrilling and avant-garde as Mabel

Dodge's "Evenings" had been a decade earlier. At the height of the Harlem Renaissance, James Weldon Johnson's novel *The Autobiography of an Ex-Colored Man* was reprinted under his own, now very well-known name, by the prestigious Alfred A. Knopf.

Although Grace allegedly looked down on A'lelia Walker and refused to attend her famously decadent parties, she and James were equally well known as hosts. Sometime in the 1920s a party was thrown in their honor at the Greenwich Village studio of Charles Studin, a lawyer who worked pro bono for the NAACP—the invitation, depicting a jitterbugging couple in silhouette on bright orange card, was illustrated by the young Harlem Renaissance artist Aaron Douglas.[32] In 1930, James Weldon Johnson wrote Claude McKay reminiscing about a party he hosted just before the latter left for Russia, "We often speak about that party back in '22, wasn't it. Do you know that was the first getting together of the white and black literati on a purely social plane. Such parties are now common in New York, but I doubt if any since has been more representative." He named a few guests, including Heterodoxy's Ruth Hale and her husband Heywood Broun, the drama critic of the *New York World* who was a fixture of the Algonquin Round Table, plus Freda Kirchwey of *The Nation*, and "on our side," Du Bois, Walter White, and the literary critic of *The Crisis*, Jessie Redmon Fauset. "I think the party helped to start something," he added. Claude McKay also remembered the occasion as "the first of the Bohemia-elite interracial parties in Harlem which became so popular during the highly propagandized Negro renaissance period."

Claude also described a far more raucous event held around the same time, downtown at the home of Inez Milholland's widower, Eugen Boissevain, in Greenwich Village. Max and Crystal Eastman were there, along with Doris Stevens and her new husband, and for added glamour, Charlie Chaplin, who was an acquaintance of Max. "The party was warming up with Jamaica rum cocktails and snatches of radical gossip," when the political activist Hubert Harrison arrived, in the company of a working-class Black sex worker. In his description of the party, Claude makes the woman the butt of several uncomfortable jokes as she pursues Charlie Chaplin throughout the evening for an autograph and gives out her business card in an effort to entice the radicals uptown. Giving a hint of how far propriety and dignity still constrained Harlem socializing, Claude notes with some satisfaction that this story infuriated the "elite of Harlem," who insisted the Negro race had been betrayed.[33]

Greenwich Village's entwined commitment to creative and political progress in the 1910s continued to be an inspiration to other bohemias, both uptown and farther afield. Harlem and the "New Negro" emerged as a cultural beacon, a physical yet mythologized location to rival pre-war Greenwich Village and its iconic inhabitant, the New Woman. The freedom to embody *the new* might have been limited by class, in particular, but the existence of a pattern or a model of a different way to live could resonate far beyond a few privileged individuals.

Chapter 15

THE FUTURE OF FEMINISM

IN THE WAKE OF THE SUFFRAGE VICTORY IN 1920, THE FRAGILE unity among the different forces fighting for women's rights splintered. Feminists and women's rights activists disagreed on where they ought to focus their fight moving forward, with some pushing for an Equal Rights Amendment, and others for less obviously gender-based causes. Ideological differences that had been laid aside for the sake of the vote now opened up like cracks in the pavement. "All we can say is that the suffrage movement is ended," Crystal Eastman remarked in 1921. Coming away disappointed and bitter after a three-day Woman's Party convention that celebrated the suffrage victory but refused to engage with any ongoing issues of injustice, Crystal outlined her own vision for a truly equal future. Her manifesto contained many goals—from state-sponsored maternity benefits to full birth control access—for which feminists are still fighting today.[1] She was far from alone in grappling with the question of what women's rights now meant.

In an effort to promote her own broader vision of feminism, Crystal organized the Women's Freedom Congress in New York in March 1919, which brought together more than five hundred attendees to hear speakers on topics including labor law, cooperative living, birth control, and the future of Black women. On this subject the speaker was Minnie G. Brown, a clubwoman and NAACP member who was an active promoter of Black musical talent, and herself a soprano nicknamed "the human mockingbird." Crystal's own speech, "Feminism," focused on the way women were held back by "restrictive legislation" (at the time, they still didn't have the vote) and "repressive social custom." She argued that it was the combination of both that "halts them in almost every field of endeavor, and effectually marks them as an inferior class."[2] This was a familiar refrain for her. Though she might have rejected the military metaphor, the point was that the wide range of seemingly separate battles in which feminists were occupied was, in fact, an interconnected front in a much bigger war. The question was whether any meaningful victory was on the horizon.

The speaker roster at the Freedom Congress included several of Crystal's Heterodoxy friends and veterans of the previous decade's feminist battles, including Elizabeth Gurley Flynn, Henrietta Rodman, and Elinor Byrns. A fellow NYU law graduate some years older than Crystal, Elinor had helped to organize the first major New York suffrage parade but had been moved by the urgency of the war years to focus more fully on peace. In the mid-1920s, she would draft and lobby for a constitutional amendment declaring war illegal and banning the United States from manufacturing or selling weapons or training soldiers; she believed war was fundamentally gendered, an activity that had "enslaved" men, and that the "outlawry of war" was thus a naturally feminist project.[3] Elinor called Heterodoxy "the nicest place I know" and declared she was "proud to be a part of it."[4] Nevertheless, she differed from Crystal and the WPP in her embrace of nonresistance, the principle of opposing all violence (better known today as nonviolent resistance and associated with Gandhi). This went well beyond the NYC-WPP's opposition to World War I in particular.[5]

For the *New York Times*, writer Helen M. Wayne attended the conference and produced a report that offers a chilling glimpse of the brewing conservative, women-led backlash against progressive feminism—a backlash as influential, in its insidious way, as the brute-force external crackdowns of the Red Scare.[6] It was typical of the way post-suffrage feminist concerns were mocked as trivial while also being attacked as threats to the family and the whole foundation of society. Noting first that she has missed the morning session featuring "Greenwich Village notables," the writer comforts herself with the thought that "each speaker was either an avowed Socialist or anarchist," and therefore predictable in her arguments. "I could be sure that each one had used her particular hobby or grievance—as the case might be—to urge Socialist measures of improvement." She goes on to record an overheard conversation between two women, one with long hair and the other a "bobbed-hair type," parenthetically noting how "the ugly ones are more ugly for the bobbing!" The point of the purported conversation is not its substance, a racist deliberation over the marital attitudes of Jewish women, but the conclusion from the long-haired woman that "it takes a pretty radical person to be even a little conservative in these wild days." A later speaker, coming after a "pretty woman . . . hurling at us her views on birth control," is another conservative, a teacher of "sex hygiene" who advocates for teaching "old-fashioned virtues" rather than contraception. Following several speakers advocating for day care and communal housekeeping schemes, a pair of "despised conservatives" protest in the name of traditional values. Even though these speakers apparently got the biggest applause, the continued emphasis of the piece is how daring and outspoken these "radical-conservatives" are, despite sharing a stage, and what sounds like a robust debate, with the progressives. Concluding her report—she skips Louise Bryant's presentation on Soviet Russia—the writer wonders aloud to her male companion whether there is "German stuff" or Bolshevism behind it all.[7]

The Freedom Congress did not become a regular event. It had gone over budget, and its platform was judged too radical by the leaders of the Woman's Peace Party, which had become the Women's International League since the end of the war. They also judged its wide-ranging talks to have strayed too far from the central issue of pacifism, and Crystal resigned her leadership position in the organization. The organization folded, and what had been the WPP was absorbed into the larger Women's International League for Peace and Freedom. Pacifism had been a difficult, divisive, and often lonely cause, yet it inspired deep reflection on what it meant to be a woman, and a citizen, at a time of national crisis. Her peace activism led Crystal to join with Norman Thomas and Roger Baldwin—who married her friend Madeleine Doty in 1919—to found the organization that would become the American Civil Liberties Union (ACLU). Alarmed by the overreach of the government against its citizens during the war, they believed that safeguarding the right of dissent was of paramount importance in an unstable new world.

In the first flush of the suffrage victory, politicians were still interested in courting women's rights leaders as an influential voting bloc. This allowed the National Consumers League to push for legislation that (modestly) funded healthcare for mothers and children. The Sheppard-Towner Act, passed in 1922, was the first welfare legislation passed in a generation. It was only in effect for a few years, however, and came under sustained assault from conservatives, including the Daughters of the American Revolution, founded in 1890 to promote a patriotic (and highly selective) version of American history. After joining the large pro-suffrage coalition, it wheeled sharply to the right in the 1920s and attacked the act as "an entering wedge of communism."[8] It was also a harbinger of what would be the major split in the women's movement in the 1920s, between those who wanted to carve out special protections and provisions under the law for women and children and those who believed that guaranteeing women's equality with men was the only way to guarantee their freedom.

Also in 1922, the National League of Women Voters, led by Inez Haynes Irwin's old friend from Radcliffe, Maud Wood Park, pushed to pass the Married Women's Independent Nationality Act. This was an effort to undo a piece of glaringly sexist legislation, the 1907 Expatriation Act, which stripped US citizenship from American women who married foreign men, while entitling the alien wives of American men to naturalization. Both Crystal Eastman and Inez Milholland had fallen foul of this law: Crystal, when she married the British Walter Fuller in 1916; and Inez, on marrying Eugen Boissevain, who was Belgian, in 1913. Because it was retroactive, the law also ensnared suffrage leader Harriot Stanton Blatch, who'd married an Englishman in 1902. Women in Harriot's situation were not even notified of the change, so many did not even know they had lost their citizenship until they attempted to travel or register to vote in one of the states where it was legal—evidence of how unimportant women's independent legal identities were considered at the time. The clear inequity of the Expatriation Act sharpened the attention of many suffragists toward the second-class status of women under American law. There had been several efforts to amend or overturn the act during the 1910s, including a push by Jeannette Rankin, but nothing was done until after the war. Even then, the new act carried its own racist exclusion for American women who married Asian men; until 1931, those women still lost their citizenship. This was a compromise with the nativist forces that were in the ascendant at the time, and a sign of things to come: bills in 1921 and, especially,

1924 dramatically curtailed US immigration with quotas and exclusions.

The issue of a woman keeping her name upon marriage continued to preoccupy Heterodoxy for its social, professional, and legal implications. In 1921, Ruth Hale, a writer for *Vogue* and *Vanity Fair*, gathered a new group, the Lucy Stone League, named in honor of the radical nineteenth-century women's rights activist, under the rallying cry "My Name Is the Symbol of My Identity, and Must Not Be Lost." The charter membership reads like a "Heterodoxy roster" and included Katharine Anthony, Crystal Eastman, Zona Gale, Susan Glaspell, Fannie Hurst, Fola La Follette, Alice Duer Miller, Ruth Pickering, Grace Potter, Mary Shaw, and Marie Jenney Howe, who refused to call herself, in accordance with convention, "Mrs. Frederic Howe." Its honorary vice president, naturally, was Charlotte Perkins Gilman.[9] The campaign to keep one's own name on marriage spoke to a real and fraught question of what women were: citizens, people, their "full human selves," in Marie Jenney Howe's phrase, or eternal adjuncts to men? As the writing of this book has proven, figuring out what to call a much-married woman, who published under more than one name, is no easy task.

In 1911, when Ida Rauh married Max Eastman, she was profiled in the New York *World* under the headline A Miss, Though Married. In the article she strongly hints that she would have preferred to avoid marriage altogether: "It was with us a placating of convention, because if we had gone counter to convention, it would have been too much bother for the gain." Her young husband, by contrast, sounded full of zeal over the principle of the thing, telling the reporter that he got "quite cross" at his wife being known simply as "Mrs. Eastman," and insisting, "I do not want to absorb my wife's identity in mine."[10]

When Fola La Follette married George Middleton, also in 1911, at the age of twenty-nine, she made the same decision, declaring, "The point is that the name I was given at birth, the name under which I established my identity, should be mine through life." Onstage at Cooper Union in 1914, Fola had argued that all women, regardless of marital status, should be known as Miss. It was, to her, a question of independence and identity: complicated for Fola, nevertheless, by the fact that her surname connected her to her very famous father. Five years later, at Crystal's Freedom Congress, Fola reiterated her points—which resonated very differently after her father's public war opposition and her own experience of notoriety under her own name. (The *New York Times* reporter in the audience mocked her for her "pathetic earnestness" and judged her to be anti-men.)[11]

Marriage was a defining factor in women's citizenship. After the passage of the Nineteenth Amendment, NWP activist Doris Stevens undertook a substantial research project to compile and analyze data on women's citizenship laws around the world. In 1921, she married Dudley Field Malone, the lawyer who staunchly defended the White House pickets in court, and who had quit his prestigious, presidential-appointed post as Collector of the Port of New York in protest at Wilson's treatment of the women. Doris kept her name when she married, and when the couple divorced at the end of the decade, she refused to accept any financial support.

Madeleine Doty made the same choices when she married ACLU cofounder Roger Baldwin and made her vows public. "We deny without reservation the whole conception of property in marriage," the couple announced, linking their partnership instead to "the great revolutionary struggle for human freedom, so intense, so full of promise today." Her divorce announcement, seven years later, was just as bold: she told newspapers that "marriage is a link, not a handcuff" and that alimony was an admission that a woman could not provide for herself. Without children to consider, "No self-respecting feminist would accept alimony," she vowed.[12]

The best-known effort toward securing women's status as full citizens in the wake of the Nineteenth Amendment was the Equal Rights Amendment, drafted by Alice Paul, with help from Crystal Eastman, Doris Stevens, and other National Woman's Party members, and submitted to Congress in 1923. The amendment was the outcome of the continued single-mindedness of the NWP leader, who had turned away African American women who wanted her party's help in battling disenfranchisement efforts in the South, enraging those who had thrown in their lot to help win the vote.[13] Ending legal discrimination against women was the plain and simple (and single) goal, and the wording of the proposed amendment—that "men and women shall have equal rights throughout the United States"—equally plain. But it was far from simple in effect. What did *equal rights* encompass? Could all *men* in the United States be said to have equal rights under the law? The breadth of the amendment meant that opposition didn't simply come from conservatives. Plenty of women's rights activists who believed in protective legislation feared that women's special status would be swept away. What kind of victory would it be if it meant that employers were now free to treat women as poorly as men?

The ERA would continue to be introduced and finally passed in 1972 at the height of second-wave feminist activism, when Alice Paul was eighty-eight years old, though it failed at the ratification stage thanks to determined pushback from antifeminist women. The split deepened between those who believed in equality and those who considered women a protected class. The WTUL, opting to support protective laws, was no longer a vibrant, cross-class sisterhood of women working on behalf of the laboring woman. Its allies were replaced by paid workers, and its "faith in sisterhood was forgotten."[14] It was no longer an inspiring ideal. Without the single goal of suffrage to sustain them in overcoming their differences, the unified march of women melted into a crowd.

Women's political participation in the 1920s was a patchwork of advance and retreat. Black women continued to press for their rights to vote and to run for office, taking their case to the Supreme Court. There were other hurdles for women to fight for: the rights to serve on juries and to run for elected office. None of these battles had the yes/no simplicity of the suffrage question, reducible to a simple narrative of pro or anti. A woman who dared to run for office, meanwhile, found that she was answerable both for her sex as a whole and for herself as an individual, a double burden that suffragists had not faced. Men who had been content to let women access the ballot box recoiled at the idea that they might enter the halls of power; aside from Jeannette Rankin, most of the small handful of women in Congress in the 1920s were widows occupying their husbands' seats.[15]

After the Nineteenth Amendment, the term *feminism*, unyoked from *suffragism*, began to toss more freely in turbulent cultural waters. It remained a defining feature of Heterodoxy, but its members no longer felt so securely that they were in the vanguard of a rushing tide. Instead, countercurrents pulled their former allies, and the rising new generation, in quite different directions. Many members of the club turned away from the leadership that had come naturally and found themselves looking for answers to the private dilemmas of their own lives.

Undoubtedly it was their public roles that first brought together the Heterodites: Marie Jenney Howe gathered them for their achievements, their fame, their willingness to stand up and be heard. But it was their personal journeys that bonded them. The club presented an opportunity to connect their pasts with

their present, to understand their own feminist journeys in retrospect. There is some dispute about this—Rheta Childe Dorr
claimed that the meetings' subjects were never personal, while
Inez Haynes Irwin and other members recalled semiregular
background talks, during which "a member told whatever she
chose to reveal about her childhood, girlhood, or young womanhood."[16] It's possible that Rheta, constructing a persona as a
daring, adventurous foreign correspondent in her memoir, chose
to downplay these exercises in navel-gazing; or perhaps those
were meetings she was happy to skip. In putting her early life up
for discussion, the club member was effectively making herself
available for psychoanalysis within the group, by women steeped
in the latest psychological theories—whether professionally, like
Beatrice Hinkle and Grace Potter, or simply out of curiosity.

Charlotte Perkins Gilman had given her own "background
talk" at Heterodoxy, but she grew increasingly impatient with
the club's infatuation with Freud, whom she linked with a new
spirit of sexual licentiousness in the 1920s. In big cities, especially, she complained that women were adopting "the vices of
men," and although the "moral relaxation" of the flapper era
could be understood as the natural response of "any servile class
suddenly set free," she thought it was holding them back. She
hoped that within a few years, liberated women would overcome
"the mental indecencies of a sex-sodden psychoanalysis" and live
up to their potential. Surprisingly, her language for this was more
in line with Ellen Key's celebration of the maternal than what
we might expect from Charlotte's more economically oriented
vision of equality. "Women are first, last, and always mothers,"
she concluded. Her meaning was not entirely literal, trailing
with it a larger metaphor of women as mothers of the human
race, but the language was nonetheless striking. After all that,
it seemed to imply, women *were* different: their moral standards
higher than men's, and their responsibilities to humanity greater.

Perhaps that felt to some feminists like growth, like change, like progress. For others, who had flocked to psychoanalysis not for sexual license but for the license to explore *themselves*, it could not help but sound like a voice calling from the past.[17]

Katharine Anthony did not write publicly of her upbringing or her feminist journey from an Arkansas frontier town to Greenwich Village—her interest was in the lives of other women. Beginning in 1920, she published an influential series of biographies of women, including feminist heroines like Susan B. Anthony and Margaret Fuller, the writer Louisa May Alcott, and—her biggest best sellers—the powerful and notorious rulers Catherine the Great, Elizabeth I, and Marie Antoinette. (The only time she wrote about a man was in a joint biography of siblings Henry and Catherine Lamb, and then, she said, only because the brother kept shoving his way into the sister's story.) Nevertheless, her feminist biographies pursued what was arguably Heterodoxy's unifying question: How did a woman break free of her upbringing to become her "whole human self," and how could she continue to grow and develop beyond the limits society placed on women? In her first biography, a "psychological" study of the Transcendentalist author and feminist Margaret Fuller, Katharine explained that she was not trying to tell a new story, to "unearth fresh material or discover unpublished evidence."[18] Instead, her goal was to look at the existing material with new eyes, enlightened by Freud and feminism. As Marie Jenney Howe wrote approvingly in her review, "It is this analysis—the reconstruction of character from old material—which gives distinction to her biography."[19] Marie herself defined feminism as "a changed psychology" and "the creation of a new consciousness in women."[20] It was little use changing the world if women could not change how they saw themselves within it. Marching up Fifth Avenue might have been thrilling, but winning the vote, the outward sign of emancipation, was not enough. The true liberation from the expectations of a patriarchal culture happened inside.

The idea that an all-female social group might be a place to help that liberation along made perfect sense to the women of the club. In her biography of Fuller, Katharine had written quite plainly that "the feminism of women, like the corresponding form of sex-solidarity among men, is based on a social impulse which is in turn, rooted in an erotic impulse towards others of one's own sex." It was "neither possible nor desirable," she went on, to destroy that impulse.[21] Such a claim—that feminism and same-sex desire were inextricable at the root—might not have shocked Heterodites, most of whom had been educated at the turn of the century in the romantic intimacy of all-female colleges and had had passionate entanglements with both men and women. But it shocked everyone else.

As the decade advanced, and with it the cultural familiarity with sexological theories of deviance, fears of that *erotic impulse* began to undermine same-sex solitary and community. The term *feminist* no longer easily covered, and explained, all women who wanted careers and resisted marriage. Now, there was another term—lesbian—in circulation, and increasingly, feminists acted on the impulse to distance themselves from it. They declared their interest in heterosexual marriage and motherhood (on modern terms of equality and efficiency, of course), and disdained women-only clubs and gatherings as old-fashioned, at best.[22]

Despite these currents, Heterodoxy in the 1920s continued to offer a haven for radicals, artists, oddballs, dreamers, and "resistants," in a far-reaching sense. Mary Margaret McBride, a farmer's daughter from Missouri, became a journalist in New York and, beginning in the late 1930s, a famous radio personality and interviewer; she maintained a discreet, lifelong relationship with her business partner, Stella Karn. The suit-wearing Wall Street trailblazer Kathleen de Vere Taylor, who opened her own brokerage firm in the 1920s exclusively staffed by and catering to women, credited Heterodoxy and particularly its founder with creating a far-reaching safe space: "Many are the fine things that you have done for women, Marie, but to my mind the finest is this: You have helped some of us who were timid and unsure to be ourselves, fully and freely—and in so doing to find happiness and fulfillment."[23]

Throughout the next two decades, the women of Heterodoxy continued to play a part in New York City's cultural and intellectual life, but the dissolution of the Village as a radical epicenter affected their ability to influence larger conversations. Other coteries and communities supplanted vanished meeting places like the Liberal Club. The new downtown literary scene in the 1920s was anchored by the Algonquin Round Table—which included Heterodoxy's Ruth Hale and her good friend, the comic poet Alice Duer Miller—and *The New Yorker* magazine. These venues embodied the decade's firmly mixed-sex culture and emphasis on wit and style over political radicalism.

Heterodoxy journalists continued to write, edit, and promote one another's work. They reviewed each other's books, interviewed one another, and kept their friends' names in circulation. If money was short, as it often was in the years after editors soured on the thrilling adventure of feminism, they could extend each other this cultural credit—and for as long as the group was in the avant-garde, that credit was good. But it was not quite the same as institutional security or literary canonization. The words of one researcher about Katharine Anthony could be applied to any number of women in the club when she marvels at the contrast between "the countless statements attesting to her talent, wit, and notoriety from the first half of the twentieth century" and her "near-invisibility today."[24]

Susan Glaspell's feminist theatrical experiments with the Provincetown Players ended in 1922, when the original company acrimoniously dissolved under the pressure of its own success. As the theater grew in stature, and the fame of Eugene

O'Neill, in particular, skyrocketed, its members fought over the familiar dilemma facing "little" creative endeavors that make it big: whether it was worth it to trade the principles of experimentation and autonomy for money and fame. Edna Kenton in particular fought fiercely to preserve its humble, amateur roots in the Village, even as the Village itself commercialized and gentrified beyond recognition. But Susan and Jig no longer felt that the Provincetown Players was truly their creation. Jig, whose playwriting contributions were sporadic and largely unpopular, resented the greater success that other writers—particularly Susan and Eugene—were enjoying, and his attention, never very consistent, was soon directed elsewhere. In 1922, the couple left New York for Greece, with the intention of living a rustic life more closely in tune with the ancient world Jig still romanticized and yearned for. It would not last long—he died in 1924, and Susan returned to Provincetown, where she and Mary Heaton Vorse both settled for the long term.

Mabel Dodge decamped farther afield, to New Mexico, with Elsie Clews Parsons, who wanted to pursue her anthropological fieldwork among the Native American population. Mabel soon left her third husband, the artist Maurice Sterne, for Anthony Luhan (or Lujan), whose status as a total outsider to her world—a Taos Pueblo man who helped design and build her house—apparently allowed enough air in for the relationship to survive. "Tony was whole and young in the cells of his body, with his power unbroken and hard like the carved granite rock, yet older than the Germanic Russian whom the modern world had destroyed," Mabel wrote, with her inimitable flourish.[25] As the hostess and patron of a vibrant creative community in Taos, Mabel found her purpose at last. Along with the famous guests she would welcome—D. H. Lawrence and his wife Frieda, Georgia O'Keeffe, Willa Cather, Dorothy Parker—she also played hostess to many creative Heterodites over the years, including

Ida Rauh, Inez Haynes Irwin, and the California-based novelist Mary Hunter Austin, who settled in Santa Fe and produced a book about Taos in collaboration with Ansel Adams.[26]

In Paris, where the bohemian torch passed after Prohibition, the flamboyant American socialite Natalie Barney's salon, far more open in its embrace and celebration of lesbianism, welcomed several Heterodoxy members. During World War I, Natalie's weekly salon at 20, Rue Jacob on the Left Bank had been a haven for pacifist and anti-war intellectuals, and Natalie hosted a women's peace congress; through those connections, she met Fola La Follette, who stayed with Natalie in Paris in the early 1920s.[27] To the great surprise of her friends, Marie Jenney Howe moved there in 1926 to research her feminist biography of George Sand, subtitled *The Search for Love*, which she dedicated to Rose Young. She went on to translate Sand's journals into English, and she and Rose wrote a play together, *Impossible George*, based on the novelist's life. While the nature of Marie's relationship with Rose is unclear, they were extremely close, and friends treated Rose as an intimate at least as important as Marie's husband, Fred. Mabel Dodge characterized Marie's marriage as one of "sterility," blaming Fred's preoccupation with his work ("he was one of those husbands who seems to be perpetually engrossed in thought and never on the spot"). She claimed that after reading the first draft of his autobiography, Marie turned to him and wryly asked, "Why, Fred, were you never married?"[28] Yet in the published book, Fred talked a great deal about Marie, and the book's dedication is fulsome, placing Marie at the center of his life:

TO HER MOST OF MY HAPPINESS IS DUE

FROM HER I HAVE GOT FAR MORE THAN I HAVE TOLD

WITHOUT HER THIS NARRATIVE WOULD NOT HAVE BEEN WRITTEN

PERHAPS THERE WOULD HAVE BEEN NO STORY WORTH TELLING

THEREFORE THIS IS NOT A MERE STORY OF MY LIFE
BUT A GRATEFUL ACKNOWLEDGEMENT OF LOVE
AND DEBT TO A COMPANION AND
CO-WORKER THROUGH TWENTY YEARS.[29]

With so little record of Marie's own voice, we have no way of knowing how she felt, on her side of the relationship, or whether she shared Fred's sentiments. But unlike her friends in truly "sterile" or otherwise unsatisfactory marriages, Marie never sought a divorce.

THE STORY OF feminism over the past century has been one of victory and reversal, advance and retreat. No matter how publicly popular its basic principle might be, that people ought not to be held back by their sex from pursuing the life they want to live, the reality and consequences of that principle at work still inspire vicious opposition. As the women of Heterodoxy discovered, however, it was easier to ride out those ups and downs in the company of friends.

The "charmed circle" continued to meet, every other week, and to talk for hours. No doubt, over time, those conversations were about the past just as much as the future, what they had all done, together, not what they had yet to do. Their friendships would deepen with time, the discovery of each other's new ideas and projects now, sprinkled in among the discussion of well-trodden topics: their children, their partners, their work. And then perhaps, their grandchildren, their memories, their weak hearts, "game knee[s] and other signs of senility."[30]

In one of her last letters, Marie Jenney Howe wrote to Fola La Follette with news of their mutual friends: a litany of aging, grieving, and dying, but also of travel and work. She reports that Doris Stevens "is in Uraguay [sic] for six weeks at the Pan American Convention" while another member, Signe Toksvig, "has just published a fascinating biography of Hans Christian Andersen."[31] For those who were most deeply connected to the club, Heterodoxy encompassed its members' whole lives, in public and in private, in success and in despair. It helped them shape who they wanted to be, as feminists and as women, and it helped them understand, in retrospect, how they got there. And more simply, it gave them joy. In 1940, Mary Ware Dennett wrote to her fellow club member Netha Roe, whose husband was the liberal lawyer who defended *The Masses* in court all those years before, to assure her that, even without Marie's warm presence at the head of the table, the club endured—"not that all the old atmosphere is evident all the time, but on the whole, it has been fine." It remained for Mary, at almost sixty-eight, "a pleasure that is unique, and for which there is no substitute that I know of."[32]

Heterodoxy gave its unusual, prominent, spiky, and adventurous members the vital company of other women who could inspire them to greater things, and comfort them in the isolation of their radical positions. When Inez Irwin looked back on the adventure of her life and her activist days in the 1910s, few of her memories are as heartfelt as her tribute to the women who spurred her on through that adventure: "What women I met! What fights I joined! How many speeches I made! How many words I wrote! But best of all—what women I met!"[33]

EPILOGUE

Tucked away in the Schlesinger Library on the History of Women in America at Harvard University's Radcliffe Institute, in the papers of writer Inez Haynes Irwin, is a scrapbook covered in a patchwork brocade, a brown tile pattern through which peeps a shining chinoiserie print in shades of gold, green, and blue: cranes in flight, and dragons' heads, and curling leaves. The book is thick and heavy and filled with photographs and messages, the ink turning brown, the pages yellowed, the edges foxed and faded. Assembled out of love and nostalgia, to honor relationships and preserve a moment in time, to commemorate a singular network of love and friendship among women, this album is the most substantial piece of evidence we have about Heterodoxy. The bulk of the content comes from 1920, the year Marie Jenney Howe turned fifty, so the album may have originated as a birthday gift for her. Other materials were added later, in the mid-1930s, perhaps as a memorial after she died in 1934. Some members were careful to mark the date and to caption the pictures they contributed—others simply plunged ahead with their tribute.

To turn the pages of the album is to discover the impact that the club had on the lives of its members and the lasting emotional bond that they forged with one another and with Marie. On the first page, in calligraphy inspired by medieval illuminated manuscripts, someone has carefully inked the dedication: *Heterodoxy to Marie*. In a self-deprecating introduction, probably written by Inez Irwin, the members pay tribute to their leader's almost mystical power to produce "unity" out of their differences and create a collective spirit stronger than the sum of its parts: "a warm and friendly and staunch spirit, in which our conglomerate personalities all have a share."

There are photographs of Marie: in one, she looks rather young, and rather ill, and sits listlessly in a chair in a cluttered Victorian parlor, with a guitar propped against her leg, facing another woman across a small table set with tea things. In another, she is several years older, sitting on what looks like a park bench in New York, wearing a fur coat and hat and petting the dog that stands on the bench next to her looking at the camera. (Dogs were a strong bond among the Heterodites—several women, including Elisabeth Irwin, chose photos that immortalize their pups along with themselves.) There is a third picture of a grandmotherly Marie with an unidentified child, possibly her great-niece: the picture is captioned "the mother-tree and the youngest twig." In a series of bold sketches, titled "Our Fearless Leader: Futurist School," cartoonist Lou Rogers captures Marie's strong, dark eyebrows, set mouth, and intense gaze.

The album's pages introduce these "women who did things" through snapshots, inscriptions, clippings, sketches, jokes, and tributes. Many of them pasted in photographs of themselves in the midst of their activities, whether that was appearing on stage, marching in a protest, or reporting from the front line of a war zone. Katharine Anthony's page shows two photographs: in the first, she appears as young woman in a pale, lace-trimmed gown holding a spray of roses, smiling rather vacantly for the camera. In the second, she is older, sitting at a desk piled with books,

On her page in the "Heterodoxy to Marie" album, biographer Katharine Anthony charts her evolution from a society "butterfly" to an intellectual chrysalis. (*Credit: Schlesinger Library, Harvard Radcliffe Institute*)

wearing practical clothes, captured in the fervor of thinking and writing. Anthony labeled the photographs "the evolution of a butterfly into a chrysalis"—a reverse flowering that transforms her from a decorative creature into a hard-shelled organism, full of potential.

Bertha Kunz Baker, "who gave interpretations of dramatic and other literary masterpieces" and taught the art of public speaking, is posed on a cliff face, arm raised mid-declamation against the sky. Dr. Jo Baker, in her preferred androgynous attire of collar and tie and pince-nez glasses, cracks a joke on the club's name, a play on the slang term "doxy," meaning prostitute: "'Orthodoxy' is my doxy, 'Heterodoxy' is another man's doxy." After Dr. Jo comes roving reporter Bessie Beatty, who includes a portrait and two snapshots showing her grinning at the camera, flanked by a large group of uniformed soldiers. Her caption reads, "Barbed wire and other entanglements on the Russian front."

And that only takes us up to the letter *B*.

Scholars of literature, feminism, and politics who encounter the "Heterodoxy to Marie" album will feel jolts of recognition as they turn these pages, but most casual readers won't be familiar with the names of most of the hundred or so women who, over the years, made up "this hydra-headed Heterodoxy." The heroic self-aggrandizement—by oneself and one's peers and disciples—necessary to qualify as a biographical subject is elusive. Many of these women did their most important work in groups and organizations in which individual glory was frowned upon or deemed irrelevant; by political inclination many of them were socialists, dedicated to shared improvement. Then again, their gender pushed against the standard narratives of historical fame, of biographical worthiness: their energies were diverted into family life, or they were eclipsed by the men they worked alongside. In a few cases, their lives were cut short by ill health or accident, and for others, the glow of fame simply faded over time.

In 1982, feminist historian Judith Schwarz published a small study, just over a hundred pages long, titled *The Radical Feminists of Heterodoxy*. Gleaned primarily from the album of photographs, letters, and ephemera dedicated to Marie Jenney Howe, it is a document of passionate frustration, full of gaps and question marks, unknown birth and death dates, information that's been muddled or lost. Her effort in pulling together the scattered archive of the club and its members was nothing short of heroic, but for too long it stood alone as a record of this club that made a vital impact in the lives of dozens of prominent women. Schwarz begs her historical inheritors to track down what's missing and to fill in those blanks, to round out the record of the Heterodites in fields as diverse as social work, anthropology, education, law, applied arts, theater, literature, and politics.

During the so-called second wave of feminism in which Schwarz was writing, writers and scholars dug into the lives of individual Heterodoxy women, especially those who left voluminous archives and whose lives touched many other notable people's, and whose battles to be heard, respected, understood, and remembered resonated with the struggles of women who grew up in the 1950s and were reclaiming the feminist idea and labels for themselves. Charlotte Perkins Gilman, Mabel Dodge, and Susan Glaspell, in particular, became the subjects of several biographies and edited collections of their writing, while Rose Pastor Stokes and Elizabeth Gurley Flynn were restored to positions of prestige in the history of the American Left. In the emerging academic field of women's history, in the 1970s and 1980s, Heterodoxy offered an important model of early feminist cooperation, although its political importance was eclipsed by a focus on suffrage as the defining feature of the first wave. As I hope to have demonstrated in these pages, suffrage and feminism were overlapping movements, but they had very different purviews and goals. Today, neither is "over" in any meaningful sense. Voting rights are under sustained assault, and feminists continue to turn out into the streets in the thousands to demand rights that the Heterodites were also fighting for—as well as some that they could only have dreamed about.

It can be disheartening to look back, over the course of more than a century, at a world limping under the strain of rampant capitalism, racist violence, misogyny, and a crippling pandemic and to see how far we haven't come. But we can also take comfort, I think, in the past, and in the ways that people have always found to live in dark times. "I don't know exactly what people mean by disillusionment," wrote the irrepressible Lou Rogers in 1927. "I love to live and the longer I keep at it the greater capacity I have for living, and when I die, if it be so arranged that I lose my individual entity, I pray that I may become the lightning that snaps and crackles and whips through a thunder-storm."[1]

If there is hope to be found for feminism today, and I believe there is, it has to lie in the way we come together, to reexamine the past and redefine the future. There is more awareness than ever of the ways that women, together, can create change and how much we have to learn from listening to one another's stories. This is not the same as looking for heroines and role models, which is a limiting and isolating framework into which women biographical subjects are too often squeezed. I was drawn to this story less for the individuals within it, though there are plenty of stories left to tell (Grace Nail Johnson and Ida Rauh, at least, are crying out for their own biographies . . .), than for the evidence it offered, over and over again, of the importance of friendship in shaping who we are and what we become. In burnishing our ambition as we rise, in helping catch us as we fall. In pushing us to become nothing less than our whole, big, human selves.

ACKNOWLEDGMENTS

I WROTE MOST of this book during the COVID-19 pandemic and the lockdown in New York that began two weeks after I gave birth. Those two events shaped my writing profoundly. Over the course of the next year and a half, I learned a great deal about living in interesting historical times, and I restructured this book to, as far as possible, reflect that experience. Rather than one damn thing after another, recent history has felt like every damn thing at once, and it is an experience that deeply informed how I thought about the women in this book, torn between multiple battles and doing their best to keep up.

The pandemic also materially affected my research, making it impossible to travel to several archives that I had hoped to visit. I was able to continue thanks to the peerless remote research resources of the New York Public Library, and I am also grateful to staff at Yale's Beinecke Library and the Schlesinger Library, who digitized material for me and provided photographs. The "Heterodoxy to Marie" album, in the Inez Haynes Gillmore Irwin papers at the Schlesinger, is fully digitized and I encourage everyone to seek it out.

I first encountered Heterodoxy in the course of researching an exhibition for the New-York Historical Society's Center for Women's History, "Hotbed," which marked the centennial of women's right to vote in New York State. I am indebted to Valerie Paley, the center's director, for her mentorship and support, and to the brilliant team she gathered, who taught me so much. To my co-curator Sarah Gordon, thank you for all the Central Park strategy sessions, coffee dates, inspiration, and friendship, and for giving this book the benefit of your rigorous eye. I'm honored to have had the chance to meet and learn from the scholarly advisory council at the center, headed by Alice Kessler-Harris, and from individual scholars, particularly Lara Vapnek and Blanche Wiesen Cook. Many fellow biographers and historians of women's lives have helped to shape my thinking on what a feminist biography can be, and I am honored by their support and encouragement of this project. Thanks to Elaine Showalter, Anne Boyd Rioux, Carla Kaplan, Imani Perri, Ruth Franklin, Amy Aronson, Francesca Wade, Alexis Coe, Michelle Dean, Lauren Elkin, and the members of the CUNY Women Writing Women's Lives seminar.

My agent, Kate Johnson, has been an unstinting champion of my work, a careful reader, and a loyal guide through many vagaries of publication. I have been lucky to work with wonderful editors, Katie Adams and now Claire Potter, whose patience, insight, and cheerleading ensured this book actually got finished. To Claire, Abigail Mohr, and the whole team at Seal Press, thank you for giving Heterodoxy a welcoming home.

It felt appropriate to dedicate this book about women's friendships to my own charmed circle, but the network that makes it possible is much bigger. I am fortunate to be able to bring both a book and a baby into a generous and loving extended family—thank you to Dave, Rob, Bud, Eva, Andrew, and Rose, and most of all to my kind and brilliant mother, Andrea, who was my earliest feminist inspiration. Our pandemic saviors included the best friends and neighbors in the world, Sam Meyer and Bari Dulberg. Thank you also to the artists, curators, and staff of Socrates Sculpture Park, who created a lockdown lifeline.

While we wait for affordable feminist apartment complexes with Montessori schools on the roof, or governments that take childcare and caregivers seriously enough to fund them, I have to thank the teachers and staff of Bright Start, our dedicated and loving local day care, without whom this book would simply not exist. To my beautiful Felix, for making me work harder, think harder, and feel harder than ever, thank you. To Tony, for making our bubble so joyful and always believing in this book, and in me, and for not being like 90 percent of the husbands in this book, I owe you every day, for everything.

NOTES

Introduction: A Little World for Us

1. As historian Gerald W. McFarland and others point out, the area known to middle-class bohemians as "Greenwich Village" had several other names more commonly used by its immigrant communities, including Little Africa and Little Italy, and was officially made up of sections of New York's Sixth and Ninth Wards. Its precise borders and boundaries were always in flux.

2. This description is adapted from Steven Watson's colorful account, a hybrid of several contemporary sources, in *Strange Bedfellows*, 155.

3. Hulme, "The Liberal Club and Its Jamaican Secretary," 13. Hulme reproduces a club flyer showing that this is the correct phrase—not "a meeting place" as most histories have it.

4. Letter from Crystal to Max Eastman, quoted in Aronson, *Crystal Eastman*, 68.

5. Dedication, most likely written by Inez Haynes Irwin, in unpublished "Heterodoxy to Marie" scrapbook album, Schlesinger Library. Judith Schwarz draws heavily on her account and calls her the "unofficial club historian" (Schwarz, *Radical Feminists*, iii).

6. Irwin, *Adventures of Yesterday*, 414. This unpublished autobiography offers the fullest account we have of Heterodoxy's members and operation.

7. Anonymous source, quoted in "With the Members Sworn to Secrecy, Forty of New York's Prominent 'Advanced' Women Band into 'the Heterodoxy' and Meet to Eat and Decide Their Position on Problems of the Day," *New-York Tribune*, November 24, 1914.

8. Irwin, *Adventures of Yesterday*, 413.

9. The phrase is Mabel Dodge Luhan's, *Movers and Shakers*, 143.

10. Ida Proper entry, "Heterodoxy to Marie" scrapbook.

11. "With the Members Sworn to Secrecy," *New-York Tribune*, November 24, 1914.

12. The group didn't meet over the summer. In an era before air conditioning, most New Yorkers who could afford it decamped in the hottest months.

13. Most accounts place the Liberal Club at 137 MacDougal. As the next chapter will show, there is a great deal of accreted myth around the institution, but I am persuaded by Hulme's account, which reproduces the club's letterhead from 1913, placing it at 135. The four houses at 133, 135, 137, and 139 form a remarkable nucleus of activity in the prewar Village. Hulme, "Liberal Club," 13.

14. Schwarz, *Radical Feminists*, 1, 17–18. The shift to Tuesday evenings is apparent from the later additions to the "Heterodoxy to Marie" album.

15. Dorr, *Woman of Fifty*, 271.

16. Letter from the Missouri Anti-Suffrage League, quoted in Cott, *Grounding of Modern Feminism*, 13.

17. Dorr, *Woman of Fifty*, 268.

18. Quoted in Cott, *Grounding of Modern Feminism*, 40.

19. Cott, 13. The popular meaning of "vampire" at the time came from an 1897 poem by Rudyard Kipling that rages against a woman—or rather, "a rag and bone and a hank of hair"—whose crime is that she is indifferent to a man's devotion. Theda Bara, born Theodosia Goodman, in Cincinnati, Ohio, established herself as an "exotic" screen icon by embracing that role, soon shortened to "vamp," in films with titles like *Siren of Hell*, *The Devil's Daughter*, *The Vixen*, and *The She-Devil*.

20. Alice Duer Miller, "Feminism," in *Are Women People?* 64.

21. "Edna Kenton Says," *The Delineator*, July 1914, 17.

22. Quoted in "Feminists Ask for Equal Chance," *New York Times*, February 21, 1914.

23. Marie Jenney Howe, "Feminism," *New Review* 2, no. 8 (August 1914): 441–442.

24. Watson, *Strange Bedfellows*, 143.

25. Recent biographies of Crystal Eastman and Rose Pastor Stokes are encouraging exceptions to this rule.

26. Showalter, *Inventing Ourselves*, 120.

27. As Linda J. Lumsden puts it in her biography of Inez Milholland, "College women across the nation quoted *Women & Economics* like the Bible." Lumsden, *Inez*, 2.

28. Davis, *Charlotte Perkins Gilman*, 339.

29. Marie Hoffendahl Jenney to Charlotte Perkins Gilman, quoted in Gilman, *Living of Charlotte Perkins Gilman*, xxxvi.

30. Gale, Foreword, in Gilman, *Living of Charlotte Perkins Gilman*, xxxvii.

31. Paula Jakobi and Inez Haynes Irwin entries, "Heterodoxy to Marie" scrapbook.

32. I use the lowercase "socialist" rather than "Socialist" in this book to distinguish between the open-ended belief system, widespread in the 1910s, and the narrower case of membership in the male-dominated Socialist Party. Although several Heterodoxy members belonged to the SP, for most, the label "socialist" was more akin to "feminist" than to, say, Democrat or Republican, especially since they had no power to vote party members into office.

33. Elizabeth Gurley Flynn entry, "Heterodoxy to Marie" album.

34. It is this spirit of friendship and intimacy that I hope to capture by referring to the women by their first names. As we will see, names were of enormous significance for Heterodoxy women, and the desire to be known as themselves, not in relation to fathers or husbands, meant that identifiers were already fraught, even before the fact that many of the married Heterodites had more than one husband.

Chapter 1: Way Down South in Greenwich Village

1. Howe, *Confessions of a Reformer*, 233.

2. Howe, *The City*, 8.

3. Newton Baker to Tom L. Johnson, October 5, 1910. Quoted in Miller, *From Progressive to New Dealer*, 138.

4. The exact nature of Marie's illness is not known, although it seems to have been some kind of gastric ailment. In the summer of 1909, she spent time at a sanatorium in Carlsbad, Germany, where she was diagnosed with a stomach ulcer. The treatment helped, but there are continued references to bouts of illness and exhaustion in her surviving letters. Miller, *From Progressive to New Dealer*, 98–99.

5. Miller, *From Progressive to New Dealer*, 166.

6. Howe, *Confessions of a Reformer*, 240.

7. Symbolically, the Abyssinian Baptist Church closed its doors on Greenwich Village's Waverly Place in 1902 and eventually moved to Harlem, where during the 1920s it became a vital community landmark. For a fuller account of the history of Little Africa, see McFarland, *Inside Greenwich Village*, 11–25.

8. Vorse, *I've Come to Stay*, 3. The novel is subtitled "A Love-Comedy of Bohemia."

9. Arens, *Little Book of Greenwich Village*, 16.

10. Vorse, *I've Come to Stay*, 3.

11. "Mellow brick houses," in Vorse, *I've Come to Stay*, 3; Barnes, "Greenwich Village As It Is," in *Djuna Barnes's New York*, 225.

12. Vorse, *I've Come to Stay*, 4.

13. Irwin, *Adventures of Yesterday*, 407.

14. McFarland, *Inside Greenwich Village*, 120–123.

15. Quoted in Aronson, *Crystal Eastman*, 64.

16. Quotations are from Carl Zigrosser's 1971 memoir, *My Own Shall Come to Me*, in Stansell, *American Moderns*, 91. Stansell claims that Patchin began to meet in 1915, but Simonson provides convincing evidence that the group began earlier, around 1910. Elizabeth Westwood died suddenly in 1915, at the age of thirty-five, and, according to Zigrosser, the Patchin group began to deteriorate before dissolving in 1917. Simonson, *"Féminisme Oblige,"* 158, 267.

17. Simonson, *"Féminisme Oblige,"* 199.

18. "The Day in Bohemia" was privately printed in 1912 and is reproduced in Mabel Dodge, *Movers and Shakers*, 171–185, 175. She says it was the first she heard of her future lover. (One assumes that "they" did *ask* for the rent, they just didn't always get it.)

19. Glaspell, *Road to the Temple*, 247, quoted in Ben-Zvi, *Susan Glaspell*, 40.

20. Arens, *Little Book of Greenwich Village*, 10. Vorse's naming is cited by Garrison, *Mary Heaton Vorse*, 64.

21. Watson, *Strange Bedfellows*, 127–128.

22. Vorse, *I've Come to Stay*, 86–87.

23. Descriptions of the club are gleaned from Christine Stansell, *American Moderns*; William M. Scott and Peter B. Rutkoff, *New York Modern*, 74; and Watson, *Strange Bedfellows*, 154–155.

24. Sarah Addington, "Who's Who in New York's Bohemia," *New-York Tribune*, November 14, 1915.

25. Levin, "Bohemians," 122.

26. Dell, *Love in Greenwich Village*, 18. Quoted in Harris, *Around Washington Square*, 187–188.

27. "Dr. Grant Quits the Liberal Club," *New York Times*, September 12, 1913. Retraction, September 16, 1913. Henrietta's battle with the Board of Education is detailed in Chapter 7.

28. These inconsistencies are untangled in Peter Hulme's article, "The Liberal Club and Its Jamaican Secretary." The complications include the fact that there were, by Hulme's count, four different "Liberal Clubs" in New York in a fifty-year period, with frequently overlapping memberships. Hulme, "The Liberal Club," 5.

29. Dee Garrison estimates there were fourteen Heterodites out of twenty-three women members (Garrison, *Mary Heaton Vorse*, 72). For

both clubs, definitive records are lacking, and membership meant different things to different people. However, the numbers indicate the extent of the overlapping circles and how dominant Heterodoxy was among prominent Village women.

30. The story is found in club secretary W. Adolphe Roberts's memoir *These Many Years*, quoted in Hulme, "The Liberal Club," 11.

31. Levin, *Bohemia in America*, 347.

32. Quoted in Schwarz, *Radical Feminists of Heterodoxy*, 64.

33. Quoted in Murphy, *Provincetown Players*, 8.

34. Irmscher, *Max Eastman*, 94. The brusque wording of this note is widely quoted, but biographer Amy Aronson highlights Crystal's pivotal role in boosting Max's profile, Aronson *Crystal Eastman*, 65.

35. Irwin, *Adventures of Yesterday*, 291.

36. Vorse, *Footnote to Folly*, 42.

37. Susan Glaspell, *The People*, 3.

38. Lumsden, *Inez*, 58.

39. Vorse, *Footnote to Folly*, 32.

40. Ami Mali Hicks, *Everyday Art*, 45.

41. Irwin, *Adventures of Yesterday*, 281.

42. Interview with Ida Rauh, 1966. Quoted in Sochen, *New Woman*, 5–6.

Chapter 2: The Type Has Changed

1. "Vassar Students Are Now Radicals," *New York Times*, May 9, 1909, 8.

2. The term "New Woman" is usually cited as first appearing in a story by Irish writer Sarah Grand in 1894. It rapidly entered the lexicon on both sides of the Atlantic, to denote an educated, middle-class, and culturally rebellious young woman. Most of the older members of Heterodoxy, born in the 1870s and 1880s, would have qualified. The term "feminist" appeared later and was considered much more threatening.

3. Bzowski, "Spectacular Suffrage," 65*n*.

4. Irwin, *Adventures of Yesterday*, 452.

5. "Mrs Belmont Home for Suffrage War," *New York Times*, September 16, 1910.

6. Lumsden, *Inez*, 16.

7. Jean Torry Milholland, "Miss Inez Milholland," *New York Times*, March 2, 1909. The distinction between "suffragist" and "suffragette" was a fraught one. The latter term was embraced by the British, but the American movement leaders shunned it, as both demeaning and indicative of

extremism. "Suffragette" in the American press at the time, therefore, is usually a clue that the coverage is skeptical, at best.

8. "Vassar Students Are Now Radicals," *New York Times*, May 9, 1909, 8.

9. Baker, *Fighting for Life*, 196.

10. Leah Cates, "Harriot Stanton Blatch," *Vassar Encyclopedia*, www .vassar.edu/vcencyclopedia/alumni/harriott-stanton-blatch.html.

11. Elizabeth Adams Daniel, "The Suffrage Movement at Vassar," *Vassar Encyclopedia*, originally published 1983. www.vassar.edu/vcencyclopedia /interviews-reflections/the-suffrage-movement.html.

12. "American Girl Harried Oxford and Cambridge," *St. Louis Post-Dispatch*, October 3, 1909, A9.

13. Baker, *Fighting for Life*, 192.

14. Baker, *Fighting for Life*, 28.

15. Mabel Potter Daggett, "Votes for College Women," *The Key: Kappa Kappa Gamma* 28, no. 3 (May 1911): 213.

16. Goodier and Pastorello, *Women Will Vote*, 120.

17. Max Eastman, "Confessions of a Suffrage Orator," *The Masses* Suffrage Issue, October–November 1915. Quoted in Kroeger, *The Suffragents*, 172.

18. "American Girl," A9.

19. "Miss Milholland Won't Surrender," *New York Times*, October 24, 1909.

20. Bzowski, "Spectacular Suffrage," 72.

21. Baker, *Fighting for Life*, 197.

22. Bzowski, "Spectacular Suffrage," 74. The British suffrage colors were purple, green, and white, also sometimes seen in New York, but yellow soon became synonymous with the American movement. For more on the history and symbolism of suffrage colors, see https://womenatthecenter .nyhistory.org/the-many-official-colors-of-the-suffrage-movement/.

23. "Suffragists March in Procession Today," *New York Times*, May 6, 1911, 13.

24. Baker, *Fighting for Life*, 193.

25. Quoted in Cobrin, *From Winning the Vote*, 55.

26. Bzowski, "Spectacular Suffrage," 78.

27. "Suffrage Parade to Be 'Best Ever,'" *New-York Tribune*, November 9, 1912.

28. "Chinese Girl Wants Vote," *New-York Tribune*, April 13, 1912, 3.

29. "Women Parade and Rejoice," *New York Times*, May 7, 1911.

30. Ronald Shaffer, "The New York City Woman Suffrage Party, 1909–1919," *New York History* 43, no. 3 (1962): 272.

31. The participation of nonwhite women in the suffrage movement, neglected for decades by white historians, has recently been the subject of a surge of scholarly and popular interest. See, especially, Cathleen D. Cahill, *Recasting the Vote*, and Martha S. Jones, *Vanguard*.

32. Mrs. John E. Milholland, "Talks About Women," *The Crisis*, December 1910, 28. Jean Milholland had a regular column in *The Crisis* for the first year of its existence.

33. Editorial, *The Crisis*, April 1913, 1.

34. Irwin, *Adventures of Yesterday*, 453.

35. Baker, *Fighting for Life*, 197.

36. "Mary Shaw Dies: Noted Ibsen Player," *New York Times*, May 19, 1929, 27; Schanke, "Mary Shaw, a Fighting Champion," 105–106; "Ernest Shipman Presents America's Leading Emotional Actress, Mary Shaw," Cincinnati: US Lithograph Co. Photograph, ca. 1907, Library of Congress, www.loc.gov/item/2014635859/.

37. Quoted in "Why We Must Win: By Men and Women of the Stage," *The Woman Voter* Dramatic Number, December 1914, 8.

38. "Pledge Actresses to Suffrage Parade," *New York Times*, April 22, 1912, 11. It's unlikely this announcement got much attention, however: the newspaper was full of stories about the tragedy of the *Titanic* sinking, less than a week earlier.

39. Hernando Real, "A Luncheon for Suffrage," 81.

40. Marie Jenney Howe, "An Anti-Suffrage Monologue," in Schwarz, *Radical Feminists of Heterodoxy*, 110–114.

41. Mary Shaw, "The Woman of It," in Bettina Friedl, *On to Victory*.

42. Irwin, *Adventures of Yesterday*, 453.

43. "Twenty-Five Answers to Antis: Five-Minute Speeches on Votes for Women by Eminent Suffragists" (pamphlet, National Woman Suffrage Publishing Company, 1912), 40.

Chapter 3: The Rebel Girls and the Mink Brigade

1. Descriptions adapted from Enstad, *Ladies of Labor, Girls of Adventure*.

2. Shavelson, "Remembering the Waistmakers General Strike, 1909," 301.

3. Dorr, *Woman of Fifty*, 55–56.

4. "Edna Kenton Says," *The Delineator*, July 1914, 17. Kenton is quoting the contemporary literary critic James Huneker.

5. Quoted in "Feminist Apartment House to Solve Baby Problem," *New York Times*, January 24, 1915.

6. Ida Rauh, "The Wooden Spools," *New York Evening Call*, August 12, 1908, 5; Ida Rauh, "A Protest," *New York Evening Call*, September 21, 1908, 4. Quoted in Dye, *As Equals and As Sisters*, 54.

7. Hochschild, *Rebel Cinderella*, 73.

8. Miller, *From Progressive to New Dealer*, 56–60.

9. Hochschild, *Rebel Cinderella*, 48.

10. Henry Street is still a vital community center and recently marked its 125th anniversary. www.thehouseonhenrystreet.org.

11. McFarland, *Inside Greenwich Village*, 60.

12. McFarland, 45–58.

13. McFarland, 59.

14. Detailed in Aronson, *Crystal Eastman*, 85.

15. Cook, "Female Support Networks and Political Activism," 44; Faderman, *Odd Girls*, 24–28.

16. Dye, *As Equals and As Sisters*, 41.

17. Judith Schwarz speculates that Rose and Marie were lovers, and there is evidence for a long, intimate relationship, including sharing a house together during at least one summer, and Marie dedicating her biography of George Sand to Rose.

18. Names drawn from Dye, *As Equals and As Sisters*, and Schwarz, *Radical Feminists of Heterodoxy*.

19. Lumsden, *Inez*, 44.

20. Dye, *As Equals and As Sisters*, 67.

21. The term, *one-off*, is Clara Lemlich's.

22. Note that the name meant the workers *made* ladies' garments, not that the workers *were* ladies—on the contrary, most of the ILGWU leadership was male, and grudging or hostile toward women members.

23. Hochschild, *Rebel Cinderella*, 105.

24. Dye, *As Equals and As Sisters*, 90–92.

25. George Middleton autobiography, quoted in Schwarz, *Radical Feminists of Heterodoxy*, 31.

26. Quoted in Edge, *We Stand as One*, 78.

27. Quoted in Lumsden, *Inez*, 51.

28. Hochschild, *Rebel Cinderella*, 108.

29. Dye, *As Equals and As Sisters*, 93.

30. *Daily Worker*, June 20, 1943, reprinted in Baxandall, *Words on Fire*, 189.

31. "Stokes Says 'Twas a Union of Souls," *Hartford Courant*, April 7, 1905, 11.

32. Hochschild, *Rebel Cinderella*, 81.

33. "The Uprising of the Girls," *Collier's*, December 25, 1909, 14.

34. Hochschild, *Rebel Cinderella*, 106.

35. Quoted in Downey, *Woman Behind the New Deal*, 34.

36. Garrison, *Mary Heaton Vorse*, 49.

37. Downey, *Woman Behind the New Deal*, 35.

38. Quoted in Stein, *Triangle Fire*, 26.

39. Dye, *As Equals and As Sisters*, 144.

40. Martha Bensley Bruere, "The Triangle Fire," *Life and Labor*, May 1911, 137.

41. Schneiderman's speech was carried in *The Survey*, April 8, 1911. Reprinted in Stein, *Out of the Sweatshop*, 196–197.

42. Quoted in Downey, *Woman Behind the New Deal*, 36.

43. David von Drehle, "Uncovering the History of the Triangle Shirtwaist Fire," *Smithsonian Magazine*, August 2006.

44. Aronson, *Crystal Eastman*, 78.

45. Aronson, 58–60.

46. "Portia Appointed by the Governor," *New York Herald*, April 24, 1910.

47. Aronson, *Crystal Eastman*, 93–95.

48. Crystal Eastman, "Three Essentials for Accident Prevention," in Cook, *Crystal Eastman*, 282.

Chapter 4: The New Abolitionists

1. Lumsden, *Inez*, 25; Lumsden also cites Carolyn Wedin, *Inheritors of the Spirit: Mary White Ovington and the Founding of the NAACP* (New York: John Wiley & Sons, 1997), 66.

2. Mary Heaton Vorse oral history, 1957, quoted in Schwarz, *Radical Feminists of Heterodoxy*, 31. "The Beautiful Strunsky Sisters" are listed among the who's who in Arens, *Little Book of Greenwich Village*, 23. "Papa Strunsky" in Schwarz, *Radical Feminists of Heterodoxy*, 126.

3. William English Walling, "The Race War in the North," *The Independent* 65, no. 3118 (September 3, 1908): 529–534, 534.

4. "NAACP: A Century in the Fight for Freedom: Founding and Early Years," Library of Congress, www.loc.gov/exhibits/naacp/founding-and-early-years.html.

5. For a detailed account see Bernstein, *First Waco Horror*.

6. Chapman, *Prove It on Me*, 48.

7. Perry, *May We Forever Stand*, 26.

8. See also Imani Perry's concept of "Black formalism," in *May We Forever Stand*, 1–24.

9. Quoted in Nowlin, "Race Literature, Modernism, and Normal Literature," 505.

10. Johnson, *Along This Way*, 203.

11. Quoted in Nowlin, "Race Literature, Modernism, and Normal Literature," 509.

12. Dowling, "A Marginal Man in Black Bohemia," 128.

13. Johnson, *Along This Way*, 210.

14. "Grace Nail Johnson," in *Carl Van Vechten's Harlem Renaissance Portraits* (online exhibition, Beinecke Rare Book and Manuscript Library, Yale University Library, New Haven, CT, https://vanvechten.beinecke.library.yale.edu).

15. Johnson, *Along This Way*, 274.

16. Booker T. Washington, *The Negro in Business* (Boston: Herschel Jenkins, 1907), 197–205; Camille Heung, "John E. Nail: 1883–1947," Black Past, 2008, www.blackpast.org/african-american-history/nail-john-e-1883-1947/.

17. Johnsons and John E. Nail photographs, box 108, folder 938, James Weldon Johnson and Grace Nail Johnson papers, Beinecke Rare Book and Manuscript Library, Yale University, New Haven, CT.

18. Marie Jenney Howe to Grace Nail Johnson, September 18, 1918, box 30, folder 86, James Weldon Johnson and Grace Nail Johnson papers, Beinecke Rare Book and Manuscript Library, Yale University.

19. Miller, *From Progressive to New Dealer*, 233.

20. Aronson, *Crystal Eastman*, 204.

21. Irwin, *Adventures of Yesterday*, 412.

22. In the 1920s, W. E. B. Du Bois led a campaign to capitalize the word as a marker of dignity and respect. In the wake of renewed racial justice protests in 2020, many publishers adopted the upper-case "Black" as standard usage, as I have in this book.

23. Irwin, *Adventures of Yesterday*, 446.

24. Although the word was known to be demeaning, in 1905 it was in common use. The stories were popular enough, and their title unremarkable enough, to be cited in full in Rose's *New York Times* obituary, July 8, 1941. For comparison, the white writer and Harlem Renaissance booster Carl Van Vechten's 1926 novel *N—r Heaven* was titled to be deliberately provocative, and both his Black and white friends reacted with anger.

25. McKay, *Long Way from Home*, 28.

Chapter 5: What We Want Is a Revolution

1. Vorse, "Elizabeth Gurley Flynn," 175–176.

2. Vorse, "Elizabeth Gurley Flynn," 175.

3. Vorse, "The Trouble at Lawrence," *Harper's Weekly*, March 16, 1912, 10.

4. Baxandall, *Words on Fire*, 15.

5. Luhan, *Movers and Shakers*, 89. Mabel's venom may have been rooted in jealousy, as her lover John Reed was enthralled by Haywood as a masculine ideal. Green, *New York 1913*, 98.

6. Quoted in Hochschild, *Rebel Cinderella*, 122.

7. Vorse, *A Footnote to Folly*, 8.

8. Flynn, "Memories of the Industrial Workers of the World" speech given November 8, 1962, Northern Illinois University, www.sojust.net /speeches/elizabeth_flynn_memories.html.

9. Vorse, "The Trouble at Lawrence," *Harper's Weekly*, March 16, 1912, 10.

10. Baxandall, *Words on Fire*, 16.

11. Baxandall, 16.

12. Hochschild, *Rebel Cinderella*, 128.

13. Mattina and Ciavattoni, "Striking Women," 158.

14. Dye, *As Equals and As Sisters*, 105.

15. Lara Vapnek emphasizes this connection throughout her biography of Flynn.

16. Vapnek, *Elizabeth Gurley Flynn*, 7–18.

17. Grace Potter, "Max Eastman's Two Books," *New Review* 1, no. 20 (September 1913): 797.

18. Vorse, "Elizabeth Gurley Flynn."

19. Miller, *From Progressive to New Dealer*, 92.

20. Quoted in Vapnek, *Elizabeth Gurley Flynn*, 52.

21. Quoted in Hochschild, *Rebel Cinderella*, 81

22. Hochschild, 112.

23. Flynn, *I Speak My Own Piece*, 140.

24. Flynn, 280.

25. Vorse, *Footnote to Folly*, 14.

Chapter 6: To Dynamite New York

1. Flynn, *I Speak My Own Piece*, 141.

2. "Young Woman Leads the Waiters' Strike," *New York Times*, January 14, 1913.

3. Catherine A. Paul, "Paterson Silk Strike, 1913," Social Welfare History Project, Virginia Commonwealth University, https://social welfare.library.vcu.edu/organizations/labor/paterson-silk-strike-1913/.

4. Golin, *Fragile Bridge*, 22.

5. Frederick Sumner Boyd, *Pageant of the Paterson Strike* [microform] (New York: Success Press, 1913), 4, https://archive.org/details/pageant ofpaterso00unse/page/n1/mode/2up). Sumner Boyd also gives details of the IWW's arrest strategy.

6. Quoted in Baxandall, *Words on Fire*, 17.

7. Sumner Boyd, *Pageant of the Paterson Strike*, 4.

8. Golin, *Fragile Bridge*, 137.

9. Elizabeth Gurley Flynn, in *Pageant of the Paterson Strike*.

10. Quoted in Lena Rubin, "Artists in Revolt, Form New Society: The 1913 Armory Show," www.villagepreservation.org/2021/02/17/artists-in-revolt-form-new-society-the-1913-armory-show/.

11. Woolf, "Mr. Bennett and Mrs. Brown," in *Collected Essays*, 320. The phrase has been picked over innumerable times and is the title of at least one book.

12. Lois Rudnick, Introduction, in Luhan, *Movers and Shakers*, ix.

13. Fola stayed with Barney in 1920, most likely connected through a shared interest in pacifism rather than each other—her husband George Middleton was also there.

14. Rudnick, *Mabel Dodge Luhan*, 24–25.

15. Rudnick, 26.

16. Wanda M. Corn, Introduction, in Rudnick and Wilson-Powell, *Mabel Dodge Luhan and Company*.

17. Stein, *Selected Writings*, 121.

18. Stein, "Portrait of Mabel Dodge at the Villa Curonia," in *Selected Writings*, 527–530.

19. Quoted in Rudnick, *Mabel Dodge Luhan*, 69.

20. Luhan, *Movers and Shakers*, 10.

21. Cheryl Black is unusual in naming Neith as a member of Heterodoxy—she is more usually described as a friend of the group who was often preoccupied taking care of her home and children. Black, *Women of Provincetown*, 13.

22. Luhan, *Movers and Shakers*, 23.

23. Luhan, 83.

24. Luhan, *European Experiences*, 100.

25. Watson, *Strange Bedfellows*, 136.

26. Luhan, *Movers and Shakers*, 86.

27. Luhan, 87.

28. Luhan, 92.

29. Mabel Dodge, "Speculations, or Post-Impressionism in Prose," *Arts & Decoration*, March 1913, 173–174.

30. Luhan, *Movers and Shakers*, 35.

31. Luhan, 36.

32. Quoted in Green, *New York 1913*, 186.

33. Luhan, *Movers and Shakers*, 36.

34. Hapgood, *Victorian in the Modern World*, 340.

35. Quoted in Garrison, *Mary Heaton Vorse*, 24.

36. Garrison, 75.

37. See Chen, *"The Sex Side of Life,"* for a full account of Mary's remarkable life.

38. Dennison, "Babies for Suffrage," 24–30.

39. Stein, "Autobiography of Alice B. Toklas," in *Selected Writings*, 111–112.

40. Luhan, *Movers and Shakers*, 186.

41. Green, *New York 1913*, 197.

42. Luhan, *Movers and Shakers*, 205.

43. Hochschild, *Rebel Cinderella*, 143.

44. Quotes via Blake, "A New Social Art."

45. Potter, "Max Eastman's Two Books," 795.

46. Descriptions from the *Pageant of the Paterson Strike* program.

47. Potter, "Max Eastman's Two Books," 795.

48. The phrase is Linda Nochlin's, from "The Paterson Strike Pageant of 1913," *Art in America* 62 (May–June 1974): 64–68. Cited in Glassberg, *American Historical Pageantry*.

49. Bzowski, "Spectacular Suffrage," 84.

50. Luhan, *Movers and Shakers*, 204.

51. Green, *New York 1913*, 212.

52. Vorse, *Footnote to Folly*, 53

Chapter 7: Femi-*what?*

1. Quotes from "Talk on Feminism Stirs Great Crowd," *New York Times*, February 18, 1914.

2. Floyd Dell, "Confessions of a Feminist Man," *The Masses*, March 1914, 8.

3. "Talk on Feminism Stirs Great Crowd," *New York Times*, February 18, 1914.

4. "What Is Feminism?" *New-York Tribune*, February 15, 1914.

5. Ida Tarbell, "Interesting People: Nina Wilcox Putnam," *American Magazine*, May 1913, 34.

6. "'Advanced' Women Scolded in Church," *New York Times*, March 11, 1914.

7. Inez Milholland, "A New Department for Women: The Changing Home," *McClure's Magazine*, March 1913, 206.

8. Young, "What Is Feminism?"

9. Florence Guy Woolston, "Marriage Customs and Taboo Among the Early Heterodites," in Schwarz, *Radical Feminists of Heterodoxy*, 107–109.

10. Young, "What Is Feminism?" 216, 219.

11. Quoted in Schwarz, *Radical Feminists of Heterodoxy*, 67. Schwarz draws on Harry Hollingworth's biography to suggest that Leta remained sadly trapped in traditional femininity. But to write a full-length biography of her at all, bringing her work to a wide readership, does not strike me as the action of a man who considers his wife a mere helpmeet.

12. Telegram from Fola La Follette to Grace Nail Johnson, June 9, 1938, Grace Nail Johnson papers, box 32, folder 134, Beinecke Rare Book and Manuscript Library, Yale University.

13. Irwin, *Adventures of Yesterday*.

14. Waitt, "Katharine Anthony," 73. Though the term *gay* didn't come widely into use to refer to homosexual people—especially women—until after World War II, slang is notoriously slippery, and given the sophisticated circles the women moved in, it is likely the wink was deliberate.

15. Quoted in Simonson, "*Féminisme Oblige*," 226.

16. Wylie, *My Life with George*, quote via "'My Life with George: An Unconventional Autobiography, by I. A. R. Wylie,'" Neglected Books, May 27, 2012, https://neglectedbooks.com/?p=1379.

17. In the "Heterodoxy to Marie" album, the women share a joint page, illustrated with caricatures drawn by Lou, and a poem that announces: "Here comes Lou and here comes Liz." Marriage detail and "love is good" quote via Showalter, *These Modern Women*, 104.

18. This is especially noticeable in Judith Schwarz's study, based on her personal experience.

19. Report in the *Brooklyn Daily Eagle*, September 3, 1913. Via Hugh Ryan, "How Dressing in Drag Was Labeled a Crime," History.com, June 25, 2019, www.history.com/news/stonewall-riots-lgbtq-drag-three-article-rule. See also Eskridge, *Gaylaw*, 52–55.

20. Baker, *Fighting for Life*, 64–65.

21. Woolston, "Marriage Customs and Taboo," in Schwarz, *Radical Feminists of Heterodoxy*, 107.

22. "Few in Trousers at Feminist Ball," *New-York Tribune*, December 27, 1914.

23. "No Real Trousers at Feminist Ball," *New York Times*, December 27, 1914. Patricia A. Carter identifies Alice as a lesbian. Carter, "From Single to Married," 52.

24. Quoted in finding aid to the Carl Zigrosser papers, Kislak Center for Special Collections, Rare Books, and Manuscripts, University of Pennsylvania, Philadelphia. Maud Muller was the farm-girl heroine of a popular nineteenth-century poem by John Greenleaf Whittier.

25. "No Real Trousers," *New York Times*, December 27, 1914.

26. Quoted in Jones, *Heretics and Hellraisers*, 35.

Chapter 8: Does Mr. Freud Live in the Village?

1. Watson, *Strange Bedfellows*, 157. Chapter title quotation "over-heard" by Arens, *Little Book of Greenwich Village*, 19.

2. Quoted in Showalter, *These Modern Women*, 3.

3. Quoted in Adickes, *To Be Young*, 141–142.

4. Adickes, 142.

5. Quoted in Alexandra Sacks and George Makari, "Freud in the New World," *American Journal of Psychiatry* 166, no. 6 (June 2009): 662.

6. Grace Potter, "The Purpose of Mating," *Birth Control Review*, April 1922.

7. Wittenstein, "The Feminist Uses of Psychoanalysis," 41.

8. Anthony, *Feminism in Germany and Scandinavia*, 231.

9. Wittenstein, "The Feminist Uses of Psychoanalysis," 45.

10. Beatrice Hinkle, "Woman's Subjective Dependence on Men," *Harper's*, January 1932.

11. Quoted in Jones, *Heretics and Hellraisers*, 34.

12. Parsons, *Journal of a Feminist*, 51.

13. Parsons, *Fear and Conventionality*, 76.

14. Quoted in Wittenstein, "The Heterodoxy Club," 36.

15. Rowbotham, *Dreamers of a New Day*, 14.

16. Stansell, *American Moderns*, 91.

17. Quoted in Simonson, "*Féminisme Oblige*," 160.

18. Elsie Clews Parsons, "Facing Race Suicide," *The Masses*, June 1915, 15.

19. Hale, *What Women Want*, 273–274.

20. Simonson, "*Féminisme Oblige*," 348; Pinchot letter, quoted in Cott, *Grounding of Modern Feminism*, 158.

21. Quoted in Wittenstein, "The Heterodoxy Club," 35.

22. Milford, *Savage Beauty*, 163.

23. Dell, *Homecoming*, 283.

24. Boyce and Hapgood, *Intimate Warriors*, 110.

Chapter 9: Suppressed Desires

1. Garrison, *Mary Heaton Vorse*, 57.

2. Schwarz, *Radical Feminists of Heterodoxy*, 122.

3. Dorr, *Woman of Fifty*, 74.

4. Mickenberg, *"The Bolshevik Revolution Had Descended on Me,"* xiv. Job ads in the United States were gender segregated until the 1960s.

5. Quoted in Fahs, *Out on Assignment*, 40.

6. Bogard, preface to Kenton, "Provincetown Players," 7.

346   Notes to Chapter 9

7. Ben-Zvi, *Susan Glaspell*, 128.

8. Quoted in Hernando Real, "Luncheon for Suffrage," 76.

9. Quoted in Matthews, "The New Psychology and American Drama," 149.

10. The characterization of Broadway versus the little theater is drawn from Fred Matthews.

11. Glaspell, *Road to the Temple*, quoted in Brenda Murphy, *Provincetown Players*, 11.

12. Langner, *Magic Curtain*, 91.

13. Schwarz, *Radical Feminists of Heterodoxy*, 64.

14. Adele Heller, "The New Theatre," 228.

15. Cook, "Female Support Networks and Political Activism," 52.

16. Crowley, *Neighborhood Playhouse*, 31.

17. Kenton, "The Provincetown Players," 17.

18. Kenton, 19.

19. Kenton, 78.

20. "New York Notes," *Christian Science Monitor*, February 5, 1918.

21. Widely repeated (and disputed), the scene originates with Glaspell herself, in *The Road to the Temple*, 253–254.

22. Barnes, "The Days of Jig Cook," 388.

23. "Workers Should Produce Their Own Plays," *New York Call*, February 29, 1920. Quoted in Black, *Women of Provincetown*, 86.

24. Interview with Rauh, December 11, 1962. Quoted in Black, *Women of Provincetown*, 106.

25. Quoted in Black, 106.

26. Black, 125.

27. Black, 25.

28. Irwin, *Adventures of Yesterday*, 414.

29. Hapgood, *Victorian in the Modern World*, 377. Quoted in Wittenstein, "The Heterodoxy Club," 28, and also in Schwarz, *Radical Feminists of Heterodoxy*, 3. Schwarz takes strong exception to the implication that the club was little more than "a coffee-klatch for half-crazed mystics," but Wittenstein, rightly I think, argues that heightened emotion was characteristic of the club's meetings, and in no way seen by Heterodoxy as antithetical to intelligence.

30. Edna Kenton, in her essay on feminism, makes this connection explicit.

31. Black, *Women of Provincetown*, 67.

32. Glaspell, *Road to the Temple*, 252–253.

33. Susan Glaspell, "Joe," *The Masses*, January 1916, 3.

34. Garrison, *Mary Heaton Vorse*, 102–105.

35. Edna Kenton and Rose Pastor Stokes were two recipients of such fundraising efforts in the early 1930s.

Chapter 10: "The Baby Is the Great Problem"

1. Howe and Howe, "Pensioning the Widow and the Fatherless," 282–291.

2. Carter, "From Single to Married," 42.

3. "Feminists Debate Plans for a House," *New York Times*, April 22, 1914, 12.

4. "Marriage Under Two Roofs," in Cook, *Crystal Eastman*, 76–83.

5. "Fannie Hurst Wed; Hid Secret Five Years," *New York Times*, May 4, 1920.

6. Charlotte Perkins Gilman, "How Home Conditions React upon the Family," 1909. In Gilman, *Families, Marriages, and Children*, 22.

7. Quoted in Carter, "From Single to Married," 50.

8. Marguerite Mooers Marshall, "Wage Earning Mother Social Phenomenon Will Not Abandon Her Chosen Career," *Evening World* (New York), January 13, 1915.

9. Laura Fay-Smith, "That Feminist Paradise Palace," *New York Times*, April 25, 1915, 6.

10. George MacAdam, "Feminist Apartment House to Solve Baby Problem," *New York Times* (Sunday Magazine), January 24, 1915, 9.

11. Parsons, *Old-Fashioned Woman*, 83.

12. Discussed in Jones, *Heretics and Hellraisers*, 66–69.

13. Review by Gail West, quoted in Simonson, "*Féminisme Oblige*," 202.

14. Katharine Anthony, *Mothers Who Must Earn*, 129. Statistics and analysis via Simonson, "*Féminisme Oblige*," 204–205.

15. For a detailed discussion of Rodman's educational theories and the classes she taught at Wadleigh High, see Carter, "Guiding the Working-Class Girl."

16. Brooklyn and the other boroughs became part of the metropolis of New York City in 1898.

17. Dorr, *Woman of Fifty*, 278.

18. Quoted in Carter, "Henrietta Rodman," 161.

19. Mrs. and Mr. John Martin, "The Woman Movement and the Baby Crop," *New York Times Magazine*, August 29, 1915.

20. Charlotte Perkins Gilman, "Freedom of Speech in the Public Schools," *The Forerunner*, March 6, 1915, 72–74.

21. Young, "What Is Feminism," 680. Italics original.

22. Black, *Women of Provincetown*, 17. Stella's son Ian founded the publishing imprint Ballantine Books.

23. Garrison, *Mary Heaton Vorse*, 75–76.

24. *The Woman Voter*, February 1915, 12.

25. Carter, "Henrietta Rodman," 166–167. According to Patricia Carter, who was able to trace via the census two-thirds of the twenty-seven

teacher-mothers who fell under the school board's scrutiny in 1914, all but three were still teaching in 1920, and more than half by 1930, along with several of their daughters. In their own lives, these teachers proved the feminists' point—that women wanted to combine work and family.

Chapter 11: How Long Must We Wait?

1. Baker, *Fighting for Life*, 191.

2. Hurst, *Anatomy of Me*, 246.

3. Kroeger, *Fannie*, 21. It would be nearly twenty years before Fannie Hurst published the novel for which she's best remembered now, the melodrama of racial passing and mother-daughter conflict *Imitation of Life*, the basis for Douglas Sirk's classic 1959 weepy.

4. Baker, *Fighting for Life*, 194.

5. Bzowski, "Spectacular Suffrage," 87.

6. Dorothy's photograph was widely circulated, and she made several front pages, including the *Topeka (KS) State Journal*, November 6, 1915, under the headline "Creates Sensation with Suffrage Plea Painted on her Pretty Back." Sadly, it does not appear she was able to translate her moment of notoriety into any lasting fame.

7. Dye, *As Equals and As Sisters*, 122–138.

8. Details of Lou's life are drawn from Alice Sheppard, "Suffrage Art and Feminism," and Lou's personal narrative, "Lightning Speed Through Life," in Showalter, *These Modern Women*, 97–104.

9. "Lou Rogers, Cartoonist," *Woman's Journal and Suffrage News* 44, no. 31 (August 2, 1913): 1–2.

10. Alice Sheppard, "Political and Social Consciousness in the Woman Suffrage Cartoons of Lou Rogers and Nina Allender," *Studies in American Humor* 4, no. 1/2 (Spring/Summer 1985), 42.

11. Jill Lepore describes the striking parallel between this illustration and early depictions of the comic-book heroine Wonder Woman, originally drawn by Harry George Peter, Lou's colleague at *The Judge*, where the cartoon first appeared. Lepore, *Secret History of Wonder Woman*, 84–86.

12. For a more detailed look at this contest, see Joanna Scutts, "The Great Everywoman Outfit Contest of 1915," *Narratively*, September 12, 2019.

13. Dye, *As Equals and As Sisters*, 136–137.

14. Sarah Addington, "Who's Who in New York's Bohemia," *New-York Tribune*, November 14, 1915. Crystal's first married name was Benedict, although she did not use it herself.

15. "Emma Goldman's Defense," *The Masses*, June 1916, 27.

16. Quoted in Wittenstein, "The Heterodoxy Club," 39.

17. "Birth Control in the Feminist Program," in Cook, *Crystal Eastman*, 46–49. Originally published in *The Birth Control Review*, January 1918.

18. Katharine Anthony was both a critic and a booster of Ellen Key's ideas, and she has been called the Swedish feminist's "chief American publicist," Buhle, *Feminism and Its Discontents*, 39.

19. Quoted in Simonson, "*Féminisme Oblige*," 226.

20. Adickes, *To Be Young*, 128–129.

21. See, for example, Chesler, *Woman of Valor*, 97–98.

22. "With Members Sworn to Secrecy," *New-York Tribune*, November 24, 1914.

23. Sochen, *New Woman*, 65–66.

24. *The Masses*, January 1917, 6.

25. Comstock died in September 1915.

26. Gertrude Marvin, "Anthony and the Devil," *The Masses*, February 1914, 16. Over the issue of belief in a literal devil, the exchange struck me for how closely it mirrors one between the late Supreme Court justice Antonin Scalia and a female journalist, Jennifer Senior, almost a century later. "In Conversation with Antonin Scalia," *New York Magazine*, October 4, 2013.

27. Dorr, *Woman of Fifty*, 271; Rudnick, *Mabel Dodge Luhan*, 86.

28. Mary Ware Dennett, *The Sex Side of Life: A Guide for Young People* (private printing, 1919), 14.

29. Craig, "The Sex Side of Life," 159.

30. Craig, 149.

31. Craig, 161.

32. Stokes speech, "The Right to Control Birth," reprinted in Michels, *Jewish Radicals*, 104–109.

33. Adickes, *To Be Young*, 127.

34. Hochschild, *Rebel Cinderella*, 162.

Chapter 12: A Woman's War Against War

1. Garrison, *Mary Heaton Vorse*, 86–87.

2. "Silent as Women March for Peace," *New-York Tribune*, August 30, 1914, 10. The number of Black women in the parade varied with the reports, from as few as 20 to as many as 250. Unlike other papers, the *Tribune* report correctly distinguishes between their leader, Rosalie Jonas, a Black poet, and Rosalie Jones, a white socialite and suffragist,

who was also marching and famous for her suffrage hikes to Albany and Washington, DC.

3. Aronson, *Crystal Eastman*, 124.

4. Quoted in Wittenstein, "The Heterodoxy Club," 44.

5. Quoted in Jones, *Heretics and Hellraisers*, 87.

6. Stevens, *Jailed for Freedom*, 77.

7. Aronson, *Crystal Eastman*, 113–114.

8. Garrison, *Mary Heaton Vorse*, 88–89.

9. Garrison, 82.

10. Aronson, *Crystal Eastman*, 122.

11. Details via Lumsden, *Inez*, 135–139, and Kraft, *Peace Ship*, 301, 304.

12. *New York Evening Post*, March 13, 1915.

13. Inez Milholland, "Censorship," *The Crisis*, January 1917 (published posthumously).

14. Perry, *May We Forever Stand*, 26–29.

15. Bzowski, "Spectacular Suffrage," 88.

16. The radicals, Thomas Mooney and Warren K. Billings, were both finally pardoned in 1939.

17. Aronson, *Crystal Eastman*, 150.

18. Aronson, 142–144. Details of her wedding to Walter Fuller, 155.

19. Hochschild, *Rebel Cinderella*, 155.

20. Jones, *Heretics and Hellraisers*, 70.

21. Stevens, *Jailed for Freedom*, 81–82.

22. Cook, *Crystal Eastman*, 17.

23. Inez Milholland to Eugen Boissevain, quoted in Nicolosi, "'The Most Beautiful Suffragette,'" 306.

24. Nicolosi, "'The Most Beautiful Suffragette,'" 306.

25. Quoted in Lumsden, *Inez*, 165.

26. Aronson, *Crystal Eastman*, 156.

Chapter 13: Pacifism Versus Patriotism

1. Stevens, *Jailed for Freedom*, 100.

2. Irwin, *Adventures of Yesterday*, 460.

3. Stevens, *Jailed for Freedom*, 106.

4. Cassidy, *Mr. President*, 174.

5. Stevens, *Jailed for Freedom*, 108.

6. Simonson, "*Féminisme Oblige*," 265–267.

7. In February 1918, they were thinly rewarded when a paternalistic and class-prejudiced version of suffrage was passed, which allowed only

property-owning women over the age of twenty-eight to vote. It would be another decade before the franchise was extended to all women.

8. Cott, *Grounding of Modern Feminism*, 60.

9. Quoted in Hochschild, *Rebel Cinderella*, 189.

10. Davis, *Charlotte Perkins Gilman*, 339n70.

11. A December 26, 1920, letter from Marie Jenney Howe to Grace Nail Johnson has "C.P. Gilman" scheduled to speak on January 22. Box 30, folder 86, James Weldon Johnson and Grace Nail Johnson papers, Beinecke Rare Book and Manuscript Library, Yale University.

12. Dorr, *Woman of Fifty*, 280.

13. Wilson, *New York and the First World War*, 94.

14. Details from Kuhlman, "'Women's Ways in War,'" 80–100.

15. Hochschild, *Rebel Cinderella*, 174.

16. John Reed, "Whose War?" *The Masses*, April 1917, 11.

17. Hochschild, *Rebel Cinderella*, 176.

18. Simonson, "*Féminisme Oblige*," 264.

19. Davis, *Charlotte Perkins Gilman*, 330.

20. Quoted in Simonson, "*Féminisme Oblige*," 269.

21. Hochschild, *Rebel Cinderella*, 192. Hochschild notes that of fifteen hundred Americans arrested under this bill, only ten were actually charged as German agents.

22. Cassidy, *Mr. President*, 96.

23. Stansell, *American Moderns*, 315.

24. Baker, *Fighting for Life*, 182. It's unknown who this "worried member" might have been.

25. Hochschild, *Rebel Cinderella*, 183.

26. Luhan, *Movers and Shakers*, 144.

27. Vorse, "Elizabeth Gurley Flynn," 176.

28. Quoted in Baxandall, *Words on Fire*, 25.

29. Baxandall, 29.

30. Quoted in Jones, *Heretics and Hellraisers*, 106.

31. Stevens, *Jailed for Freedom*, 128.

32. Stevens, 162.

33. Stevens, 158.

34. Doty, *Society's Misfits*, 8.

35. Stevens, *Jailed for Freedom*, 203–204.

36. See Saidiya Hartman, *Wayward Lives, Beautiful Experiments*, for a powerful evocation of the impact of vagrancy laws on Black women in this era, assembled via the fragmentary surviving records of lives treated as inherently criminal and expendable.

37. Stevens, *Jailed for Freedom*, 204.

38. Negro Silent Protest Parade petition, James Weldon Johnson and Grace Nail Johnson papers, Beinecke Rare Book and Manuscript Library, Yale University.

39. Quoted in Bzowski, "Spectacular Suffrage," 90.

40. Stevens, *Jailed for Freedom*, 301–316.

41. Cassidy, *Mr. President*, 222.

42. Quoted in DuBois, *Suffrage*, 271.

43. Weiss, *Woman's Hour*, 329. Weiss gives a detailed, dramatic account of the ratification fight in Tennessee, which lays bare the racism inherent in the opposition to voting rights.

44. Quoted in DuBois, *Suffrage*, 278.

45. DuBois, 279.

Chapter 14: Red Scare, Red Summer

1. Quoted in Simonson, "*Féminisme Oblige*," 270.

2. Beatty, *Red Heart of Russia*, 480.

3. Madeleine Z. Doty, "Revolutionary Justice," *The Atlantic*, July 1918, 129–139. Quoted in Mickenberg, "*The Bolshevik Revolution Had Descended on Me*," xxvi.

4. Dearborn, *Queen of Bohemia*, 44–45. Dearborn's account implies that Sara Bard Field was a member of Heterodoxy, but she isn't listed in Schwarz or the "Heterodoxy to Marie" album. Being based on the West Coast, she would have been a less frequent visitor and was perhaps an honorary member.

5. "Classic Dispatches: The Battalion of Death," *MHQ—the Quarterly Journal of Military History* 32, no. 2 (Winter 2020), adapted from Bessie Beatty's *The Red Heart of Russia*.

6. Dorr, *Inside the Russian Revolution*, 242–243.

7. Beatty, *Red Heart of Russia*, 358.

8. Arens, *Little Book of Greenwich Village*, 22–32.

9. Floyd Dell, "The Villager's Lament," in *The Liberator*, quoted in Arens, *Little Book of Greenwich Village*, 15.

10. Chauncey, *Gay New York*, 147.

11. Quoted in Heise, "Degenerate Sex," 250.

12. McKay, *Long Way from Home*, 83.

13. Quoted in Jones, *Heretics and Hellraisers*, 70.

14. Hochschild, *Rebel Cinderella*, 193. Hochschild notes that it was Rose's "habit of meticulously correcting any errors in press coverage" that led to her arrest.

15. Rose Pastor Stokes entry, "Heterodoxy to Marie" album.

16. Simonson, "*Féminisme Oblige*," 297–299.

17. Hochschild, *Rebel Cinderella*, 215.

18. The information about Marie's arrest comes via a letter from Senator Robert La Follette to his wife, quoted in Davis, *Charlotte Perkins Gilman*, 330.

19. Baxandall, *Words on Fire*, 26.

20. Hochschild, *Rebel Cinderella*, 219.

21. Hochschild, 223.

22. Hochschild, 243–244.

23. Quoted in Baxandall, *Words on Fire*, 30.

24. Perry, *May We Forever Stand*, 56.

25. Marie Jenney Howe to Grace Nail Johnson, date unclear [September 20?], 1919, box 30, folder 86, James Weldon Johnson and Grace Nail Johnson papers, Beinecke Rare Book and Manuscript Library, Yale University.

26. Perry, *May We Forever Stand*, 56.

27. Terborg-Penn, "African American Women's Networks," 148–161.

28. Marie Jenney Howe to Grace Nail Johnson, n.d., box 30, folder 86, James Weldon Johnson and Grace Nail Johnson papers, Beinecke Rare Book and Manuscript Library, Yale University.

29. NAACP Papers, Part 7: The Anti-Lynching Campaign, 1912–1955, Series B: Anti-Lynching Legislative and Publicity Files, 1916–1955, Library of Congress.

30. Letter from Mary B. Talbert to Mary White Ovington (October 21, 1922), NAACP Papers, Part 7: The Anti-Lynching Campaign, 1912–1955, Series B: Anti-Lynching Legislative and Publicity Files, 1916–1955, Library of Congress.

31. Baxandall, *Words on Fire*, 27.

32. Muriel Draper papers, n.d., Beinecke Rare Book and Manuscript Library, Yale University.

33. Letter from Johnson to Claude McKay, August 21, 1930, box 4, folder 118, Claude McKay Collection, Yale Collection of American Literature, Beinecke Rare Book and Manuscript Library, Yale University; McKay, *Long Way from Home*, 96.

Chapter 15: The Future of Feminism

1. "Alice Paul's Convention," in Cook, *Crystal Eastman*, 57–63.

2. Quoted in Aronson, *Crystal Eastman*, 223.

3. Alonso, *Women's Peace Union*, 53. The amendment was introduced by Republican senator Lynn Joseph Frazier of North Dakota in 1926 but drafted earlier, with Caroline Lexow Babcock, another former suffragist.

"Outlawry of War" was the name given to a specific branch of global pacifism in the 1920s and 1930s.

4. Byrns entry in "Heterodoxy to Marie" album.

5. Alonso, *Women's Peace Union*, 9.

6. See Delegard, *Battling Miss Bolsheviki*, for a fuller account of the role played by conservative women in the backlash to radicalism.

7. Helen M. Wayne, "Bobbed Hair and Names for Wives!" *New York Times*, March 30, 1919.

8. DuBois, *Suffrage*, 285.

9. Wittenstein, "The Heterodoxy Club," 48.

10. "A Miss, Though Married," *Washington Post*, November 20, 1911.

11. Wayne, "Bobbed Hair and Names for Wives!"

12. Quoted in Mickenberg, *"The Bolshevik Revolution Had Descended on Me,"* xxii.

13. DuBois, *Suffrage*, 287.

14. Dye, *As Equals and As Sisters*, 165.

15. The first woman in the Senate, Rebecca Felton, was appointed and served one day in 1921. It was not until 1932 that a woman—also a political widow—was actually elected: Hattie Caraway, a Democrat from Arkansas.

16. Irwin, *Adventures of Yesterday*, 414.

17. "The New Generation of Women," first published 1923. In Gilman, *Charlotte Perkins Gilman*, 288.

18. Quoted in Simonson, *"Féminisme Oblige,"* 34.

19. Marie Jenney Howe, "A Woman's Woman," review of *Margaret Fuller: A Psychological Biography*, by Katharine Anthony, in *The Woman Citizen*, December 18, 1920, 804.

20. Marie Jenney Howe, "A Feminist Symposium," *New Review* 2, no. 8 (August 1914): 441.

21. Anthony, *Margaret Fuller*, 58–59.

22. See Faderman, *Odd Girls and Twilight Lovers*, 37–51, for a fuller account of the impact of sexology on cultural understandings of intimacy between women.

23. Quoted in Schwarz, *Radical Feminists of Heterodoxy*, 91.

24. Simonson, *"Féminisme Oblige,"* 11.

25. Mabel Dodge Luhan, *Edge of Taos Desert*, 193.

26. Ida and Inez appear in photographs in the Mabel Dodge Luhan papers, Yale Collection of American Literature, Beinecke Rare Book and Manuscript Library, Yale University Library.

27. Rodriguez, *Wild Heart*, 222–223.

28. Dodge, *Movers and Shakers*, 143. Fred's autobiography, *Confessions of a Reformer*, is actually very revealing of his relationship with Marie,

particularly his own inability to move past the conventions of his upbringing and support her ambitions in public life.

29. Quoted in Miller, *From Progressive to New Dealer*, 271.

30. Marie Jenney Howe to Fola La Follette, December 13, 1933, La
Follette Family Papers, Library of Congress. Quoted in Schwarz, *Radical
Feminists of Heterodoxy*, 101.

31. Schwarz, 101.

32. Letter from Mary Ware Dennett to Gwyneth (Netha) Roe, March
28 1940, La Follette Family Papers, Library of Congress. Quoted in
Schwarz, 4.

33. Irwin, *Adventures of Yesterday*, 463.

Epilogue

1. Lou Rogers, "Lightning Speed Through Life," in Showalter, *These
Modern Women*, 104.

WORKS CITED AND CONSULTED

Adickes, Sandra. "Sisters, Not Demons: The Influence of British Suffragists on the American Suffrage Movement." *Women's History Review* 11, no. 4 (December 2002): 675–690.

———. *To Be Young Was Very Heaven: Women in New York Before the First World War*. New York: St. Martin's Press, 1997.

Alonso, Harriet Hyman. *The Women's Peace Union and the Outlawry of War, 1921–1942*. Syracuse, NY: Syracuse University Press, 1997.

Anthony, Katharine. *Feminism in Germany and Scandinavia*. New York: Henry Holt, 1915.

———. *Margaret Fuller: A Psychological Biography*. New York: Harcourt, Brace, 1920.

———. *Mothers Who Must Earn*. New York: Survey Associates, 1914.

Arens, Egmont. *The Little Book of Greenwich Village*. New York: Washington Square Bookshop, 1918.

Aronson, Amy. *Crystal Eastman: A Revolutionary Life*. New York: Oxford University Press, 2020.

Atkinson, Diane. *Rise Up, Women! The Remarkable Lives of the Suffragettes*. London: Bloomsbury, 2018.

Baker, Jean H., ed. *Votes for Women: The Struggle for Suffrage Revisited*. Oxford: Oxford University Press, 2002.

Baker, S. Josephine. *Fighting for Life*. New York Review Books Classics. New York: New York Review Books, 2013. Originally published 1939.

Barnes, Djuna. "The Days of Jig Cook." In *The American Stage: Writing on Theater from Washington Irving to Tony Kushner*, 385–389. New York: Library of America, 2010. Originally published in *Theatre Guild Magazine*, January 1929.

————. *Djuna Barnes's New York*. Edited with commentary by Alyce Barry. Los Angeles: Sun & Moon Press, 1989.

Barnet, Andrea. *All-Night Party: The Women of Bohemian Greenwich Village and Harlem, 1913–1930*. Chapel Hill, NC: Algonquin Books of Chapel Hill, 2004.

Baxandall, Rosalyn. *Words on Fire: The Life and Writing of Elizabeth Gurley Flynn*. New Brunswick, NJ: Rutgers University Press, 1987.

Beatty, Bessie. *The Red Heart of Russia*. New York: Century, 1918.

Becker, Susan D. *The Origins of the Equal Rights Amendment: American Feminism Between the Wars*. Contributions in Women's Studies, no. 23. Westport, CT: Greenwood Press, 1981.

Ben-Zvi, Linda. *Susan Glaspell: Her Life and Times*. New York: Oxford University Press, 2005.

Bernstein, Patricia. *The First Waco Horror: The Lynching of Jesse Washington and the Rise of the NAACP*. College Station: Texas A&M University Press, 2006.

Bird, Stewart, Dan Georgakas, and Deborah Shaffer. *Solidarity Forever: An Oral History of the IWW*. Chicago: Lake View Press, 1985.

Black, Cheryl. *The Women of Provincetown, 1915–1922*. Tuscaloosa: University of Alabama Press, 2009.

Blake, Casey Nelson. "A New Social Art: The Paterson Strike Pageant." The Armory Show at 100, New-York Historical Society, June 4, 2013. http://armory.nyhistory.org/a-new-social-art-the-paterson-strike-pageant/.

Borda, Jennifer L. "The Woman Suffrage Parades of 1910–1913: Possibilities and Limitations of an Early Feminist Rhetorical Strategy." *Western Journal of Communication* 66, no. 1 (Winter 2002): 25–56.

Boyce, Neith, and Hutchins Hapgood. *Intimate Warriors: Portraits of a Modern Marriage, 1899–1944: Selected Works of Neith Boyce and Hutchins Hapgood*. Edited with an introduction by E. K. Trimberger. New York: Feminist Press at CUNY, 1991.

Boylan, James R. *Revolutionary Lives: Anna Strunsky & William English Walling*. Amherst: University of Massachusetts Press, 1998.

Brown, Nikki. *Private Politics and Public Voices: Black Women's Activism from World War I to the New Deal*. Bloomington: Indiana University Press, 2006.

Bryant, Louise. *Six Red Months in Russia*. New York: George H. Doran, 1918.

Buhle, Mari Jo. *Feminism and Its Discontents*. Cambridge, MA: Harvard University Press, 1998.

————. *Women and American Socialism, 1870–1920*. Urbana: University of Illinois Press, 1983.

Bzowski, Frances Diodato. "Spectacular Suffrage; Or, How Women Came Out of the Home and into the Streets and Theaters of New York City to Win the Vote." *New York History* 76, no. 1 (1995): 56–94.

Cahill, Cathleen D. *Recasting the Vote: How Women of Color Transformed the Suffrage Movement.* Chapel Hill: University of North Carolina Press, 2020.

Cameron, Ardis. "Bread and Roses Revisited: Women's Culture and Working-Class Activism in the Lawrence Strike of 1912." In *Women, Work and Protest: A Century of US Women's Labor History,* edited by Ruth Milkman, 42–61. New York: Routledge and Keegan Paul, 1985.

Carter, Patricia A. "From Single to Married: Feminist Teachers' Response to Family/Work Conflict in Early Twentieth-Century New York City." *History of Education Quarterly* 56, no. 1 (2016): 36–60.

———. "Guiding the Working-Class Girl: Henrietta Rodman's Curriculum for the New Woman." *Frontiers* 38, no. 1 (2017): 124–155.

———. "Henrietta Rodman and the Fight to Further Women's Economic Autonomy." In *Women Educators, Leaders and Activists: Educational Lives and Networks 1900–1960,* edited by Tanya Fitzgerald and Elizabeth M. Smyth, 152–178. London: Palgrave Macmillan UK, 2014.

Cassidy, Tina. *Mr. President, How Long Must We Wait?: Alice Paul, Woodrow Wilson, and the Fight for the Right to Vote.* New York: 37 Ink/Atria, 2019.

Chapman, Erin D. *Prove It on Me: New Negroes, Sex, and Popular Culture in the 1920s.* New York: Oxford University Press, 2012.

Chapman, Mary. *Making Noise, Making News: Suffrage Print Culture and U.S. Modernism.* Oxford Studies in American Literary History 6. Oxford: Oxford University Press, 2014.

Chapman, Mary, and Angela Mills, eds. *Treacherous Texts: U.S. Suffrage Literature, 1846–1946.* New Brunswick, NJ: Rutgers University Press, 2011.

Chauncey, George. *Gay New York: Gender, Urban Culture, and the Making of the Gay Male World, 1890–1940.* Updated edition. New York: Basic Books, 2008.

Chen, Constance M. *"The Sex Side of Life": Mary Ware Dennett's Pioneering Battle for Birth Control and Sex Education.* New York: New Press, 1996.

Chesler, Ellen. *Woman of Valor: Margaret Sanger and the Birth Control Movement in America.* New York: Simon & Schuster Paperbacks, 2007.

Cobble, Dorothy Sue, Linda Gordon, and Astrid Henry. *Feminism Unfinished: A Short, Surprising History of American Women's Movements.* New York: Liveright/W. W. Norton, 2014.

Cobrin, Pamela. *From Winning the Vote to Directing on Broadway: The Emergence of Women on the New York Stage, 1880–1927.* Newark: University of Delaware Press, 2009.

Committee of Fourteen Records 1905–1932. New York Public Library Manuscripts and Archives Division. https://archives.nypl.org/mss /609.

Cook, Blanche Wiesen, ed. *Crystal Eastman on Women and Revolution.* New York: Oxford University Press, 1978.

———. "Female Support Networks and Political Activism: Lillian Wald, Crystal Eastman, Emma Goldman." In *Social and Moral Reform*, edited by Nancy F. Cott, 35–53. Berlin: De Gruyter Saur, 1994.

Cooney, Robert P. J., ed. *Remembering Inez: The Last Campaign of Inez Milholland, Suffrage Martyr.* Half Moon Bay, CA: American Graphics Press, 2015.

Cooper, Brittney C. *Beyond Respectability: The Intellectual Thought of Race Women.* Women, Gender, and Sexuality in American History. Urbana: University of Illinois Press, 2017.

Cott, Nancy F. *The Grounding of Modern Feminism.* New Haven, CT: Yale University Press, 1987.

Craig, John M. "The Sex Side of Life": The Obscenity Case of Mary Ware Dennett." *Frontiers: A Journal of Women Studies* 15, no. 3 (1995): 145–166.

Crowley, Alice Lewisohn. *The Neighborhood Playhouse: Leaves from a Theatre Scrapbook.* New York: Theatre Arts Books, 1959.

Davis, Cynthia J. *Charlotte Perkins Gilman: A Biography.* Stanford, CA: Stanford University Press, 2010.

Deacon, Desley. *Elsie Clews Parsons: Inventing Modern Life.* Women in Culture and Society. Chicago: University of Chicago Press, 1997.

Dearborn, Mary V. *Queen of Bohemia: The Life of Louise Bryant.* New York: Houghton Mifflin Harcourt, 1996.

Degen, Marie Louise, and Lella Secor Florence. *The History of the Woman's Peace Party.* New York: Burt Franklin Reprints, 1974.

Delahaye, Claire. "'A Tract in Fiction': Woman Suffrage Literature and the Struggle for the Vote." *European Journal of American Studies* 11, no. 1 (June 2, 2016).

Delap, Lucy. *The Feminist Avant-Garde: Transatlantic Encounters of the Early Twentieth Century.* Ideas in Context 84. Cambridge: Cambridge University Press, 2007.

Delegard, Kirsten Marie. *Battling Miss Bolsheviki: The Origins of Female Conservatism in the United States*. Politics and Culture in Modern America. Philadelphia: University of Pennsylvania Press, 2012.

Dell, Floyd. *Homecoming*. New York: Farrar and Rinehart, 1933.

———. *Love in Greenwich Village*. New York: George H. Doran, 1926.

———. *Women as World Builders: Studies in Modern Feminism*. Chicago: Forbes and Company, 1913.

Dennison, Mariea Caudill. "Babies for Suffrage: 'The Exhibition of Painting and Sculpture by Women Artists for the Benefit of the Woman Suffrage Campaign.'" *Woman's Art Journal* 24, no. 2 (2003): 24–30.

Derleth, August. *Still Small Voice: The Biography of Zona Gale*. New York: Appleton-Century, 1940.

Dorr, Rheta Childe. "A Convert from Socialism." *North American Review* 224, no. 837 (1927): 498–504.

———. *Inside the Russian Revolution*. New York: Macmillan, 1917.

———. *A Woman of Fifty*. New York: Funk & Wagnalls, 1924.

Doty, Madeleine Z. *Society's Misfits*. New York: Century, 1916.

Dowling, Robert M. "A Marginal Man in Black Bohemia: James Weldon Johnson in the New York Tenderloin." In *Post-Bellum, Pre-Harlem: African American Literature and Culture, 1877–1919*, edited by Barbara McCaskill and Caroline Gebhard, 117–132. New York: New York University Press, 2006.

Downey, Kirstin. *The Woman Behind the New Deal: The Life of Frances Perkins, FDR's Secretary of Labor and His Moral Conscience*. New York: Nan A. Talese/Doubleday, 2009.

Dresner, Zita. "Heterodite Humor: Alice Duer Miller and Florence Guy Seabury." *Journal of American Culture* 10, no. 3 (September 1, 1987): 33–38.

Dubofsky, Melvyn. *We Shall Be All: A History of the Industrial Workers of the World*. 2nd ed. Urbana: University of Illinois Press, 1988.

DuBois, Ellen Carol. *Feminism and Suffrage: The Emergence of an Independent Women's Movement in America, 1848–1869*. Ithaca, NY: Cornell University Press, 1999.

———. *Suffrage: Women's Long Battle for the Vote*. New York: Simon & Schuster, 2020.

Dye, Nancy Schrom. *As Equals and As Sisters: Feminism, the Labor Movement, and the Women's Trade Union League of New York*. Columbia: University of Missouri Press, 1980.

———. "Creating a Feminist Alliance: Sisterhood and Class Conflict in the New York Women's Trade Union League, 1903–1914." *Feminist Studies* 2, no. 2/3 (1975): 24.

Eastman, Crystal. *Work-Accidents and the Law*. New York: Russell Sage Foundation, 1910.

Eastman, Max. *Enjoyment of Living*. New York: Harper, 1948.

Easton, Eric E. *Defending the Masses: A Progressive Lawyer's Battles for Free Speech*. Madison: University of Wisconsin Press, 2018.

Eckhaus, Phyllis. "Restless Women: The Pioneering Alumnae of New York University School of Law." *NYUL Review* 66 (1991): 1996.

Edge, Laura B. *We Stand as One: The International Ladies Garment Workers Strike, New York, 1909*. New York: Twenty-First Century Books, 2010.

Edwards, I. N. "Marriage as a Legal Cause for Dismissal of Women Teachers." *Elementary School Journal* 25, no. 9 (May 1925): 692–695.

Eisenstein, Sarah. *Give Us Bread but Give Us Roses: Working Women's Consciousness in the United States, 1890 to the First World War*. London: Routledge & K. Paul, 1983.

Enstad, Nan. *Ladies of Labor, Girls of Adventure: Working Women, Popular Culture, and Labor Politics at the Turn of the Twentieth Century*. New York: Columbia University Press, 1999.

Erenberg, Lewis A. *Steppin' Out: New York Nightlife and the Transformation of American Culture, 1890–1930*. Chicago: University of Chicago Press, 1984.

Eskridge, William N. *Gaylaw: Challenging the Apartheid of the Closet*. Cambridge, MA: Harvard University Press, 2002.

Evans, Stephanie Y. *Black Women in the Ivory Tower, 1850–1954: An Intellectual History*. Gainesville: University Press of Florida, 2007.

Faderman, Lillian. *Odd Girls and Twilight Lovers: A History of Lesbian Life in Twentieth-Century America*. New York: Columbia University Press, 1991.

Fahs, Alice. *Out on Assignment: Newspaper Women and the Making of Modern Public Space*. Chapel Hill: University of North Carolina Press, 2011.

Fink, Augusta. *I-Mary, a Biography of Mary Austin*. Tucson: University of Arizona Press, 1983.

Finnegan, Margaret Mary. *Selling Suffrage: Consumer Culture and Votes for Women*. New York: Columbia University Press, 1999.

Fishbein, Leslie. *Rebels in Bohemia: The Radicals of The Masses, 1911–1917*. Chapel Hill: University of North Carolina Press, 1982.

Fleming, Robert E. *James Weldon Johnson*. Boston: Twayne Publishers, 1987.

Flexner, Eleanor, and Ellen F. Fitzpatrick. *Century of Struggle: The Woman's Rights Movement in the United States*. Cambridge, MA: Belknap Press of Harvard University Press, 1996.

Flynn, Elizabeth Gurley. *I Speak My Own Piece: Autobiography of the "Rebel Girl."* New York: Masses & Mainstream, 1955.

———. *Rebel Girl: My First Life, 1906–1926*. New York: International Publishers, 1986.

Foner, Philip S. *Women and the American Labor Movement*. 2nd ed. Chicago: Haymarket Books, 2018.

Frankel, Noralee, and Nancy Schrom Dye, eds. *Gender, Class, Race, and Reform in the Progressive Era*. Lexington: University Press of Kentucky, 1991.

Frankfort, Roberta. *Collegiate Women: Domesticity and Career in Turn-of-the-Century America*. New York: New York University Press, 1977.

Friedl, Bettina, ed. *On to Victory: Propaganda Plays of the Woman Suffrage Movement*. Boston: Northeastern University Press, 1987.

Gallagher, Julie A. *Black Women and Politics in New York City*. Urbana: University of Illinois Press, 2012.

Garrison, Dee. *Mary Heaton Vorse: The Life of an American Insurgent*. Philadelphia: Temple University Press, 1989.

———, ed. *Rebel Pen: The Writings of Mary Heaton Vorse*. New York: Monthly Review Press, 1985.

Giddings, Paula. *When and Where I Enter: The Impact of Black Women on Race and Sex in America*. New York: W. Morrow, 1984.

Gilfoyle, Timothy J. *City of Eros: New York City, Prostitution, and the Commercialization of Sex, 1790–1920*. New York: W. W. Norton, 1994.

Gilman, Charlotte Perkins. *Charlotte Perkins Gilman: A Nonfiction Reader*. Edited by Larry Ceplair. New York: Columbia University Press, 1991.

———. *Families, Marriages, and Children*. Edited by Michael R. Hill. New Brunswick, NJ: Transaction Publishers, 2011.

———. *The Living of Charlotte Perkins Gilman: An Autobiography*. Wisconsin Studies in American Autobiography. Madison: University of Wisconsin Press, 1991.

———. *Suffrage Songs and Verses*. New York: Charlton, 1911.

———. *What Diantha Did*. Introduction by Charlotte J. Rich. Durham, NC: Duke University Press, 2005.

———. *The Yellow Wall-Paper, Herland, and Selected Writings*. Penguin Classics Edition. Introduction by Kate Bolick. New York: Penguin Random House, 2019.

Gilman, Charlotte Perkins, and Beth Sutton-Ramspeck, ed. *Herland and Related Writings*. Broadview Editions. Peterborough, Ontario: Broadview Press, 2013.

Glaspell, Susan. *The People and Close the Book: Two One-Act Plays*. New York: Frank Shay, 1918.

————. *The Road to the Temple: A Biography of George Cram Cook*. New York: Frederick A. Stokes, 1927.

Glaspell, Susan, Patricia L. Bryan, and Martha Celeste Carpentier. *Her America: "A Jury of Her Peers" and Other Stories*. Iowa City: University of Iowa Press, 2010.

Glassberg, David. *American Historical Pageantry: The Uses of Tradition in the Early Twentieth Century*. Chapel Hill: University of North Carolina Press, 1990.

Glenn, Susan A. *Female Spectacle: The Theatrical Roots of Modern Feminism*. Cambridge, MA: Harvard University Press, 2000.

Goldsby, Jacqueline Denise. *A Spectacular Secret: Lynching in American Life and Literature*. Chicago: University of Chicago Press, 2006.

Golin, Steve. *The Fragile Bridge: Paterson Silk Strike, 1913*. Philadelphia: Temple University Press, 1988.

Goodier, Susan, and Karen Pastorello. *Women Will Vote: Winning Suffrage in New York State*. Ithaca, NY: Cornell University Press, 2017.

Gordon, Linda. *The Second Coming of the KKK: The Ku Klux Klan of the 1920s and the American Political Tradition*. New York: Liveright/ W. W. Norton, 2017.

Gottlieb, Agnes Hooper. "The Reform Years at Hampton's: The Magazine Journalism of Rheta Childe Dorr, 1909–1912." *Electronic Journal of Communication* 4, nos. 2–4 (1994).

Grand, Sarah. "The New Aspect of the Woman Question." *North American Review* 158, no. 448 (1894): 270–276.

Grant, Thomas. "Feminist Humor of the 1920s: The 'Little Insurrections' of Florence Guy Seabury." In *New Perspectives on Women and Comedy*, 157–167. Philadelphia: Gordon and Breach, 1992.

Grasso, Linda M. "Differently Radical: Suffrage Issues and Feminist Ideas in the *Crisis* and the *Masses*." *American Journalism* 36, no. 1 (January 2, 2019): 71–98.

Green, Barbara. "Around 1910: Periodical Culture, Women's Writing, and Modernity." *Tulsa Studies in Women's Literature* 30, no. 2 (2011): 429–439.

Green, Martin. *New York 1913: The Armory Show and the Paterson Strike Pageant*. New York: Collier Books, 1988.

Greenwald, Richard A. *The Triangle Fire, the Protocols of Peace, and Industrial Democracy in Progressive Era New York*. Philadelphia: Temple University Press, 2005.

Gutek, Gerald Lee, and Patricia Gutek. *Bringing Montessori to America: S. S. McClure, Maria Montessori, and the Campaign to Publicize Montessori Education*. Tuscaloosa: University of Alabama Press, 2016.

Hale, Beatrice Forbes-Robertson. *What Women Want: An Interpretation of the Feminist Movement.* New York: Frederick A. Stokes, 1914.

Hale, Nathan G. *Freud and the Americans: The Beginnings of Psychoanalysis in the United States, 1876–1917.* Vol. 1, *Freud in America.* New York: Oxford University Press, 1971.

———. *Freud and the Americans: The Rise and Crisis of Psychoanalysis in the United States, 1917–1985.* Vol. 2, *Freud in America.* New York: Oxford University Press, 1995.

Hapgood, Hutchins. *A Victorian in the Modern World.* New York: Harcourt, Brace, 1939.

Hare, Peter H. *A Woman's Quest for Science: Portrait of Anthropologist Elsie Clews Parsons.* Buffalo, NY: Prometheus Books, 1985.

Harris, Luther S. *Around Washington Square: An Illustrated History of Greenwich Village.* Baltimore: Johns Hopkins University Press, 2003.

Hartman, Saidiya V. *Wayward Lives, Beautiful Experiments: Intimate Histories of Social Upheaval.* New York: W. W. Norton, 2019.

Hayden, Dolores. *The Grand Domestic Revolution: A History of Feminist Designs for American Homes, Neighborhoods, and Cities.* Cambridge, MA: MIT Press, 1983.

Heise, Thomas. "Degenerate Sex and the City: Djuna Barnes's Urban Underworld." *Twentieth Century Literature* 55, no. 3 (2009): 287–321.

Heller, Adele. "The New Theatre." In *1915, the Cultural Moment: The New Politics, the New Woman, the New Psychology, the New Art & the New Theatre in America*, edited by Adele Heller and Lois Palken Rudnick, 217–232. New Brunswick, NJ: Rutgers University Press, 1991.

Heller, Adele, and Lois Palken Rudnick, eds. *1915, the Cultural Moment: The New Politics, the New Woman, the New Psychology, the New Art & the New Theatre in America.* New Brunswick, NJ: Rutgers University Press, 1991.

Henry, Susan. *Anonymous in Their Own Names: Doris E. Fleischman, Ruth Hale, and Jane Grant.* Nashville, TN: Vanderbilt University Press, 2012.

Hicks, Ami Mali. *Everyday Art.* New York: E. P. Dutton, 1925.

Hochschild, Adam. *Rebel Cinderella: From Rags to Riches to Radical, the Epic Journey of Rose Pastor Stokes.* New York: Houghton Mifflin Harcourt, 2020.

Hollingworth, Harry L. *Leta Stetter Hollingworth.* Lincoln: University of Nebraska Press, 1943.

Howe, Frederic C. *The City: The Hope of Democracy.* New York: Charles Scribner's Sons, 1905.

———. *Confessions of a Reformer.* New York: Scribner, 1925.

Howe, Marie Jenney. "An Anti-Suffrage Monologue." In *The Radical Feminists of Heterodoxy: Greenwich Village, 1912–1940*, edited by Judith Schwarz, 110–114. Lebanon, NH: New Victoria Publishers, 1982.

Howe, Marie Jenney, and Frederic C. Howe. "Pensioning the Widow and the Fatherless." *Good Housekeeping* 57 (September 1913): 282–291.

Hulme, Peter. "The Liberal Club and Its Jamaican Secretary." Unpublished manuscript, March 2017. PDF. https://essex.academia.edu/PeterHulme/Drafts.

Hurst, Fannie. *Anatomy of Me: A Wonderer in Search of Herself.* London: Jonathan Cape, 1959.

Irmscher, Christoph. *Max Eastman: A Life.* New Haven, CT: Yale University Press, 2017.

Irwin, Inez Haynes (Gillmore). *Adventures of Yesterday.* Unpublished autobiography. Inez Haynes Gillmore Irwin papers, Schlesinger Library, Radcliffe College, Cambridge, MA.

———. *The Story of the Women's Party.* New York: Harcourt, Brace, 1921.

Johnson, James Weldon. *Along This Way: The Autobiography of James Weldon Johnson.* New York: Viking Press, 1933.

———. *The Autobiography of an Ex-Colored Man: Authoritative Text, Backgrounds and Sources, Criticism.* A Norton Critical Edition, edited by Jacqueline Goldsby. New York: W. W. Norton, 2015.

———. *The Book of American Negro Poetry.* Cleveland: Duke Classics, 2012.

———. *Writings.* New York: Library of America, 2004.

Jones, Margaret C. *Heretics and Hellraisers: Women Contributors to The Masses, 1911–1917.* Austin: University of Texas Press, 1993.

Jones, Martha S. *Vanguard: How Black Women Broke Barriers, Won the Vote, and Insisted on Equality for All.* New York: Basic Books, 2020.

Jordan, Elizabeth Garver, Mary Austin, Samuel Merwin, Henry Raleigh, et al. *The Sturdy Oak: A Composite Novel of American Politics by Fourteen American Authors.* New York: Henry Holt, 1917.

Keire, Mara L. "The Committee of Fourteen and Saloon Reform in New York City, 1905–1920." *Business and Economic History* 26, no. 2 (Winter 1997): 573–583.

Kennedy, Jeff. "Experiment on Macdougal Street: The Provincetown Players' 1918–1919 Season." *Eugene O'Neill Review* 32 (2010): 86–123.

Kenton, Edna. "The Provincetown Players and the Playwrights' Theatre." Edited by Jackson R. Bryer, Travis Bogard, and Bernadette Smyth. *The Eugene O'Neill Review* 21, no. 1/2 (1997): 4–160.

Kessler-Harris, Alice. *Out to Work: A History of Wage-Earning Women in the United States.* 20th anniversary ed. Oxford: Oxford University Press, 2003.

Klein, Ann G. *A Forgotten Voice: The Biography of Leta Stetter Holling-worth*. Scottsdale, AZ: Great Potential Press, 2002.

Kraditor, Aileen S. *The Ideas of the Woman Suffrage Movement, 1890–1920*. New York: W. W. Norton, 1981.

Kraft, Barbara S. *The Peace Ship: Henry Ford's Pacifist Adventure in the First World War*. New York: Macmillan, 1978.

Krasner, David. *A Beautiful Pageant: African American Theatre, Drama, and Performance in the Harlem Renaissance, 1910–1927*. New York: Palgrave Macmillan, 2002.

Kroeger, Brooke. *Fannie: The Talent for Success of Writer Fannie Hurst*. New York: Times Books, 1999.

———. *The Suffragents: How Women Used Men to Get the Vote*. Albany: State University of New York Press, 2017.

Kuhlman, Erika. "'Women's Ways in War': The Feminist Pacifism of the New York City Woman's Peace Party." *Frontiers: A Journal of Women Studies* 18, no. 1 (1997): 80–100.

Ladd-Taylor, Molly. *Mother-Work: Women, Child Welfare, and the State, 1890–1930*. Urbana: University of Illinois Press, 1995.

Lagemann, Ellen Condliffe. *A Generation of Women: Education in the Lives of Progressive Reformers*. Cambridge, MA: Harvard University Press, 1979.

Lange, Allison K. *Picturing Political Power: Images in the Women's Suffrage Movement*. Chicago: University of Chicago Press, 2020.

Langner, Lawrence. *The Magic Curtain: The Story of a Life in Two Fields, Theatre and Invention*. New York: Dutton, 1951.

Lears, T. J. Jackson. *Rebirth of a Nation: The Making of Modern America, 1877–1920*. New York: HarperCollins, 2009.

Lepore, Jill. *The Secret History of Wonder Woman*. New York: Alfred A. Knopf, 2014.

Lerner, Elinor. "Jewish Involvement in the New York City Woman Suffrage Movement." *American Jewish History* 70, no. 4 (1981): 442–461.

Levin, Joanna. *Bohemia in America, 1858–1920*. Stanford, CA: Stanford University Press, 2010.

———. "Bohemians: Greenwich Village and The Masses." In *American Literature in Transition, 1910–1920*, edited by Mark W. Van Wienen, 117–130. New York: Cambridge University Press, 2018.

Linett, Maren Tova, ed. *The Cambridge Companion to Modernist Women Writers*. Cambridge: Cambridge University Press, 2010.

Loomis, Erik. *A History of America in Ten Strikes*. New York: New Press, 2020.

Lovett, Laura L. *Conceiving the Future: Pronatalism, Reproduction, and the Family in the United States: 1890–1938*. Chapel Hill: University of North Carolina Press, 2007.

Luhan, Mabel Dodge. *European Experiences: Volume Two of Intimate Memories*. New York: Harcourt, Brace, 1935.

———. *Movers and Shakers: Volume Three of Intimate Memories*. New York: Harcourt, Brace, 1936.

———. *Edge of Taos Desert: An Escape to Reality, Volume Four of Intimate Memories*. New York: Harcourt, Brace, 1937.

Lumsden, Linda J. *Inez: The Life and Times of Inez Milholland*. Bloomington: Indiana University Press, 2016.

Makowsky, Veronica A. *Susan Glaspell's Century of American Women: A Critical Interpretation of Her Work*. New York: Oxford University Press, 1993.

Marsh, John. "Labor: The Lawrence Strike in Poetry and Public Opinion." In *American Literature in Transition, 1910–1920*, edited by Mark W. Van Wienen. Cambridge: Cambridge University Press, 2017.

Matthews, Fred. "The New Psychology and American Drama." In *1915, the Cultural Moment: The New Politics, the New Woman, the New Psychology, the New Art and the New Theatre in America*, edited by Adele Heller and Lois Palken Rudnick, 146–156. New Brunswick, NJ: Rutgers University Press, 1991.

Matthews, Jean V. *The Rise of the New Woman: The Women's Movement in America, 1875–1930*. Chicago: Ivan R. Dee, 2003.

Mattina, Anne F., and Dominique Ciavattoni. "Striking Women: Massachusetts Mill Workers in the Wake of Bread and Roses." In *The Great Lawrence Textile Strike of 1912: New Scholarship on the Bread and Roses Strike*, edited by Robert Forrant and Jürg K. Siegenthaler, 153–171. New York: Routledge, 2017.

McCarter, Jeremy. *Young Radicals: In the War for American Ideals*. New York: Random House, 2017.

McCaskill, Barbara, and Caroline Gebhard, eds. *Post-Bellum, Pre-Harlem: African American Literature and Culture, 1877–1919*. New York: New York University Press, 2006.

McFarland, Gerald W. *Inside Greenwich Village: A New York City Neighborhood, 1898–1918*. Amherst: University of Massachusetts Press, 2001.

McGirr, Lisa. *The War on Alcohol: Prohibition and the Rise of the American State*. New York: W. W. Norton, 2015.

McKay, Claude. *A Long Way from Home*. Edited with an introduction by Gene Andrew Jarrett. New Brunswick, NJ: Rutgers University Press, 2007. First published 1937.

Michels, Tony. *Jewish Radicals: A Documentary Reader*. Goldstein-Goren Series in American Jewish History. New York: NYU Press, 2013.

Mickenberg, Julia L. *American Girls in Red Russia: Chasing the Soviet Dream*. Chicago: University of Chicago Press, 2017.

———. *"The Bolshevik Revolution Had Descended on Me": Madeleine Z. Doty's Russian Revolution*. Bloomington, IN: Slavica, 2019.

Milford, Nancy. *Savage Beauty: The Life of Edna St. Vincent Millay*. New York: Random House, 2001.

Milkman, Ruth, ed. *Women, Work, and Protest: A Century of US Women's Labor History*. London: Routledge and Kegan Paul, 1987.

Miller, Alice Duer. *Are Women People? A Book of Rhymes for Suffrage Times*. New York: George H. Doran, 1915.

Miller, Kenneth E. *From Progressive to New Dealer: Frederic C. Howe and American Liberalism*. University Park: Pennsylvania State University Press, 2010.

Mitchell, Juliet. *Psychoanalysis and Feminism*. New York: Pantheon Books, 1974.

Mitchell, Koritha. *Living with Lynching: African American Lynching Plays, Performance, and Citizenship, 1890–1930*. Urbana: University of Illinois Press, 2012.

Morrissette, Noelle, ed. *New Perspectives on James Weldon Johnson's "The Autobiography of an Ex-Colored Man."* Athens: University of Georgia Press, 2017.

Murphy, Brenda. *The Provincetown Players and the Culture of Modernity*. Cambridge: Cambridge University Press, 2006.

Neuman, Johanna. *Gilded Suffragists: The New York Socialites Who Fought for Women's Right to Vote*. New York: New York University Press, 2017.

Nicolosi, Ann Marie. "'The Most Beautiful Suffragette': Inez Milholland and the Political Currency of Beauty." *Journal of the Gilded Age and Progressive Era* 6, no. 3 (2007): 287–309.

Nowlin, Michael. "The Color Line: Racial Inequality in the Literary Field." In *American Literature in Transition, 1910–1920*, edited by Mark W. Van Wienen, 74–88. New York: Cambridge University Press, 2018.

———. "Race Literature, Modernism, and Normal Literature: James Weldon Johnson's Groundwork for an African American Literary Renaissance, 1912–20." *Modernism/Modernity* 20, no. 3 (2013): 503–518.

Oelberg, Sarah. "Marie Hoffendahl Jenney." In *Standing Before Us: Unitarian Universalist Women & Social Reform, 1776–1936*, edited by Dorothy May Emerson, 542–544. Boston: Skinner House Books, 2000.

O'Neill, William L. *Divorce in the Progressive Era*. New Haven, CT: Yale University Press, 1967.

Orleck, Annelise. *Common Sense and a Little Fire: Women and Working-Class Politics in the United States, 1900–1965*. Chapel Hill: University of North Carolina Press, 1995.

Parker, Alison M. *Unceasing Militant: The Life of Mary Church Terrell*. Chapel Hill: University of North Carolina Press, 2021.

Parry, Albert. *Garrets and Pretenders: A History of Bohemianism in America*. New York: Covici-Friede, 1933.

Parsons, Elsie Clews. *The Family: An Ethnographical and Historical Outline*. New York: Putnam, 1906.

———. *Fear and Conventionality*. New York: G. P. Putnam's Sons, 1914.

———. *The Journal of a Feminist*. With a new introduction and notes by Margaret C. Jones. Bristol, UK: Thoemmes Press, 1994.

———. *The Old-Fashioned Woman: Primitive Fancies About the Sex*. New York: Putnam, 1913.

Passet, Joanne Ellen. *Sex Radicals and the Quest for Women's Equality*. Women in American History. Urbana: University of Illinois Press, 2003.

Pauley, Garth E. "W.E.B. Du Bois on Woman Suffrage: A Critical Analysis of His *Crisis* Writings." *Journal of Black Studies* 30, no. 3 (2000): 383–410.

Paull, John. "The Women Who Tried to Stop the Great War: The International Congress of Women at The Hague 1915." In *Global Leadership Initiatives for Conflict Resolution and Peacebuilding*, edited by A. H. Campbell, 249–266. Bellevue, NE: International Peace and Leadership Institute, 2018.

Payne, Elizabeth Anne. *Reform, Labor, and Feminism: Margaret Dreier Robins and the Women's Trade Union League*. Women in American History. Urbana: University of Illinois Press, 1988.

Perry, Imani. *May We Forever Stand: A History of the Black National Anthem*. Chapel Hill: University of North Carolina Press, 2018.

Petty, Leslie. *Romancing the Vote: Feminist Activism in American Fiction, 1870–1920*. Athens: University of Georgia Press, 2006.

Pfister, Joel, and Nancy Schnog, eds. *Inventing the Psychological: Toward a Cultural History of Emotional Life in America*. New Haven, CT: Yale University Press, 1997.

Pickens, Donald K. *Eugenics and the Progressives*. Nashville, TN: Vanderbilt University Press, 1968.

Player, Tiffany A. "The Anti-Lynching Crusaders: A Study of Black Women's Activism." Master's thesis, University of Georgia, 2008.

Real, Noelia Hernando. "A Luncheon for Suffrage: Theatrical Contributions of Heterodoxy to the Enfranchisement of the American Woman." *Revista de Estudios Norteamericanos* 16 (2012): 75–90.

Rhodes, Jane. "Pedagogies of Respectability: Race, Media, and Black Womanhood in the Early 20th Century." *Souls* 18, nos. 2–4 (October 2016): 201–214.

Roberts, Brian Russell. "Passing into Diplomacy: US Consul James Weldon Johnson and the Autobiography of an Ex-Colored Man." *MFS Modern Fiction Studies* 56, no. 2 (2010): 290–316.

Roberts, W. Adolphe. *These Many Years: An Autobiography*. Edited by Peter Hulme. Kingston: University of the West Indies Press, 2015.

Rodriguez, Suzanne. *Wild Heart: Natalie Clifford Barney's Journey from Victorian America to Belle Epoque Paris*. New York: Ecco, 2003.

Rosenberg, Rosalind. *Beyond Separate Spheres: Intellectual Roots of Modern Feminism*. New Haven, CT: Yale University Press, 1982.

Rowbotham, Sheila. *Dreamers of a New Day: Women Who Invented the Twentieth Century*. London: Verso, 2010.

Rudnick, Lois P. *Mabel Dodge Luhan: New Woman, New Worlds*. Albuquerque: University of New Mexico Press, 1987.

Rudnick, Lois P., and MaLin Wilson-Powell, eds. *Mabel Dodge Luhan and Company: American Moderns and the West*. Santa Fe: Museum of New Mexico Press, 2016.

Ryan, Hugh. *When Brooklyn Was Queer*. New York: St. Martin's Press, 2019.

Sacks, Alexandra, and George Makari. "Images in Psychiatry: Freud in the New World." *American Journal of Psychiatry* 166, no. 6 (June 2009): 662–663.

Salem, Dorothy. "Black Women and the NAACP, 1909–1922: An Encounter with Race, Class, and Gender." In *Black Women in America*, edited by Kim Vaz, 54–70. Thousand Oaks, CA: SAGE Publications, 1995.

Santangelo, Lauren. *Suffrage and the City: New York Women Battle for the Ballot*. New York: Oxford University Press, 2019.

Saville, Deborah. "Dress and Culture in Greenwich Village." In *Twentieth-Century American Fashion*, edited by Patricia Cunningham and Linda Welters, 33–56. Dress, Body, Culture 6. Oxford: Berg Publishers, 2005.

Sawyers, June Skinner, ed. *The Greenwich Village Reader: Fiction, Poetry, and Reminiscences, 1872–2002*. New York: Cooper Square Press, 2001.

Schaffer, Ronald. "The New York City Woman Suffrage Party. 1909–1919." *New York History* 43, no. 3 (1962): 269–287.

Schanke, Robert A. "Mary Shaw, a Fighting Champion." In *Women in American Theatre*, eds. Helen Krich Chinoy and Linda Walsh Jenkins, 98–107. New York: Crown, 1981.

Schwarz, Judith. *Radical Feminists of Heterodoxy: Greenwich Village, 1912–1940*. Lebanon, NH: New Victoria Publishers, 1982.

Scott, Anne Firor. *Natural Allies: Women's Associations in American History*. Women in American History. Urbana: University of Illinois Press, 1991.

Scott, William M., and Peter B. Rutkoff. *New York Modern: The Arts and the City*. Baltimore: Johns Hopkins University Press, 1999.

Shavelson, Clara Lemlich. "Remembering the Waistmakers General Strike, 1909." In *A Documentary History of the Jews in the United States, 1654–1875*, edited by Morris U. Schappes. New York: Schocken Books, 1971.

Sheppard, Alice. *Cartooning for Suffrage*. Albuquerque: University of New Mexico Press, 1994.

———. "Suffrage Art and Feminism." *Hypatia* 5, no. 2 (1990): 122–136.

Showalter, Elaine. *Inventing Herself: Claiming a Feminist Intellectual Heritage*. London: Picador, 2002.

———, ed. *These Modern Women: Autobiographical Essays from the Twenties*. New York: Feminist Press, 1989.

Sicherman, Barbara, and Carol Hurd Green, eds. *Notable American Women: The Modern Period: A Biographical Dictionary*. Cambridge, MA: Belknap Press of Harvard University Press, 1980.

Simkhovitch, Mary Kingsbury. *Neighborhood: My Story of Greenwich House*. New York: W. W. Norton, 1938.

Simmons, Christina. *Making Marriage Modern: Women's Sexuality from the Progressive Era to World War II*. Studies in the History of Sexuality. Oxford: Oxford University Press, 2009.

———. "Women's Power in Sex Radical Challenges to Marriage in the Early-Twentieth-Century United States." *Feminist Studies* 29, no. 1 (2003): 169–198.

Simonson, Anna. "*Féminisme Oblige*: Katharine Susan Anthony and the Birth of Modern Feminist Biography, 1877–1929." PhD diss., CUNY, 2017.

Smith-Rosenberg, Carroll. "The New Woman as Androgyne: Social Disorder and Gender Crisis, 1870–1936." In *Disorderly Conduct: Visions of Gender in Victorian America*, 245–296. New York: Alfred A. Knopf, 1985.

Sochen, June. *Movers and Shakers: American Women Thinkers and Activists, 1900–1970*. New York: Quadrangle, 1973.

————. *The New Woman: Feminism in Greenwich Village, 1910–1920*. New York: Quadrangle Books, 1972.

Soderlund, Gretchen. *Sex Trafficking, Scandal, and the Transformation of Journalism, 1885–1917*. Chicago: University of Chicago Press, 2013.

Solomon, Barbara Miller. *In the Company of Educated Women: A History of Women and Higher Education in America*. New Haven, CT: Yale University Press, 1985.

Stamp, Shelley. *Movie-Struck Girls: Women and Motion Picture Culture After the Nickelodeon*. Princeton, NJ: Princeton University Press, 2000.

Stannard, Una. *Mrs Man*. San Francisco: Germain Books, 1977.

Stansell, Christine. *American Moderns: Bohemian New York and the Creation of a New Century*. New York: Metropolitan Books, 2000.

Stein, Gertrude. *Selected Writings of Gertrude Stein*. Edited with an introduction and notes by Carl Van Vechten. New York: Vintage, 1990. First published 1962.

Stein, Leon, ed. *Out of the Sweatshop: The Struggle for Industrial Democracy*. New York: Quadrangle/New Times Book Company, 1977.

————. *The Triangle Fire*. New York: Carroll & Graf/Quicksilver, 1962.

Stevens, Doris. *Jailed for Freedom*. New York: Boni and Liveright, 1920.

Stevens, Hugh, and Caroline Howlett, eds. *Modernist Sexualities*. Manchester, United Kingdom: Manchester University Press, 2000.

Stovall, James Glen. *Seeing Suffrage: The Washington Suffrage Parade of 1913, Its Pictures, and Its Effect on the American Political Landscape*. Knoxville: University of Tennessee Press, 2013.

Stowell, Sheila. *A Stage of Their Own: Feminist Playwrights of the Suffrage Era*. Manchester, United Kingdom: Manchester University Press, 1992.

Strausbaugh, John. *The Village: 400 Years of Beats and Bohemians, Radicals and Rogues: A History of Greenwich Village*. New York: Ecco, 2013.

Tax, Meredith. *The Rising of the Women: Feminist Solidarity and Class Conflict, 1880–1917*. New York: Monthly Review Press, 1980.

Terborg-Penn, Rosalyn. *African American Women in the Struggle for the Vote, 1850–1920*. Blacks in the Diaspora. Bloomington: Indiana University Press, 1998.

————. "African-American Women's Networks in the Anti-Lynching Crusade." In *Gender, Class, Race, and Reform in the Progressive Era*, edited by Noralee Frankel and Nancy Schrom Dye, 148–161. Lexington: University Press of Kentucky, 2015.

Tyler, Gus. *Look for the Union Label: A History of the International Ladies' Garment Workers' Union*. Labor and Human Resources Series. Armonk, NY: M. E. Sharpe, 1995.

Van Vechten, Carl. *Generations in Black and White*. Edited by Rudolph P. Byrd. Athens: University of Georgia Press, 2014.

Van Wienen, Mark W., ed. *American Literature in Transition, 1910–1920*. American Literature in Transition. New York: Cambridge University Press, 2018.

Vapnek, Lara. *Breadwinners: Working Women and Economic Independence, 1865–1920*. Women in American History. Urbana: University of Illinois Press, 2009.

———. *Elizabeth Gurley Flynn: Modern American Revolutionary*. Lives of American Women. Boulder, CO: Westview Press, 2015.

Vassar College Encyclopedia. "Distinguished Alumnae/i." www.vassar.edu/vcencyclopedia/alumni/.

Vorse, Mary Heaton. "Elizabeth Gurley Flynn." *The Nation* 1, no. 3163 (February 17, 1926): 175–176.

———. *A Footnote to Folly: Reminiscences of Mary Heaton Vorse*. New York: Farrar & Rinehart, 1935.

———. *I've Come to Stay: A Love Comedy of Bohemia*. New York: Century, 1918.

Vorse, Mary Heaton, Adele Heller, and Jill O'Brien. *Time and the Town: A Provincetown Chronicle*. New Brunswick, NJ: Rutgers University Press, 1991.

Waitt, Alden. "Katharine Anthony: Feminist Biographer with the 'Warmth of an Advocate.'" *Frontiers: A Journal of Women Studies* 10, no. 1 (1988): 72–77.

Ware, Susan, ed. *American Women's Suffrage: Voices from the Long Struggle for the Vote, 1776–1965*. Library of America Series 332. New York: Library of America, 2020.

———. *Why They Marched: Untold Stories of the Women Who Fought for the Right to Vote*. Cambridge, MA: Belknap Press of Harvard University Press, 2019.

Watkins, Valethia. "Votes for Women: Race, Gender, and W.E.B. Du Bois's Advocacy of Woman Suffrage." *Phylon* 53, no. 2 (2016): 3–19.

Watson, Steven. *Strange Bedfellows: The First American Avant-Garde*. New York: Abbeville Press, 1991.

Weiss, Elaine. *The Woman's Hour: The Last Furious Fight to Win the Vote*. New York: Viking, 2018.

Werbel, Amy. *Lust on Trial: Censorship and the Rise of American Obscenity in the Age of Anthony Comstock*. New York: Columbia University Press, 2018.

Wetzsteon, Ross. *Republic of Dreams: Greenwich Village: The American Bohemia, 1910–1960*. New York: Simon & Schuster, 2002.

Wheeler, Leigh Ann. "Where Else but Greenwich Village? Love, Lust, and the Emergence of the American Civil Liberties Union's Sexual Rights Agenda, 1920–1931." *Journal of the History of Sexuality* 21, no. 1 (2012): 60–92.

Wheeler, Marjorie Spruill, ed. *One Woman, One Vote: Rediscovering the Woman Suffrage Movement.* Troutdale, OR: NewSage Press, 1995.

Wilson, Ross. *New York and the First World War: Shaping an American City.* Ashgate Studies in First World War History. Farnham, United Kingdom: Ashgate, 2014.

Wittenstein, Kate E. "The Feminist Uses of Psychoanalysis: Beatrice M. Hinkle and the Foreshadowing of Modern Feminism in the United States." *Journal of Women's History* 10, no. 2 (1998): 38–62.

———. "The Heterodoxy Club and American Feminism, 1912–1930." PhD diss., Boston University, 1989.

Woolf, Virginia. *Collected Essays I.* London: Hogarth Press, 1966.

Wylie, I. A. R. *My Life with George, an Unconventional Autobiography, by I. A. R. Wylie.* New York: Random House, 1940.

Yellin, Jean Fagan. "Dubois' 'Crisis' and Woman's Suffrage." *Massachusetts Review* 14, no. 2 (1973): 365–375.

Young, Rose. "What Is Feminism?" *Good Housekeeping* 58, no. 5 (May 1914): 679–684.

Zumwalt, Rosemary Lévy. *Wealth and Rebellion: Elsie Clews Parsons, Anthropologist and Folklorist.* Publication of the American Folklore Society. New Series. Urbana: University of Illinois Press, 1992.

Zurier, Rebecca. *Art for The Masses: A Radical Magazine and Its Graphics, 1911–1917.* Introduction by Leslie Fishbein. Philadelphia: Temple University Press, 1988.

INDEX

Page numbers in *italics* indicate illustrations.

Credit: Sarah Klock

Joanna Scutts is a literary critic, historian, and author of *The Extra Woman*. She has written for the *New York Times*, *Washington Post*, *New Yorker*, and the *Paris Review* series "Feminize Your Canon." She holds a PhD from Columbia University and lives in New York.